NORTHERN EXPOSURE

Tim Quelch

NORTHERN EXPOSURE

A Fifty-Year Diary of Watching
Burnley FC

First published by Pitch Publishing, 2022

Pitch Publishing
9 Donnington Park,
85 Birdham Road,
Chichester,
West Sussex,
PO20 7AJ
www.pitchpublishing.co.uk
info@pitchpublishing.co.uk

© 2022, Tim Quelch

Every effort has been made to trace the copyright.
Any oversight will be rectified in future editions at the
earliest opportunity by the publisher.

All rights reserved. No part of this book may be reproduced,
sold or utilised in any form or transmitted in any form or by
any means, electronic or mechanical, including photocopying,
recording or by any information storage and retrieval system,
without prior permission in writing from the Publisher.

A CIP catalogue record is available for this book
from the British Library.

ISBN 978-1-80150-190-3

Typesetting and origination by Pitch Publishing
Printed and bound in Great Britain by TJ Books Ltd, Padstow

CONTENTS

Many Thanks	7
Introduction	9
Part 1: Whatever Happened to 'The Team of the Seventies'? 1970 to 1979	11
1. First Game: 1969/70 Season	12
2. The Disastrous 1970/71 Season	19
3. Post-Relegation Blues 1971/72	46
4. Champions Again 1972/73	56
5. Back in the Big Time 1973/74	69
6. Indian Summer 1974//75	80
7. Wild Day in Blackpool 1975/76	112
8. Harry's Game 1976/77	118
9. 'Big Stevie Wonder' 1977/78	130
10. Cup Winners Again 1978/79	141
11. The End of the Seventies	153
Part 2: On the Road to Oblivion 1980 to 1987	155
1. A New Low 1979/80	156
2. A Brief Revival 1980/82	161
3. Cup Fever/League Lament 1982/83	175
4. Lost Hope 1983/84	183
5. Supping at the Last-Chance Saloon: 1985 to 1987	186
Part 3: 'Things Can Only Get Better' 1988 to 1994	191
1. Wembley Way 1987/88	192
2. 'Jimmy Mullen's Claret and Blue Army': 1991 to 1994	197
3. Back at Wembley 1994	210
Part 4: On a Wild Rollercoaster. 1994 to 2002	217
1. The Calamitous 1994/95 Season	218
2. Backs against the Wall 1995 to 1999	256
3. Back among the Big Boys 1999 to 2000	276
4. The End of the Nineties and What Came After	289

Part 5: Missed Glory and Beating The Retreat.
2000 to 2007   293
    1. Premier Ambitions 2000 to 2002   294
    2. On the Back Foot 2002 to 2007   316
    3. The Dream Soars   374

Part 6: Capital Punishment. 2008 to 2009   351
    1. 'Fake It To Make It' The Coyle Way   352
    2. Wembley Triumph 2009   370

Part 7: Decline and Fall. 2010 to 2012   379
    1. The Dream Sours and Dies: 2010   380
    2. What Goes Up …   387
    3. New Broom and Sweeping Changes: 2011/12   393

Part 8: The Dyche Factor. 2012 to 2022   409
    1. 'To Succeed You Must Start at the Back'   410
    2. 'Room at the Top'   418
    3. Boarding the Orient Express   444
    4. 'My Zero'   456
    5. Back to Basics   458
    6. 'You Want It Darker?' Covid Calls 2020   464

Epilogue: Will the North Rise Again?   468
References   474

MANY THANKS

This book has been written to raise funds for Asthma + Lung UK. All my royalties will be donated to this national charity to assist in combating lung diseases such as those that brought about the premature deaths of two friends. It seems an appropriate charity to support at this time given the vulnerability of those with lung conditions to coronavirus infections.

Although this book is essentially a personal diary, I am indebted to the memories of many others who have shared some or all of this 50-year journey, notably the contributors to the excellent London Clarets magazine, *Something to Write Home About*. I would like to thank the Burnley footballers and managers listed here for their past reflections including: Steve Kindon, Brian Miller, Martin Dobson, Geoff Nulty, Jimmy Adamson, Harry Potts, Arthur Bellamy, Les Latcham, Colin Waldron, Ralph Coates, Brian Laws, Paul Fletcher, Ian Britton, Jimmy Robson, Ian Wright, Ian Moore, Gareth Taylor, Glen Little, Mike Conroy, Roger Eli, David Eyres, Brian Jensen, Robbie Blake, Wade Elliott, Steven Caldwell, Graham Alexander, Frank Sinclair, Clarke Carlisle, Andy Payton, Keith Treacy, Gerry Harrison, Danny Ings, Kieran Trippier, Dean Marney, Eddie Howe, Stan Ternent, Harry Potts, Jimmy Mullen, Sean Dyche, Ashley Barnes, Ben Mee, Charlie Austin, Jason Shackell, Martin Paterson, Michael Keane, Steven Defour, Sam Vokes, Stephen Ward, and Tom Heaton.

I am also indebted to present and former board members, including Barry Kilby, Clive Holt, Frank Teasdale, John

Banaszkiewicz, and Ray Griffiths, whose contributions also featured in my previous book *From Orient to the Emirates*, short extracts of which have been reused here. I would also like to thank existing board member Mike Garlick and for his past and present contributions, extracts of which I have used here.

I am grateful to other Burnley writers for use of brief segments of their work, notably Dave Thomas, Ray Simpson, former club historian, Tony Scholes of Up the Clarets website, Darren Bentley, the former Burnley media manager, and Phil Whalley, co-editor of *Something to Write Home About* and curator of The Claret Archives. I am indebted to the local press, particularly the *Burnley Express* and *Lancashire Telegraph* for their past match reports which have helped jog my memory.

A big thank you to Matthew Riley, for use of his superb photographs of Burnley players; to Dave Hird for use of his superb historical Burnley videos; to Darren Bentley for re-use of his stunning Burnley images; and to Paul Fletcher for his personal Burnley shots. Finally, thank you to everyone at Pitch for your valued help and guidance. I am particularly grateful to Duncan for his superb graphic design work and to Katie Field for her rigorous and thoughtful editing.

In the reference section I have listed all sources which have assisted my recollections.

INTRODUCTION

I went North in 1968, arriving at Lancaster University in a dank, glum autumn. Yet I fell in love with the north, with its people, its moors, fells, and lakes, once I had learnt to cope with its petrifying cold and insurgent damp. I also developed a soft spot for one of its struggling football teams, Burnley FC, set well away from the national motorways in its isolated Pennine valley. My first visit was on a cold and wet Saturday in March 1970. Despite the grubby post-industrial dereliction, I warmed to the Burnley fans' chirpy resilience. Having seen their side come from behind to beat West Bromwich in front of a sadly depleted crowd, my head was turned. This born-again allegiance has stayed with me wherever I have lived and worked since – in Rochdale, Halifax, Leicester, Bristol, and London before returning to the north in 2010, following retirement. Now I can watch my team – pandemic excepting – without the exhausting journeys I made for much of my working life, sometimes with my wife, Liz, who was as keen as I during the seventies, and sometimes with our daughter, Lydia, who developed a fondness for the Clarets during her nineties' adolescence. My work colleague, Andrew, often came with me too as we drove the length and breadth of the country to watch Burnley play.

Because it is impossible to cram the experience of watching Burnley for a half-century into a book of moderate size, I have chosen to provide an overview of the club's progress that traces its wildly fluctuating fortunes, from the aftermath of its sixties glory days, through its subsequent decline in the late seventies and threatened extinction in the latter eighties, before a bumpy recovery took place, which ultimately led it back, quite improbably, to top-flight football. Here, it became the smallest and least wealthy Premier League club to earn a place in a European competition.

To put more flesh on these bones I have chosen to dwell on four momentous periods in the club's recent history. I have gone back to my early adulthood, when I first became a Claret, when Jimmy Adamson boasted that his talented young Burnley side would become 'the team of the seventies'. Having watched Burnley regularly for much of this decade I examine what became of this vaunted team, helped by the views of some of those who played under Adamson. Moving on, I have revisited the early nineties when Jimmy Mullen raised the flagging spirits of Burnley fans by choosing to play exciting, attacking, and entertaining football, helping the club rise from the lower reaches of Division Four to the second tier, only to falter once there. Thirdly, I look at the essential contributions made by former manager Stan Ternent and ex-chairman Barry Kilby in establishing the club's firm foothold in the Championship despite severe financial pressures, notably those caused by the collapse of ITV Digital broadcasting. Their estimable efforts in the late nineties and early noughties paved the way for the club's rise into the Premier League. Finally, I focus on the eight incredible seasons that Burnley have spent playing in the Premier League since 2009, seven of these under the club's remarkable manager, Sean Dyche, six consecutively. Sadly he lost his job on 15 April 2022, almost ten years after his appointment.. The song titles are included because of their personal associations on this 50-year journey.

Tim Quelch, June 2022

PART 1

WHATEVER HAPPENED TO 'THE TEAM OF THE SEVENTIES'?

1970 to 1979

'Where Have All the Good Times Gone?'

1. FIRST GAME: 1969/70 SEASON

Burnley 2 West Bromwich Albion 1
21 March 1970

'In a Broken Dream'

My first trip to Burnley seemed inauspicious. Stepping out of our car onto a greasy cobbled street, the gusting wind propelled icy rain into our screwed-up faces. We wondered whether we should have stayed in Lancaster. Burnley appeared broken. Around us were the scars of industrial blight: the derelict mills; the oily canal; the empty unwanted housing; and the rusted, weed-strewn marshalling yards. Yet overlooked by drab, rain-darkened moors, the occupied stone-terraced houses appeared snug and welcoming. Their flickering fires left an impression of homeliness. The packed pubs were inviting, too, with the Burnley fans amusing us with their sharp, ribald banter.

The football club, like its town, was a declining force. Frank Casper's £30,000 signing from Rotherham in 1967 marked the start of a new era when it was no longer possible for the club to rely upon an endless supply of youthful talent. With the bigger clubs turning the heads of bright, young players and their parents, proffering attractive enticements, Burnley found it harder to compete. Yet the club still attracted some gifted young players such as David Thomas, Steve Kindon, Mick Docherty, and Leighton James who thought there were earlier first-team opportunities here. But increasingly Burnley needed to recruit experienced players from other clubs, such as

1. FIRST GAME: 1969/70 SEASON

Colin Waldron and Jim Thomson. To afford these purchased players and balance the books, one or more of the club's better players had to be sold each season. Their aged ground required urgent renovation too, placing further pressure on the bottom line. By the late sixties Burnley were no longer First Division heavyweights. In the four seasons leading to the start of the seventies, the Clarets became ensconced in 14th place. Heavy defeats were no longer a surprise although there were enough stirring victories to avoid the drop.

Meanwhile the local economy, once dominated by textile manufacturing and coal mining, was in sharp decline. Despite Prestige and Michelin offering replacement manufacturing, with Lucas still a local engineering giant, these businesses were undermined by the economic downturns of the sixties and early seventies, leaving them prey to ruthless takeovers. Because these businesses were subsidiaries of parent companies, they were more vulnerable to cost-saving restructuring, closures, and subsequent job losses. Rolls Royce at nearby Barnoldswick was more resilient, being specialist producers of aircraft engines and parts. Lest we forget, Britain led the world in aeronautics during the fifties before being overtaken by foreign competition, notably from America.

Unabashed, club chairman, Bob Lord, built an all-seated stand at the western end of Turf Moor, backing onto the Burnley cricket club. The original specification included oil-fired heated seats but with the sharply rising cost of oil after the Arab/Israeli Six-Day War, this idea was junked. Meanwhile, on the southern flank of the ground was an unsightly cordoned-off demolition site. The eastern end remained open to the elements, frequently bringing about over-crowding on the covered Longside in bad weather. Yet here there was often dripping water from its rusty girders. As for its toilet, this was utterly insanitary. In step with these austere surroundings, the local kids exuded nonchalant toughness. It was not so much their bovver boots or their scuffed scarves, tied tightly to their wrists, that marked them out as hardy souls. None of them wore coats. They seemed oblivious to winter's late riposte.

Burnley's 1959/60 championship-winning manager, Harry Potts, was no longer in charge. He had been pushed 'upstairs' as general manager in February 1970, allowing former captain, coach, and favourite son, Jimmy Adamson, to take over team affairs. Harry's move was made by Lord to keep ambitious Adamson at the club. Adamson was well thought of as a coach. Bobby Charlton rated him highly having seen him in action during the 1962 World Cup in Chile. Adamson had been schooled for the England job, but turned it down, preferring to continue his playing career at Burnley.

Chairman Bob Lord thought that a Potts–Adamson partnership was his dream ticket, pairing Potts's impressive managerial track record with Adamson's vaunted coaching skills. Besides, as manager and skipper, they had complemented one another splendidly during the club's glory years. In 1963, Adamson even recommended Potts as a part-time adviser to new England manager, Alf Ramsey. But after Adamson was appointed as first-team coach one year later, their relationship became strained.

Adamson was steeped in modern tactical thinking. Potts was more of an old-school thinker, wedded to what had worked well for him in the past, not appreciating, perhaps, that he no longer had the surfeit of talent, which could make up for any tactical deficiencies. Whereas the excitable and enthusiastic Potts rarely gave detailed instruction about how he wanted his team to play, the ostensibly cooler Adamson was specific and demanding, using training-ground drills and blackboard diagrams to make his points.

But it was not just a clash of ideas that was the problem. The club's fortunes were fading as was its support. Ten years before, when Burnley were Football League champions, they

1. FIRST GAME: 1969/70 SEASON

drew an average crowd of 26,869 for their home league games. But in 1969/70 this average figure had fallen by almost 11,000 to 16,072, the lowest in the top flight. There were only 12,801 diehards at the West Bromwich game, and 1,000 fewer for the ensuing midweek home fixture with Southampton. With Burnley compelled to sell their principal assets, the cracks in the Potts–Adamson relationship began to widen. Their differences in personality and style started to grate.

One-club man Brian Miller was a Potts fan. He based his future management style upon Potts's way, allowing his players to play according to their intuitions. Miller was aware of Harry's tactical limitations but warmed to Potts's freer style and his unremitting care for his players.

Former left-back Les Latcham remembered the souring of the relationship between Potts and Adamson. He said, 'Adamson wanted sole control. This was not an unnatural ambition. He had his own theories, tactics, and aspirations but it led to a growing confusion about who was in charge. If there is one thing that footballers want it is clarity. But this was becoming blurred. This once happy club split into pro-Adamson and pro-Potts camps. Adamson once told ace midfielder Ralph Coates that he would start the next game, after playing well in a previous one. However, Potts over-ruled this. This divisive situation was damaging morale. In February 1970 Lord appointed Adamson as team manager and Potts was 'pushed upstairs'. The decision was made just after Burnley had thrashed Nottingham Forest 5-0 at home. It was Burnley's fourth win in a five-match unbeaten run. Without doubt this was a planned decision, although Potts had not been consulted. Potts graciously acknowledged Adamson's accession, saying, 'I could not hand over to a better fellow.' But he was devastated to be excluded from the Gawthorpe training ground. Potts never lost his love of the place, rubbing his hands on icy mornings, excitedly exclaiming, 'It's just like Switzerland.'

Potts found it hard to adjust to the role of general manager. He had been a father figure to many of his younger players, having rescued Steve Kindon when he was thrown out by his landlady, and comforting Ralph Coates during a family bereavement. Harry's wife Margaret harboured a grudge about the affair, feeling that her husband had been stabbed in the back. When she and Harry were denied a top-table place at the club's annual dinner, she had no hesitation in speaking her mind. What had been a happy, close-knit, family club began to fragment.

The team was changing markedly. Only full-back John Angus remained from the 1959/60 championship-winning side. Their title-winning goalkeeper Adam Blacklaw had moved on and central defender Brian Miller had retired through injury. But still young hearts ran free. Wingers Kindon and Dave Thomas were the newish kids in town, complementing established home-grown stars such as Coates, Brian O'Neil, and Martin Dobson. Kindon and Thomas had graduated from the youth team that had won the FA Youth Cup in 1968. In his programme notes for the Albion game, Potts purred about Adamson's gifted youngsters, who had performed so well in the 3-3 midweek draw at Old Trafford. Potts wrote, 'Congratulations to Jimmy Adamson and his team on a fine performance. We have a most promising set of players. Next season looks likely to be an important, exhilarating one for this club and its supporters. Two-up after five minutes and 3-1 ahead at the break, it certainly seemed to be our night. It was just our luck that Manchester United pulled one back midway through the second half and grabbed another in the final minutes.' Potts picked out Kindon and Thomas as his men of the match. Kindon drilled in the first goal from 25 yards while Thomas's quick feet accounted for the other two. 'Breathtaking footwork,' said Potts.

Not that Potts's pre-match euphoria inhibited West Bromwich. With Jeff Astle's probing runs pulling the Burnley defenders about, Tony 'Bomber' Brown broke free giving the

1. FIRST GAME: 1969/70 SEASON

visitors a 21st-minute lead with a skidding strike. This was a nasty setback, for Burnley were still in relegation trouble in 18th position. That midweek point at Old Trafford had been a good result but did little to ease their worries about the drop. Stung by this early blow, Burnley set about wresting control from the Baggies, who were two points better off. Gradually, the collective industry of flitting Coates, twinkling Thomas, terrier-like O'Neil, and dogged Bellamy forced the visitors to concede the soggy centre ground as increasing pressure was placed upon Albion's suspect defence.

Kindon had been a hat-trick hero against Forest in February. He was in 'a runaway wardrobe' mode here too. Making light of the heavy conditions, he powered in from the left, uninhibited by surface water, squelching mud, and despairing tackles, launching muscular assaults on Osborne's goal. Warming to his efforts, the home crowd set aside their groaning and moaning, and threw themselves wholeheartedly into the fray. Belligerently bellowing their side on, they were suitably rewarded in the 36th minute when Kindon's powerful running enabled him to break through the left side of the Baggies' defence. Not slowing to take aim, from 18 yards out, Kindon lashed home a fierce, rising drive that screamed into the roof of the net. Albion goalie Osborne was left standing by the visceral force of the shot. This unleashed a leaping tumult on the Longside terracing as the sullen away supporters were treated to the home fans' jabbing derision.

The rain grew in intensity as a premature dusk descended. The glare of the floodlights flashed and twinkled in the muddy pools appearing all over the pitch. As the second half progressed, the game became, quite simply, a trial of strength. It was a challenge that Burnley's youngsters were determined to win. By the time that Bellamy's slithering long-range effort had evaded a thicket of legs and found goal, there were only five minutes left. Neat football had been abandoned. The objective was to propel the ball far forward and chase it in dogged pursuit. Hacking it clear of the mud and puddles required Herculean power. We felt exhausted by association.

The 12,000 or so Burnley fans continued to urge their team forward, hurling encouragement and invective in equal measure, but the Clarets could not find another way through. It did not matter. By then, West Brom had lost their way. Little did I realise it then, but a claret and blue potion had been injected into my veins. From that sodden day onwards, my compass would automatically point north for I had winter in my blood. Although I was born and bred in Sussex the north became my spiritual home.

Burnley stayed up that season. The two points they took off West Bromwich meant that only two more were required from their final six fixtures. Two more victories over Newcastle (1-0) and Chelsea (3-1), plus a hat-trick of 1-1 draws, made that task a formality. Adamson crowed, 'We have a wonderful set of young players at Turf Moor and although we haven't won any senior honours we are soon going to. Mark my words. Our potential is better than that of all other clubs and I do mean all. Some First Division managers would give their right arms for our teenagers.'

Adamson was so confident about his young guns that he paraded all of them in the 1-1 Good Friday home draw with Stoke. Coates, at 23, was the oldest team member.

2. THE DISASTROUS 1970/71 SEASON

'Won't Get Fooled Again'

Before the 1970/71 season Adamson announced, 'Burnley will be "the team of the seventies." We are building one of the finest stadiums in the country and we have a great young team to go with it. In the next few years, we will win the Championship not once but several times.' Not to be outdone, chairman, Bob Lord, revealed his intention of adding capacity to the Bee Hole End terracing during the summer break, costing £88,000. He also proposed raising the total ground capacity to 40,000.

Perhaps Lord was so dazzled by Adamson's euphoria that he allowed himself to be carried away, speculating too about building an entertainment centre as part of the projected all-seated new stand on Brunshaw Road. So bullish was he, that when announcing the club's £46,000 annual loss he confidently assured the shareholders this was not something 'to lose sleep over'. How were such developments to be paid for, particularly when the average home attendance continued to fall? It seemed to be pure folly.

Perhaps Adamson regretted his outlandish predictions given that if Lord pursued all his aims, more players would be sold. However, he gained an assurance from Lord that prized asset Ralph Coates would remain. But there was a price to be paid. Lord sold dynamic midfield enforcer, Brian O'Neil, instead. The 'Bedlington Terrier' had played a key part in protecting Burnley's porous defence with his combative, 'muck and bullets' aggression. He joined Southampton in the summer of 1970 for a £75,000 fee, a record signing for the Saints. O'Neil's loss was considerable. Had he remained for one more year Burnley might have just survived the drop.

The season got off to a bad start with Martin Dobson breaking a leg in a friendly game and goalkeeper Peter Mellor dislocating his shoulder, forcing experienced player-coach, Tony Waiters, to deputise in 35 first-team games. There was little continuity. Collins made only 14 appearances in midfield while Kindon, a striking winger, was unavailable for 30 per cent of games. Veteran right-back Angus and centre-half Waldron were present in most games. But the left-back position remained problematic, with Merrington, Ray Ternent, Nulty, Thomson, and Cliff filling in uneasily until Latcham reclaimed the position in January 1971.

Full-back Jim Thomson deputised at centre-half alongside Colin Waldron in the opening nine games of this season, whereas Dave Merrington, an experienced centre-back, with over 100 first-team appearances for Burnley in that role, was asked to play at left-back. Merrington lost confidence so badly that he asked to be replaced as team captain. When Dobson returned from injury, in November, he became Waldron's partner in central defence, also taking the captain's band. It was only then that stability was restored at the back.

Not only were Burnley vulnerable in defence, they also lacked punch up front. Leading striker, Frank Casper, missed the start of the season with illness and thereafter struggled to find form and fitness, playing in only half of Burnley's league fixtures, and scoring merely four goals. Goalscoring was a perpetual problem. Only 29 league goals were scored in 1970/71, almost 50 per cent fewer than in the previous season. Strapping speedster Steve Kindon had been the club's top striker in 1969/70 with 17 goals – no one else reached double figures. Yet in 1970/71 he contributed just three. These missing goals would seal Burnley's dismal fate.

2. THE DISASTROUS 1970/71 SEASON

Burnley 1 Liverpool 2
15 August 1970
'Tears of a Clown'

The season opened with Liverpool as visitors. A bumper crowd of 25,783 watched. But with only 11 minutes gone, Waiters boobed, overlooking the 'four-step rule', a measure introduced to curb goalkeepers' timewasting. Having gifted Liverpool a needless indirect free kick, Waiters was unsighted when the ball cannoned off the Burnley wall allowing Alun Evans to tuck away the lucky rebound. Liverpool instantly seized control. Their tricky international left-winger Peter Thompson ran the Burnley defence ragged with his sinuous incursions. Fortunately for Burnley, the Liverpool strikers spurned his gold-tap service, wasting a succession of simple chances. Missing the composure of Dobson, Waldron's clearances were too often wild and wasteful, inviting further Liverpool pressure. Then, with only four minutes remaining of a one-sided first half, Burnley sprang unexpectedly into life. Coates and Kindon tore down the left flank, by-passing their markers with a snappy exchange of passes, and setting up David Thomas for an exquisitely curled equaliser that left Ray Clemence dumbfounded. The second half was mostly an insipid affair with Burnley defending with greater resilience and Liverpool creating fewer chances. But in the 77th minute Adamson's men conceded another costly free kick. Given sight of a chink in a shabby Burnley wall, Emlyn Hughes belted in the winner.

Everton 1 Burnley 1
18 August 1970
'All Right Now'

At reigning champions, Everton, Burnley defended stoutly after Dave Thomas had given them an eighth-minute lead with a rasping, acute angled shot. Despite Johnny Morrissey's equaliser Burnley fully deserved a share of the points. Burnley's centre-half Colin Waldron was outstanding, neutralising the threat from young centre-forward Joe Royle.

Manchester City 0 Burnley 0
22 August 1970
'54-46 Was My Number'

City manager Joe Mercer and his first-team coach, Malcolm Allison, forged a highly successful partnership at Maine Road, winning the First Division in 1968, the FA Cup in 1969, and the Cup Winners' Cup in 1970. But when Allison made a bid for the hot seat, this caused instability on the pitch. Burnley took advantage of this malaise, nicking another welcome point against a side which had crushed them 0-7 only two seasons before.

Burnley 0 Manchester United 2
25 August 1970
'Mama Told Me Not to Come'

Manchester United were not in a settled place either. Their new manager, Wilf McGuinness, struggled to establish himself after Matt Busby's retirement. United's ageing team came into this game after a 0-4 hiding by Arsenal at Highbury. Injury-prone Denis Law was on the transfer list while his colleagues were misfiring. Despite battering the United defence for much of this game, Burnley conceded two soft second-half goals both scored by Denis Law.

Burnley 0 Leeds 3
29 August 1970
'Get Up (I Feel Like Being a) Sex Machine'

There was no mistaking Leeds's superiority here. Two up in 11 minutes, Leeds added a third before half-time, ensuring the second half was irrelevant. Not even James Brown's pounding funk could lift my mood after this mauling.

2. THE DISASTROUS 1970/71 SEASON

Burnley 0 Chelsea 0
1 September 1970
'Give Me Just a Little More Time'

If Chelsea thought there were easy pickings to be had here, they were in for a rude surprise. Coates made repeated inroads while Kindon and Thomas were a constant menace. Bonetti was by far the busier goalkeeper although Burnley let themselves down with their woeful finishing. Kindon spanked a fierce shot against a post, Thomas's goal-bound effort was deflected wide by Harris at full stretch, and the returning Casper shot wastefully wide from close range. Chelsea had their moments, too, with Weller and Hudson hitting the woodwork and Osgood at his slick, marauding best. Thankfully, Tony Waiters was in top form. This goalless stalemate meant that Burnley had not scored in 443 minutes of play.

Ipswich Town 3 Burnley 0
5 September 1970
'Ohio'

Burnley travelled to Portman Road on 5 September in good heart. Ipswich were in bottom place with the Clarets just above them. It was hoped that the recovery would start here. But despite Kindon's probing runs, his team-mates failed to rise to the occasion. Ipswich's victory allowed them to leapfrog over Adamson's side. With Ipswich centre-back Billy Baxter overpowering Casper, Adamson replaced him at half-time with midfielder Arthur Bellamy but without improvement. Adamson seemed to be whistling in the dark, describing this abject defeat as 'a cause for concern but not a crisis'. Keith McNee, sports editor at the *Burnley Express,* agreed, writing: 'Relegation is written all over the current Turf Moor scene in large, ugly black letters. They must surely buy someone before long.' The national press men said much the same.

Burnley 1 Arsenal 2
12 September 1970
'(To Be) Young, Gifted and Black'

The demoralising defeat at Ipswich was followed by six more, although a 0-0 home draw with Coventry interrupted this sorry sequence. Here, the Clarets lost to Arsenal, who had made a steady start to their double-winning season. Dispiritingly Burnley conceded a fourth-minute goal to young Ray Kennedy. Although Roberts's own goal on the half-hour let Burnley back into the game, John Radford seized the points with a late strike. Another early goal, yielded at Derby, on 19 September, led to a further defeat. Not once during the 1970/71 season did Burnley come from behind to win.

Burnley 2 Wolves 3
26 September 1970
'You Can Get It If You Really Want'

Burnley put up a brave fight against visiting Wolves, though. Defying their soft underbelly, they twice recovered to level, thanks to Thomas's 49th-minute penalty and a rare goal from defender Colin Waldron, only for Wolves to snatch the winner with 12 minutes left.

West Ham 3 Burnley 1
3 October 1970
'Kick Out the Jams'

An error-strewn performance at West Ham gifted their hosts a 0-3 first-half lead. Coates's 82nd-minute goal was pointless. Adamson commented: 'I am afraid that we are still making too many elementary individual mistakes, and this cost us today as it did against Wolves.'

2. THE DISASTROUS 1970/71 SEASON

Liverpool 2 Burnley 0
17 October 1970

'Down on the Street'

As expected, Liverpool proved too strong at Anfield. Imposing centre-half Ron Yeates scored just before the interval, and gazelle-like Steve Heighway added a second shortly after. Burnley hardly figured in this regulation home win.

Southampton 2 Burnley 0
24 October 1970

'Ball of Confusion'

Having been shut out at Anfield, Burnley were trampled on at The Dell. The Saints' bruising defenders, John McGrath, Joe Kirkup, Denis Hollywood, and David Walker, were eagerly reinforced by three snapping hard men in midfield, Brian O'Neil, formerly of Burnley, Jimmy Gabriel, and Hugh Fisher. They collectively erected a craggy wall that the Burnley attackers could not penetrate, whereas the Saints had a formidable, international strike force, comprising Mick Channon, Ron Davies, and Terry Paine. Davies was a battering-ram centre-forward, dominant in the air, feeding off Paine's precise crosses, while fleet-footed Channon was Davies's mobile strike partner. Davies and Channon contributed 35 of Southampton's 54 league goals in 1970/71. As for O'Neil, he had more in his locker than a club. He set up Channon to breeze through Burnley's flimsy defence to score almost on the stroke of half-time. O'Neil also laid on Channon's second, just before time. Channon capitalised upon O'Neil's perfectly weighted pass to force the ball past hapless Waiters.

It was rumoured that Burnley chairman Bob Lord was prepared to raise Adamson's recruitment budget by an unprecedented £100,000. Yet Lord's response to this wretched defeat, Burnley's tenth in 14 fixtures, was not encouraging. He stated, 'We are not prepared to make the rat race any bigger.

There will be no panic buys.' Lord also berated the abolition of the maximum wage, having originally welcomed it. He told the PFA that 'top players were taking too much out of the game, not caring one iota for lower division players'. Lord had not expressed dissent when Burnley were one of the First Division top dogs in the early sixties. In fact, he recommended a top-flight cartel with no promotion or relegation, ostensibly to preserve the highest standards of football, free from fear of the drop. With Burnley now at risk of relegation, he changed his tune. This threat eventually pushed him to loosen the purse strings. But as is the case now, it was difficult to attract players to a struggling club. Besides, Burnley, the place, was difficult to sell to prospective recruits.

Jimmy Adamson constantly urged the disgruntled Burnley fans to keep the faith, explaining: 'the odds are stacked against us for a variety of reasons which include misfortune with injuries and the failure of willing players to do themselves justice. But everyone at Turf Moor, and this includes the players, of course, are convinced that our policy is on the right lines and that we will move away from the brink of disaster to stage a cheering recovery.' A 3-1 home win over Hearts in the Texaco Cup was hailed as the start of this 'cheering recovery' only for the Clarets to lose the second leg 1-4.

Burnley 2 Crystal Palace 1
31 October 1970

'Paranoid'

Burnley eventually broke their duck on 31 October when Crystal Palace came to Turf Moor. Eric Probert was the hero with two match-winning goals before half-time. His first came in the 21st minute when he headed in Coates's precise cross. His second, another header, came five minutes later but this time he was indebted to Palace's Alan Birchenall, who unwittingly deflected the ball past goalie Jackson. Thomas was given the opportunity to put Burnley out of sight with a penalty, awarded when Sewell sent superb Coates crashing. Alas, nerves got the better of him as he fired his spot kick high and wide. This spurned chance nearly cost Burnley dearly. Following a brief period of Burnley pressure at the resumption, during which Kindon wasted two inviting chances, Palace finally shed their first-half lethargy. Prompted by Kember and McCormick, they mounted a series of dangerous raids. One of these led to Taylor's goal. Somehow this scratch Burnley defence held out, ably marshalled by Waldron.

At last, 12,000 or so Burnley fans went home happily. Roared on by the home crowd from start to finish, Dave Thomas remarked: 'It was more like a 40,000 crowd inside the ground. I've never known such support and all the lads spoke about this.' Coates added: 'The supporters' encouragement did not cease throughout, not even when Thomas missed his penalty. I think it was because they realised we were doing our best and that their vocal support makes the team stronger and more confident, more prepared to attempt things that otherwise would not be on.' A euphoric Adamson announced that Burnley were certainly staying up!

Tottenham Hotspur 4 Burnley 0
7 November 1970

'War'

Had Burnley turned a corner? If so, they stepped out into the path of a Spurs juggernaut. Their old foe simply flattened them after Chivers had opened the scoring in the 15th minute. He was Spurs' executioner in chief, having all the time and space he needed to whip in two right-foot drives from crosses supplied by Peters and Gilzean. Spurs' third goal was a thing of beauty, albeit conceded through my gritted teeth. A polished exchange of passes involving England, Gilzean, and Peters gave industrious Perryman the freedom to run at the heart of the Burnley defence. Once at the edge of the Burnley box, Perryman played a one-two with Pearce so swiftly and exactly that his markers were confounded. This left Perryman, Spurs' tiny midfielder, with the space to burst between Waldron and Nulty and pull the trigger. His crisp cross-shot found goal to the right of Waiters's dive.

I did not stay to witness the Clarets' final indignity. With the result no longer in doubt I caught an early train home, wallowing in a slough of despondency. After this roasting I had little doubt that Burnley were destined for the drop. Adamson reflected: 'Ironically on a day when Mellor, Dobson and Jones returned to action in a reserve fixture, we suffered another heavy, disappointing defeat on a ground that has become almost a graveyard for us. Not only did we lose 0-4 but we returned with Michael Docherty nursing a painful ankle strain. We were in the game for about an hour and could have had a couple of goals but then Spurs got well on top, and the hopes of our young and enthusiastic youngsters were sadly crushed. It is always a hard match here and currently they are something special [Spurs would win the inaugural UEFA Cup a year later]. Only Leeds have looked a better, more professional and efficient side.'

Mr Harrison, a Burnley supporter, wrote to the editor of the Burnley *Claret and Blue* matchday magazine stating: 'I think the reason behind Burnley's defeats – injuries apart – is that they are trying TOO HARD to justify Mr Adamson's statement that they are going to be the 'team of the seventies' and in their eagerness, they are making silly mistakes.' I am sure Mr Harrison was not the first or the last Claret to voice concern about a Burnley team being overburdened by false expectation.

Burnley 2 Huddersfield 3
14 November 1970
'Voodoo Chile'

In the matchday programme for the home Huddersfield game on 14 November the £1 letter prize was awarded to James Needham who wrote: 'In recent weeks there has been a lot of talk about

2. THE DISASTROUS 1970/71 SEASON

Burnley's scoring potential or lack of it. Because of the present financial position of the club, the fans must accept that Burnley cannot afford to buy new players. However, I believe that the present playing staff is more than capable of doing a good job. The forward line has rarely been settled enough to produce the goals and results that the Burnley fans have become accustomed to. But I am sure that if it were possible to field the same forward line, with Dobson and Mellor back, then the goals and results will come back.'

On a sunny, late-autumn afternoon, Burnley did recover their scoring touch, against newly promoted Huddersfield. In this leanest of seasons two goals were as good as it got. Unfortunately, Huddersfield scored one more. Midfielder Bobby Hoy was responsible for two of Huddersfield's goals, but it was 'playboy' Frank Worthington who was the star performer. Playing as a deep-lying centre-forward he pulled the strings with a breezy swagger.

Once again Burnley conceded a sloppy early goal allowing Hoy to net with a simple lob in the 12th minute. Burnley's best moment came 13 minutes later when their playmaker, Alan West, scored a fine equaliser. The build-up was immaculate. Casper fed Coates on the right wing who instantly passed sideways to Probert inviting the midfielder to sprint along the vacant inside-right channel. Meanwhile West found unmolested space inside Huddersfield's box, allowing Probert to slide the ball into his path. With impressive composure, West dummied a shot prompting goalie Poole to shift to his right whereupon West rolled the ball into the opposite corner. It was a goal of sublime craft and execution, so rare in this star-crossed season.

Just as it seemed as if Burnley were possible victors, Hoy and Lawson took Huddersfield out of reach with goals in the 66th and 74th minutes. Thomas's belated right-wing surge and cross created a frantic goalmouth scrimmage with Kindon slamming the loose ball home at point-blank range. Alas, time was up.

It was another hammer blow to the Clarets who, in the heavy conditions, deserved better, having played exciting, expansive football. The exasperated Burnley Longsiders chanted fatuously: 'There's going to be a riot' and 'There'll not be many going home', whereas 2,000-plus Huddersfield fans left the ground unimpeded and unharmed. Years later, Frank Worthington remarked: 'It was a smashing game that left both sets of supporters feeling good.' Whatever were you on, Frank?

Burnley 2 Nottingham Forest 1
21 November 1970
'Woodstock'

Burnley also scored another brace of goals against visiting Forest on 21 November. Helped by the return of Dobson and Mellor, this time two strikes were enough. Goals from Geoff Nulty in the 34th minute and Eric Probert immediately after the interval gave Burnley the points despite the visitors reducing the deficit seven minutes after the break. The Clarets' main talking point was the brilliant debut of young Welsh winger, Leighton James. He deputised for Ralph Coates who was sidelined for four weeks following an ankle injury.

Newcastle United 3 Burnley 1
28 November 1970
'Black Night'

It was one step forward and three back as the Mags defeated Burnley at St James' Park. Although Newcastle took a sixth-minute lead through Moncur, Probert equalised 14 minutes later. Burnley were still in the game with only 15 minutes to go, playing stylishly, but then Ford struck for the Magpies, with 'Pop' Robson rubbing salt into the Clarets' wounds in the final minute. 'Wor' Jackie Milburn reported that, 'Burnley had run rings around their opponents before Ford's goal.' Fellow press man Len Shackleton agreed. There was no consolation here, just frustration. Adamson's response was to urge the abolition of the offside rule, complaining that 'defenders have too many advantages, always outnumbering the opposing forwards and having the offside rule as an extra weapon'. Not content with that he recommended widening the goal posts, too!

Burnley 1 West Bromwich Albion 1
5 December 1970
'Everyday People'

Burnley should have won this ragged home game against West Bromwich after taking a 54th-minute lead. Visiting goalkeeper, Jim Cumbes, could not hold Leighton James's lusty drive, leaving Kindon to put away the rebound. Exasperatingly, with 20 minutes left, Tony Brown seized upon Waldron's weak back pass and flicked in the equaliser.

Stoke City 0 Burnley 0
12 December 1970
'After the Gold Rush'

At Stoke, Burnley parked the bus, easily holding their hosts at bay despite Jimmy Greenhoff's bustling belligerence. For Burnley, Collins and West provided skilful industry but without any discernible attempt to push forward. This must have been at Adamson's behest as his players appeared content to knock the ball around innocuously in midfield. Although the game ended as a bore draw, Burnley might have won when Kindon was put through on goal with just Banks to beat. Annoyingly, he fluffed this glaring opportunity. He was taken off later because of injury, with James replacing him. However, Burnley could consider themselves fortunate that the referee subsequently ruled out a Stoke goal, having first pointed at the centre spot.

Burnley 0 Manchester City 4
19 December 1970
'Moondance'

As for Jimmy Adamson's belief that the game would benefit from wider goalposts, Manchester City found the Turf Moor goals wide enough, winning easily with two goals from Colin Bell and one apiece from Francis Lee and Mike Summerbee. Bell and Waldron were close friends having been team-mates at Bury. We can only speculate what impact this thrashing had upon their relationship.

Blackpool 1 Burnley 1
26 December 1970
'Venus in Furs'

At least a point was won at partners in distress, Blackpool, on Boxing Day in a hard-fought derby. Frank Casper, who had largely languished in the reserves since October, scored a 65th-minute equaliser after Blackpool had taken a ninth-minute lead. But the ensuing FA Cup tie at Oxford on 3 January was a disaster with the Second Division side, led by 'Big Ron' Atkinson, trouncing Burnley 3-0, thereby presenting them with a hat-trick of cup losses in 1970/71.

Burnley 2 Everton 2
9 January 1971
'What's Going On'

Undeterred, Burnley battled well against reigning champions Everton at Turf Moor. Casper gave Burnley a sixth-minute lead only for Henry Newton and David Johnson to turn the game around with goals in the 52nd and 56th minutes. Martin Dobson's 79th-minute strike secured a share of the spoils, though. In the match programme Jimmy Adamson took issue with the reporters who thought some of his players were 'uninterested', 'not firmly behind him', and 'unconcerned whether the Clarets stayed up or went down so long as the money rolled in'. Adamson retorted angrily: 'Burnley players DO care. If I thought differently about anyone of them, he would not be on the books. If we go down, it will be heartbreak for them. Some, admittedly, have had a bad time and not played as well as they can – BUT NOT BECAUSE THEY DO NOT CARE.'

Such allegations are often made when a team is in trouble, along with rumours of players' late-night drinking, and other improprieties. As part of the tiresome dance it becomes, the predictable refutations are wheeled out to meet these.

Prime Minister Ted Heath was in the firing line, too. Curbing the power of the unions was as troublesome as it had been in the final years of Harold Wilson's 1964–70 administration. In 1971 Heath was faced by two one-day stoppages in protest at his industrial relations policy. Unemployment was mounting. By April there were 814,819 people on the dole, many of them living in post-industrial areas, such as Burnley. Even Rolls Royce was threatened with bankruptcy, alarming their 'cotton towns' employees. A heavy December snowfall gave us a rare white Christmas, but it did not feel at all cosy. 'Glam rock' was here but the prevailing mood was glum.

Manchester United 1 Burnley 1
16 January 1971

'Fortunate Son'

At Manchester United Matt Busby was back in charge after the sacking of Wilf McGuinness in December. United's glory days were well behind them, though. The contretemps with an increasingly unreliable George Best had not helped. The truth was that Manchester United were on a downward curve, with their promoted youths not yet as good as their predecessors had been. It was rumoured that Busby was prepared to invest in new blood; 20-year-old Kindon placed himself in the shop window here, with a supposed £100,000 price on his head. *The*

Sun named others on Busby's possible shopping list, including Newcastle striker Wyn Davies, Sunderland's classy defender Colin Todd, and Ipswich's accomplished right-back Mick Mills. Typically, it was just 'paper talk' although Wyn 'The Leap' did join United later.

The game began with Coates, Kindon, and Thomas swarming all over United's beleaguered defenders. Only the goalkeeper, Stepney, prevented Burnley from taking an unassailable lead. He twice denied Kindon, bravely diving at his feet, while Thomas narrowly blazed over. Time was catching up with Charlton, though, despite being the only United player capable of lifting this siege. Thankfully, his long, raking passes were largely wasted by his docile attackers. Although not as fast as he had been in his pomp, he retained his sharp-shooting ability, forcing Waiters to push over a trademark thunderbolt. Burnley were understandably frustrated, though, going in scoreless at half-time. Once again, they paid for their wastefulness. Within a minute of the restart Aston put United ahead, having capitalised on a pass by Law. However, the Burnley players were incensed that referee Johnson allowed the goal, complaining that Aston had used his hand to control the ball before scoring. But Johnson was unmoved.

With Burnley committing themselves to all-out attack, their defence became depleted, not that United threatened it much. Coates, Kindon, and Thomas repeatedly bombarded the partisan Stretford End, forcing Stepney into making several spectacular saves. But the home fans behind him became increasingly agitated and rightly so. Stepney was compelled to concede a corner in the 74th minute, having made another stupendous save. But from the corner kick Waldron rose highest and headed downwards towards the penalty spot. In the ensuing scramble, Crerand inadvertently blocked Edward's attempted clearance. Fortuitously, the ball ran loose to Dobson who poked it through a cluster of legs and past Stepney for a richly deserved equaliser.

2. THE DISASTROUS 1970/71 SEASON

Charlton was so dispirited that with five minutes left, he passed his loose boot to the referee, signifying he had had enough. It was understandable. His long passes and urgent breaks were the only flickering candles in this Old Trafford gloom.

Burnley 1 Newcastle United 1
30 January 1971
'Brown Sugar'

Newcastle came to Turf Moor and it was the same sorry story of another squandered point. Probert put Burnley ahead in the 20th minute but debutant Newcastle winger Stewart Barrowclough snatched an equaliser with only six minutes remaining.

West Bromwich Albion 1 Burnley 0
6 February 1971
'Whipping Post'

West Bromwich's free-scoring midfielder Tony Brown put paid to Burnley's chances with a habitual goal, scored on the brink of half-time. Brown had scored against the Clarets in each of their three preceding fixtures. He completed the season with 28 league goals, an incredible haul for a midfielder. How Burnley could have done with these!

Nottingham Forest 1 Burnley 0
20 February 1971
'Let It Be'

Nottingham Forest were there for the taking as Burnley bore down upon their suspect defence. Kindon and Probert led the charge with industrious Dobson probing in midfield, but – disappointingly – once Ian Storey-Moore had snatched a 29th-minute lead, helped by Neil Martin's head on, the balance of play shifted. With the home defence tightened, Coates's strenuous efforts were snuffed out. Adamson was particularly disappointed with this defeat, saying: 'We played quite well at relegation rivals

Forest, but were unable to hit back after Ian Moore scored. He is a fine striker, but once again we did not cash in on our earlier superiority.'

Burnley 1 Stoke City 1
23 February 1971
'It's Too Late'

Against injury-ravaged Stoke, it was déjà vu. Stoke had a wretched away record this season with just one league victory on the road. But Terry Conroy quickly exposed the indecision of the Burnley defenders, giving Stoke a 13th-minute lead. With their confidence boosted, Stoke City applied increasing pressure on the Clarets' shaky back line, using a more direct route to goal. Fortunately, their dominance did not yield further goals. As for Burnley, only Coates exhibited any driving force while his colleagues meandered ineffectually.

After the break Kindon followed Coates's example, using his scorching pace and hefty power to good effect. This presented a greater challenge for the Stoke defenders. Unfortunately, his goal-bound header was beaten away, as was Dobson's shot in a goalmouth scrum. But in the 66th minute Burnley's efforts were rewarded when Dobson equalised with a header, helped by Gordon Banks's slip when trying to punch away Coates's cross. Despite Burnley being on top for much of the second half, had Burrows's shot not cannoned off Waiters's outstretched leg, their efforts would have been in vain. The point Burnley won here lifted them off the bottom for the first time since early September, albeit by only one place.

Crystal Palace 0 Burnley 2
27 February 1971
'For What It's Worth'

At last Burnley achieved their first away win with a powerful display of counter-attacking. In the sixth minute Bellamy forced his way past three Palace defenders to reach their goal line. Having cut the ball back into the crowded home box it was inadvertently deflected into Coates's path by Palace goalkeeper, Jackson. Coates instantly clipped the loose ball into the empty net with Jackson struggling to regain his ground. The second goal was scored by Dobson 20 minutes later. Probert improbably outjumped the Palace centre-backs and headed out to Kindon on the left wing. Kindon powered along the touchline before crossing potently to Dobson who unhesitatingly fired past Jackson. It was vindication of Adamson's attacking strategy in which Dobson was encouraged to push forward. Kindon ran riot with his strength and speed, while the Palace strikers, Queen and Birchenall, had little change out of the Burnley defenders who were well supported by Waiters.

Burnley 0 Southampton 1
6 March 1971

'Fire and Rain'

With Bob Lord recognising that team strengthening was imperative, Bolton's 20-year-old centre-forward Paul Fletcher was signed in March 1971 for a club record fee of £60,000. After looking at 34 different players, Adamson was cock-a-hoop with his acquisition. He said: 'I am sure he is going to be a great asset for a long time to come. He has been under the microscope for some time, but Bolton were reluctant to sell him.' Because Bolton were in grave danger of being relegated to Division Three, they were persuaded to cash in. Adamson continued: 'I am sure the Burnley supporters will give Paul great encouragement but recognise he may not set the ground alight immediately. Even so we hope that he will soon be on the goal trail.' There were only 12 games left though. Avoiding relegation, their first since 1930, seemed a very tall order.

Nevertheless, the signing of a new striker generally stirs excitement among a club's supporters. So, when Southampton came to sunny Burnley there was an air of optimism, buoyed by Burnley's heart-warming win over Palace and Fletcher's signing. It was announced that Fletcher was to make his debut in this game. As a result, the home gate rose to 15,786, over 3,000 higher than for the midweek home game with Stoke. The Burnley youth team were roundly applauded too, having disposed of Hull in an FA Youth Cup quarter-final tie. Could this mean there were further home-grown stars in the making?

Many years later when Paul Fletcher became CEO at Turf Moor, he told Tony Scholes of the Up the Clarets supporters' website: 'Adamson told me when he signed me for Burnley that my job was not to score goals. "I have better players than you who can do that. You just head the ball towards the penalty spot, and they'll score the goals."' Really?! Disappointingly, Fletcher did not set the ground alight, neither did his colleagues, while a Mick Channon goal in the 82nd minute, celebrated with his bloody wheeling arm, sent the Saints home with both points.

Huddersfield Town 0 Burnley 1
13 March 1971
'Working Class Hero'

Adamson now had to pursue victories at home and away. At a grey and misty Huddersfield, he chose a 4-3-3 formation with Thomas, Fletcher, and Kindon up front, Dobson, Coates, and Bellamy in midfield and Angus, Waldron, Nulty, and Latcham in defence. It was intended to be a fluid set-up with Dobson having liberty to forage in advanced positions while Coates was expected to pull the Huddersfield defenders around with his bustling pace and trickery. Bellamy was instructed to retain a holding role. But it was the solidity of Burnley's back four, adeptly marshalled by Waldron, that enabled us to win this crucial game. Waldron even headed the winner. The *News of the World* reporter wrote: 'Despite a rather hectic and at times nervous second half, Burnley were full value for their two points. They took the game to Town in those vital early stages, unnerving the home side, and taking a 28th-minute lead, which held firm until the final whistle.' The *Daily Telegraph* added: 'The combined talents of Dobson, the highly promising Fletcher, Thomas and Kindon, backed by the ferocious industry of Coates, always promised a goal.' Adamson thought the Palace victory was a better performance but described the Huddersfield win as 'a memorable team effort'. The gap between Burnley and relegation rivals West Ham had reduced to three points, after the Irons lost at Molineux. There was still a slender chance of avoiding the drop. What's more, Burnley were due to meet West Ham at Turf Moor in an Easter 'four-pointer'.

Burnley 0 Tottenham Hotspur 0
20 March 1971
'Northern Sky'

Two home games followed, although Burnley had not won at Turf Moor in four months. Their first opponents on 20 March were high-riding Spurs. Although Burnley began nervously, exhibiting greater urgency than skill, they soon found their feet and proceeded to batter the Spurs goal. Unfortunately, they found Pat Jennings in superb form, denying three headers from Fletcher and further efforts from Thomas and Kindon. Kindon bossed the show with his muscular raids, frequently splitting the Spurs defence. Meanwhile, Waldron held the back line imperiously, completely dominating Chivers. While a 0-0 draw was a creditable result, a single point was not enough, given Burnley's parlous position.

Burnley 2 Ipswich 2
27 March 1971
'While My Guitar Gently Weeps'

The week after, Burnley faced lowly Ipswich at Turf Moor. Waldron hardly eased their nerves by blasting a penalty well wide. But Casper rectified this by giving his side a 54th-minute lead. Alas, 16 minutes later, Lambert equalised with his first kick, having replaced the injured Collard. Then in the 70th minute Morris turned the game on its head with a brutal 25-yard drive that flew into the top corner. Burnley replaced their unwell right-back, Angus, with Collins but could not recover their earlier zest. With only seconds left, though, a miscued shot from Collins was well off target before ricocheting from Nulty's head and finding goal, although bemused Ipswich goalie, Laurie Sivell, should have saved it.

Leeds United 4 Burnley 0
3 April 1971
'Get It On'

Leeds mercilessly humiliated Burnley here. Alan Clarke scored all four goals, having scored twice in the Turf Moor fixture. His first came from a quick throw-in by Lorimer near the half-way line. Clarke was on it in a flash, rounding Nulty, and slipping the ball past Waiters after the Burnley goalkeeper had injudiciously raced to the edge of his box. The second came when Madeley's shot was headed off the line by Latcham whereupon Lorimer instantly set up Clarke to score easily. For his third, Clarke received Sprake's goal kick on the half-way line. With the Burnley defence AWOL, Clarke raced through to complete his hat-trick. The fourth came eight minutes before the end following a slick exchange of passes. While Coates laboured in vain, Fletcher showed an impressive turn of pace. As for Kindon, his powerful running caused spasmodic concern in the Leeds defence. It was not nearly enough, though. Having watched Colchester bundle Leeds out of the FA Cup in January, I had hoped for more. West Bromwich proved it was possible to overthrow Leeds at their citadel, albeit helped by some controversial refereeing.

2. THE DISASTROUS 1970/71 SEASON

Burnley 1 Blackpool 0
10 April 1971
'Double Barrel'

A week later, on a sunny Easter Saturday, Burnley finally gained their first home win in 1971, a 1-0 victory over relegation-bound Blackpool. It was a dreadful, scrappy game, redeemed for Burnley, at least, by one shining moment ten minutes before time. After Waiters had foiled a Blackpool attack, he threw the ball quickly to right-back Docherty. Seeing a huge gap before him, Docherty instantly fired a long, low, diagonal pass into this vacant space. Fletcher was quickest to the ball, brushing aside Blackpool's centre-half Glyn James and making for goal. As he approached the Blackpool box, Fletcher shot immediately. His left-foot effort lacked pace, but it had pinpoint accuracy, finding the right-hand corner of the net at the Cricket Field End. It was Fletcher's first goal for Burnley and well deserved, after he had been thwarted repeatedly by last-ditch saves. This victory was a close-run thing, though. Before Fletcher stole the game for Burnley, Craven had come close to giving Blackpool the lead. His first effort was kneed away awkwardly by Nulty, and his second slammed against the bar. Waiters also made a flying save to stop a thunderbolt from Johnny Johnson, two minutes after Fletcher had scored.

Burnley 1 West Ham 0
13 April 1971
'Whole Lotta Love'

Three days later Burnley won again, thanks to Geoff Nulty's soaring header in the 67th minute. Once more Coates was the instigator of victory with his extraordinary bursts of speed. Local reporter Keith McNee remarked: 'Coates is the player Burnley look to in the "Let's go forward" department whether home or away. He has often been an outstanding raider with those sword thrusts on right and left, using his extraordinary ability to burst quickly past defenders.' Alas, Coates's time left at Burnley was now short as he was about to move to Spurs for a club record fee of £190,000. Relegation made this move a necessity with the deal completed secretly in a motorway service station.

Coventry 3 Burnley 0
17 April 1971
'Changes'

At Coventry, Adamson went for a 4-4-2 formation with Casper and Fletcher playing up front. It did not come off, but not for the want of trying. Adamson commented: 'I just want to say to all our supporters that they should be proud of the way the team fought against Coventry. They ran themselves into the ground, battled magnificently and did not surrender without a terrific effort. Just as we were getting on top, Ernie Hunt surprised us with a 40-yard lob, in the 53rd minute, that caught Tony Waiters off his line. Coventry's final two goals came in the last two minutes. I agree with a national pressman who awarded his "man-of-the-match" to Coventry goalkeeper, Bill Glazier. Why do they always do this against us?'

Arsenal 1 Burnley 0
20 April 1971
'If Not for You'

Three days later Burnley were relegated at league-champions elect Arsenal in front of a 47,591 crowd at Highbury. The Gunners were about to secure their first 'double'. Charlie George, who became an Arsenal hero at Wembley when he scored the FA Cup-winning goal, sent Burnley down with a spot kick.

2. THE DISASTROUS 1970/71 SEASON

Burnley 1 Derby County 2
24 April 1971
'LA Woman'

In front of a 10,373 crowd at Turf Moor, Casper opened the scoring, but mid-table Derby under Clough and Taylor completed the turnaround with nine minutes remaining. A year later Derby would become First Division champions.

Chelsea 0 Burnley 1
26 April 1971
'Famous Blue Raincoat'

Chelsea were destined for European Cup Winners' Cup glory but were surprisingly beaten 1-0 at Stamford Bridge where a profligate Kindon put away his third gilded chance of the game. The season ended on 1 May at Wolverhampton where Burnley lost to a second-half goal by flamboyant showman Derek Dougan, formerly with Burnley's arch rivals, Blackburn Rovers.

Adamson believed that Burnley were relegated because they exhibited 'too much tension and anxiety after a bad start.' He thought that Dobson's injury was 'the biggest setback.' What was indisputable was Burnley's poor goalscoring record, just 29 goals in 42 league fixtures, easily the worst record in the First Division. Eric Probert 'top-scored' with just five goals. Apart from Coates, only Waldron had a distinguished season having 'tidied up his image' as Burnley journalist Keith McNee put it. McNee chose Waldron as his 'player of the season' principally because of his aerial prominence and grit, reckoning he might have won an England Under-23 cap had Burnley not been in a relegation battle. As for the others, there were too many fitful performances. They were certainly hampered by injury to key players but also by their erratic performances. Had target man Paul Fletcher been signed earlier, he might have helped them to hold up the ball in advanced positions.

Unabashed, Bob Lord insisted: 'My dream of a "Real Madrid style super club" on the Lancashire moors is still intact despite the club's relegation.' He refuted any suggestion that relegation meant a big cut-back in his £1m-plus renovation scheme for making Turf Moor the cutting edge of football and recreational stadia. He also rejected claims that there would be cuts in staff and substantial economies. He was surely just shooting the breeze though. No longer benefitting from the lucrative visits of Liverpool, Manchester United and City, and Leeds, each of whom added around 10,000 to Burnley's average gate, it was likely that the club would have to rely upon gates in the order of 14,500 to survive.

Before Coates's transfer to Spurs, Lord insisted 'none of our stars will be sold'. Lord was an astute businessman. He must have known that this was nonsense. The replacement Brunshaw Road stand was then estimated to cost around £500,000. Perhaps it was a deliberate bluff to obtain the best sale prices for his players, while discouraging desertion of existing season ticket holders. The reality was that the young players Adamson proudly unveiled for the Stoke game, on Good Friday 1970, would be sold or released in the ensuing four years. These comprised: Peter Mellor (21 years old); Mick Docherty (19); Ray Ternent (21); Wilf Wrigley (20); Martin Dobson (22); Alan West (18); David Thomas (19); Ralph Coates (23); Geoff Nulty (21); Eric Probert (18); and Steve Kindon (19).

Yet for Burnley's 'sell to survive' policy to work there needed to be a constant stream of talented young players joining the club who could be developed sufficiently to replace the club's departing stars before being sold off in turn. Given the enormous 'wastage' rates among football clubs' apprentices, this was a formidable challenge. Even after Coates had departed to Spurs in the summer of 1971, Bob Lord continued to talk up the deal and its benefits. He argued: 'We did not want to sell him but had to. What we received in return, £190,000, represented one of the finest pieces of business enterprise ever pulled off by a football club. If we are going to remain a first-class club, we have to offer our players first-class contracts.'

I did not buy Lord's boasts, assurances, and expansive ambitions. I am sure I was not alone. Given the huge costs of running a football club with relatively small attendances, as was the case at Burnley, it seemed preposterous that he could create a super stadium with such limited resources available to him. By the time of the next annual shareholders' meeting, Bob Lord confessed, announcing the shelving of his plan for a new stand and entertainment centre. Relegation had proved costly as a £27,000 loss was recorded. It was only the sixth time in 24 post-war seasons that Burnley had sustained an annual loss. But all clubs other than the wealthiest ones were struggling to break even, let alone make a profit. Between 1949 and 1969, First Division attendances had declined by almost 20 per cent while player wages and transfer fees continued to increase. This was well before the days of £100m annual TV payments when gate revenue contributed no more than eight per cent of annual receipts.

3. POST-RELEGATION BLUES 1971/72

Burnley 0 Hull City 2
12 February 1972
'Can't Find My Way Home'

It was a bleak mid-winter. In the damp, cold days of February, we had to contend with daily power cuts as Prime Minister Heath slugged out a losing battle with the miners. Heath never got to grips with the trade unions. His Industrial Relations Act was a disaster. Eleven million days were lost to strikes in 1970, the highest total since the General Strike of 1926. The National Union of Miners (NUM) had not been a militant organisation in post-war Britain, quite the contrary. But its members became increasingly frustrated by their comparatively low wages and appalling conditions at the coal faces. In January 1972, the miners began their industrial action armed with a new, decisive tactic – the 'flying picket'. Saltley was its crowning glory; it was a vindication of Arthur Scargill's shrewd planning. Helped by sympathetic local car workers, the Birmingham-based coke depot was closed as 10,000 pickets overwhelmed the few hundred policemen deployed to keep the coke supplies flowing. Thousands of factories were forced to work a three-day week. Millions were laid off. The public were urged to restrict electrical usage to one room at home. Only the hospitals were spared the power cuts, although Burnley's Marsden hospital had to borrow an army power generator to keep it going. After seven weeks of misery, Heath capitulated.

3. POST-RELEGATION BLUES 1971/72

But the bloodiest conflict of that winter took place in Londonderry on Sunday 30 January when 13 unarmed civilians on a civil rights demonstration were shot dead by soldiers of the Parachute Regiment. The sectarian violence escalated quickly and 72 innocent civilians, 43 soldiers, 11 policemen, and five members of the Ulster Defence Regiment died in the 1972 Northern Ireland 'Troubles'. It was the worst annual death toll of the Ulster conflict.

Burnley made a promising start to life in Division Two. In their opening game at Cardiff on 14 August, second-half goals from a rejuvenated Casper and Dobson pulled back a 0-2 half-time deficit. A week later they beat Luton in front of 13,365 home supporters. It was noteworthy that Adamson was permitting a more direct style of play, unlike before, capitalising upon the speed of Casper, Kindon, and Fletcher. In the 55th minute Waiters passed the ball out to Dobson, ten yards in front of him. Dobson immediately launched a long ball down the middle which Casper received at pace. Bursting past three bemused Luton defenders loitering on the edge of their box, he scored with a searing shot before they or the Luton goalkeeper could react. Two minutes later Bellamy released Kindon. At full speed Kindon charged down the inside-left channel, leaving his markers for dead before rounding the advancing goalie and slipping the ball into the unguarded net from an acute angle.

Despite disappointing losses at Oxford (1-2), Charlton (0-2), and Norwich (0-3) Burnley beat Preston at Deepdale (3-1) and had emphatic victories against Carlisle (3-0) and Orient (6-1) at home. Burnley midfielder Bellamy scored a hat-trick against Orient, while Cardiff were undone at Turf Moor by a second brace from Casper (3-0). Meanwhile, Welsh winger Leighton James had emerged as a major talent, scoring seven times in his first 11 games. He was twice on target as visiting Middlesbrough were thumped 5-2 on 13 November.

Here, Burnley's joint star performer was 'super sub' Steve Kindon. He created havoc in Middlesbrough's defence with his bullish power and thoroughbred pace. At that point Burnley were in fourth position and challenging hard for a promotion place. But in their next 19 fixtures they won just five games, losing 11. This disappointing decline did little to lift the glum mood around the club and town. Kindon's erratic performances troubled Adamson most. He told James Lawton of the *Daily Express* 'There is no more powerful runner in English football than Steve Kindon. When he is feeling good in himself, he frightens opposing defences right out of their skins.' Yet a few weeks later an exasperated Adamson told Kindon: 'You are either brilliant or rubbish. I cannot afford to gamble with you currently.'

It was reported that Bert Head of Crystal Palace and Malcolm Allison of Manchester City were prepared to offer £180,000 for the unsettled Kindon, although nothing transpired. But Kindon was not the only mercurial star in Adamson's side. England Under-23 winger David Thomas also performed spasmodically. While he sometimes lit up a game with his brilliant footwork, at other times he seemed distracted. After First Division strugglers Huddersfield dismissed Burnley from the FA Cup at a windy Turf Moor in January 1972, one reporter carped, 'Thomas seemed to be trying wastefully to win the match on his own.'

Young goalkeeper Peter Mellor was proving less reliable, too. It was his mistake which gifted Huddersfield their winning goal. With Waiters retiring, Adamson was permitted to sign a replacement goalie – Alan Stevenson, the Chesterfield and England Under-23 international. Almost half of his £50,000 fee was recouped when Mellor moved to Fulham.

The left-back problem had not been solved, either. Adamson tried four players in this position: youngsters Harry Wilson and Eddie Cliff, former Chelsea right-back Jim Thomson, and utility player Geoff Nulty, all without success. Adamson's patience was

3. POST-RELEGATION BLUES 1971/72

sorely tried, not only by his stars' inconsistency but also by the impatience of the home fans. He was so incensed at the fans' criticisms of Harry Wilson's performance against Fulham in March 1972 that he snapped, 'He is only a youngster and yet they expect him to play like Terry Cooper. Look at Peter Mellor, a confident, composed goalkeeper – because he was playing for Fulham. He got so much stick here we had to sell him. There is a message there, surely?' Former Blackburn, Everton, and England full-back Keith Newton would solve the left-back problem, but he did not arrive until the season was over.

Glowering clouds squatted above Burnley on a grisly 12 February day, deluging the town with icy rain. I met Liz, my wife, at her family home in Leeds – she was training to be a teacher in Manchester, while I was undergoing social-work training in the East Midlands. We borrowed her mother's car to go to the game. Cowering under our plastic macs, we made for the shelter of the Longside where most of the meagre 11,751 crowd had gathered. It might have been worse. Surely, only the hated power cuts could have driven so many from their cold homes? The derelict Brunshaw Road stand remained boarded up – an unsightly accusation – while chairman Bob Lord glumly contemplated the indigestible cost of its replacement.

At the Bee Hole End, there was a morose gathering of misanthropes, folded over their chosen barriers, stoically defying the inclement weather. A distorted version of T. Rex's 'Telegram Sam' emerged erratically from the club's PA system. With personal warmth a distant memory, many stamped and blew into their hands. Much of the pre-match talk focused on work shortages and the hated cuts. Once the game started, these gripes drained away, leaving embattled Jimmy Adamson to face the fans' mounting objections.

Visitors Hull City were having a poor season. Despite thrashing bottom-placed Watford 4-0 at home on the previous Saturday, they remained in 20th position, where they had been for almost two months. They were only two points better off than Cardiff – a promotion rival just 12 months before – who had a game in hand. Hull had recorded just one league win away from home – a 2-1 victory at doomed Watford. Yet they had recently eliminated First Division Coventry from the FA Cup.

After ex-Burnley, Everton, and Preston manager Cliff Britton had 'moved upstairs' in 1970, Terry Neill, his 28-year-old replacement, applied sterner defensive disciplines. Neill had been a top defender with Arsenal and Northern Ireland. As a player-manager at Boothferry Park, Neill led by example, helping make the Tigers' defence tighter.

Former centre-forward Chris Chilton had been indispensable to both Britton and Neill. In his 11-year career at Hull, Chilton scored 222 goals in all competitions. So, when the strapping 28-year-old striker left for Coventry at the start of the 1971/72 season, for a fee of £90,000, his presence was sorely missed. A 22-year-old local lad, Stuart Pearson, had been groomed to fill his boots but he made a slow start, not helped by the Hull fans' impatience.

Pearson was a different kind of centre-forward to Chilton. Whereas Chilton had muscular presence, Pearson had express pace and quicksilver mobility. Once he had found his feet, Pearson showed he had more in his locker than his predecessor. He could forage menacingly as a lone striker, creating space for himself and others. His first touch was sure. He was nimble but also strong, able to resist thuggish defenders at his back. He could bring others into the game with his accurate layoffs. Although he did not have Chilton's aerial power, Pearson was competent with his head. He possessed a fierce shot to boot. Pearson was Hull's leading goalscorer in this spluttering season, netting an impressive 15 league goals. Soon his detractors were singing his praises. So was eagle-eyed Tommy Docherty, snaffling Pearson for his resurgent Manchester United side in 1974, for a fee worth

3. POST-RELEGATION BLUES 1971/72

£200,000. Pearson would eventually play 15 times for England, scoring five goals.

Although Pearson represented a welcome introduction of youthful talent, Hull City's side was ageing. Two thirds of Neill's first-team squad were aged around the 30 mark, including: Ian McKechnie, a former Arsenal reserve goalkeeper; centre-back Bill Baxter, a First Division championship winner at Ipswich under Alf Ramsey; and John Kaye, a midfielder, although formerly a striker with Scunthorpe and West Bromwich. However, Hull's full-backs Frank Banks and Roger Devries were in the early stages of their careers. Seasoned midfielder Ken Knighton was unavailable for the Burnley game, so his place was taken by another experienced squad member, 29-year-old Billy Wilkinson. At Turf Moor, Wilkinson and the industrious Malcolm Lord played in central midfield, while fiery Scot Jimmy McGill played on the right. McGill had made over 170 league appearances with Arsenal and Huddersfield before joining Hull in 1971. Playing on Hull's left flank was 28-year-old Ian Butler, who had racked up almost 400 league appearances at Hull and Rotherham. Up front, Ken Wagstaffe partnered Pearson. Wagstaffe had scored almost 250 league goals for Hull and Mansfield.

Burnley were in the middle of a goal drought, having scored just three goals in their previous five games. But lifted by their feisty victory over Norwich, Adamson selected an unchanged, attacking side, including David Thomas, Frank Casper, Paul Fletcher, Steve Kindon, and Leighton James. I wondered whether they would get in the way of one another. The Hull defensive wall troubled them more. Burnley created just one chance in the first half. It came soon after kick-off. Fletcher – normally so ruthless in the air – unaccountably headed wide from Alan West's perfect cross. While James continued to impress on the left wing, Dave Thomas had a wretched game on the right. The drab first half was goalless. With so little entertainment on view, it was hard to suppress the increasing cold. Liz and I wondered whether we would have been better off staying at her family home – power cuts or not.

But just two minutes after the restart, the Tigers showed they could bite as well as tame. Neill played a free kick to Wagstaffe who quickly relayed the ball into the path of the advancing full-back, Banks. He instantly sent over a low skidding cross which eluded everyone except Hull City left-winger, Butler, who slid the ball in at the far post.

Burnley tried to raise the tempo. Despite their spluttering form, chances came and went with Casper, Kindon, and James the worst culprits. However, Fletcher was unlucky with a goal-bound header which beat Hull goalkeeper McKechnie, only for the full-back, Devries, to head the ball over the bar. Not that Hull were restricted to all-out defence. They exerted periodic pressure, using long passes to good effect. Stevenson had to make athletic saves from Pearson and Lord and was at full stretch to prevent Colin Waldron scoring an own goal. But he was helpless when Wagstaffe scored Hull's second goal, two minutes from time. With Burnley committed to a final all-out assault, Wagstaffe seized upon Casper's misplaced pass just inside the Burnley half, and raced through for a fine individual goal. The Longside supporters immediately began chanting 'Adamson out! Potts in!' Their demonstration lasted for several minutes after the game. Adamson offered no excuses. He told *Burnley Express* sports editor Keith McNee, 'It was a poor game and one we shouldn't have lost. Generally, we had too many important players below par. When Hull scored, the players got anxious, the crowd got anxious, and we could not recover. Our supporters were fully justified in their criticisms. We cannot put on an exhibition like that and hope to get away with it. We are entertainers and we must do a heck of a lot better than this. But this is part of the hazards of being a manager and I have got to take it on the chin.'

3. POST-RELEGATION BLUES 1971/72

Adamson had been in charge for 88 games. He had won just 27 per cent of these. The *Daily Mirror* football correspondent reckoned that 'Burnley needed someone like Jimmy Adamson out on the park, someone who can take stock, point the way and calm their hell-for-leather approach.' The *Daily Express* football reporter thought that Burnley's problems were due to a lack of mental toughness. He wrote: 'In short, Burnley's prodigies always look hurt and surprised if their dazzling footwork fails to bring goals. Lesser players than Terry Neill and Ken Wagstaffe smack their lips when they see that.' Burnley supporters' letters to the local newspaper were unequivocally critical. One wrote, 'The booing of Jimmy Adamson has been on the cards for some time. In my opinion, Mr Adamson could bring internationals to play at Burnley and within a month they would be unrecognisable, wondering where they have come to.' Another added, 'The youth policy is a dead loss. I am honestly worried we will finish in the Third Division. What a disappointment this team is.' Yet another Burnley fan commented, 'Players valued at half a million pounds are giving Central League performances. What a disaster for the "Team of the Seventies".'

In the face of mounting supporter criticisms, Bob Lord retorted, 'It is not Jimmy's fault, it's the players who are not getting the results. The fans will not get their way. Our team did not play well. Jimmy Adamson has done a lot for Burnley and will do a lot more in the future.' Colin Waldron added: 'There were 11 guilty men on Saturday. It was our worst display and we deserved to lose. But we feel the chanting is unjustified. We wouldn't have minded if it was directed at us.'

Keith McNee reflected in the *Burnley Express*: 'The manager and the team must expect to share a bitter reaction. Where the Clarets go from here, especially in their strained relationships with their own followers, remains to be seen, but the present mood is black indeed and only a massive improvement on the field of play can move that monster cloud on to someone else's patch of sky.' After a subsequent defeat at promotion-bound Birmingham City, Burnley dropped to tenth place.

Belatedly, Adamson discovered his best team. Neither Kindon nor Thomas featured but Billy Ingham did, as a scrapping, fetching-and-carrying midfielder. Crucially, too, Martin Dobson was released to play a creative midfield role, with Jim Thomson moved to centre-back to accompany Colin Waldron. The final six fixtures were won with 12 goals scored and only two conceded. This was more like it! A promotion-winning side was taking shape. Regrettably, Adamson's apparent inability to communicate with Thomas and Kindon about their value to the club left both players with bitter memories of him, souring their subsequent departures. As for Frank Casper this season was a welcome return to form with 18 league goals, his best seasonal haul for Burnley. It had been sad seeing this classy forward struggle so badly during the previous season.

Dave Thomas told his namesake, author of *No Nay Never: A Burnley Anthology*: 'Jimmy Adamson was years ahead of his time with his free-kick routines and tactics. Maybe it was me; I have a determined streak and stood up to him when he wanted his own way. He always thought he was number one, always thought he was right. He was a sort of "get your hair cut" sort of a bloke and he could be arrogant. Harry Potts, if he passed you by, always had something to say or a greeting. Adamson sometimes walked straight by. You never knew what mood he would be in.'

Steve Kindon recalled, 'Towards the end of the '71/72 season, Jimmy Adamson sought me out. He put his arm around my shoulders and told me, "Next season I'm going to build a team around you, Steve." It surprised me a bit because I never thought I was really his sort of player. I was the knock-and-run type whereas Adamson wanted the tippy-tappy team-playing sort. Dave Thomas did not fit in either because he was too individualistic. My fiancée and I decided to marry on 3 June, and we were thinking about buying a house locally. I asked Adamson

3. POST-RELEGATION BLUES 1971/72

whether I should buy or rent as I did not want to commit myself to a mortgage if I was about to move on. He told me emphatically that I should buy. Assured by this, we went ahead and bought a place. I spent the summer doing it up. Then, just eight days after our wedding, I was transferred to Wolves for a £100,000 fee. Jimmy Adamson is a two-faced so and so.'

But Steve would make a stunning return to Burnley five years later, having been brought back by another returning hero, Harry Potts. Potts left his general manager post at Burnley in that summer of 1972 with a £28,000 pay-off in recognition of his loyal and glorious 14-year service. The next time there was a crisis of confidence in Adamson's management, in January 1976, Bob Lord was not at all supportive.

4. CHAMPIONS AGAIN 1972/73

'I Can See Clearly Now'

The last US combat unit quit Vietnam. Hanoi had emphatically won both the 'French War' and the 'American War', albeit with the loss of well over three million lives. In 1972 Britain also had an international conflict of their own to resolve. This was the spat with Iceland about fishing rights. Two British trawlers were sunk. Although the Royal Navy was summoned, the Icelandic gunboats continued to cut the trawlers' nets in courageous if reckless, darting, high-seas raids. This was done right under the noses of the supposed protectors, Royal Navy frigates. It was a bad year for terrorism too, as at the Munich Olympics a Palestinian group, Black September, killed all nine of its hostages, while at Tel Aviv airport, three kamikaze Japanese hitmen killed 26 people. Although the sectarian violence in Northern Ireland persisted, at least the Baader-Meinhof reign of terror was brought to an end.

Because of the demands of my social-work training, I saw few Burnley games in the 1971/72 and 1972/73 seasons. This training entailed long shifts at a Midland children's home. I became increasingly reliant upon radio, television, and press coverage for updates. What I gathered, from a distance, was that Adamson had a much more settled side. Six players – Stevenson, Newton, Waldron, Thomson, Casper, and James – played in all 42 league games. Dobson missed only one game and Fletcher two. Adamson had never had this luxury during the 1970/71 and 1971/72 seasons, and the lack of continuity had shown in

4. CHAMPIONS AGAIN 1972/73

his team's performances and results. My first sighting of Burnley in 1972/73 was at Fulham in August.

Fulham 1 Burnley 1
19 August 1972
'Silver Machine'

Jimmy had been at it again. He predicted: 'We'll be among the promotion contenders', oblivious to the fate of his previous predictions. The fans seemed unconvinced though as the first four home fixtures drew, on average, crowds of little more than 13,000. It had not helped that Burnley were abruptly eliminated from the Watney Cup by Third Division Bristol Rovers. As seen on BBC *Match of the Day*, Burnley were rolled over by 'Smash' and 'Grab', the lethal strike partnership of Alan Warboys and Bruce Bannister. Sadly, Kindon had left, with Thomas about to depart. Also, 1959/60 hero John Angus had called it a day after fighting a losing battle with injury. However, veteran England international left-back, Keith Newton, joined the ranks on a free transfer. His contribution would be immense.

The opening game was at Carlisle on 12 August where Burnley twice came from behind to secure a 2-2 draw, with goals from James and Thomas. Having a rare weekend off from childcare responsibilities, on Saturday 19 August I hitched to London and back for the match at Fulham.

It was a sparkling day. But the game was the icing on the cake. It was a belter! In the second minute Doug Collins and Dave Thomas exchanged passes deep inside Fulham's half. With Burnley left-back Keith Newton moving up in support, Collins laid the ball back to him. Newton immediately swung in a diagonal cross that cleared the heads of the Fulham defenders but fell into James's path. He was on it in a flash, blasting the ball past ex-Claret Peter Mellor. The Fulham defenders protested that James was offside, to no avail. Soon afterwards, James attacked down the left flank, feeding the overlapping Newton who produced another brilliant cross. With several players leaping to meet it, the ball ran loose to Collins, whose fierce volley was grasped by Mellor. This was looking good.

But Fulham soon found their feet and began making menacing raids on Stevenson's goal. Mullery pushed a free kick towards Callaghan whose shot narrowly cleared the bar. Then, following an interlude of head tennis, involving three Fulham players, Barrett suddenly claimed the ball and made for goal. Once he reached the Burnley box he shot immediately. Stevenson dived to his right to grab the grubbing effort. Next, Lloyd burst down the middle, before releasing Brown to his right. Brown's shot was powerful but fizzed into the side netting. Lloyd's free kick on Fulham's left flank caused consternation, too. It reached Richardson at the far post and he headed back across goal, where Dobson was well placed to nod it over the bar for a corner, with Mullery ready to pounce. Having withstood this relentless pressure, the Burnley players were pleased to hear the half-time whistle.

On the resumption, Fulham picked up where they left off. A neat combination between Callaghan, Richardson, and Lloyd on their left flank allowed Lloyd the space to transfer the ball to Mullery on the right of the Burnley box. He pushed it instantly into the path of overlapping Moreline whose shot was deflected wide for a corner by the alert Newton. Mullery's corner kick was aimed at the near post where 'man mountain' Paul Went used his mighty strength to part his markers and head in via the underside of the bar. Fifty minutes had gone, and Burnley had lost their slender lead. Now with their tails up Fulham pressed forward in greater numbers. Prompted by Barrett, Lloyd suddenly found himself in space on the edge of the Burnley box. His looping shot looked as if it was going in, but thankfully dipped into the top netting.

Although this entertaining game featured much fluent football, neat skills, deft touches, and crisp passing, it had its

4. CHAMPIONS AGAIN 1972/73

fair share of agricultural tackling, too, resulting in several yellow cards being shown, mostly to the besieged Burnley players. I was pleased to see greater ruggedness in the Clarets' play. There had been too little of this during the 1970/71 season. But midway through the second half Burnley were awarded a free kick around 40 yards from goal. Thomas clipped it towards the far post where Fletcher outjumped the Fulham defenders and headed towards goal, forcing Mellor to punch the ball away at full stretch. James immediately let fly with a fierce volley. Luckily for Mellor the ball zipped into the side netting.

Fulham returned to the attack and Stevenson had to be at his best, claiming a high cross above the heads of the inrushing Fulham attackers. He then had to dive at the feet of a Fulham forward who was intent upon converting a whistling cross. Fletcher routinely bolstered his defenders at set pieces, demonstrating impressive aerial strength. His headed clearances frequently carried 25 yards or more. Today, this is commonplace but then it was less evident. Keith Newton was also immaculate in defence. He thwarted one raid along the left goal line with a perfectly timed sliding tackle, not only dispossessing the Fulham attacker, but also preventing the ball running out for a corner kick. Quicker in regaining his feet than his sprawling adversary, Newton calmly took the ball away from danger.

With only a few minutes left, Burnley should have claimed both points. Casper was sent free, cutting the ball back after reaching the goal line. With the Fulham defenders at sixes and sevens, James spotted his chance, striding in between them and getting his shot away before he could be stopped. Alas, he lifted the ball over the bar from close range. This miss might have been costly, for only seconds later Thomson made a hash of a back pass, forcing Stevenson to hurl himself across his goal twice to avert danger. First, he pushed away the miscued back pass just before it crossed his goal line, and then he threw himself at the feet of an aggressive attacker, denying him a tap-in. As hairy moments go, this was as heart-stopping as they come.

I left the ground drained but delighted. Burnley were not at their best, but they gained a worthy point. Fulham's new riverside stand lifted their ground's total capacity to 40,000. Bob Lord must have been beside himself with envy. My reward was a tortuous hitch back to the Midland care home.

Burnley 4 Aston Villa 1
26 August 1972
'You Wear It Well'

I relied on *Match of the Day* for this one, making sure I did not stumble upon the result before the highlights were shown. As at Fulham, James gave us a flying start. In the third minute he picked up a pass from Thomas and raced 60 yards, outpacing everyone in his path. Having reached the edge of the Villa box, instead of going for goal, he pushed the ball to Collins on his left. Collins shot instantly with his left foot. The ball barely left the ground as it rocketed past Worcestershire cricketer Jim Cumbes.

However, Villa were soon back in the hunt. In the 15th minute left-back Charlie Aitken crossed high and diagonally towards the far post. Ex-Claret Andy Lochhead, as combative as ever, headed powerfully across goal for Chico Hamilton to poke the ball past Stevenson at the near post.

Not to be outdone, in the 28th minute overlapping Keith Newton found Casper with a left-wing cross. Casper headed the ball down for Fletcher, whose half-volley flashed into the net, leaving goalkeeper Cumbes a mere spectator. Burnley were ahead once more.

Thomas was next to make his mark, in the 32nd minute, when he took a corner on the left flank. After exchanging a swift, short pass with Casper, Thomas bamboozled two Villa defenders with his sinuous dribbling before crossing to the near post where a dazed Dobson outjumped Aitken and headed in.

4. CHAMPIONS AGAIN 1972/73

At half-time this superb Burnley team left the field to rapturous applause from over 14,000 Clarets fans. The game was wrapped up in the 76th minute. Stevenson cleared high and long into the Villa half. Fletcher headed the ball on and Casper rifled in Burnley's fourth. Burnley moved into sixth place. Subsequent 2-0 victories over Preston and Portsmouth put them in pole position. Adamson was awarded the Second Division manager of the month prize. However, in September Burnley fell back into third place after a series of draws. They also almost let slip a 4-0 lead over Blackpool at Turf Moor on 23 September. When Blackpool scored their third goal there were just four minutes left. Fortunately, Burnley recovered their composure, helped by the substitution of gritty Nulty for Thomas.

Luton Town 2 Burnley 2
30 September 1972
'Mama Weer All Crazee Now'

A friend drove me to this game, which was bathed in glittering autumn sunshine. The Saturday press had headlined with the plight of the Ugandan Asians seeking refuge in Britain, having been expelled by Idi Amin, supposedly a 'decent chap' according to one British diplomat. Many of these refugees had been successful businessmen and women in Uganda but were then compelled to find new homes and work in Britain. Many turned to Luton and Leicester. It was my first visit to Kenilworth Road. The ground seemed ramshackle and shabby, whereas Luton's team were certainly not, being highly combative and skilful. We made for the shaded terraces at the town end, mainly populated with home fans. In those days I saw no reason to stick with my fellow supporters if there was a better vantage point.

At the opposite end Leighton James opened the scoring in the third minute. His 30-yard shot dipped and bent, and somehow found a way past Willie Carrick in the Luton goal. However,

13 minutes later Luton equalised. A penalty was awarded after Collins was judged to have blocked Rodney Fern's shot with his right hand. The Burnley players complained vociferously but the referee ignored them. An emotionless John Aston, formerly with Manchester United, slid the ball past Stevenson, before contemptuously clearing his nose.

The second period began quietly until Colin Waldron's careless back pass, in the 54th minute, was eagerly intercepted by Vic Halom, who put Luton ahead. In the remaining 36 minutes there were chances at both ends, but I sensed that if Burnley were going to get anything from this game it was going to come from James. He was everywhere, confounding his opposing defenders with pace and trickery, but also riling the Luton crowd with his petulance. They reacted by booing him each time he was on the ball, not realising perhaps that this only increased his desire to make them suffer. With barely a minute left he cut in from the right, outpacing his markers again and making for goal. Just as it looked as if he was heading into a cul-de-sac, he unleashed a fierce dipping drive. Carrick had no chance as the ball whizzed into the left-hand corner. With discretion seeming the better part of valour, I muffled my joy while James continued to taunt the home supporters with his extravagant celebrations. You must be very good to get away with such stunts.

The game at Luton was Dave Thomas's last for Burnley before he departed to QPR, with the Hoops shelling out a club record £165,000 fee. Although his time at Burnley ended sourly, with a fine, he was genuinely sad to leave. However, his career took off at Loftus Road, just as Burnley coach, Brian Miller, predicted. His lucrative sale persuaded Bob Lord to announce that the club would proceed with their original plans to build an all-seated stand on the site of the demolished Brunshaw Road stand. The new stand's revised cost had fallen to £200,000.

On 7 October Burnley returned to the top when they beat Swindon 2-1 at Turf Moor, with goals from Fletcher and Dobson.

4. CHAMPIONS AGAIN 1972/73

They would hold this position until early March. A week later the *Match of the Day* cameras were enticed to Hillsborough. Wednesday were going well in second place. They had two dangerous wingers in Scottish international Willie Henderson and former West Ham FA Cup winner John Sissons. They also had Jimmy Mullen in defence. He would later play a big part in Burnley's future. Once again, James excelled. In the 54th minute his long-range Exocet flew into the top-right corner of the net in front of the uncovered Kop to grasp both points. Burnley won six and drew five of their next 11 games. A Fletcher hat-trick downed Cardiff 3-0 on 21 October. A brace from Casper overcame depleted Blackpool at Yuletide. And a late recovery at Middlesbrough enabled Burnley to escape with a 3-3 draw, after an 80th-minute goal from Fletcher and an 87th-minute one from Dobson. The only blot on their progress came on 11 November when Gerry Queen's late goal at Turf Moor enabled Orient to seize the points.

Aston Villa 0 Burnley 3
6 January 1973

'The Jean Genie'

For many Clarets this was Burnley's best performance of the season. I used some of my Christmas money to go. It was a dreary, grey day, not cold though. It was at the end of a week in which Ted Heath had taken us into the EEC without explaining that the European Court of Justice would have jurisdiction over British courts. It was also the week when 400 Londonderry children attacked British troops.

There were almost 40,000 fans in Villa Park. The ground seemed to vibrate with their collective strength. Hemmed in by febrile home fanatics, this was not the place to put my head above the parapet. But the Burnley lads were oblivious to the partisan din. In only the seventh minute Burnley took the lead. Billy Ingham, who had an outstanding game, was fouled on the edge of the Villa box, following a penetrating run from midfield. He tricked the Villa wall by preparing to shoot, but instead pushed the ball left to Keith Newton, who rifled it into the net. Cumbes got a hand to the ball, but the power of the shot was too much for him. This stunned the Villa supporters, although they soon recovered their voices, urging their team on with their flat invective. Although Stevenson saved Alun Evans's speculative shot, he was largely untroubled during the first half. Cumbes was much the busier goalkeeper.

In the 23rd minute Burnley scored their second goal. Frank Casper hustled down the right flank and centred. Fletcher timed his leap to perfection, heading Casper's cross downwards towards the penalty spot where Nulty volleyed home with relish. I rarely relax at Burnley games. Normally my forehead remains furrowed, with my nails dug into my palms. But watching Burnley here was like admiring the purring power of a Rolls. Burnley could have been out of sight by half-time. James was anxious not to be excluded from the action. Having lobbed the ball over the heads of two Villa defenders, he raced around them catching the ball on the half-volley. Only a brilliant save from Cumbes denied him.

At the resumption Burnley immediately won a corner. This was partially cleared only to be returned with interest. James was first to the loose ball, but the erratic bounce confounded him, resulting in a sliced shot. However, Ingham sprang upon his miscued effort, diverting the ball into the Villa net. For the remaining 45 minutes, Burnley closed ranks and sucked up periodic Villa pressure with Dobson in authoritative form. It was only in the final minutes that Villa made more challenging assaults on the Burnley goal. Both Graydon and Rioch broke through the Burnley back line only for Stevenson to produce eye-catching saves.

While several press men took Burnley's promotion for granted after this superlative victory, Adamson did not. He said:

4. CHAMPIONS AGAIN 1972/73

'Our target is to get two points from every match. Aston Villa are one of our challengers and we have widened the gap between us and them. This is obviously what we want to do. Although this was one of the best performances of the season, it was not the best. I thought we played better at Orient in September where we could have won by six goals but had to rely on Frank Casper's equaliser in the last few minutes to gain a point. Sometimes you can't justify the score line.'

Queens Park Rangers 2 Burnley 0
27 January 1973
'Wishing Well'

As if to reinforce Jimmy's caution, two weeks later Burnley lost 0-2 at promotion rivals Queens Park Rangers. I watched the brief highlights on ITV. The weather at Loftus Road was sunny but Burnley's performance was not. Rangers opened the scoring in the 15th minute when their midfielder, Delve, was allowed to control a pass from Thomas and turn. Having no one to close him down he floated a high right-wing cross towards the far post where Mike Leach outjumped the Burnley defenders and headed in powerfully. Five minutes later Collins dithered in midfield, waiting for Casper to retreat from an offside position. Leach dispossessed him with a sliding tackle and released Givens. With no one to block his path Givens raced forward and shot firmly past Stevenson. Burnley were still in top spot but only by one point, although they did have a game in hand over Rangers.

Burnley were quickly back in the saddle, though, with a 2-1 home win over Huddersfield and a 4-1 victory at Hull, with Ingham scoring twice. There were setbacks against Sheffield Wednesday (0-1) and Forest (0-3). But these defeats were brushed aside with victories at Swindon and Cardiff (both 1-0 wins). Portsmouth were also thrashed 4-0 at Turf Moor with Casper scoring twice. Millwall were beaten 2-1, too, after Burnley came from behind, before Burnley completed the double over Huddersfield at Leeds Road (2-0). Then on 16 April promotion was assured after eventual FA Cup winners Sunderland were defeated 2-0 at Turf Moor. Fletcher scored both goals in front of almost 23,000 fans. Burnley not letting up, Oxford were then beaten 2-0 and Brighton and Luton were seen off with a pair of 3-0 victories. But Adamson wanted the championship, as did QPR who had tracked Burnley all the way to the tape. This was the time of the Watergate scandal. It was also the time to bid farewell to Bobby Charlton who bowed out at Chelsea. Meanwhile Denis Law left Old Trafford on a free transfer.

Preston North End 1 Burnley 1
28 April 1973
'Cum On Feel the Noize'

This April day was blessed with scintillating spring warmth, fitting weather for Burnley to celebrate winning the Second Division championship. But they had to get past Preston first. Having restored Preston to Division Two in 1971, former manager Alan Ball Senior struggled to keep them there. Despite bringing in experienced recruits such as Hugh McIlmoyle, from Middlesbrough, and Neil Young and David Connor, from Manchester City, Preston spluttered. They finished the 1971/72 season in 18th position, just four points above the drop. Nevertheless, Preston had started the 1972/73 season well. A 2-0 win at Oxford at the end of October lifted Preston into fourth place. But a 1-6 defeat at Carlisle on Boxing Day signalled the start of an alarming decline. Only two victories were achieved in their next 20 games, 12 of which were lost. Gates plummeted. Merely 6,230 watched their 0-5 drubbing by lowly Portsmouth on 10 February. It was Alan Ball Senior's last game in charge. Their only cause for cheer was the emergence of fledgling Scottish striker Alex Bruce, who topped the Preston league scoring chart with 13 goals.

4. CHAMPIONS AGAIN 1972/73

On 28 April Preston needed to deny Burnley to be sure of survival. It was said that Preston had narrowed their pitch to curb the threat from Leighton James's wing play. As it turned out, no one was disappointed. Preston took a 43rd-minute lead when Bruce shot past Stevenson, having capitalised on a 40-yard run by Alan Lamb. This was classic counter-attacking, for Burnley had dominated possession in the first half only to be thwarted by Preston's unusually stout defence. With Burnley fans comprising at least half of the 21,550 crowd, nothing was going to spoil their rowdy party. Ten minutes after the break, Waldron's header rebounded to him 25 yards from goal. Without hesitation he struck a sweet left-foot volley high into the Preston net. Cue party time. Thereafter, Burnley and Preston eliminated the risk of an adverse result by playing pat-a-cake.

Burnley supporter Vini Corrigan recalled: 'Let us say the game fizzled out for about half an hour of very timid midfield play.' Mark Pickering added: 'apart from Waldron's goal, my main memory is of James standing by the corner flag with his foot on the ball and the Preston players just staring at him until the referee eventually got bored and blew his whistle'. As that jubilant moment grew closer, massed ranks of Burnley fans gathered on the touchline, crouching in readiness for their exuberant charge. Once referee Hunting's whistle sounded, on they poured, an excited, heaving churn of Bay City Roller-like pubescence. 'Shang-a-Lang's shenanigans would not trump this, though.

Jimmy Adamson was named the Second Division manager of the year while Martin Dobson was chosen as Granada TV's player of the year. Adamson had achieved promotion using only 14 players, one of whom – Eddie Cliff – played only three times. The first-team squad sailed off to a well-deserved break in Majorca. Burnley were back with a vibrant young side, led by one of the best coaches in the country. A salutary note came from the bottom line, though. On average, only 14,083 fans were drawn to

Turf Moor during this triumphant season – 2,000 down on the 1970/71 figure, in a dismal relegation year. Burnley's population was continuing to fall, too. In 1971, around 77,000 lived in the town, five per cent less than in 1961. Taken as a whole, there had been a 30 per cent decline in Burnley's population since the end of the World War One. Like Barrow, Burnley FC had to beat an inexorable economic and demographic retreat. Each week they needed to punch well above their weight and be prepared to punch harder and harder as that weight declined. But such challenges were for tomorrow, for this beautiful day was one of exultant joy.

5. BACK IN THE BIG TIME
1973/74

The winter of 1973/74 did for Prime Minister Ted Heath. He had turned to the country for a firmer mandate to deal with striking miners, power workers and railwaymen, and to halt the runaway inflation fuelled by the oil crisis following the Yom Kippur War. Heath asked who should be running the country. With the nation replying, 'Not you mate', Harold Wilson's Labour Party was returned to power, albeit by a slender margin, as in 1964. The constant electricity cuts that plagued this season almost did for small football clubs. Floodlit games were only permissible with a generator. Burnley bought one for £30,000, although chairman Bob Lord reacted grumpily when fewer than 19,000 turned up for its christening. A vast majority of lower-division teams were forced to play their midweek fixtures in daylight. Gates fell through the floor. Just 450 people went to Spotland in February 1974 to watch relegation-bound Rochdale take on Cambridge in a Third Division game. But the top flight was not immune either. A midweek league game between Chelsea and Burnley in March 1974 attracted only 8,131 fans.

The season began brightly though with a victory in the FA Charity Shield at Maine Road on a glimmering summer afternoon. Burnley's set play dazzled, too. With my wife and me now qualified and earning a wage, we resumed watching them regularly at the start of the 1973/74 season. Up until Christmas, Burnley valiantly tracked Leeds's hot pace. Initially, the crowds returned in droves. By mid-November home gates were averaging 25,000, the best figures for over ten years. Despite Turf Moor being reduced to three sides, on account of the reconstruction of the Brunshaw Road stand, 40,000 wriggled in to see the tough 0-0 draw with Leeds on 10 November. Burnley was buzzing once more.

Although the national press picked out sturdy young striker Ray Hankin and pint-sized midfielder Brian Flynn as exciting prospects, the Burnley production line was not delivering the volume of young talent that it had during the sixties. The emerging Bob Lord stand began to assume a spectral presence as Burnley's 'sell to survive' policy faltered. Burnley needed to sell over £200,000 worth of talent each season to keep the wolf from the door. It seemed an impossible task.

As talented as his side was, Jimmy Adamson knew that he needed sharper game plans to prosper in the top flight. One area which Adamson prioritised was set plays. It was something that both he and Jimmy McIlroy had worked upon in the fifties and early sixties.

Burnley captain Martin Dobson told me in our meeting in 2010: 'In 1973 we played Manchester City twice. The first game was staged at Maine Road in the Charity Shield Final. Here, we used a set-play routine that worked to perfection. A free kick was awarded just outside the City box to the right of centre. We had a couple of lads standing over the ball – playmaker Dougie Collins was one. There was a bit of shuffling around – a false start – as if there was confusion between them as to what the plan was. In fact, the two of them started a mock argument, blaming one another for fouling up the routine.

'Well, of course, that caused the City defenders to relax and lose concentration. They thought our guys didn't know what they were doing. And just as the City lads had dropped their guard, Dougie suddenly clipped a lofted ball to the back of the six-yard box. "Waldo" [Colin Waldron], our centre-half, anticipated the move. Unseen, he ran around the back of the City defence and met Dougie's chip with a diving header. It was the Charity Shield-winning goal.

'A few months later, we were due to play City again. This time it was in the league at Turf Moor. Jimmy Adamson said to us before the game: "Remember that free-kick routine that worked so well at Maine Road?" And we said: "Yes boss, but we can't pull that stunt again. They won't fall for it twice." But Jimmy replied: "But they might if we change the players involved. They might be fooled into thinking it is a different set play." Well, we did as he suggested. This time "Fletch" – Paul Fletcher – was the target. He, too, scored with a diving header at the far post and we won easily by 3-0. That was typical of Jimmy Adamson's brilliance as a tactician.'

Although Burnley prospered during the autumn months the receding local economy tightened its grip upon attendances, which by December had dropped to 13,000.

Burnley 2 Liverpool 1
26 December 1973

'Roll Away the Stone'

The Christmas period provided a welcome boost, though. On Boxing Day, 24,000 fans braved the torrential rain to see Liverpool beaten in the Turf Moor mud. Fleet-footed Leighton James repeatedly roasted Liverpool hard man Tommy Smith. Smith was playing out of position at right-back, filling in for the injured Lawler. Paul Fletcher put Burnley ahead in the third minute, beating Clemence with a bullet header from a hissing James corner, that Dobson had flicked on at the near post. Fletcher's header had so much force that water droplets sprayed from the bulging net like a wet dog shaking itself. Meanwhile little Billy Ingham was having the game of his life, tirelessly harrying his opponents from start to finish. Liverpool were rattled, so much so that Keegan fluffed his second-half penalty kick. Although Cormack eventually equalised in the 84th minute, Burnley were not done. Ingham wriggled into the Liverpool box, which was inches deep in mud, before offloading the ball to burly Hankin who scrambled a winner. This exciting victory over Liverpool appeared to represent the summit of Burnley's league achievements for, despite an encouraging FA Cup run, helped by some fortuitous pairings, league form dipped alarmingly in the new year. Burnley failed to register a further league win until 16 March when Everton were defeated with a late three-goal burst, helped by Leighton James's sensational wing play. But Leeds were next up. Surely this would be a different matter?

Leeds United 1 Burnley 4
23 March 1974

'Jet'

Incensed by their 1973 FA Cup Final defeat by massive underdogs Sunderland, and frustrated again in their bid for the league title, Leeds took the First Division by storm in 1973/74. They extended their unbeaten league run to 29 games, playing superlative football. But the psychological burden of leading the pack for so long started to eat away at them. At Stoke on 23 February 1974 Leeds's unbeaten run was ended after the Potters recovered from a 0-2 deficit to win 3-2. Bristol City had also surprisingly eliminated Leeds from the FA Cup in a replay at Elland Road. Nevertheless, Leeds were still unbeaten at home in the league when Burnley arrived on 23 March.

Despite the mounting pressure, Don Revie was not worried about Burnley. In fact, he was uncharacteristically dismissive in an ITV interview given before the game. His programme notes made no reference to the Clarets, directing his attention at the appalling hooliganism at St James' Park during an FA Cup tie with Forest. This shameful event would have unwelcome repercussions for Burnley's FA Cup fortunes.

5. BACK IN THE BIG TIME 1973/74

There had been a lot of ill feeling between Burnley and Leeds prior to this Elland Road fixture. The spat between Burnley chairman, Bob Lord and his Leeds counterpart, Manny Cousins, hardly helped. This followed Lord's crass remark made at a formal dinner a year earlier when he said: 'We have to stand up against a move to get soccer on the cheap by the Jews who run television.' Lord had several Jewish friends. At this time the term was sometimes used in a colloquial sense, denoting stinginess. However, it is understandable that Manny Cousins, who was a Jew, should find Lord's comment deeply offensive. Although Lord subsequently apologised, Cousins would have none of it and banned him from the Elland Road directors' box. Lord took umbrage and forbade anyone from his club to go to the game except the team, manager, and physio.

Adamson prepared his players carefully, running through the niggling ploys used by the Leeds players, designed to disturb their opponents and to pressurise the match officials. Martin Dobson told me: 'Jimmy used to brief us carefully before big games. I remember the build-up to the Leeds game particularly well. He stressed that we must not let ourselves become intimidated by the likes of Hunter and Bremner. He warned us about their gamesmanship. Jimmy insisted that we should not become involved in any fracas, no matter what provocation was used. That was firmly drilled into us from the start. He would always fine us if we retaliated. He would even discipline us if we used bad language. If anyone used expletives in training, Jimmy would stop the play and make the offender do five press-ups. He would certainly not tolerate any of us sounding off to a referee. But he was equally insistent that we competed against these physically robust sides. The strange thing is that Leeds were such a good team they did not need to trade in these rough-house antics. We believed they would have been better still had they not done so. Brian Clough was probably right on that score.'

Paul Fletcher told me that he said to Adamson in a jocular fashion: 'It's all right for you, boss, sat in the dugout, we've got wives and families to think about!' During the 0-0 draw at Turf Moor the Leeds players had targeted one Burnley player in particular: inventive midfielder Doug Collins. They told him they would 'break his legs' in the return game. Adamson heard the threat and filed it away. Burnley centre-half Colin Waldron said: 'Collins was not the most physically robust of players, he was no hard man. The Leeds players knew this. At Elland Road, Adamson told the referee of the threats that the Leeds players had made, in front of Don Revie. Revie was furious.' This game promised to be a joy.

Just before the game began, the powerful brassy introduction to 'Jet' boomed out of the Elland Road PA system. I wasn't much of a Macca (Paul McCartney) fan once the Beatles had fragmented, particularly after his abysmal 'Mull of "Kindire"'. But the stirring opening to 'Jet' fitted this pumped-up occasion perfectly. 'Jet' remains stapled on my memory of that sparkling spring afternoon.

Burnley started the game brightly, attacking the Scratching Shed End in the warm sunlight. They looked sharp and nimble, finding one another with quick, precise passes, dodging the arresting grabs and jabs like Muhammad Ali in his prime. Don Revie turned to Les Cocker with a troubled, puckered expression, conceding: 'By – they're a good side going forward.' It might have been a different story had Lorimer's 13th-minute shot found goal rather than the full face of the crossbar or had Stevenson not denied both Clarke and Lorimer at close range soon after Burnley had taken the lead. But this was to be Burnley's day.

Lightning quick Leighton James gave Leeds full-back Reaney a hard time during the opening exchanges. Reaney was not the sort of guy to thrive on public embarrassment, so, shortly after the quarter-hour mark he felled James as the Welshman threatened to break free on the left. Unperturbed by the snarling

5. BACK IN THE BIG TIME 1973/74

remarks of the Leeds players, Doug Collins trotted over to take the free kick. Doug was not quick, but he was adroit; the accuracy and incisiveness of his passing was sublime. He rarely wasted a set play, and he did not here. Floating the ball into the crowded Leeds box, Casper climbed above the ruck to head the ball back across the goalmouth. As quick as a flash, Fletcher nipped in to prod the loose ball past Leeds goalkeeper David Harvey.

Fletcher had nearly missed the game. He explained: 'I had been in bed all week with flu and only a Dr Iven special anti-flu jab, two gallons of penicillin injected with a red-hot poker, had got me to the game. After I scored, Billy Bremner, foaming at the mouth, said to me, "What are your chances of playing at Hillsborough next Saturday, Fletch [in the FA Cup semi-final] against Newcastle, with two broken legs?" "Well done, Billy," I replied, "where did you learn to put a FULL sentence together?" I don't think he heard; he was too busy going over the ball and performing a vasectomy on Martin Dobson.'

Fletcher's goal was merely a catalyst. Supine Leeds reverted to 'Super Leeds', intent on bloody retribution. Roared on by an incensed crowd, they threatened to score with each attack. Thanks to some desperate, full-tilt defending and Stevenson's frantic agility, somehow Leeds were repelled; that is, until six minutes before half-time. Forcing their fifth corner in quick succession, Bremner clipped a sharp head-high cross towards the near post. Although right-back Noble attempted to bundle the ball away, he failed to clear his lines, allowing Clarke to clatter in, his header sneaking over the heavily defended goal line. The whole ground trembled with the vocal power of the home crowd, chanting: 'Leeds! Leeds! Leeds! Leeds!' punctuated by the shuddering of so many stamping feet. Serious suffering seemed imminent.

But what happened next completely threw us. Almost directly from the restart, Noble made progress along the right flank. Nulty and McQueen contested his centre, the ball flicking off both their heads towards Fletcher who had his back to goal. Despite Hunter's close attention, Fletcher performed a stunning bicycle kick. The ball flew past Harvey in a blur. The cacophonous clamour that had greeted Clarke's goal was instantly silenced. The eerie quietness was surreal. The ecstatic celebrations of the Burnley players made it even more so. We had watched but had not recognised. We had seen but had not comprehended. It was left to an unusually audible tannoy announcer to confirm the reality – 'the scorer of Burnley's second goal was number nine, Paul Fletcher'. The adjacent Leeds fans glared at me maliciously. Not that my thoughtful response helped. For having regained my faculties but taken leave of my senses, I chirped: 'I bet you won't see a better goal than that in the next ten years.'

I am rarely as wound up as I was on that afternoon. I put it down to the provocative 'big club' syndrome. I've no problem with those fans who have hacked it through the hard times, whether with a so-called 'big club' or not. It's the success groupies that get to me; those who indulge their flaccid egos by tagging on to vicarious glory. I guessed some of those around me were 'Johnny come latelys'. I hoped so. Nothing beats the odour of crushed invincibility on those who deodorise with hubris.

Meanwhile, out on the pitch the hero of the moment, Paul Fletcher, was exultant but suffering. He later explained: 'I was feeling awful. The week in bed was telling on my stamina. I had launched myself into an overhead kick thinking either the ball or Hunter's head would go flying into the net. In mid-air I felt my left foot come into perfect contact with a round, empty object – and for a moment I thought I'd kicked Hunter in the head. But as I landed, I saw the ball crash into the net.' Jimmy Adamson's team started to rip Leeds apart.

The second half was a breeze. Just past the hour, Martin Dobson dispossessed Paul Madeley in midfield. Like a smoothly orchestrated relay, the ball was passed along a line of Burnley players seeking space. It was shifted from Dobson to Casper to Fletcher and finally to Collins slitting open Leeds's defence like the proverbial can of sardines. This fluent move left Dougie Collins in oceans of space to do his worst. Dougie sized up his opportunity. He was 20 yards or more outside the Leeds box. Harvey was off his line. Dougie wasn't the best finisher at the club, often giving gravity too much to do. But this effort was well and truly nailed. His delicate chip sent the ball sailing over the remaining home defenders, over the furiously back-pedalling Harvey, before plopping into the back of the rippling net. Collins, targeted as a bottler by the Leeds bullies, had made his riposte. His tightly screwed-up expression conveyed the intensity of his satisfaction. He thrust both arms aloft, his fists clenched like a triumphant boxer. This was merited vindication. Having just scored the 'goal of the decade', Paul Fletcher conceded that Dougie's effort was 'the goal of the game'.

Burnley's fourth goal came with 20 minutes remaining. Once again Collins was instrumental in its execution, his hat-trick of 'stuff yous'. Burnley midfielder Geoff Nulty said: 'We had some really sharp dead-ball routines in our repertoire. We reckoned that if we were awarded a free kick within 35 yards of our opponents' goal, we had a decent chance of scoring. At Elland Road we were awarded a free kick about 30–35 yards away from goal on our right. Doug Collins took the kick but instead of knocking it towards the far post as the Leeds defenders were expecting him to do, he chipped it towards the near post. Colin Waldron anticipated Doug's intentions and made a late run towards the near post. Here, he back-headed the ball across the face of the goal where I nodded it in, on all fours, at David Harvey's feet. At 4-1 up we were home and dry.' I can still see them now, Colin Waldron and Geoff Nulty, standing in front of the Leeds Kop, their arms upstretched, totally oblivious of the seething, feral surge coming their way. Today, it would have been stopped but back then footballers had the freedom to indulge their moments of supremacy. 'What a joke!' sneered a nearby homer. I had to agree. It was Leeds's heaviest home defeat since returning to the First Division ten years before.

Peter Noble, Burnley's midfielder and makeshift right-back, said, 'We paralysed Leeds. We could have scored seven. The performance was so good it worried Jimmy Adamson.' Noble remembered Jimmy Adamson saying to their team after the game: 'I've got to bring you down again. You think you are a good team. But you still need to perform at Hillsborough. You know you cannot live next Saturday on this Saturday's result.' Leeds boss Don Revie admitted to feeling 'terrible' after the game, adding that he didn't think the ball was rolling for his side at that moment. He added: 'It will be tight now, but Liverpool have still to win their two away games in hand. It is up to us to make the most of our last seven games.'

The only sour note of this game concerned the serious injury suffered by Frank Casper after a reckless tackle by Norman Hunter. It would shortly bring his career to a premature end. Hunter was wound up and just lost it because Burnley had humiliated them. Paul Fletcher told me years later, 'In those days, if a player could smack another player and get away with it, he would. And our Waldo could dish it out. We had this rule. If the ref didn't see it then it is OK. A foul is only a foul if the referee sees it. I certainly knew one player on my side who was told to smack an opponent hard on the side of the head in the first few minutes just to rattle him. He was assured that his boss would accept responsibility and pay the fine if the player was sent off. Today, the game is like netball, nobody is allowed to touch another player. The thing with Leeds was they did that kind of thing in every position. Most teams had one or two assassins, but with Leeds, it was the whole team. But OK, Hunter, you would have him in your team. He won the players' award. Yes, he did the things he did, but you'd have him in your team.'

5. BACK IN THE BIG TIME 1973/74

Paul Fletcher concluded: 'We were already a good team, a very good team, and had the makings of being a great team. We had skills, we had commitment and, perhaps above all, we had team spirit. We would have walked through walls for each other. And Jimmy Adamson, who had done so much to create that spirit, wanted to build upon it. All the players of that side had an incredible admiration for him. I asked him: "What will happen next season?" He replied: "I want to build a team, but the chairman wants to build a stadium and I think he will win."'

The sad thing about this result was that it counted for so little. Leeds went on to win the championship at a canter. Burnley failed to qualify for Europe, and a week later lost a game of much greater significance: an FA Cup semi-final against Newcastle. However, just play me the opening bars of 'Jet' and I am immediately suffused with a warm, lingering glow.

6. INDIAN SUMMER 1974/75

'It's Only Rock 'n' Roll (But I Like It)'

Do you remember the 1974 World Cup? England were not there, of course. Everyone was raving about the Dutch team's 'total football'. Every one of their outfielders could play. Their roles were fluid. It was fabulous, fluent, balletic even. The pundits drooled. Yet the bloody Germans won. Method 2 Style 1. It was scant consolation that the Poles played well. Elimination by them still hurt.

'Tricky Dicky' Nixon had been sent packing too. This should have been his time of triumph. He had initiated détente with the Soviets, agreeing a Strategic Arms Limitation Treaty (SALT) with Leonid Brezhnev. He had opened communication with the isolationist Chinese, too. Trade with both powers seemed possible. To top it all he had finalised an elusive peace deal with North Vietnam, belatedly keeping his electoral promise. But then he was embroiled in the Watergate scandal.

Patty Hearst, the abducted heiress turned terrorist, was indefensibly compromised too. Was she a villain or victim? The US court had no doubt, summing up with a seven-year sentence. Stockholm syndrome was not widely understood then. This is a condition in which hostages develop a psychological bond with their captors. Such emotional ties appeared to form between the hostages and their captors after a Stockholm bank robbery in 1973. The captives' reaction seemed irrational given the potential dangers they faced. A similar phenomenon occurred after South Moluccan terrorists hijacked a Dutch train in 1977. Two captives and six terrorists were killed when attempts were made to free them. And yet some captives were sympathetic to their captors' cause.

This seems to be the deal. You are given a bad, bad time. You lose all sense of worth and being. You have no one or thing to turn to except those who are giving you this bad, bad time. It is your only hope, your only identity. If you have ever followed your team through thin and thinner knowing that relegation is inevitable, but you are nevertheless clinging on to your sinking ship for dear life, then you might recognise what is said here.

At Burnley, the pre-season news was bad. Casper and Docherty were still injured, and the club had sustained an annual loss of £224,000 during the previous year despite its successes. Eleven players were earning over £10,000 per year for the first time in Burnley's history. That figure is now multiplied ten-fold *per week* for many current Premier League footballers.

Burnley 1 Wolverhampton Wanderers 2
17 August 1974

'Sweet Home Alabama'

It was a day of blazing sunshine. We should have been on our holidays. So should 40,000 other Brits but we were left high and dry as tour firms Clarkson's and Horizon went bust. Burnley's 18-year-old striker, Ray Hankin, looked fit to bust. Jimmy Adamson wrote in his programme notes: 'He grows half an inch and puts on a pound every night.' Liz and I believed him. We asked ourselves (jokingly) whether he ate anything other than steroids. More like the 'Incredible Hulk' than the gangly teenager we first saw at the start of the previous season, Hankin roughed up the Wolves defence. He thundered in a towering header, too, but sadly it counted for nothing. John Richards poached an early goal for Wolves and Geoff Palmer grabbed a ludicrous winner with a 40-yard lob. *Evening Star* reporter

Keith McNee exonerated our usually brilliant goalkeeper Alan Stevenson, but I was in a meaner mood. Still, Carlisle sprang a massive surprise, winning 2-0 at Chelsea in their first top-flight game. Bumpkins or pumpkins? Who cares! Good luck to them, but I silently implored them to leave us with four points.

Burnley 1 Chelsea 2
27 August 1974
'When Will I See You Again'

The Turks had driven the Greek Cypriots out of Famagusta leaving a barbed-wired no man's land. Weirdly, it enclosed a row of once plush beach hotels full of stranded suitcases, abandoned clothing, yellowed newspapers, and spectacles, after the tourists were hounded out in a wild rush. Today, this corner of Famagusta resembles a ghost town, frozen in time and populated with rusting, undriven Hillman Avengers. Meanwhile, back in Burnley, the bank appeared to be driving favourite son Martin Dobson out of town. He complained: 'I am just a pawn in this game. It is just like a cattle market.' He was a prize steer though worth the £300,000 that Everton paid for him. This cleared the £210,000 cost of the new stand and significantly reduced the £224,000 loss incurred during the previous season.

I wondered about that loss. Hadn't we done well last season? Jimmy Adamson explained that Burnley had been 'defying the game's law of gravity'. Bob Lord might have been relieved at Dobson's departure, but no one else was, least of all the players, who lost 1-2 to undistinguished Chelsea. Chelsea had severe financial pressures, too, having erected a massive cantilever stand which left them with ruinous debt. James gave us the lead from the penalty spot, but Chelsea retaliated with two late goals from Bill Garner and Ian Hutchinson. Burnley had distinguished themselves at Stamford Bridge six days before, coming back from a 0-3 first-half deficit to draw 3-3 with goals from Hankin, Dobson, and Fletcher. Adamson's explanation for the home loss was that his team were 'over-motivated, too determined to prove themselves after the departure of Dobson.' I had a bad feeling about this season. Meanwhile Spurs boss Bill Nicholson resigned, having become disillusioned with 'money-grabbing players'. Denis Law also called it a day, having sent his beloved United down with a back-heel. I thought he should be canonised.

Burnley 3 Coventry City 0
31 August 1974
'Search and Destroy'

New skipper Colin Waldron made a rousing address to his team-mates, urging them to put aside their sadness at Dobson's departure and focus on the task before them, for two points were desperately needed. His reinvigorated team rose to the occasion splendidly. Peter Noble excelled in Dobson's midfield position; Newton stifled tricky Scottish winger Hutchison and Waldron and Thomson kept a tight rein on Colin Stein and Brian Alderson. Meanwhile, Carr and Mortimer were starved of space and opportunity in midfield. But this was James's day. He humiliated Coventry right-back Peter Hindley, setting up net-busting headers from Hankin and Noble, and wrapping things up with an unstoppable drive.

Arsenal 0 Burnley 1
7 September 1974
'Shake Some Action'

Heath had been done over by the deadly duo, union might and economic blight. Wilson was not doing much better. Inflation was getting out of hand and EEC sceptics were pushing for a referendum about Britain's continuing membership. Keith Joseph believed monetarism was the answer. I decided fanaticism was my answer as I caught a train for London. Standing at the Clock End I had an uninterrupted view as Noble volleyed in Fletcher's downward header. Noble was brilliant, so was Ian Brennan, in an attacking left-back role, while Newton switched to right-back with aplomb. Only Jimmy Rimmer's agility in the Arsenal goal prevented further goals from Fletcher and Ingham.

Burnley 2 Leeds United 1
14 September 1974
'Saturday Night's Alright for Fighting'

The IRA had stepped up their mainland campaign having placed bombs in Pall Mall and at Marble Arch. Chia Chia and Ching Ching were not getting it on at London Zoo while Ted Heath, apparently a celibate, too, arrived at Turf Moor to open the Bob Lord stand, aka the 'Martin Dobson' stand. Brian Clough arrived with his grumpy Leeds side. It was a day of radiant sunshine. Lorimer put Leeds in front with an angled drive, but Burnley turned the game around in the second half thanks to Fletcher's fierce shot and James's penalty. It was quite a scrap, which Hankin and McQueen took literally, resulting in their dismissals.

Liverpool 0 Burnley 1
24 September 1974
'This Town Ain't Big Enough for the Both of Us'

My useless, rusted pile of crap that masqueraded as a car, was in dock again. So, I persuaded a new social worker to drive Liz and me to Anfield this evening. I did not stop to ask him whether he was interested in football or had other pressing commitments. The game was decided with a shell of a shot from Ian Brennan in the 37th minute. Clemence could only watch as the ball clipped the inside of his right-hand post and zoomed into the net. Incensed at Burnley's audacity Liverpool threw everything they had at them. But Waldron and his men stayed cool and strong as wave after wave of attacks bore down upon them. Half-time passed but there was no letting up. A scouser insisted I should 'stop Waldron making unnatural advances on Boersma

6. INDIAN SUMMER 1974/75

and Kennedy'. I declined. It was too amusing. Every Burnley outfielder was camped inside their area, deflecting goal-bound shots wide, heading crosses clear, hurling their bodies into the heart of the action. Stevenson was called upon to make some sharp saves, but the battle raged largely in front of him. Waldron and Rodaway were brilliant in central defence. At the end my scouse neighbour exclaimed: 'How the f**k did that happen?'

Burnley 3 West Ham United 5
28 September 1974

'What Becomes of the Brokenhearted'

'Pretty team, but not enough bottle.' That was what many pundits said about Greenwood's Hammers. But John Lyall's version was a lot tougher. New signings Keith Robson and Billy Jennings epitomised the new order – a team of scrappers who could play a bit. They had scored 15 goals in their three previous games, and they added another five here with Robson (twice), Brooking, Jennings, and Bonds on target. In reply Fletcher scored two and Noble one but with Stevenson having a stinker, Burnley had no chance of competing on a farmyard of a pitch.

Tottenham Hotspurs 2 Burnley 3
5 October 1974

'Money'

Five died and 65 were injured in the Guildford pub bombings. A leaked memo from Army Intelligence stated that terrorism could not be beaten. I wondered how bright you had to be to join Army Intelligence. I decided, though, that the IRA was not going to keep me from White Hart Lane. It was a cool day of sunshine and heavy showers. Burnley's midfield, comprising Ingham, Collins, and Flynn, was inspired. Ingham worked his socks off, fetching and carrying, offering much more than just hard graft. Flynn had a sure touch, was clever on the ball and had a good range of accurate passes. Meanwhile, Collins displayed terrific vision, found spaces, and repeatedly created enticing openings. Brennan set the ball rolling in the seventh minute with a cross that England could only divert into his own net. John Pratt then deflected Fletcher's shot past Jennings. Had Jennings not made two fantastic saves from Noble and Rodaway before the break, Burnley would have been beyond catching. Spurs emerged for the second half in a more determined mood, but it took them until the 78th and 80th minutes to eliminate their deficit, with Pratt and England redeeming themselves. Spurs looked as if they might snatch the points, but Flynn had other ideas. His perfectly executed pass to James set Taffy up for a shot that found goal off Pratt's heel.

Burnley 2 Manchester City 1
12 October 1974
'Big Eyed Beans from Venus'

The press were getting very jumpy about union agitators, restrictive practices and 'excessive wage claims'. Redistribution of wealth had little political support. Higher taxes had no more support among the working classes than with the stockbrokers. So, what did Labour stand for? Paul Fletcher gave us an early lead against third-placed Manchester City but Tueart levelled before the break with a penalty. But today was about a redistribution of points as Jeff Clarke's sliced own goal generously swelled our mounting tally. Pity Spurs, our former nemesis. After losing to Chelsea today, they fell into bottom place.

Burnley 1 Ipswich Town 0
15 October 1974
'Reelin' In the Years'

This was a tough battle tonight. Fletcher put us ahead with a venomous drive, but Burnley had to fight hard to stay in front. Clive Woods was outstanding for the visitors. Burnley's 1-0 victory lifted them into sixth place, but it was floodlight robbery.

6. INDIAN SUMMER 1974/75

Stoke City 2 Burnley 0
19 October 1974
'The Night'

Keith Joseph called for better birth control. He wanted to curb allegedly 'irresponsible breeding among the poor'. *Grandstand* did not help him much though. Their TV cameras attempted to avoid coverage of a Durex-sponsored sports car. It was a lost cause. The Durex car romped home by a country mile. However, Burnley did not. Alan Hudson was inspirational in midfield, well supported by powerful Salmons and grafting Mahoney. Stoke were two up at the break. Stoke full-back Marsh belted in the first goal following a nine-man move. Then Geoff Hurst headed a second. Burnley pulled themselves together after the break. Newton made a series of overlapping runs and Fletcher scraped the top of the bar with a whiplash header. Farmer in the Stoke goal played a blinder, brilliantly denying James and Noble. The *Sunday Express* correspondent was impressed with Burnley, writing, 'they may well win the championship'. I was dubious, on account of our thin squad. Docherty was on the comeback trail, but Casper had broken down again.

Burnley 1 Everton 1
26 October 1974
'Living for the City'

It was a grey miserable day. I spent the morning reading about an allegation that MI5 were plotting to bring down Harold Wilson. I have always found conspiracy theories difficult to swallow. I cannot imagine anything or anybody being that well organised. But Martin Dobson was. He was at his best in his return to Turf Moor. He was so elegant, so unhurried, gliding around in midfield as if carried on a cushion of air. He set up the opening goal too, creating space for a right-wing cross, enabling Mick Lyons to head back across goal for Gary Jones to nod in. Everton's lead was short-lived. Keith Newton gained his revenge for his miserable time at Goodison. Perhaps his former teammates did not rate him for they seemed to ignore his oblique cross. Hankin did not, though, sending a flashing header past Dai Davies. And that was the way it stayed.

Leicester City 1 Burnley 0
2 November 1974
'Killer Queen'

Muhammad Ali was world heavyweight champion again. No longer the 'floating butterfly', Ali won this fight by sheer force of will, allowing George Foreman to punch himself out in the 'rumble in the jungle'. This seemed to be Leicester's tactic too. Burnley were superb, at the top of their game, playing gloriously fluent football throughout, which matched the superb autumn weather. A James scorcher almost holed goalie Wallington, Waldron hit a post and Brennan caused constant panic in the Leicester box with his salvoes and penetrating crosses. Somehow, Leicester hung on. Sammels pinched the points with an eye-catching 49th minute drive.

Burnley 2 Birmingham City 2
9 November 1974
'Virginia Plain'

A pub in Woolwich was bombed. There was one fatality and 28 were injured. It was soon to get worse. Burnley's assistant secretary, John Timson, died during this week. Everyone at the club was terribly upset. Burnley were well below par here. Birmingham were without leading goalscorers Trevor Francis and Bob Hatton but it was Burnley who struggled. Howard Kendall was in terrific form, and combative Kenny Burns battled well up front. Rodaway's error gifted Brum a 19th-minute lead, although Hankin headed an equaliser two minutes later. But immediately after the break, Gordon Taylor restored his side's lead with a deflected shot, celebrating wildly. Newton had been

6. INDIAN SUMMER 1974/75

goading Taylor throughout the first half, dispossessing him at will, waltzing around him with a wink and a grin. Taylor became increasingly ruddy and riled. Adding to Taylor's exasperation, we were egging Keith on. No wonder Taylor was so pumped up after scoring Brum's second goal. It only took Hankin a further eight minutes to poop his party though.

Manchester United 3 Burnley 2 (League Cup) 13 November 1974
'Walk on the Wild Side'

Lord Lucan's nanny had been murdered but he was nowhere to be found. A neighbour blubbed: 'Oh dear, what a pity. Nannies are so hard to come by.' On this night, our schadenfreude ended. United were back with a vengeance, with around 45,000 screaming for our blood. Docherty's men even twice tossed us the lead and still beat us in this League Cup tie. Morgan's chip was sublime and Macari's two drives were blistering. I would not admit it then, but this game was one of the best I had seen since following Burnley. The pace and intensity of this contest was breathtaking as was the skill on show. Throw in the relentlessly deafening roar and we had an experience that I recall sharply almost 50 years later.

Sheffield United 2 Burnley 2 16 November 1974
'Personality Crisis'

The sweeping, russet moors looked spectacular as we crossed Woodhead in the dazzling autumn sun. Better still, there was Ward's real ale on tap at a moorside pub. Real ale was then as rare as red squirrels thanks to bloody keg, better known as 'Wonderloaf' on draught. With Liz driving, I could fill my boots. In those days football was always better watched half pissed; pissed enough to stoke up the euphoria and pissed enough to numb the pain. Chemically enhanced or not, this game was a belter in front of a large, hostile crowd. Billy Rodaway poked in the opening goal in the 14th minute only for bustling Tony Field to equalise 15 minutes later. Tony Currie was in immaculate form, darting here, there, and everywhere but with the coolness to produce defence-splitting passes at will. Bramall Lane still had an open flank to accommodate county cricket in the summer months, but this did nothing to dissipate the huge roar after Billy Dearden had stabbed in the Blades' second soon after the resumption, capitalising upon a misunderstanding between Stevenson and his defenders. Stevenson redeemed himself by keeping Burnley in the game with his great agility. Waldron and returning Docherty were excellent in defence, too. With 11 minutes left, Fletcher stole a point, blasting the ball into the roof of Jim Brown's net, sending us home happy.

Burnley 4 Newcastle United 1
23 November 1974
'Solid Air'

The IRA inflicted their worst mainland atrocity, as 17 people were killed at the Mulberry Bush and the Tavern in the Town pubs in Birmingham's city centre. Within 24 hours five suspects were arrested. A work colleague asked me what I thought about the Renault 5. Without thinking I said 'guilty'. It was a wet, grey day when the Toon came to town. Around 90 minutes later they wished they had not, for Burnley thrashed the Mags in the second half after James had given us a 12th-minute lead. I could not remember seeing such a ruthless Burnley performance. The Villa game in January 1973 came closest but that was suave and accomplished. Here, it was about cudgels. It was revenge for the Hillsborough FA Cup defeat and perhaps a payback for Noble, too, who had been foolishly released by Newcastle when in his youth. His response was a hat-trick of headers which finished off these woeful visitors. Barrowclough pulled one back, but his side were lucky to get away with a 4-1 drubbing as Burnley turned up the heat on Newcastle's shell-shocked defenders. It was hard to believe that this rabble had mauled Chelsea 5-0 only seven days before. Sadly, the occasion was besmirched by the stoning of the Newcastle coach by some local idiots. Newcastle's John Tudor had to go to hospital to have 12 stitches in a facial wound.

Luton Town 2 Burnley 3
30 November 1974

'Needles in the Camel's Eye'

The Prevention of Terrorism Act became law. It allowed for suspects to be detained for up to seven days without charge. It was reported to be a civil rights disaster but whose civil rights were more in jeopardy, the innocent suspects, or the terrorists' victims'? And what about the witnesses who were silenced before they reached court? Over the next ten years, only six per cent of the 5,800 detained suspects were found guilty of any offence. It seemed too much of a scattergun approach but was this a necessary price to be paid?

Stupidly, I expected beleaguered Luton to roll over. They were rock bottom with only nine points, four adrift of Carlisle in the other relegation place. But had Stevenson not made a string of outstanding saves from ex-Claret Alan West, 'new boy' Peter Spiring, John Ryan, and Peter Anderson, Burnley would have lost. It was no siege, though, for Burnley pressed forward whenever possible, playing an equal part in a pulsating, toe-to-toe contest played on a tiring, muddy surface. Burnley struck the first blow on the half-hour. James and Collins combined to release Brennan on the left wing. Pausing briefly to steady himself, Brennan curled over a pacy cross that Hankin headed in powerfully at the far post. Stung by this setback, Luton hit back, winning a corner six minutes later. John Aston's cross was headed away by Newton at the near post, only for Luton centre-back Faulkner to head it back with interest. With the right-hand post unguarded, Stevenson was unable to prevent the ball crossing the goal line. It was 1-1 at the break.

Burnley had no intention of abandoning their attacking instincts. Four minutes after the restart, James cut in from the right wing, exchanging crisp passes with Billy Ingham on the edge of the Luton box, before letting fly with a shot that had too much pace and accuracy for Luton goalie, Keith Barber. The Hatters' heads did not sink, though. Strapping Adrian Alston, a 'Socceroo', was brought on for Jimmy Husband and immediately put himself about. But it was £70,000 new signing Peter Spiring who levelled the scores in the 51st minute. Luton full-back John Ryan overlapped on Luton's right flank and crossed with height and power to the far post where Spiring sprinted in and headed emphatically past Stevenson. Parity lasted just two minutes. Collins picked up a loose ball in midfield and swung it across to James on the right wing. James's low cross was dummied by Ingham, allowing Hankin to pick his spot with a bobbling finish. Despite Luton's frantic efforts they were unable to wrest Burnley's advantage from them. I then spent a boozy night in the East End with friends. Here I met a West Ham fan chuffed with his side's 2-0 victory at QPR. Suddenly, his expression became sombre as he doubted the prospects of smaller clubs. Quaintly, he regarded his side as one of these. He claimed that everything was ruled by cash. I was too pumped up with the Luton victory to debate his morose thoughts.

Burnley 3 Queens Park Rangers 0
7 December 1974
'You Ain't Seen Nothing Yet'

This was a fabulous performance, lighting up a dismal afternoon. Two weeks previously, the Magpies had been battered with a mallet. On this occasion, QPR were taken apart with a scalpel. QPR's stars, Gerry Francis, Stan Bowles, and ex-Claret David Thomas, were snuffed out by the eager

Burnley markers. Newton took special care of Thomas, who had starred in a midweek European Championship qualifier, against Czechoslovakia. Thomas had turned that game around with his sparkling footwork and pinpoint crossing, vindicating Don Revie's estimation. But here Newton made him look like a nervous novice. Collins had one of his best games for the club, showcasing his range of raking passes and deft touches, also chipping a sublime 33rd-minute goal. Burnley were gifted their first goal, though, a 20th-minute own goal from QPR full-back Dave Clement. With ten minutes left, Waldron wrapped up this brilliant team performance with a goal of his own. QPR were unable to cope with the quality and speed of Burnley's passing, with their players finding the space to permit this. When Ron Kennedy of the *Sunday Express* interviewed Adamson after the game, Jimmy harped on about how marvellous the re-laid pitch was and what good value it had been at £60,000. After watching Burnley buried alive by Derby several months later, I was less enamoured with his 'bargain pitch'. Besides, Jimmy made no mention of Burnley's superb performance here. I chuntered, 'Come on Jimmy. Get a grip!'

Wolverhampton Wanderers 4 Burnley 2
14 December 1974

'Lonely This Christmas'

In the first half, Wolves twice took the lead, with goals from Kindon and Richards. But James twice pegged them back, his second coming from a penalty just before the interval. We knew this mid-game parity was precarious and so it proved. Five minutes after the restart, Wolves's arch poacher Richards scored again. Even James could not rescue us this time, and 20 minutes later Kindon finished us off with a brutal shot following a defence-busting sprint. Kindon's form at Wolves had been erratic, but on this grey, grimy afternoon, he was too hot to handle. With his storming pace and muscular physique, he drove all before him. It was no wonder that the Wolves fans dubbed him 'tank'. One in the eye for Adamson perhaps after his bitter departure from Turf Moor. Afterwards Liz and I went to a party organised by a college friend. Our host thought we needed only one single for the party to swing – Slade's 'Merry Christmas Everybody'. After its umpteenth repetition, I pleaded in desperation: 'All right Noddy, we've had our fill of Black Country punishment, can we move on please?' Burnley fell to eighth.

Burnley 1 Middlesbrough 1
21 December 1974
'20th Century Boy'

Burnley played as if they had forgotten their Christmas shopping. Their minds seemed elsewhere. Fletcher gave Burnley a 15th-minute lead which they somehow clung on to until the final minute, when David Armstrong levelled. It was no more than Jack Charlton's side deserved. With players like Souness, Boam, Maddren, and Foggon in Boro's ranks, they were bound to battle for everything. They were neat, robust, and well knit and, regrettably, still above us. We had sold Geoff 'versatility' Nulty to Newcastle for £120,000. I suspected that we would regret this, and how we did, in spades.

Leeds United 2 Burnley 2
26 December 1974
'Gimme Danger'

We spent Christmas in Leeds. With my brother-in-law a devout Leeds fan, we slagged and blagged our way through the booze-boosted festivities. By Boxing Day afternoon, we were barely capable of staggering into Elland Road, but we somehow managed to find our separate entrances. Leeds had recovered from the Clough fiasco and found some promising form under new manager Jimmy Armfield. Hunter was out with a knee injury. I wished him a slow recovery. Frankie Gray, brother

6. INDIAN SUMMER 1974/75

of Eddie, was the new starlet, playing at left-back. Showman Duncan McKenzie was impressing up front. Blackburn boss, Gordon Lee, dismissed him as a 'piss pot' player but I'd rather have him in my side than not. Judging by the gushing plaudits from the *MOTD* pundits, I was not alone.

Strangely, but generously, Jimmy Armfield gave our Jimmy a decent amount of column space in the programme. Adamson began by putting the offside law to rights. Then he moved on to the curse of football hooliganism, proclaiming: 'The answer lies in stiffer penalties by the courts.' Ah! Another problem passed off as someone else's responsibility when the remedy surely required a collective effort. Then, well into his stride, Jimmy turned to his criticism of the excessive cost of player contracts, believing these 'threatened the life of British football, leaving many footballers out of a job'. I presumed Jimmy had taken his enhanced wage without qualm in 1961, when the maximum wage was abolished? Almost 30 per cent of registered players lost their jobs then because of the resultant club economies.

But this was no time to be dwelling upon the rights and wrongs of British football. I was tanked up and ready to rock. The fire on the pitch soon turned to fire in our bellies. For this was a truly nasty, petulant game. Last year's thrashing still rankled with the Leeds players, while Hunter's reckless career-ending tackle on Casper had incensed the Burnley faithful. Seven combatants were booked, some for settling old scores, a few by proxy. Given Armfield's hospitable welcome, Adamson's aggressive summing up seemed crassly ill-mannered. Adamson railed: 'We were provoked, and we retaliated. It has happened with Leeds for the past ten years.' Had he forgotten that the Revie era was over? Armfield was a decent guy. So much for festive goodwill.

In between the fights there were four goals. Joe Jordan put Leeds ahead in the 13th minute arousing a cacophonous roar among the 34,724 crowd, only for James to equalise six minutes later. Although Leeds restored their lead through Lorimer in the 68th minute, James snatched another equaliser with five minutes left. Squeezed into a half-renovated section of the old 'Scratching Shed', we were beside ourselves with joy, leaping and throwing our arms all over the place. That is the great thing about rancorous games. Being pumped up as hell, there is a tendency to hit the stratosphere when a vital goal is scored. Once home again, the red mists evaporated. With the excess booze sourly churning in our stomachs, we were nicely primed for the *Morecambe and Wise Christmas Special*.

Burnley 2 Carlisle United 1
28 December 1974
'Proud to Be (a Honky Woman)'

The cost of living was rocketing with a 20 per cent rise in the previous 12 months. Wages were up by 26 per cent. Even the wrongly maligned teachers received a 32 per cent pay rise. There was a big hike in petrol prices as well. Given that supporting Burnley meant supporting my local Thrust petrol station, it was disturbing to note that the price of Four Star had risen from 42p to 72p per gallon in six months. Not that we had far to travel on this day. The game was a steal. Carlisle deserved to come away with something but did not. Burnley played as if they wanted to get their hangover in before the New Year festivities began. That scrap at Leeds had been draining. Carlisle took a deserved first-half lead through winger Dennis Martin. However, James came to our rescue yet again with an equaliser five minutes after the break, leaving Collins to fashion a late winner. Burnley rose to seventh place.

Burnley 0 Wimbledon 1 (FA Cup third round)
4 January 1975
'Angie'

Oh God! What could I say? I could not face work. I could not face anyone. The Khmer Rouge were besieging Phnom Penh but all I could think about was the shame, the indignity of losing. Ray Hankin said he was never going out again. All right, Wimbledon were incredible, terrific organisation and composure. They also became the first club to shackle James during this season, employing two clued-up, aggressive midfielders to slow him down with a third to dispossess him. Their strategy, based upon extensive intelligence, was executed to perfection. As much as Burnley bombarded the Wimbledon goal, they were too predictable. With their frustration mounting, Burnley reverted to a long-ball game that was simply food and drink to the Dons' beefy defenders. Without James performing his magical skills, Burnley looked lost. Sure, there were opportunities to win. Thomson, Fletcher, and James missed easy chances although Dickie Guy, in the Wimbledon goal, was superb. But it was not just 'backs to the wall' defending that pulled Wimbledon through, they looked good on the break as well. One of these resulted in Mahon giving Wimbledon the lead shortly after half-time. Burnley pushed forward relentlessly but could not break down the stubborn Dons. Adamson said afterwards: 'The players gave everything they had but their skills were off.' But it was not just about the players. Jimmy was too slow in adjusting to the Dons' tactics. Having said that, I admired him for saying anything, for I became as mute as a Trappist monk. To prove this result was no fluke Leeds needed two games before overcoming the Dons in the next round.

Queens Park Rangers 0 Burnley 1
11 January 1975
'The Wall Street Shuffle'

It was a day of wan, filtered sunlight. Two Windscale workers died of leukaemia this week, arousing further doubts about the safety of nuclear power. The battered and bruised English tourists had doubts about the safety of Test cricket, too, having been trapped in a fast lane created by speed kings

Lillee and Thomson. Ducking and diving seemed a sensible policy.

Burnley had a score to settle in west London, which they did, albeit controversially. They were without Waldron, who was serving a one-match ban, and Brennan, who was injured. Rodaway partnered Thomson in central defence with Noble filling in at left-back, while young Colin Morris made his debut on the right wing.

QPR pushed forward menacingly from the off. Their strikers Givens and Bowles were supported by Gerry Francis, in an advanced midfield role, and serviced by Thomas's crosses and Don Masson's penetrative passing. QPR had won all four of their previous games, scoring ten goals. With their Turf Moor humiliation still rankling, they were out for blood.

Under pressure from the outset, Burnley needed everyone behind the ball to quell Rangers' dangerous raids. Newton hacked down Thomas after the ex-Claret made a fast break, also heading out a goal-bound effort just beneath the crossbar. Burnley's block count rose dramatically. But with QPR committing so many in attack, Burnley were able to hit them on the break with James on top form. Whenever Burnley ventured upfield, James and Morris caused consternation in the Rangers defence. Hankin was a menace, too, using his height and weight to good effect, holding the ball up in advanced positions. Meanwhile his strike partner, Fletcher, frequently supplemented his under-fire defence. Stevenson was by far the busier goalkeeper throughout, making several acrobatic saves and bravely diving at the feet of the QPR forwards. Yet it was Burnley who took the lead in the 59th minute. The goal was hotly disputed. QPR left-back Gillard was left prostrate outside the home box after a heavy challenge. But while the QPR players stood still, expecting the referee to halt play, Morris transferred the ball quickly to James, who advanced along the goal line to set up Hankin for a tap-in at the far post. I thought QPR goalie Parkes should have blocked

6. INDIAN SUMMER 1974/75

James's goal-line run. With the home fans angrily berating them, Burnley closed ranks to preserve their fortunate lead. But there was no cooling of the action, with frantic scrambles at both ends. Stevenson had to palm away a fierce shot from John Beck while Fletcher's soaring header needed to be tipped over by Parkes. Rodaway and Thomson were drawn into sliding challenges that would have been penalised today, while Stevenson caused an angry outcry when he wasted time by throwing the ball into the crowd behind him. James played a vital part in defence too, using his speed and dribbling skills in taking the ball far up field.

On the tube, I read the *Evening Standard* reports. The headlining match was ailing Spurs' 5-2 win at Newcastle with a match-winning hat-trick from Alfie Conn. Burnley's game received a one-word review, 'dour'. I took issue with this, believing I had seen a pulsating, high-tempo contest. But having no one to share my blarney with, I talked to myself. Burnley were up to sixth. So, who cares about Wimbledon? A week is a short time in football.

Burnley 1 Luton Town 0
18 January 1975

'Marcus Garvey'

The IRA ended their Christmas truce. It was another straw flung into the wind, as was Willie Whitelaw's doomed power-sharing initiative. On a bright, tingling afternoon, Billy Ingham scored the game's only goal in the 34th minute. It should have settled Burnley down, but it did not. Bucked up by three festive victories, Luton played all the football. Luton centre-forward Ron Futcher would later become a Burnley cult hero known as 'Rocket Ron'. His apparent lethargy was deceptive, just as it was years later, when in claret and blue, for he was an accomplished striker. He had made that clear during the Christmas period, when he grabbed a hat-trick in a 3-2 home victory over Wolves. Burnley were hard-pressed to keep him and his team-mates out. Meanwhile, his brother Paul was authoritative at centre-back. Luton had the luck that blesses downbound teams – nowt. Burnley were lucky but they were now third!

Birmingham City 1 Burnley 1
1 February 1975
'No Woman No Cry'

The cost of a black and white TV licence had risen sevenfold from £1 to £7 whereas a colour TV licence had increased from £6 to £18. Who needed colour? Well, Birmingham might have. It seemed a drab place, haunted by horrific IRA violence. The overcast weather hardly helped. At least the game provided fair entertainment. The Blues had become particularly goal-shy over the recent months, falling to 17th position. Nevertheless, a long-range shot from Gary Emmanuel gave them a 22nd-minute lead. Then James burst into life. It was his precise right-wing cross in the 44th minute which enabled Hankin to outjump Roger Hynd and plant his header wide of Dave Latchford in the Brum goal. After the break Burnley stepped up their efforts at grasping both points but were resisted by Birmingham's tough defenders. Burnley dropped to fourth. I began to worry that Burnley were over-dependent upon James. He completed the season as leading goalscorer with 16, ahead of Hankin with 14 and Fletcher with ten, although Fletcher missed the last eight fixtures with a knee injury. Also, many of Burnley's goals came with his assistance. If ever James became injured, or worse, left, the team would be in the mire, having no obvious replacement.

Burnley 2 Leicester City 0
8 February 1975
'Make Me Smile (Come Up and See Me)'

The government could not have been worried about Windscale. They had just commissioned two nuclear power stations at Sizewell and Torness Point. I should not have worried about

6. INDIAN SUMMER 1974/75

Leicester. They were second from bottom, having drawn four and lost nine of their 13 league games since beating Burnley in November. But any team featuring Frank Worthington and Keith Weller had to be reckoned with. They had just bought brawny Jeff Blockley from Coventry to help shore up their leaking defence. On another cold, sunny afternoon it was like a replay of the Luton game but without a first-half goal. Burnley looked dreadful and so did Leicester. Neither side was troubled in defence. Blockley was a lot better than I had envisaged. Then almost out of the blue, Hankin scored. Although there were 37 minutes left, Leicester looked crestfallen and beaten, but forced by necessity to push forward, gaps opened. With only three minutes remaining, Keith Newton struck a rare goal, much to our relief. Burnley were back in third place.

Newcastle United 3 Burnley 0
15 February 1975
'Born to Run'

Thatcher replaced Heath as leader of the Tory party. She announced: 'I owe nothing to women's lib.' 'Thank God for that,' sighed the relieved feminists. She seemed too intent upon excluding the male eunuch to be concerned with the female kind. Heath's response was to embark upon a record-breaking sulk. At lunchtime I sank a lot of McEwan's, but obviously not enough. Like a crap anaesthetist I failed to get the booze/wooze ratio right. With the salty Tyne wind making early inroads I had far too little to muffle the pain. Newcastle were fresh from their midweek thrashing of Liverpool. Their blood was up and their talons still famished. Only a few weeks beforehand, their manager Joe Harvey had demanded better protection for his players from referees. With his attack so hot, protection was superfluous. Trust Burnley to turn up too late. Burnley were never in this game, played in front of 40,000 baying Geordies. Malcolm 'Supermac' Macdonald slammed in his first after a quarter of an hour and his second 15 minutes later. Quick, strong, and skilful, he played with a knowing swagger. Burnley did not know the question let alone the answer. Nulty was excellent in the Mags midfield. How we could have done with him in ours. With three minutes left, Barrowclough wrapped up this sorry affair. Liz drove us home while I slept. This reality stung too much for my liking.

Burnley 2 Sheffield United 1
22 February 1975

'Superstar'

What a difference a week makes! Burnley were not brilliant, but they did not need to be, despite the Blades being fellow title contenders. The first half was nondescript although the Blades striker Tony Field had a goal ruled out for offside. James reserved his magic for the second half when he reverted to the left wing. In the 77th minute he clipped a right-foot cross high into the Blades' goalmouth. Both Noble and Blades centre-back Colquhoun competed for the flighted ball. As they went up together, the ball flicked off both their heads and flew over Jim Brown for the opening goal. The ITV replay suggested it was an own goal, but Noble was having none of that, promptly claiming it for himself. Suitably aroused, James flew down the left wing before crossing for Fletcher to head in forcefully. Although the prematurely greying Alan Woodward joined the heading contest, his far-post effort came too late to affect the result. A gorgeous sunset greeted our rise into second place. Driving home, we heard prim Karen Carpenter deliver a groupie's lament in 'Superstar'. Really?

Coventry City 0 Burnley 3
1 March 1975

'Dreamer'

It had been a bloody week. PC Tibble was killed by the IRA after stumbling upon one of their operations. Then the Moorgate tube

6. INDIAN SUMMER 1974/75

disaster claimed 35 lives. A doctor on duty remarked: 'If there's a hell, I've seen it.' I started to read the report but could not finish it. On the way to Coventry, we met a truck driver while eating spongey-form sandwiches at a motorway service station. Having asked where we were heading, he responded: 'You don't want to go to Coventry. It's full of Belgians!' There was greater evidence of Germans, though. But what the Luftwaffe began, the city's lugubrious planners had finished. The result was unremittingly grim. In contrast the game was a shining beacon of attacking football, at least from my partisan perspective. Coventry began well but were progressively pushed back by Burnley's pressure. James was strafed with abuse from the home fans, a sure sign of respect, whereas being roughed up by the Coventry defenders was a sure sign of desperation. The first occasion James was given a scrap of space, he rifled in an unstoppable, rising drive. Any hope City had of a second-half recovery was stifled at birth. Noble was first to a right-wing corner, heading in decisively at point-blank range. With only two minutes remaining, Fletcher headed in Flynn's corner unchallenged. The Coventry PA announcer described Burnley's supercharged performance as 'rampant'. We graciously agreed.

Burnley 1 Liverpool 1
8 March 1975

'Street Life'

Burnley had a credibility gap to straddle. Few hacks rated them as potential champions despite being in second place behind Billy Bingham's boring Everton. Liverpool were not out of the race, either. They were three points adrift with a game in hand. Nearly 32,000 turned up, easily Burnley's biggest home gate of the season. It was not a good game. The dry, bumpy surface did not help, but a fluent contest was unlikely given what was at stake. Burnley made the most of limited pickings when Hankin stooped to head in James's cross on the half-hour.

After growing second-half pressure, though, Terry McDermott's low drive evaded Stevenson's grasp. We tried to contain our disappointment. After all, Burnley were still in second place.

West Ham United 2 Burnley 1
15 March 1975
'Pressure Drop'

Would dustmen be the catalyst to spark a revolution? Glaswegians might have thought so as their rubbish piled up during a nine-week strike. In the end the troops moved in and carted off 70,000 tons of waste. They could have taken my bloody car while they were at it. The damn thing broke down on the motorway as we were heading for London. The recovery vehicle did not get us back home until 3am. Obviously this was a bad omen, but we did not heed it. By nine we were at Manchester Piccadilly waiting to board a London-bound express.

It was a day of steady rain. The pitch was more suited to military manoeuvres, but Burnley adapted superbly. Despite their exciting FA Cup run, West Ham's league form had gone down the drain. During the first half Burnley played the Hammers off their mudheap, helped by Billy Bonds's early exit. To cap it all, Doug Collins chipped a superb goal a minute before the break. The North Bank crowd was compressed, surging, urging, swaying, and baying, the sour smell of damp clothing mingling with the whiffs of tobacco. Despite being crushed together with the heaving home fans, we felt perfectly at ease, euphoric even. This was to be a perfect day after all. Then it all fell apart. Collins continued to probe artfully, setting up inviting opportunities that Fletcher and Hankin squandered. As against Liverpool, the Burnley midfielders were pressed back by the collective strength of their opponents. This time it was Paddon and Keith Robson supplying the beef, while Brooking and Jennings provided guile. Two of the softest goals were gifted to Robson and lightning-quick Alan Taylor, formerly of Rochdale.

6. INDIAN SUMMER 1974/75

It is always harder to stomach defeat when victory seemed so tantalisingly close. It is like tearing an encrusted plaster off a tender wound.

We stayed overnight with friends in the East End. But the longer I drank the more morose I became. It was not just the result. I was able to be gracious about that. After all, it had been a fine game. I could sense a foreboding though. I felt that something irrevocable had happened here. Paul Fletcher reckoned that our triumph at Leeds in 1974 was our turning point. Even before I was told about his serious knee injury, I knew this day was the true turning point. I had a premonition that there was only one way ahead, and this was down.

Burnley 3 Arsenal 3
22 March 1975
'I'm Not in Love'

It was a bright, blustery day. North Vietnam had invaded the South, emphasising the scale of the US's military defeat and their politicians' folly. Arsenal did not beat us on this day, but they should have done. Despite languishing in 18th position, their makeshift side ran rings around Burnley. Bertie Mee dropped Charlie George, John Radford, and Peter Storey, replacing them with Wilf Rostron, John Matthews, and Brian Hornsby who played out of their skins. Alan Ball received his customary Turf Moor welcome: 'We all hate, Ball and Ball and Ball …' sung to the '-Dam Busters'- tune. This time he brushed it aside with a blinding performance in midfield. Precocious Liam Brady flourished under Ball's faultless organisation and astute probing, as did the other Arsenal starlets. With Kidd offering experience and strength up front, the grave limitations in Burnley's defence were starkly exposed. Playing Billy Rodaway in midfield seemed to be madness. The young Arsenal players danced around him as if mocking the butt of the classroom. The lack of depth in Adamson's squad was palpably exposed. These young Gunners were certainly not 'boring, boring Arsenal'. Noble put Burnley ahead in the tenth minute following another left-wing surge from James. James's low cross was so quick, strong, and accurate that none of the Arsenal defenders could prevent Noble's firm conversion at the far post. But Arsenal were not subdued, immediately pressing Burnley back with their rapid movement and eagle-eyed passing. Rostron and Hornsby glided across the heavy Turf Moor surface as if skating. Just four minutes after going behind, Arsenal were level. Following a frantic scrum in the Burnley box, Rostron seized the loose ball and whacked it past unsighted Stevenson. Back came Burnley but their quick left-wing thrust was thwarted when Rice pushed Collins over inside the visitors' box. The referee refused to award a penalty, though, waving aside the incensed protests from the Burnley players. On the half-hour, Arsenal took the lead. A right-wing cross was knocked back into the goalmouth by Rostron for Hornsby to drill in. At the break Arsenal were still 2-1 ahead.

Jimmy Adamson used half-time to decide upon a change of plan. His side were instructed to go for goals. Within five minutes of the restart Hankin restored hope with a trademark header from Collins's high cross to the far post. Once again, the opportunity was created by James's ingenuity. The reprieve was brief as Hornsby slid the ball past Stevenson, having been put through on goal by Kidd. Thanks to the skill and industry of Waldron and Newton, Burnley just about stayed in the game. The importance of this was underlined when Burnley were awarded a dubious penalty five minutes before time. James put it away and Burnley escaped with an undeserved 3-3 draw. However, they dropped into sixth position. Even a European place looked wildly optimistic.

6. INDIAN SUMMER 1974/75

Middlesbrough 2 Burnley 0
29 March 1975
'Lady Marmalade'

Liz and I missed this one on account of the wintry Easter weather, which encased our car in a deep Pennine snow drift. It was our only absence of the season. We did not miss much. Boro were vastly superior and won 2-0 with ease. Bobby Murdoch opened the scoring in the 54th minute and Alan Foggon added a scorching second six minutes later. Apparently, Jack Charlton gave Jimmy Adamson programme space too. What did he write about? Why, Revie's school coaching plan and the offside law. To give Jimmy his due, he knew how to hammer his point home.

Burnley 2 Derby County 5
31 March 1975
'Pick Up the Pieces'

While Iraq launched new assaults upon the Kurds, Derby launched their assault upon the Clarets. A chilly thaw had begun. It caused Jimmy's vaunted pitch to cut up badly. Was it still worth £60,000 Jimmy? Derby's Panzers were much better equipped to handle this. With James bogged down, Burnley hardly showed. Derby manager Dave Mackay had inherited many of Clough and Taylor's players but fashioned them in his own image. They traded in thuggery with violence. Burnley were the latest team to be mugged by them. A blistering drive from Bruce Rioch put the Rams ahead in the first minute. Brawny Hankin was one of few Clarets capable of going toe to toe with Derby. He equalised in the 18th minute only for Derby's left-back, Nish, and centre-forward, Roger Davies, to smash in further goals in the 20th and 29th minutes. Although James pulled one back from the spot in the 66th minute, this merely provoked Kevin Hector to retaliate with a brace, taking Derby out of range. The gulf between the Ram raiders and Burnley's ewes was huge. Derby looked like worthy champions.

Their back four comprised Rod Thomas, Peter Daniel, Colin Todd, and David Nish. Here brawn stood cheek by jowl with pace and outstanding skill. Their midfield was made up of Bruce Rioch, Steve Powell, Alan Hinton, and Archie Gemmill, muscular, mobile, and menacing. Even without Franny Lee and Roy McFarland they were hard to break down while packing a tidy punch.

Carlisle United 4 Burnley 2
1 April 1975
'Fox on the Run'

April Fools' Day began brightly with soothing, swishy breezes as we drifted through the Dales. But by the time we reached Ullswater, there were no lonely clouds, and upon entering Carlisle it started to rain. Carlisle seemed dreary and unloved. The government-run pubs were as hospitable as urinals. Carlisle United were not very hospitable either. Not that they could afford to be. They were bottom despite a rousing 3-0 home victory over second-placed Everton on Easter Saturday.

Fired by this prestigious victory, Carlisle tore into Burnley from the off and were soon two up through terrier-like midfielder Les O'Neill, and sideburned striker Joe Laidlaw. Burnley's debutant goalkeeper Mickey Finn had no chance with either shot. Two other Burnley reserves made their debut, too, forward Derrick Parker, and centre-back Richard Dixey. Both were drafted in after the Derby fiasco. But with Burnley hardly managing a kick in the first half hour they seemed redundant. Then out of the blue, Parker took a swing at a loose ball. He was at least 30 yards from goal and yet the ball arched over reserve Carlisle goalie Tom Clarke and plopped into his net. We were more dumbfounded than excited. And yet we were back in the game. Shortly after half-time James put us back on terms with an expertly taken penalty. God knows, he had plenty of practice this season. But any hopes of a stirring victory were dashed in the final

6. INDIAN SUMMER 1974/75

minutes. Carlisle were by far the hungrier side and the impressive Ray Train blasted them into the lead once more with only two minutes remaining, allowing Laidlaw just enough time to seal the game from the spot. Burnley were still in seventh place but fading alarmingly. Liz and I decided this season could not end too quickly as we drove home in heavy rain and dazzling headlights.

Everton 1 Burnley 1
4 April 1975
'Rebel Rebel'

Barbara Castle tried to close all NHS private beds to reduce hospital waiting lists. Her ambition was to achieve equality in sickness and health. It was a losing battle. We thought we were in a losing battle against the current league leaders. Adamson restored Collins who had overcome the injury he had sustained at West Ham. He replaced Parker while Noble was pushed up front with Hankin. Waldron was outstanding in Burnley's improved defence, which held Everton comfortably in the first half, also carving out a few openings. But after the break, Everton turned up the heat. New boy Richard Dixey was so determined to hang on to dangerous Bob Latchford that he was prepared to grab any appendage. No wonder Latchford completed the game misshapen. But he still managed to get a sharp shot away 12 minutes after the break. It was too good for Mickey Finn, seemingly setting Everton on the path to victory. But with 11 minutes left, up bobbed Peter Noble, directing his flicked header past Davies. The Everton players and fans were stunned, their side having dominated possession. This was more like it!

Burnley 3 Tottenham Hotsput 2
12 April 1975
'Walk This Way'

Hankin was the latest casualty so Parker, a fellow Geordie, took his place. He and Noble combined well for a fourth-minute opener, with the latter's flying header whizzing past Pat Jennings. Noble broke free along the inside-right channel 18 minutes later and thumped his shot past the Irishman. However, Burnley's 2-0 interval lead was erased within 19 minutes of the resumption, with Duncan and Perryman netting with fierce shots. Driven on by Ralph Coates, Spurs seized control of the game. But Leighton James had other ideas. His penalty – his seventh of the season – was tucked away with assurance despite the heated protests of the Spurs players. As hard as Spurs tried to come back again, creating a succession of defensive scares, Burnley clung on, just.

Manchester City 2 Burnley 0
19 April 1975
'74/75'

On this sunny, spring-like afternoon, Rodaway replaced Dixey in central defence. Dixey had looked wretchedly ill at ease against Spurs strikers Chris Jones and John Duncan. However, 17-year-old Derek Scott, drafted in at right-back, did very well. Alan Stevenson was back in goal. However, once Colin Bell had cracked in a 30-yarder in the 26th minute it was City's match. Tueart's second-half goal merely confirmed that. Burnley were not disgraced but slipped to ninth position.

Burnley 0 Stoke City 0
26 April 1975
'Gloria: In Excelsis Deo'

Unemployment passed one million. It was the biggest monthly rise since World War Two. Keynesian economics had lost political currency, with the Tories insisting that spending our way out of a slump led only to a stagnant economy and runaway inflation. With the IMF calling the shots, Labour had little on offer to ease the pain. The game had a dispirited air to it as both sides fired blanks. It was an anti-climactic end to a switchback season. Jimmy Adamson was disappointed with how the season ended. He, too, identified the West Ham game as the turning point while bewailing crucial injuries in thwarting his team's bid for honours.

Surely, the reality was that Burnley's squad was too thin. Most of their reserves were too green or lacking sufficient skill to maintain a viable title challenge. Brennan had a good season, Rodaway had some good games, and Scott showed promise, but the only home-grown talents to make their mark were Hankin and Flynn. With injuries to Casper, Fletcher, Docherty, Collins, and latterly Hankin and Newton, it was almost inevitable that this team's progress would fall away during the run-in. The club's financial situation also played a strong part in the team's decline towards the end of the season; Burnley's home attendances were not high enough to sustain a title-winning side. In this season the average home gate was 19,461 – over 5,000 higher than in their 1972/73 promotion season, but nevertheless the fourth lowest in the First Division in 1974/75. This meant that player sales were needed to compensate for the below-average turnstile takings. With the supply of talented youngsters drying up, the club's 'sell to survive' policy had almost run its course.

7. WILD DAY IN BLACKPOOL 1975/76

3 January 1976
'Bohemian Rhapsody'

The previous night was wild. A violent gale rampaged across the country causing 26 deaths and £100m worth of damage. Some gusts reached 80mph. My wife and I were staying in Bristol. Throughout the night the wind buffeted the windows and growled in the grate while loose gates and shed doors groaned and slammed.

We rose early on that bright Saturday morning, unrested and irritable. The debris of the night's torment lay everywhere: fallen trees, torn branches, collapsed fences, overturned dustbins, and scattered litter. The deep-blue morning sky seemed unblemished but soon the clouds gathered.

Holding the car on course was a struggle in the fierce gale. We arrived in Blackpool just before midday. With my eyes gritty with a lack of sleep and concentrated driving, I left the car and took to the prom. There I stood, unsteadily braced against the rusted railings taking in the sea's fury. The immense, foaming waves lurched in and out of the flitting sun, their frenzied charge urged on by an icy nor'wester. Only the booming sea wall repelled them, their glinting hostages clawed back with seething resentment.

Wild weather normally stirred my torpor. But here I felt out of sorts. I returned to the car and slumped in the driver's seat, staring dully through the saline-smeared windscreen. The wind was briefly refreshing but now my eyes smarted with salt as well as fatigue. My skin was tacky, and my hair tugged on the comb. My wife prescribed a pint and hotpot. She sensed we needed fortification for what we were about to receive.

As we approached the ground, snippets of 'Bohemian Rhapsody' wafted erratically on the gusting, eddying wind. Chanting, too, was whisked above the roof tops in variable volume. I mistook this to be a celebration of 'seaside air' until twigging it was 'Seasiders'!

I used to love the pre-match routine, particularly on smarting cold winter days; the chirpy chatter in cosy, smoke-filled pubs, the unsegregated banter, the put-downs, the grotesque caricatures, the surreal tales, and outrageous gossip. But on this stormy Saturday, the pleasure stopped at foreplay.

Burnley's esteemed former boss Harry Potts was in charge at Blackpool. He desperately needed a lucrative FA Cup run. With results, resources, and crowds dwindling, his job was in peril. Besides, he had a score to settle with the current Burnley manager, Jimmy Adamson, whom he believed had wrongly usurped him at his beloved Turf Moor.

With so much at stake and both teams in wretched form, this was never going to be a fluent contest. In fact, it was truly grim. The players had huge difficulties contending with the swirling wind, which howled ghoulishly under the rusted corrugated roof, tugging at the flapping club flag. Long passes were a hostage to fortune. Ball control was an embarrassment. Chances were fewer than hardy beach boys. Before the floodlights eclipsed the fading day, the sky began to clear. Only torn tufts of cloud remained, fleeing from the north-west approaches, their crimson reflections of a raw sunset unappreciated by the anxious crowd.

Just as we were settling for an ugly 0-0 draw, Burnley's game fell apart. Hankin, our only striker of substance, was dismissed. Shortly afterwards, Blackpool's defender Bill Bentley thumped in a free header from a corner. We bowed our heads as the home fans leapt around us. With Waldron's late equaliser ruled out, there was no way back.

Harry Potts was understandably jubilant. He dismissed the reporters' comments that it had been a petulant game littered with niggling fouls and reckless challenges. His club was £4,500 better off and he had put one over his former rival. A disconsolate Jimmy Adamson lamented, 'We seemed to be playing uphill. Everything keeps going against us.' The *Burnley Express* reporter's verdict was less forgiving: 'Scraping the Barrel,' he wrote.

It was a lugubrious journey home. Liz drove. We hardly spoke. The branches of the overhanging trees still thrashed wildly in the stiff wind, their fallen leaves whipped up by the passing traffic. Outside, there was irrepressible energy but inside we felt flat and empty.

Little did we know that a bitter dressing room row was taking place. Adamson returned from his contretemps with the referee to find the dressing room door locked. It was an undignified affair. Two days later, Bob Lord requested Adamson's resignation.

Burnley's talismanic winger, Leighton James, had already left for title holders Derby. It was no surprise. His side was flagging. After lowly Wolves had buried Burnley in the Turf Moor mud in November, winning 5-1 with embarrassing ease, we knew we were facing a desperate relegation scrap. James was a top international player who was naturally ambitious. It was small wonder his head was turned. It was understandable, too, that so many of us felt resentful at his departure. We had relied upon him so much. During the previous season he had created or scored more than 40 per cent of our 68 league goals. He had also netted 81 goals in all games for the club. But his worth could not be encapsulated only in numbers. His ability to outpace almost everybody and pull the best defences apart was priceless. Burnley received a hefty £310,000 from Derby, but we

7. WILD DAY IN BLACKPOOL 1975/76

knew only a fraction of that money would be made available for incoming moves. Bob Lord did allow Adamson's replacement, Joe Brown, to spend £100,000 on novice Preston winger Tony Morley, but it was unrealistic to expect Morley to fill the gaping gap left by James, certainly in the immediate future. Morley eventually developed into a top winger, winning a European Cup medal with Villa in 1982. But given Burnley's parlous position in January 1976, the club could not afford to wait.

Burnley's plight might not have been quite so desperate had Peter Noble remained fit throughout this season. He was so adaptable. He had filled in ably at full-back when Michael Docherty was injured at the start of the 1973/74 season. He then deputised with aplomb when Martin Dobson was transferred to Everton a year later. At the start of the 1975/76 season, he was asked to become Ray Hankin's strike partner with Paul Fletcher recovering slowly from a knee injury he sustained in the previous season. It was a role which Noble relished, recording a hat-trick against Middlesbrough (4-1), and going one better against Norwich (4-4), before succumbing to injury too. This left young striker Ray Hankin with too much responsibility up front, despite netting 13 league goals, emulating Peter Noble's interrupted tally for the season.

Before the start of the 1975/76 season, Adamson had been permitted to bring in two veteran stars: former Claret Willie Morgan from Manchester United, and Mike Summerbee from Manchester City, for a combined fee of £57,000. This was to augment a squad that had been shown to be too lean towards the end of the previous season. But Morgan was merely a shadow of the player he had once been, and while Summerbee grafted in midfield, neither player was as successful as Adamson hoped. It was perhaps significant that Morgan's best performance came at Old Trafford, on 27 December 1975, the place he had been loath to leave. Morgan did perform a lot better for his next club, Bolton, helping them return to the First Division in 1978, so perhaps there were other reasons why he did not settle as well as Summerbee.

Meanwhile, the supply of bright home-grown talent had dwindled to a trickle. An unexpected 3-2 victory at snowy Everton on 31 January did feature two young hopefuls: Derek Scott, who scored one of the goals, and winger Colin Morris, but while the former established himself at right-back, Morris was passed over. With Burnley suffering one of their longest injury lists in recent times, including Casper, Collins, Morgan, and Brennan as well as Fletcher and Noble, there was little prospect of them avoiding the drop. Casper's ferocious 87th-minute free kick enabled Burnley to beat second-placed QPR in October, but sadly he could not overcome the injury that Hunter had inflicted upon him in 1974. Casper retired in February 1976, turning to coaching. For three seasons Alan Stevenson had been the club's number one goalkeeper but a series of poor performances resulted in him being replaced by Gerry Peyton, a 19-year-old acquisition from non-league Atherstone.

The new V-for-victory shirt seemed like a sick joke as the defeats piled up. Deprived of their best strikers, James, Fletcher, and Casper, Burnley managed to score only 43 league goals in this season, 25 fewer than in the previous year (a drop of 37 per cent). This team was ageing, too, and after Adamson left, so did his team's competitive spirit. Although Adamson's former assistant manager Joe Brown succeeded him, he did not appear to command the same respect, affection, authority, or loyalty as his predecessor. With the financial pressures mounting exponentially, the most promising young stars were sold. Hankin went to Leeds in September 1976 for a fee of £172,000 and Flynn followed him a year later for £175,000. Burnley's Indian summer was over. The rest of the seventies would see Burnley largely battling against a further slide into the Third Division.

Although Burnley no longer had a pool of young talent to turn to, Paul Bradshaw starred in the 3-1 win over Fulham in August

7. WILD DAY IN BLACKPOOL 1975/76

1976 but sadly did not sustain that level of performance and was transferred to Sheffield Wednesday, before succumbing to injury. Another winger, Colin Morris, was strangely overlooked, for he went on to have a successful career at Southend, Blackpool, and Sheffield United. Tony Morley was spasmodically successful, but his career did not take off until he moved to Aston Villa for a £200,000 fee, where he starred in a European Cup victory and played six times for England.

Liz and I went to almost every game during the 1975/76 season, trying hard to keep our hopes alive. Mercifully perhaps, we missed the final two home games because of a holiday organised by university friends. We felt a guilty admiration for those Burnley supporters who endured the 0-1 defeat by Manchester United which sent the Clarets down. With two thirds of Turf Moor packed with gloating United fans, it must have been unbearable.

8. HARRY'S GAME 1976/77

'Anarchy in the UK'

Temperatures topped 30°C on 21 days. Rivers dried up, ponds disappeared, trees wilted, and crops failed like Tony Greig's bruised and 'grovelling' England Test cricketers. Large crevices appeared in the baked clay beds of the receding reservoirs, including at Ladybower in the Peaks, revealing the village it had once drowned. It seemed like an exhumation. So did Joe Brown's Clarets. Waldron, Docherty, Collins, and Dixey had left on free transfers because no one was interested in buying them, while those who could attract a fee, notably Peyton and Hankin, were placed in the shop window. Relegation had cost the club £146,871 (£1m today) while debts were around £400,000 (£2.6m today) and climbing at £4,000 per week. Notwithstanding the enduring summer heat-wave, the club's graphic designer decided that gloom was chic when creating a new motif for the 1976/77 matchday programme. The front cover featured a deserted Turf Moor, apparently encased in snow. It made perfect sense, though, on a hypothermic 4 December when I had to be chipped off the Longside terraces after watching a 0-0 draw with Cardiff in freezing fog.

In sharp contrast, a 0-0 draw at a scalding Molineux on 21 August was a satisfactory start in draining conditions. A subsequent 3-1 home victory against 1975 FA Cup finalists Fulham was a sparkling display, with young winger Paul Bradshaw outstanding. But Joe's hopes of a rapid return to the top flight were quickly doused with an ensuing 1-2 home defeat

8. HARRY'S GAME 1976/77

by vastly superior Luton on the day that the rains returned. No sooner had former referee Dennis Howell been appointed Minister of Drought than the country was drenched by incessant, apocalyptic downpours. He was probably the only Labour MP of that time to be considered an unqualified success, given that the jobless total had risen to 1.5 million and Denis Healey's attempts at agreeing wage restraints with the unions, with the promise of bugger all, felt like a balancing act only Nadia Comaneci could perform. But we were still in the EEC thanks to the June 1975 referendum. So greater prosperity was just around the corner, at least according to its advocates.

Worse still, Burnley were humbled by Fourth Division Torquay in the League Cup and thrashed 0-3 by newly promoted Hereford, with arch predator Dixie McNeil scoring all three. Burnley restored a smidgen of pride by beating FA Cup winners Southampton on a suitably dank September afternoon, for it was Hankin's final home appearance before departing to Leeds. He signed off with a stooping headed goal, his 47th for the club in 110 starts. Fleeting starlet Paul Bradshaw was also on his way to Sheffield Wednesday for a £20,000 fee, while Colin Morris was transferred to Southend for £10,000. Derrick Parker would follow him on identical terms, several months later. As for 20-year-old goalkeeper Gerry Peyton, he departed to Fulham in December for £35,000 after Stevenson had reclaimed his regular place in goal on 30 October.

With the coffers benefitting from more than £200,000 in transfer fees, Joe Brown brought in Coleraine's fast and tricky right-winger Terry Cochrane for £38,000 and Malcolm Smith from Middlesbrough for £25,000, after he scored five times in eight games while on loan at Burnley. Cochrane was an immediate success, scoring on debut, but Smith's goal rush dried up as soon as he signed a permanent deal. Pools winner Danny Carr had apparently offered to buy Smith for the club, having been impressed with his strike rate during the Teessider's loan period with the club. But Lord would not hear of it. Lord would not tolerate anyone being involved in the running of the club other than board members who had bought a substantial number of shares. He even proscribed the formation of an official Burnley supporters' club on the grounds that its members were not major shareholders and therefore had no right to a say in the club's affairs.

Although Fletcher returned from injury after Hankin's departure, Burnley still struggled to score. Joe Brown adopted a 4-2-4 formation against visiting Orient on 9 October. Although Fletcher, Cochrane, and Smith gave Burnley a 3-1 lead shortly after the break, Orient hit back to earn a 3-3 draw. On the following Saturday, it was Burnley's turn to make a startling comeback against Charlton. Having been 1-4 down in the 54th minute, goals from Noble, Fletcher and Cochrane earned us a 4-4 draw. Flynn should have won the game, but he squandered a great last-minute opportunity. But this open style of play was not sustainable after a 2-5 hammering at Forest, resulting in Burnley dropping into 20th position. Ingham, Brennan, Summerbee, and Stevenson were recalled for the away game at Plymouth on a grey 30 October.

A rugged defensive display was rewarded with a 1-0 victory thanks to Smith's 54th-minute goal. Noble's penalty achieved a similar result a week later, against Oldham, lifting Burnley into 15th position. But the next five fixtures yielded only two points and a drop of four places. Having recovered from injury, Cochrane scored a wonderful solo goal against Millwall on 18 December. He ran half the length of the pitch, accelerating past several defenders, before unleashing an astonishing curling shot into the top left-hand corner of the net. It was a singular shining moment in another error-strewn display (1-3). It was just as well that we sold Peyton in December because Bob Lord had announced that the club was on the verge of bankruptcy, also suggesting that Flynn might have to be sold.

Blackburn 2 Burnley 2
27 December 1976
'Trouble Every Day'

Liz's interest had dwindled after the loss of her favourite player, Ray Hankin, leaving me to go to matches alone after the Orient game. However, she returned for this game – not that either of us was looking forward to this festive fixture. It was a grey, damp day that suddenly turned alarming when we were caught up in an angry, churning scrum of Burnley fans outside the blocked Darwen End entrances. Seeing the obvious danger, I managed to use my height and strength to free both of us before the remaining space was entirely filled. We decided to join the packed Blackburn End, realising we would need to be careful not to identify ourselves. Once in, we soon discovered there was little to cheer. Blackburn were all over Burnley. Svarc narrowly missed with a diving header. Byrom shot into the side netting; Stevenson had to hurl himself frantically to his left and right to prevent an avalanche of goals. Metcalfe's fierce drive forced him to tip over while a clever chip from Byrom required our goalie to grasp the ball above his head while being jostled by the Blackburn attackers. Parkes's shot was pushed aside for a corner which resulted in Byrom smacking the ball against a post. It seemed that every minute contained a heart-in-mouth experience. We were exhausted by half-time. How Burnley managed to survive this deluge was hard to explain. Certainly, without Stevenson's agility and bravery Burnley could have easily been six or seven goals down.

It could not last, though, and it did not. Seven minutes after the break Byrom turned in Wagstaffe's cross at the near post. We felt decidedly sheepish as the Blackburn fans leapt and screamed all around us. Fortunately, there was a crash barrier behind us otherwise we would have been flattened by the explosive surge that followed Byrom's celebrations. With his arms raised aloft, Byrom pressed himself against the perimeter wall, inviting febrile adulation from his fans, which he duly received. Ten minutes later the wretched experience was repeated. Wagstaffe's shot on goal was blocked but luckily for him the ball rebounded in his direction, allowing him to thread a ball between the scattered Burnley defenders for Byrom to slide his shot wide of Stevenson. Liz asked whether we should go home. I pleaded for more time, hoping the Blackburn lads would burn themselves out in their prolonged adrenalin rush. Liz was understandably dubious. But the game did change after winger Gordon Taylor was taken off with a badly bruised shin. This upset Blackburn's overpowering rhythm, enabling Burnley to find a precarious foothold.

Encouraged by this, they adopted a higher defensive line. With only ten minutes left, and Liz and me about to make our move, we scored! With nothing to lose Keith Newton ditched his defensive duties and pushed well forward on the left flank. Culpably, Newton was not closed down soon enough, allowing him the space to fire a stinging shot that slapped against a post. Noble pounced on the rebound and rammed it into the net via the underside of the bar. With Burnley having stolen Blackburn's ascendancy, Flynn broke away on the right wing and crossed for Brennan to fire the ball through a crowd of defenders and into the net with Blackburn goalie Bradshaw helpless. The packed Darwen End exploded with joy. Once again Liz and I had to clamp our jaws tight although our wide-eyed expressions would have given us away if anyone was looking. But their eyes were focused malevolently on the Burnley players and their celebrating supporters. All manner of threats were hurled in their direction giving us time to get away unharmed. 'It was floodlight robbery,' said Liz as we drove home. I was far too elated to care.

If we thought this unexpected revival would prompt an upturn in form, we were disappointed. The next day, Burnley drew 0-0 with promotion-seeking Blackpool, in front of a 19,682 crowd, at least half of whom were supporting the visitors. Then five days later, on a foggy, icy night at Turf Moor, Burnley capitulated pathetically to second from bottom, Plymouth. It was then that the club parted company with Mike Summerbee. Gratifyingly, Burnley responded by beating a strong Lincoln side, under Graham Taylor, in an FA Cup replay, although lowly Port Vale eliminated us in the next round. Burnley also achieved a 2-2 draw at Fulham with Fletcher and Noble on target. Then on a sunny 22 January at Turf Moor they held Second Division champions elect Wolves to a creditable stalemate. However, losses were subsequently suffered at Luton and Oldham. When relegation rivals Hereford escaped from Turf Moor with a point after a dire, toothless draw, on 12 February, Joe Brown's tenure was surely up.

Burnley 2 Carlisle 0
26 February 1977
'Blitzkrieg Bop'

Beleaguered Brown was sacked after another lame display, this time at Southampton on 19 February. Brown's side had not won a league game since beating Oldham on 6 November, 14 games before. Burnley were next to bottom. The only surprise was why Bob Lord took so long. Harry Potts had returned to Turf Moor as chief scout in the summer, much to Lord's delight, for Lord had belatedly regretted Potts's departure in 1972. With Brown gone, Lord wasted no time in reinstalling Potts as manager. This was warmly received by the dwindling Burnley faithful. The gate for the Carlisle game was 12,438, almost 4,000 more than at the wretched Hereford game. Potts remarked: 'I am convinced that there are better days ahead. This is a great club. There is nothing wrong with the training methods or team spirit. I intend to take a positive approach.' This meant 4-2-4.

Potts's first game in charge was against another side in distress, Carlisle, who had three dangerous strikers – Billy Rafferty, formerly with Coventry, Frank Clarke, brother of

Alan, and Dixie Deans, previously with Celtic. A tough game was expected. But it did not materialise. Cochrane opened the scoring shortly after the interval, while Noble secured the points with a 67th-minute penalty and Carlisle hardly fired a shot in anger. It was the first time that Burnley had scored more than one league goal at home since 16 October 1976. This game seemed like a nice stroll for Harry Potts. But subsequent heavy defeats at Notts County (1-5) and Hull (1-4) emphasised the size of the task before him. As Joe Brown found earlier in this season, playing expansive football carried considerable risk.

While Harry Potts seemed to have no qualms about returning to the fray, former Burnley star Ralph Coates remarked in a later interview with the London Clarets how het up Potts became when he was team manager. Coates said: 'On matchdays, Harry shook and sweated profusely, constantly burying his face in his hands. However, after Potts moved upstairs, becoming general manager in 1970, he was said to be a different man, asking after his players' families. The angry silences and slamming of doors disappeared.'

But here that pressure was back upon his shoulders. How would he cope? According to several Burnley players, tactics were not Potts's strongest suit. But if he thought relegation could be averted by playing attractively, he had to address the hole in midfield and tighten his porous defence. Certainly, central midfielders Noble and Flynn were too easily overrun at Notts County and Hull, not helped by the reluctance of Morley and Cochrane to back up. Also, his central defenders Thomson and Rodaway lacked pace and mobility, while his still-classy right-back Keith Newton was coming to the end of his playing days. Also, left-back Brennan was better bombing forward than in repelling a siege. Thankfully Stevenson had recovered his mojo.

Burnley 1 Sheffield United 0
12 March 1977
'Sweet Gene Vincent'

When Sheffield United came to Turf Moor on 12 March, Harry made only one change, bringing in 19-year-old centre-half Peter Robinson to replace the ageing and rather pedestrian Jim Thomson. It was a bright, breezy day and so was the football. With both the Clarets and the Blades intent upon attacking, it was an incredibly open game with many goalmouth scrimmages at both ends. The space conceded on the flanks encouraged the wingers on either side to focus exclusively upon attack. The game could have finished ten apiece but was amazingly settled by a single goal. Malcolm Smith's 67th-minute effort – a near-post header from Morley's sharp cross – snaffled the precious points.

Orient 0 Burnley 1
19 March 1977
'London Calling'

A week later Harry gained a vital 1-0 win at relegation rivals Orient. Scrapping midfielder Billy Ingham came in for Cochrane, adding robustness to Burnley's defence, helping his side claim only their second away win of the season. Harry commented: 'We put up a very good display in the first half and the highlight was a crashing 30-yard strike by left-back Ian Brennan in the ninth minute. We could have had several more as we were well on top. But injuries to Flynn, Noble and Fletcher in the second half forced us to defend our slender lead, showing a great deal of determination in securing these vital points.'

Burnley 0 Nottingham Forest 1
2 April 1977
'Hotel California'

Brian Clough and Peter Taylor's Nottingham Forest came to Turf Moor on the brink of their club's unexpected national and international triumphs. The hard, uneven playing surface and high wind did not help matters but Burnley were thoroughly outplayed. The Clarets strung few passes together and constructed even fewer scoring opportunities. This Forest team were combative, quick, strong, and well organised. They did not shine but did not need to. It seemed that one goal would be enough to settle the game and Forest scored it in the 65th minute. Noble had been deceived by a bobbling ball, allowing Woodcock to nip in and beat Stevenson. Woodcock might have joined Burnley a year before, but Bob Lord refused to pay the £15,000 fee. Whereas he paid £25,000 for Malcolm Smith.

Burnley 3 Blackburn Rovers 1
8 April 1977
'I'm Stranded'

This was a strange local derby, lacking the frenetic intensity that almost invariably characterised these contests. It seemed more like a gentle pre-season friendly. Not even a bumper crowd of 17,372 ignited much passion. Maybe it was due to the torpid weather, more suited to dozing than dog-fighting. When Malcolm Smith opened the scoring in the sixth minute it aroused no more than a brief cheer from the home supporters. It was strange, since Burnley were still in relegation trouble. As for the Blackburn fans, they remained sullenly silent, perhaps complacent with their mid-table position. Smith's opener deserved a better response from the Burnley fans, being the product of a slick five-man move, completed when Smith turned on a pass from Flynn and hammered the ball past Bradshaw from 12 yards. The disaffection of the Rovers fans was more understandable as Burnley took total control of the game. Robinson, Fletcher, and Morley went close as the Clarets penned Rovers back in their half. Yet with a minute left, in this one-sided first half, Blackburn hit back. Wagstaffe's pinpoint cross was headed into the crowded Burnley box by midfielder

Tony Parkes and Svarc forced the ball into the net. At last, the Blackburn fans responded, letting out a mighty roar.

However, the Rovers fans' listlessness returned with a resumption of play. To be fair there was little to shout about as the game descended into a sterile stalemate. Even the tackling seemed perfunctory. This hiatus was broken in the 63rd minute when Blackburn centre-back Waddington carelessly headed Fletcher's centre across his goalmouth. Noble couldn't believe his luck as he despatched the loose ball past Bradshaw, whereupon the game resumed its sleepy mood. Amazingly, three players were booked after a laboured melee. It seemed like a bout between monks. But while Burnley had only a single-goal lead, there was always the chance that Blackburn could rouse themselves and nick a point. However, six minutes from full time, Robinson erased this fear, curling a header around stranded Bradshaw after Noble had flicked on Morley's corner. It was a deserved reward, for Robinson had demonstrated maturity and skill in his impressive performance. Burnley completed a successful Easter programme, holding Blackpool to a rancorous 1-1 draw at Bloomfield Road, and shackling another promotion contender, Bolton, at Turf Moor (0-0).

Burnley 1 Chelsea 0
23 April 1977
'Heroes'

By this time, Burnley had become more proficient in front of goal and more determined to hit back when trailing. At Bristol Rovers on 16 April, Noble cracked in a deserved equaliser on the run. Then a week later Billy Ingham scored the goal of his life against promotion-bound Chelsea. Burnley had held the free-scoring Blues with ease, but a win seemed beyond them, until Ingham's decisive intervention in the 85th minute. The ball was squared to him just outside Chelsea's box. Without hesitation he flicked it over a lunging defender, brushed past him and hit the falling ball on the half-volley. He absolutely nailed it, with the ball ripping into the top corner before anyone could move. There was momentary silence until realisation dawned. Then came the Longside's explosive adulation. Ingham had performed well in shoring up the porous midfield but after this stunning goal he would always be known as the 'Ginger Pelé'.

Although Charlton gave the Clarets a 2-5 pasting at the Valley, a vital 1-0 victory was seized at Cardiff, thanks to Noble's sixth-minute strike. Security was duly attained a week later at home to Notts County. On a day of heavy May showers, Tony Morley finally came good, exceptionally good. Here was a glimpse of the outstanding talent that would flourish at Villa. He ran the County right flank ragged, drilling in two unstoppable shots. Fletcher then rounded off this emphatic victory with a rare goal. We were safe and awash with bonhomie. Briefly, ludicrously, the future seemed Claret. But like the aftermath of Dunkirk, the euphoria of escape diminished quickly as we soberly assessed our club's shrinking status, the scale of its decline, and its descending prospects.

The Queen's Silver Jubilee was celebrated in 1977. It was not one of my favourite years. But it featured the first England victory over Germany since 1966; Geoff Boycott drove us to the Ashes; Virginia Wade won at Wimbledon; Liverpool triumphed in Rome; Freddie Laker launched his cut-price Sky Train; and Anwar Sadat and Menachem Begin achieved a fragile peace deal. As for Elvis, the way was not so much down, as out; The same was true of Marc Bolan, Charlie Chaplin, and Bing Crosby, while Macca dismissed hopes of a Beatles reunion. As for me, I celebrated the emergence of punk. At its best the music buzzed with confrontational energy and savage iconoclasm, more authentic and visceral than prog rock's pompous doodling. Despite its relatively brief life span, punk seemed to be rock music's last rebel yell. That distinction passed progressively to hip hop. But my favourite memory of 1977 was

8. HARRY'S GAME 1976/77

Burnley's unexpected revival under Harry Potts, improbably lifting themselves well clear of the drop zone, having been in 21st place when Potts replaced Brown.

9. 'BIG STEVIE WONDER'
1977/78

'Wuthering Heights'

When Steve Kindon responded to the club's SOS call in November 1977, Burnley were rock bottom of the old Second Division. Jimmy Adamson had gone, along with his doomed prediction of glory. Money was too short to mention, and survival was now the name of the game. By 5 November, the Clarets had just five points from 14 games. Gates had fallen to around 7–8,000, debts were spiralling out of control and our mighty mite, Brian Flynn, was transferred to Leeds for £175,000. But out of the gloom emerged two saviours. The proceeds from Flynn's sale enabled the club to sign old-boy Kindon from Wolves and former Liverpool midfielder Brian Hall from Plymouth. The remaining booty also helped keep the wolf from the door. The mood of the club and that of its waning fans changed instantly.

Burnley 3 Notts County 1
12 November 1977

'Psycho Killer'

On 12 November Steve Kindon re-appeared in claret and blue. The visitors were Notts County, who had shaken off their early-season doldrums and were on a good run. All morning, ominous dark clouds converged over north-east Lancashire, drenching us with freezing rain. There was some doubt whether the match would be played.

9. 'BIG STEVIE WONDER' 1977/78

Attacking the Cricket Field End, Burnley were ahead within 16 minutes. Terry Cochrane's near-post cross was headed powerfully past goalie McManus by Fletcher. But this was Steve's day. While Notts County's Brian Stubbs dallied, Kindon pounced, stealing the ball from the centre-back, and setting off on a pounding run. McManus raced from his goal to intercept but Steve was too quick for him, easily rounding the goalkeeper and rolling the ball in from a tight angle. County were dangerous on the break, though, and with the weather closing in again they pulled a goal back. Peter Noble misjudged a cross in the swirling gale, causing the ball to hit his hand. A penalty was awarded, which County's right-winger, Carter, put away calmly.

As if the driving rain was not bad enough, it suddenly turned to snow. Large flakes spiralled and twirled in the glare of the floodlights. The Bob Lord and Cricket Field stands were almost opaque behind the snowy shroud. The pitch had already cut up badly. Mistakes became commonplace, but it fell to ex-Forest stalwart Bob Chapman to make a critical error. Steve caught Chapman in possession on the left touchline. Again, he was merciless. Having snatched the ball, Steve immediately found Fletcher with a low cross and he finished clinically.

Steve recalled: 'I felt really good for that game, as good as I had for any game. The conditions didn't bother me. I was equally as fast on heavy surfaces as I was on icy ones. We had two good wingers in Cochrane and Morley so I was confident we would get the opportunities to score. Paul Fletcher did well that day, too. He was not the best finisher, but he put both of his chances away terrifically. Although we were in a mess, I did not have the slightest doubt that we would pull things around. There was plenty of quality in the squad. Stevenson was a good goalkeeper, Peter Noble was a very good defensive midfielder, and Brian Hall was a good midfield signing. The main weakness was in central defence, although Jim Thomson was a better defender than many gave him credit for. I recall that back in the late sixties we were leaking a stack of goals, so Jimmy Adamson asked the first team to select their best XI and 17 of us chose Jim Thomson, who was out of the side at the time. The only one who did not was Colin Blant. He was so desperate to get a game that he put himself down for every position.'

Steve added: 'To be honest, I don't remember too much about the game apart from our goals, but what does stick was the record requested on my behalf by one of the Burnley supporters. It was Peters and Lee's 'Welcome Home', such a lovely touch. I've often wondered whether it was the same supporter who requested 'Baby Come Back' when I was in the Wolves side that drubbed Burnley 5-1 two years before.'

Luton Town 1 Burnley 2
3 December 1977
'Rockin' All Over the World'

After the euphoric victory over Notts County, Burnley lost at Cardiff, their eighth away defeat on the bounce. They also failed to beat totally besieged Orient at home. But at Luton on 3 December, Burnley could at last celebrate an away win. Harry replaced Irish winger Terry Cochrane with snapping midfielder Billy Ingham, employing a 4-3-3 formation. It worked. Both Steve and Brian Hall were on the score sheet as the middle-of-the-table 'Hatters' were beaten 2-1. Steve remembered the odds. He said: 'The bookies didn't fancy our chances. They reckoned that we had no better than a one in seven chance of winning. I told the others I'd never lost to Luton and always scored against them. I was so confident of victory that I managed to persuade everyone to put a fiver on us winning. Well, we came up trumps. I scored. Brian Hall scored, and we made £350 between us. So, everyone was pretty chuffed.'

9. 'BIG STEVIE WONDER' 1977/78

Burnley 1 Charlton Athletic 0
10 December 1977
'Go Your Own Way'

A week later Steve scored a brilliant solo goal in the 1-0 home victory over sixth-placed Charlton. Picking up the ball in midfield, Steve Kindon stormed through the centre of the Charlton defence before flicking the ball over the advancing goalie, Jeff Wood. The Charlton defenders seemed to part in the face of Kindon's juggernaut assault. Results were improving but Burnley remained stubbornly stuck to the bottom. An ensuing 0-3 defeat at Notts County reminded us how much needed to be done to avert the drop.

Burnley 2 Blackburn Rovers 3
26 December 1977
'Watching the Detectives'

On Boxing Day, Burnley faced their bitter rivals, Blackburn Rovers, at Turf Moor. The pitch was a quagmire. While Burnley were struggling against relegation, Blackburn were pursuing promotion. With so much at stake, over 27,000 turned up to watch what became a bloody contest. Capitalising on some catastrophic defensive errors, Rovers stormed into a three-goal first-half lead with Keith Fear, Noel Brotherston, and David Wagstaffe running riot. It seemed that only Steve's charismatic presence could turn this debacle around, but a Rovers centre-back made sure that wouldn't happen.

Steve explained: 'I was chasing a long ball down the left wing, in front of the Bob Lord stand, when this elbow cracked my nose. There was blood everywhere, my nose flopping against my cheek. The bone had broken in two. Jimmy Holland, the physio, had to take me off but as soon as I got to the dressing room, I yelled at him to plug the flow of blood because I was going back. I was furious, determined to exact revenge. When I re-emerged, the crowd went wild, but I could see my team-mates were worried. I heard someone say, "For Christ's sake Kindo, stay off." Blackburn defender Derek Fazackerly was even more worried. He and I were good drinking pals. So, I went straight up to him, demanding to know who was responsible. He did not want to say. Although I had guessed who it was, the Blackburn lads kept him away from me, rightly so, because I was way out of control.' Although Burnley's top gun had been spiked, they did manage a late revival. Morley scored with a spectacular solo effort and Noble put away a penalty. But even seven minutes of injury time was insufficient for Burnley to salvage a point.

Bolton Wanderers 1 Burnley 2
2 January 1978
'Lust for Life'

Only one of Burnley's three festive fixtures yielded a point – a goalless home draw with Sunderland. Burnden Park promised to be another graveyard shift. The evening was dank and cold with a spectral mist curling insidiously around the Bolton streetlights. It was as if I had blundered into *The Exorcist*. There were no 'Tubular Bells', though, and no Max von Sydow. More importantly, Bolton were top and in fine form whereas Burnley were bottom and without talismanic Kindon, thanks to the rough treatment he received in the Blackburn and Oldham games. To repel Bolton's formidable strike force, Harry chose to play with three centre-backs, Rodaway, Thomson, and Robinson, with Scott and Ingham as full-backs and Cochrane, Noble, Brennan, and Morley in midfield. This left Fletcher up front operating principally as a solitary target man. After this stirring performance, I had to revise my earlier view that Harry did not have a head for tactics.

His uses of Morley as a roaming attacker and Brennan as a left-sided marauder were inspired innovations. Burnley's movement was superb, their combativeness unrelenting and their energy levels terrific. Meanwhile, Morley dumbfounded

9. 'BIG STEVIE WONDER' 1977/78

Bolton with his darting runs, constantly switching the point of Burnley's attacks, pulling the Bolton defenders about, and creating openings that he and his colleagues could exploit. While the five-man Burnley defence stood firm, forcing the Bolton attackers to occupy the flanks and shoot harmlessly from distance, the Clarets' greater mobility and speed in counter-attacking severely troubled Bolton's back four, comprising Nicholson, Allardyce, Walsh, and Ritson. They seemed unsure which Burnley player they should be picking up. This confusion allowed Brennan the space to make regular forays along the inside-left channel which Bolton failed to stem. With Burnley maintaining a tight defensive line, and determinedly pressing the Bolton midfielders in their own half, this squeezed the supply line to Bolton front men Frank Worthington and Neil Whatmore. Burnley's energetic pressing rendered their midfield adversaries anonymous. Bolton's promotion push had owed much to their powerhouse midfielders, Reid, Train, Morgan, and Greaves, but here Burnley largely snuffed them out. The Clarets were blessed with an early opening goal which boosted their confidence while rocking the home side and their fans, for in the 14th minute Brennan broke along the left flank before moving inside and unleashing a shot so fierce and accurate that Bolton's goalie, McDonagh, could not lay a hand on the ball.

Shortly after the interval, Burnley were awarded a free kick on the edge of the Bolton box. Brennan stepped up and slammed in the second with McDonagh helpless. By this time Bolton's play had become a shambles: a miasma of petulant fouls, with repeated loss of possession, misplaced passes, and wild shots at goal. Bolton relied upon long balls to evade the Burnley press, which were easily swallowed by the Burnley defenders. The Clarets were comfortably in command. Only a careless error by Cochrane in the 89th minute let Bolton in. Whatmore prodded home after Cochrane had negligently been caught in possession. It was said that Jim Thomson took hold of Cochrane and almost throttled him. But all was well as the final whistle sounded soon after.

Bottom had beaten top, and I was buzzing, no longer cold or miserable. Bolton satisfied their wounded pride by eliminating Spurs from the FA Cup after a replay and subsequently thrashing Sheffield United 5-1 at Bramall Lane. Bolton would be promoted to the First Division alongside Spurs and Southampton. As for Burnley, they knocked Fulham out of the FA Cup before succumbing to Chelsea in the next round, although the 2-6 score flattered the Blues, at least according to Harry Potts.

Burnley 1 Stoke City 0
14 January 1978
'Lovely Day'

Stoke came to Turf Moor on a bright, shivery afternoon. They were in 15th place, having had a lean spell. On a heavy pitch, this was an attritional game with few chances, but Steve broke the deadlock in the 70th minute when he crashed through the Stoke defence to head over Stoke goalkeeper Roger Jones. This setback prompted Stoke manager Alan Durban to bring on their 19-year-old free-scoring striker, Garth Crooks. He replaced Terry Conroy, who had made little impact upon a well-organised Burnley defence. A bright future awaited Crooks. He would score 18 league goals for Stoke during this season. A brighter future was signalled for Burnley, too, as this tight victory took Burnley off the bottom, a position they had occupied since 27 August. A subsequent 1-1 draw at Crystal Palace lifted them into 20th position.

Burnley 3 Southampton 3
4 February 1978
'Uptown Top Ranking'

Kindon's pace and power had scared the pants off promotion-seeking Southampton. Burnley were twice two goals ahead

9. 'BIG STEVIE WONDER' 1977/78

in this scintillating tussle on a dark, raw afternoon, watched by 10,592 fans. Kindon had put Burnley ahead in the fifth minute after bursting through Southampton's wobbly back line. Cochrane then added a second in the 29th minute after cutting in from the right. Although Boyer pulled one back immediately after half-time, Kindon retaliated quickly with a superb solo goal. Having raced 40 yards down the left flank in typical Panzer mode, he summoned the necessary composure and sureness of touch to slip the ball past the advancing Saints goalkeeper, Ian Turner. Although Turner was way off limits, the precision of Kindon's finishing was exquisite. After benefitting three times from Southampton's defensive generosity, Burnley should have slammed their back door shut. Irritatingly, they were minded to return the compliment. Ted McDougall reduced the deficit in the 83rd minute, with Peach's last-minute piledriver denying Burnley a vital victory. The 2-2 draw at Bristol Rovers on 4 March was equally frustrating as Kindon had twice given Burnley the lead with thumping drives only for the Clarets' defence to concede a 90th-minute leveller. Burnley remained in 20th position.

Brighton & Hove Albion 2 Burnley 1
11 February 1978
'Exodus'

The mini revival came to an end at fourth-placed Brighton. The game was played on a half-thawed surface, slippery on top and hard underneath. Everyone had difficulty keeping their feet. However, Burnley adjusted to the treacherous conditions better than their hosts and were well on top for much of the first half. Yet almost on the stroke of half-time Malcolm Poskett was the beneficiary of a poor clearance and eagerly took his chance. Nevertheless, Scott restored parity soon after half-time when he thundered in a 25-yard drive. Burnley continued to dominate without finding the killer touch. They paid for this profligacy when Brennan was adjudged to have collided with hot-shot Peter Ward inside the Burnley box. A penalty was awarded which seemed particularly harsh given that the collision was caused by the slippery surface rather than by intent. Burnley protests fell on deaf ears. Brighton's midfielder Brian Horton scored coolly from the spot, leaving the Clarets only 15 minutes to save the game. However, Brighton defended doughtily to protect their narrow lead.

Burnley 4 Sheffield United 1
11 March 1978
'Staying Alive'

Kate Bush's wonderful warbling 'Wuthering Heights' topped the charts on this sunny Saturday. But for half of this game, Burnley's ill-coordinated efforts felt more like withering depths. Simon Stainrod had deservedly put the Blades ahead five minutes before the break. The visitors seemed comfortably in control. Then came a blinding second-half transformation. Cochrane equalised within ten minutes of the restart and Noble turned the game around with a coolly taken penalty in the 71st minute (he never missed one in his six and a half years at Burnley). Ingham popped up for Burnley's third with only five minutes left and Cochrane grabbed his second one minute before the final whistle. It was a devastating display of power football that left the Blades reeling. Subsequent victories over Mansfield in steady rain (2-0) and at sunny Hull (3-1) suggested that Burnley, then in 17th place, would avoid relegation, a remarkable recovery, having spent 30 games in the relegation zone, 22 of which were in bottom place.

Burnley 4 Oldham Athletic 1
25 March 1978
'Down in the Tube Station at Midnight'

Easter Saturday dawned grey, cold, and blustery with frequent showers of rain, sleet, and snow. Burnley were undeterred by the mushy conditions, crushing Oldham 4-1. Cochrane scored twice, with Brennan and Kindon sharing the other two goals. Presented with an open goal at point-blank range, a tap-in would have sufficed. Not for Steve, though, as he leathered the ball in with utmost force. Hacks often refer to net-busting efforts. Here, Steve seemed intent upon roaring real meaning into the cliché. A crowd of 13,529 turned up on this icy afternoon to watch the fireworks.

Blackburn Rovers 0 Burnley 1
27 March 1978
'Baker Street'

Easter Monday was quite different. On a bright, breezy afternoon, Donna Summer's 'I Feel Love' wafted around Ewood Park. So did Terry Cochrane's speculative shot. Twisting and erratically curling in the gusting wind, the ball's flight totally confounded John Butcher in the Blackburn goal. He groped and clawed helplessly as the ball eluded him, nestling inside the Blackburn net. Cochrane's 20th-minute strike was the only goal of the game although there were many close calls at both ends. It was a fiercely fought contest with Brotherston dismissed after a second wild tackle, this time on Cochrane. The skirmishing on the pitch was mirrored by the fans' unruly behaviour behind the goal, notably at the Darwen End, where the police intervened, removing several suspects. After achieving a well-merited 1-1 draw at rapidly declining Blackpool, Harry Potts received his second 'manager of the month' award.

In 1977/78, Steve Kindon was a colossus. Burnley's tactics were derided as 'Let Kindon chase it' but this was simply playing to his strength. Steve's speed and power were phenomenal. Neither clinging mud nor driving rain could hold him back. For all that, Harry reckoned that Steve's contribution was felt as much in the dressing room as on the field. Before his arrival, Burnley looked buried but by the end of the season this team was transformed into potential promotion contenders. His exuberant self-confidence inspired self-belief in a formerly dispirited squad, enabling them to achieve what seemed impossible in early November. Burnley completed the season in style, winning four of their six remaining fixtures, including a 2-1 win over promotion-bound Spurs and a 4-2 thumping of Cardiff.

10. CUP WINNERS AGAIN 1978/79

12 September 1978
'Summer Nights'

Steve Kindon had not finished, though. During the following season he helped Burnley win a trophy: the Anglo-Scottish Cup. This was no mean feat because in the quarter-final first leg Celtic, the Scottish giants, stood in their way. The first leg was staged at Turf Moor, Burnley. It was quite a night. Celtic were en route to the Scottish Premier title. They were expected to win easily. Some 30,000 people piled into Turf Moor, not all of them paying. It became a boozy, sectarian reconstruction of Rorke's Drift. Turf Moor's defences weren't up to the task. A closed turnstile proved no obstacle to several thousand well-oiled Celtic fans out for blood. They simply smashed their way in. Roared on by their belligerent hordes, Celtic came to slash and burn. Apparently, Burnley's part was to roll over and die but the Burnley lads torched that script. Scottish frustration, which had been stoked steadily during the first half, combusted after the break when Steve Kindon's breakaway goal put Burnley ahead. Not content with singeing the Celtic defenders, the returning Leighton James and Steve Kindon had the temerity to humiliate them as well. Surely, this would not end well.

Scottish pride had already taken a pummelling in Argentina, despite their brilliant defeat of Holland. Chrysler had pulled its TV advert featuring 'Ally's Tartan Army'. The English had scoffed, just as they had over the embarrassing Scottish failures against Peru and Iran. There were scores, ancient and modern, to settle on this hostile night. Losing to lowly Burnley was not in Celtic's prospectus.

With their team incapable of exacting the revenge that their fierce chauvinism demanded, the Celtic fans began to rampage, pulling the segregating fences out of their concrete emplacements and hurling the iron railings, like spears, onto the pitch and into the pen containing the Burnley supporters. With bottles, cans, and stones also thrown, play was held up for ten minutes while a semblance of order was restored. Steve remembered the night vividly, as well he might. He recalled: 'After the referee had taken the teams off the pitch, he suggested to both managers, Harry Potts and Billy McNeill, that they should accompany him back onto the field, linking arms to demonstrate mutual solidarity in attempting to calm the inflamed passions. You could see that Harry wasn't taken with this idea. In those days the dugout was in front of the Longside where the rioting had broken out. He was frightened, his eyes flicking nervously around the dressing room as the referee explained what he proposed to do. Then upon seeing me, Harry thought he'd found a way out. He gushed, "Steve, I think it would be a better idea if you went out with Billy and the referee. You are much more popular with the crowd." I admired his effort but had to point out, "Harry, I think you're overlooking a small detail here. It was my goal which started the bloody riot."'

Order was eventually restored, and Burnley clung on to win. Just to rub barrels of salt into Celtic's already inflamed wounds, Burnley won the away leg as well (2-1). Harry's 4-4-2 formation worked a treat. Ian Brennan and Kindon did the damage in the first half and Celtic could only manage a consolatory penalty. A crowd of 28,000 had turned up to watch the indignity continue.

The unfancied English clubs had flown the flag so furiously that all participating Scottish teams were eliminated way before the final stages. Oldham and Burnley were left as the unlikely finalists. With a glacial winter moving ever closer, the first leg

10. CUP WINNERS AGAIN 1978/79

took place at Boundary Park. Burnley had not done well there in previous seasons so few of us were prepared for what transpired. Harry rightly realised that on this hard, slippery surface the long-ball game offered the best chance of success. So, right from the off, booming long balls were struck down the middle for Steve to chase. This worked like a dream. Alan Young got a late consolation goal, but by then Burnley were four goals up with Steve responsible for two of them. The final had already been decided before the return leg.

Liz and I moved to Leicester in the spring of 1978 to be a bit closer to my ailing mother. It was a huge wrench, made sadder by our curtailed access to Burnley. We went to as many games as we could during the 1978/79 season, but this was constrained by my family care responsibilities and the severe winter weather. Before the post-Christmas ice age moved in, Liz and I went to five away games. We sullenly watched the Clarets thrashed 0-4 at Bramall Lane on a bright 16 September where an Argentinian midfielder, Alex Sabella, exhibited crushing brilliance. We also saw them overwhelmed 1-3 by a bigger and better Stoke team on 14 October. We endured a 1-2 defeat at Filbert Street by a mediocre Leicester side. We began to think we were jinxing our boys.

But before these setbacks, Burnley's 1978/79 season had begun moderately well with an unbeaten run of five games, the last one of these featuring a stirring comeback against visiting West Ham on 9 September. Here, Burnley overturned a two-goal deficit to win 3-2, thanks to Jim Thomson's 81st-minute header. *MOTD* provided TV highlights and its presenter Jimmy Hill announced that Leighton James was returning to Burnley, from QPR, for a £165,000 fee. Although Liz and I were at first excited by this news we had not yet realised that the deal was financed by Cochrane's transfer to Middlesbrough for £238,000, £50,000 of which went to Cochrane's parent club, Coleraine, under a sell-on agreement. The 25-year-old had played a leading role in Burnley's revival during the previous season and potentially had many good years ahead of him. With the club signing James, another former Burnley star, we wondered whether it was putting its past before its future, until we discovered that James was of a similar age to Cochrane. Our concern had greater truth, though, when 31-year-old Martin Dobson returned in the following summer, financed by the sale of 24-year-old Morley to Aston Villa for a £200,000 fee.

After being put to the sword at Bramall Lane, Burnley suffered the indignity of a 1-2 home loss to nine-man Sunderland on 23 September. It was an ill-tempered contest which led to an angry confrontation between Harry Potts and Sunderland boss Jimmy Adamson after the game, apparently refuelling past animosities. But a smash-and-grab raid at Millwall on 10 September put Burnley back on track, followed by a workmanlike home win over Oldham a week later. After the disappointing display at Stoke, Brighton were overrun 3-0 at Turf Moor on 21 October with Harry employing three strikers, Kindon, Fletcher, and James, although it was two-goal Ingham and Brennan who inflicted the damage from midfield. A prestigious 2-1 victory over second-placed Crystal Palace saw James at his best as he made a fool of Kenny Samson, Palace's talented right-back. Burnley were ensconced in seventh spot and looking upwards. The 1-2 setback at Leicester was righted with a 5-3 clobbering of visitors Fulham with Noble grabbing the match ball. Eventually our dismal experience on the road came to an end on 21 November as Burnley wrested a deserved point from their combative hosts, Notts County.

Cambridge United 2 Burnley 2
25 November 1978

'Oliver's Army'

On a gleaming 25 November, my 30th birthday, Liz and I drove to Cambridge to see our lads take on newly promoted

United. We travelled in hope as Burnley's recent results had been encouraging. But Cambridge had other ideas, racing into a two-goal lead with only 25 minutes gone. Cambridge 'headmaster' Bill Garner and nippy Alan Biley caused the damage. Brawny Garner won almost every aerial duel while bustling Biley fed greedily on his knock-downs and flick-ons. With the Cambridge midfield pressing forward with relish, Burnley were overwhelmed. We were not prepared for this humiliation. I took this badly. In fact, I thoroughly disgraced myself, behaving like a tethered ferret, squirming, snapping, and snarling at the surrounding Cambridge fans, who seemed more amused than offended. Normally, I am as threatening as a menopausal church warden, but here I completely lost it, angered not only by Burnley's rank ineptitude, but also by a recent spat at work. Then just before half-time Ingham made the most of a rare Burnley attack and smartly reduced the deficit. Suddenly, the home fans were not so smug. The second half was quite different, with Burnley having most of the play. On the hour Fletcher equalised with a brutal shot on the turn, prompting my delirious celebrations. Burnley were then well on top, leaving the home fans pensive and anxious. Had Fletcher's late effort found the net rather than a juddering bar we might have faced an acrimonious exit.

Burnley 2 Blackburn Rovers 1
26 December 1978

'Sultans of Swing'

On a rare visit to Turf Moor, we witnessed our first Burnley victory of this season. Typically, Burnley made hard work of it. Despite taking a two-goal lead in the first half, helped by Fletcher's fortuitous opener and Noble's deflected drive, they were nearly pegged back by relegation-bound Blackburn. Future Claret Kevin Hird played a blinder for Rovers, scoring with an exquisite chip shot in the 57th minute when goalkeeper Stevenson strayed off his line.

After a New Year stalemate with mid-table Cardiff and a demolition of languishing First Division Birmingham City in the FA Cup, ice and snow ruled out all remaining league fixtures in January. February was scarcely better with yet more postponements. In the only league games played, Burnley lost to Sunderland and upwardly mobile Stoke. Although Burnley gained revenge over Sunderland with a 3-0 victory in an FA Cup fourth-round replay, Liverpool quickly crushed their hopes of further progression.

Brighton & Hove Albion 2 Burnley 1
3 March 1979
'Transmission'

When Liz and I went to Brighton on 3 March we sensed this game might be a curtain call, or even a requiem, for Adamson's 'team of the seventies' before the decade closed. We began our support of Burnley when Jimmy Adamson was enthusing about his youngsters. Despite the setbacks, there were many fond memories, suggesting perhaps that a 'last waltz' might be a more appropriate farewell.

Sadly, this would be the last time we would see Steve Kindon play for Burnley, although I saw Burnley play at Bristol Rovers without him on 21 April. Here, Burnley sank to a tired, demoralising 0-2 defeat. That loss at Eastville began a free fall in which Burnley lost six and drew one of their final seven games.

It was a sombre if mild day. As we strolled along the empty promenade, making for the Goldstone Ground, fine rain wafted into our faces on a ruffling wind. There was an indolent feel to the day. Grubby waves staggered listlessly to the shore, collapsing onto the shingle with resigned sighs. As Burnley had been halted by the severe winter weather, they were left with a mammoth backlog of fixtures. We were sceptical whether Potts's team could summon the verve to revive their diminishing promotion hopes. Nevertheless, Burnley began this game

10. CUP WINNERS AGAIN 1978/79

brightly. The Clarets' left-winger, Leighton James, frequently outpaced Brighton's experienced full-back, Chris Cattlin, while Steve Kindon was a swift ram raider on the opposite flank. Together they ensured centre-forward Fletcher was supplied with a menacing succession of lofted crosses. Eric Steele in the Brighton goal was kept on his toes. Had he not been in such superb form, denying successive headers from Fletcher with breathtaking agility, Burnley would have been well in front at the break. After the game, Brighton manager Alan Mullery admitted to tearing strips off his team at half-time, slating their complacency and lethargy. His anger had the desired outcome as Brighton began the second half fired up.

Adopting a higher defensive line, Horton and Clark began to express themselves in the centre of the park. Wingers Ryan and O'Sullivan had more of the ball. As a result, their strikers Maybank and Ward were able to push up closer to Burnley's slow-turning central defenders. Now it was Burnley's turn to feel the heat. They were unable to commit so many men forward. Their suspect defence became sorely stretched. Five minutes after the restart, a penalty was awarded to Brighton which Horton put away decisively. But Burnley didn't buckle. Within a minute they were back on terms as Billy Ingham stole into Brighton's box, unseen, to poke home a loose ball.

The game then turned into a nip-and-tuck affair but one which began tilting Brighton's way. The contest was settled by a goal of supreme quality. Less shackled by defensive duties, Mark Lawrenson began advancing upfield. It was no wonder that Mullery had been so keen to bring him to the Goldstone. Lawrenson's sure technique and composure seemed underpinned by throbbing power. He proceeded to turn the game. In the 69th minute, he seized the ball in midfield and strode forward, effortlessly gliding through the Burnley defence as if it was an apparition. Upon reaching the edge of the Burnley box, he easily evaded Jim Thomson's desperate lunge and let fly with a skimming shot that evaded Stevenson's dive and struck the back of the net at the speed of light. A huge roar went up.

Liz and I looked at one another in resignation. This narrow defeat resulted in Burnley falling to 15th place, their lowest league ranking of the season, and yet, despite their massive fixture congestion, they embarked on a six-match unbeaten run which restored them to seventh position. But after a combative 2-1 victory at Blackburn on 14 April, a game marred by crowd violence, Burnley finally ran out of gas finishing the season in 13th place.

While Burnley subsequently embarked upon a catastrophic slide, which took them to the brink of oblivion in May 1987, Brighton seemed destined for the First Division. They deservedly secured a place in the top flight after a 3-1 victory at Newcastle in their final game of this season.

Reflecting upon the end of the seventies, a decade in which Burnley manager Jimmy Adamson expected his talented young team would flourish, three former members of that side gave their assessment of Adamson's capabilities as a coach. Burnley midfielder Arthur Bellamy said to fellow Burnley author Dave Thomas, 'Jimmy Adamson was perhaps one of the first new tacticians, the first modern-day coach and teacher. Harry Potts was a great manager, but he was not a great coach. He was a smoother of troubles. He gave players confidence. However, Jimmy Adamson taught me to do things I did not know I could do, like playing sweeper. Training under Adamson became more planned and technical. The man from the next era replaced the man of the old.'

His club colleague Martin Dobson had good reason to be grateful to Adamson, who had rescued his career after he had been rejected by Bolton. Dobson said to me, 'Jimmy had us practising set plays for hours on end. Each time we erred, he hauled us back and we would start again. The delivery had to be spot on, the positioning had to be exact, the runs needed to

10. CUP WINNERS AGAIN 1978/79

be timed perfectly. Jimmy wouldn't accept anything less than perfection.

'After spending a year as an apprentice at Bolton I could see life at Burnley was different. Everyone trained with a ball, the international players, and the younger ones. There was two-touch and "shadow" football going on. Players were going through pass-and-move drills. What impressed me was much of the training centred on developing ball skills. There was instruction in what to do, in technique, in making runs, positioning and so on. I had never seen anything like this at Bolton.

'At the heart of this activity was Jimmy Adamson. He seemed to know exactly what he wanted from his players – blowing his whistle to stop the play when the exercises were not being executed as he wanted, praising the players when they got it right and demonstrating what was missing when they did not. He was outstanding. He commanded so much respect. Everyone knew what he had achieved as a player. He had been the national Player of the Year in 1962. So, they listened closely to what he said. Adamson was steeped in modern tactical thinking.

'There was much practising of building attacks from the wing. Once again, Jimmy was meticulous about the type of cross to be supplied from the wings. We would go through a series of routines involving whipped or hanging crosses, say. He paid so much attention to detail, which, of course, paid off. I recall the intense repetition of practising flicked-on corner kicks at the near post. It involved performing decoy runs to create gaps so that the player concerned could arrive at the near post at the exact moment he was required to flick on a corner. The leap had to be right, too, so that the ball just kissed the top of his head.'

Utility player Geoff Nulty recalled in a telephone conversation with me: 'What impressed me was the training sessions were well planned. Jimmy Adamson and his assistant, Joe Brown, worked out the training schedules in advance. This was unlike what I had experienced as a young player at Stoke, where only the first team received real attention from the coaches and even their training sessions did not seem well prepared. The reserves were largely left to their own devices. But at Burnley the senior players, the reserves, and youth team players trained together, at least for most of the week.

'Jimmy Adamson and Joe Brown would divide us into mixed groups and, typically, these groups would be made up of four first-team players, four reserves, and four apprentices. Jimmy wanted everyone to be inducted into the Burnley style of play, so that when anyone stepped up, say from the youth team to the reserves or from the reserves to the first team, they were ready to make that transition.

'The mixed-group training took place on Mondays, Tuesdays, and Wednesdays. There was always a strong focus on ball work. But on Thursdays we trained in our team units in preparation for the Saturday games. As first-teamers we practised "shadow football". This is where we played against imaginary opponents. This really helped to tighten up our positional sense and interplay. Jimmy also organised a routine whereby the first team would be reduced to four defenders and a midfielder.

'They would be tasked with taking on a full reserve side. The only concession was that everyone on the reserve side was expected to fulfil their normal roles. The defenders could not become extra attackers. This exercise helped improve our defending. We had to play as one. It helped sharpen up our defensive instincts and organisation, our ability to cover for one another. We learnt how to spring the offside trap more effectively as a group. We became better attuned to one another. Having no attacking outlet, the defence was under constant pressure. This helped in getting organised. By doing this, we found we could keep the reserve sides out for some time.

'We also used this other routine designed to improve our wing play. Burnley had a string of great wingers – John Connelly, Ralph Coates, Willie Morgan, Dave Thomas, Leighton James,

10. CUP WINNERS AGAIN 1978/79

and so on. It was a key part of the club's success over many years. To make the most of these assets, Jimmy Adamson devised practice matches comprising 15 players per side with no goalkeepers. We could only score with our head. To get goals we first had to work the ball wide, so this became instinctive. We scored a lot of goals from headers in league and cup games. I am sure these practice sessions helped us in coordinating our attacks. When, say, Leighton James was attacking down one flank, the opposing defenders would be drawn over to his side to deal with the threat, so we then pushed up our full-back on the other flank to help exploit the gaps that this left.'

Nulty concluded, 'I felt well looked after at Burnley. They found me digs near to the ground. It did not matter that some of the senior players were big names. They treated the younger players like themselves.'

Yet despite his skills as a coach and tactician, Adamson was a divisive figure, eulogised by Dobson, Nulty, Bellamy, Fletcher, Waldron, and Thomson but disliked by Kindon and Thomas and others loyal to former manager Potts, such as Coates and trainer Miller. However, these rifts and allegiances need to be considered in light of the financial constraints applied by former chairman Bob Lord and the difficulty of competing with bigger and richer clubs.

With our only child on the way, Liz and I found there was much less time and money for football. Saturdays were often consumed with morose meanderings around packed supermarkets, heaving shopping centres, or, worst of all, MFI, where we bought affordable flat packs to bless with our incompetence. For the first time in my adult life football became expendable, a financially constrained choice rather than an obsessive necessity, often heard or peripherally seen, until our daughter became old and wise enough to want to go. The addiction did not expire, though. It was merely suppressed by the requisites of child care, waiting for the moment when the trailing guilt of parenthood thinned sufficiently for the urge to reappear. That prospect was hard to imagine, sat on those penal MFI benches, waiting to collect our chipboard ensembles. There, my unseeing eyes would be fixed on the cartoon channel, but my attention would be elsewhere, possibly speculating on events at the Shay or Spotland or wherever lowly Burnley were then playing. I would have to wait. The radio was always a car park away. Setting aside the contradictions in warmth, I felt like a beached ex-pat, comatosed by Spanish wine and Tenerife sun, indulging maudlin home thoughts from abroad.

11. THE END OF THE SEVENTIES

'Video Killed the Radio Star'

It has been said that the length of a skirt or the height of a building is a measure of national optimism. The mini skirt was a product of the hopeful sixties as were high-rise tower blocks. Older readers might remember that as we entered the seventies, maxi skirts became fashionable and long before we entered the eighties, many residents became disenchanted with their isolating tower blocks.

Technological advances continued apace. We had everything from the first test-tube baby to the cheap electronic calculator. Even while still in the afterglow of the 1969 moon landing, some began to question the adverse environmental implications of space exploration. British house prices increased by almost 1,000 per cent during the seventies as we became increasingly reliant upon credit. Spending had outstripped earnings, particularly after the massive hike in the price of oil, a legacy of the Yom Kippur War. This had the effect of pushing up inflation – peaking at an unsustainable 24 per cent in 1975 – creating a greater rift between the political right and left.

During the late sixties, pin-up posters of Che Guevara and Ho Chi Minh covered our college walls, reflecting our youthful idealism or pretensions, perhaps. Left-wing ideologies were treated with greater scepticism after the atrocities of the Soviet gulags, and the Killing Fields, among horrors perpetrated by other tyrants. Meanwhile at home, left-wing politics became beset with squabbles, fractious industrial relations, and economic stagnation. The EEC referendum of 1975 only achieved assent because it was thought that free access to the common market might boost our spluttering economy. Meanwhile terrorism abounded, in the Middle East, in Britain, notably in Northern Ireland, and in Germany, Italy, South and Central America, and in many former European colonies.

There was little surprise about Mrs Thatcher's rise to power. In a time of despair, quick-fix bandwagons run down careful argument. Her bandwagon was fuelled by rising exasperation with union activists and by fear and loathing in festering British cities and towns, the haunts of disaffected youths and supposed 'welfare scroungers'. In decaying Britain, punk viscerally articulated the emptiness of many young people's lives, without work or a home of their own, with little or no prospects of improvement. But for those who wanted escapism from angry reprisals, cynical iconoclasm, and glum negativity, the disco movement and club culture provided a bright, flashing, pulsating alternative; whereas Northern soul, with its exuberant dance routines and niche choice of music, created a cult following in Wigan and beyond. With the growth of MTV, vision trumped sound as a more engaging pop vehicle. 'Video Killed the Radio Star.'

PART 2

ON THE ROAD TO OBLIVION

1980 to 1987

'Livin' on a Prayer'

1. A NEW LOW 1979/80

'Message in a Bottle'

This star-crossed season was prefaced by an Atlantic storm so savage that 14 Fastnet race yachtsmen lost their lives in mountainous waves. The IRA assassinated Lord Mountbatten, while the 'Yorkshire Ripper' claimed his 12th victim. A massive relief programme was launched for ravaged Cambodia, struggling to recover after the genocide perpetrated by Pol Pot and his Khmer Rouge thugs. In defiance of the blatant folly of the Vietnam War, the Soviets invaded Afghanistan, recreating a similar miasma of brutality and widespread suffering before the Afghans retaliated forcefully. Meanwhile US Delta Force made a hash of recovering 53 US diplomats from their Iranian captors.

As for Burnley, the 1979/80 season was catastrophic, ending in a new low for the once proud club, Third Division football. The warning signs had started to flash soon after Burnley's victory at Ewood Park on Easter Monday 1979. Six of the last eight games of that season were lost, with only two goals scored. A similar pattern emerged at the start of the following campaign, culminating in the woeful 0-7 drubbing at Queens Park Rangers, which left debutant goalkeeper Billy O'Rourke in tears. He was not to blame, but his outfield colleagues were: running as if immersed in treacle, careless in distribution, weak in the tackle with no fire in their bellies. Each goal conceded appeared to be greeted by teapot gestures and mutual accusations. It was an unmitigated disgrace.

1. A NEW LOW 1979/80

Mickey Wardrobe, a reserve during that season, remarked at how easily his 'stiffs' had turned over the first team in a practice game during this dark period. Upon his return to Turf Moor in the summer of 1979, Martin Dobson was horrified at how lax training had become, remarking bitterly that Jimmy Adamson would not have tolerated such lassitude. Sadly, Harry Potts had lost his grip, with his health in jeopardy. Too many of his ageing squad had lost or were losing their potency and drive. It took Burnley 17 league games to register their first league victory of the season, a 5-3 win over nine-man Cambridge. By that time, drastic changes had been made. Steve had played his last game for Burnley and faithful retainer Brian Miller had replaced Harry Potts as manager.

Steve Kindon was a shadow of his former self in his final games with Burnley. In truth, he had never quite recaptured his phenomenal form of 1977/78. This was perhaps due to Leighton James robbing him of his favoured left-sided berth. Steve still performed an important role for the team on the right, frequently drawing away a couple of markers, but his own contributions became less prominent as his goals dried up. Also, as much as Martin Dobson's return was welcomed, this heralded a further tactical change with play being built up more deliberately through midfield. This deprived Steve of his major strength, the fast break. In short, Burnley had lost sight of how best to use him. The form of his colleagues in 1979 was scarcely better, though. However, Steve Kindon recovered his mojo instantly after moving to Fourth Division Huddersfield Town in December 1979, having become Mick Buxton's most expensive signing. He made a striking impression, scoring 35 goals in 69 games, helping the Terriers to achieve one promotion, and almost two in successive seasons. Regrettably, it ended far too quickly, with a serious knee injury forcing his premature retirement. Steve recalled: 'Brian Miller didn't want to let me go. He had to. He was told to slash the wage bill, so I had to go. There were tears in Brian's eyes when he told me.'

Leicester City 1 Burnley 1
10 November 1979
'The Eton Rifles'

Martin Dobson returned from Everton for a £100,000 fee, financed by Morley's departure. It was thought that Geoff Nulty might join Dobson until a serious injury scuppered the plan. The deficiencies Martin identified in Burnley's preparations were starkly reflected in their poor results, complicated by injuries to Noble, Fletcher, Kindon, and Stevenson. After beating Blackburn at Ewood in April 1979, Burnley failed to win any of their 24 subsequent league games. Average attendances fell to around 7,000, not helped by an entrance fee that made it cheaper to watch Manchester United and Liverpool. At least the club ditched the V-for-victory strip. I blamed that bloody shirt for every calamity suffered since 1974/75.

It was inevitable that ailing Harry Potts would lose his job. After his sad mid-October exit, Brian Miller was asked to step up, helped by Frank Casper. Despite recent failures Burnley continued to be run as a family concern. Brian had spent his entire career at Burnley, as a title-winning player, trainer, coach, and now manager. He would later become chief scout, a one-club man for sure. He knew radical changes were essential, with Scott, Noble, Thomson, Rodaway, Fletcher, and Kindon losing their places. In came full-back Tony Arins, defender Paul Dixon, striker Jeff Tate, midfielder Marshall Burke, centre-half Vince Overson, and winger Phil Cavener. Forgotten striker Malcolm Smith was recalled. Dissatisfied with reserve team football, Kindon was sold to Huddersfield in December for £55,000. Noble and Fletcher were sold to Blackpool in the new year for £25,000 and £30,000 respectively, and reserve goalkeeper Tony Norman was sold to Hull for £30,000. Kindon's sale enabled

1. A NEW LOW 1979/80

Burnley to bring in future Clarets and Northern Ireland hero Billy Hamilton, a centre-forward from QPR, for a £38,000 fee.

Only two weeks after the Loftus Road debacle, I went to Filbert Street with little hope on the back of another home defeat, this time by Orient (1-2). Leicester were champions elect with a free-scoring young centre-forward called Gary Lineker. Fittingly, it was a grey, overcast day. But despite being heavily outgunned, this young, inexperienced Burnley team competed with commendable vigour. They fought for everything. Jeff Tate and Richard Overson – a defender like his brother, Vince – appeared well out of their depth, but much to their credit they refused to be subdued. Nevertheless, Leicester should have been unreachable before half-time, which arrived goalless. James carried Burnley's sole threat. Undaunted, he worked his socks off in his team's cause. Time and again he sped along the right wing, shaking off a posse of Leicester markers who vainly attempted to close him down. His still-electric pace and quick feet repeatedly dumbfounded them. This was unlike the Leighton James of 1975 who, according to Jimmy Adamson, had under-performed to secure a transfer to a bigger club. Here, he was fully engaged, realising his inexperienced team-mates desperately needed his help. In the 65th minute, with the Leicester fans becoming increasingly restive, James espied a gap in the Leicester back ranks. Flicking into overdrive he cut in, leaving his markers in his wake, and, seeing Wallington off his line, produced a delightful left-footed chip shot which evaded the leaping goalie and plopped into the unguarded net. What a sublime goal! The 17,191 crowd were stunned, apart from a few stoical Clarets and me, leaping around deliriously.

However, Leicester's greater strength eventually told. With just 11 minutes left, ex-Oldham striker Alan Young stabbed in an equaliser, prompting an almighty roar from the relieved Leicester fans. With the rejuvenated Leicester players pursuing a winner, all ten Burnley outfielders congregated behind the ball, besieged inside their box, but frantically trying to hack the ball away as wave after wave of Leicester attacks bore down upon them. Then, horror of horrors, Leicester were awarded a penalty. It seemed so cruel, given the magnificent rearguard action mounted by the Burnley lads against the best team in the league. Young stepped up but Stevenson guessed right, only for the ball to run loose to Lineker ... who missed while Stevenson was desperately trying to recover. There is a god, after all!

Inspired by this tremendous backs-to-the-wall effort, Burnley managed to win four of their next six league games, also drawing one, which lifted them into 18th place. Alas, they were unable to maintain this momentum. As Jimmy Adamson had discovered, it is fallacious to saddle young players with such pressures, irrespective of their potential. Having beaten Fulham on a Turf Moor ice rink on 2 February, they did not win again that season. Leighton James left for upwardly mobile Swansea. Relegation to the Third Division duly followed in May 1980. This represented Burnley's lowest position in their 92-year membership of the Football League. The drop also brought about an annual deficit of £300,000, twice as much as had been lost during the 1977/78 and 1978/79 seasons. By then, Bob Lord, the self-styled 'John Bull' of English football, was broken in health and spirit, with his sold-on meat business apparently foundering. Lord's once proud empire had been reduced to ruins.

Kindon scores against QPR in January 1969.

Kindon's hot shot is saved by Arsenal's Wilson in August 1969.

Harry Potts (left) was replaced as Burnley team boss by Jimmy Adamson in 1970.

Burnley Second Division champions 1972/73. Back (from left): Nulty, Ingham, Collins, Noble. Middle: Newton, Thomson, Stevenson, Waldron, Hankin. Front: Docherty, Fletcher, Dobson, Casper, James.

Jimmy Adamson (left) celebrating winning the First Division championship in 1960

Burnley's blunt chairman, Bob Lord (left) celebrating the May 1960 victory

Ray Hankin of Burnley scoring against Derby County at Turf Moor in September 1973

Paul Fletcher scoring with a spectacular bicycle kick at Leeds, March 1974

With Burnley's debts mounting and results worsening in 1976/77 chairman Bob Lord came under fans' fire

Burnley Third Division champions 1981/82. Back (from left): Anderson, Phelan, Scott, Taylor, Wharton. Middle: Casper (coach), Dixon, Hamilton, Stevenson, Holt, Reynolds, Cassidy, V. Overson, Miller (manager). Front: Laws, Potts, Cavener, Dobson, Young, Robertson, Wood.

Starlet Trevor Steven shone for Burnley but was sold to Everton for £325,000 in 1983.

Burnley boss Miller before the 'win or bust' game in 1987.

Pint-sized Ian Britton celebrates scoring Burnley's match-winning and club-saving goal.

Miller and captain Deakin lead Burnley out at Wembley in the 1988 Sherpa Van Trophy Final.

Manager Jimmy Mullen celebrates winning the Football League Fourth Division championship at York on 28 April 1992

Burnley's success in 1991/92 was helped by Mike Conroy's 24 league goals. Here he is scoring against Wigan.

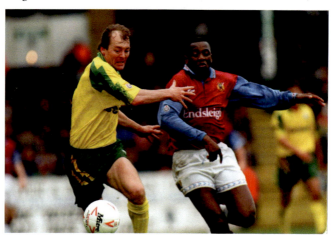

John Francis (right) scored twice in winning a Third Division play-off semi-final at Plymouth in 1994.

Burnley's goal scorers at a Wembley Play-off Final in 1994: Eyres on the left, and Parkinson.

Burnley goalkeeper Marlon Beresford performed brilliantly in the 1992/93 and 1993/94 seasons.

Steve Davis (mark two) was an outstanding member of three promotion-winning Burnley sides in 1992, 1994 and 2000.

Adrian Heath held aloft by Randall. Heath replaced Mullen as manager in 1996.

Record £400,000 signing Paul Barnes shown scoring one of his five goals against Stockport in 1996. His strike partner Kurt Nogan is far right.

After Heath's sudden resignation in 1997, Chris Waddle became his surprising replacement but his team struggled to avoid the drop.

Payton's goals (number 10) rescued Burnley from the drop in 1998 and 1999, also helping achieve promotion under Stan Ternent in 2000.

2. A BRIEF REVIVAL 1980/82

Oxford United 0 Burnley 2
6 December 1980
'Love Will Tear Us Apart'

The national unemployment figure had passed two million, the highest level since 1935. For the first time since the Industrial Revolution, we were experiencing a deficit in manufactured goods. Reflecting their troubled local economies, both Burnley and Oxford were in the Third Division. Oxford's Blackbird Leys estate, which originally housed Morris's car workers, became synonymous with social unrest, as were parts of Brixton, Tyneside, Toxteth, Burnley, and Bristol. Liz and I had recently relocated to Bristol, unaware of the mounting tensions there. During the previous decade, Oxford had dropped a division while Burnley had dropped two. Average gates had plummeted at both clubs. Ten years before, Oxford had attracted an average crowd of 11,000 to their home games. And yet only 2,526 supporters watched their 1-0 league victory over Chester in November 1980, their first home win of this season. Only a new year revival lifted their average crowd figure to 3,905. As for Burnley, their average crowd had fallen from 16,000 in 1970 to 6,500 in 1981/82.

In the Third Division, Burnley had continued to sell. Ian Brennan went to Bolton in December 1980 for £25,000. Billy Ingham went to Bradford City in August 1980 for £30,000 and young centre-back Peter Robinson went to Sparta Rotterdam for £35,000. Leighton James was also sold to First Division-bound

Swansea, for £130,000 in May 1980. It was not just the sales receipts that were needed; the wage bill was slashed as well. The departing stars were among the club's highest earners. There were rumours that Brian Laws, Burnley's richly talented right-back, was to be sold for £300,000 but nothing came of it. With the exception of Laws, Trevor Steven, Michael Phelan, Kevin Young, Phil Cavener, and Vince Overson, Burnley's well of youthful talent had almost dried up. The Clarets were forced to buy more players than they sold, albeit on more modest terms. In came Newcastle's Northern Ireland international midfielder Tommy Cassidy, for £37,500; Preston's winger Eric Potts for £20,000; Mansfield's former Bolton striker Steve Taylor, for £75,000; and Oldham defenders Ian Wood and David Holt for a combined fee of £45,000. They joined Northern Ireland international centre-forward Billy Hamilton, acquired in the previous season.

Pining for sight of Burnley once more, Liz and I decided to take our six-week-old daughter, Lydia, to the Oxford game. Liz and I had not been to a match together since the Brighton game, almost two years before. Our extended absence had not dulled our desire, though. We knew the risks of taking a young baby to a game but, perhaps rashly, thought we could manage these if we were seated in the main stand. Fortunately, Lydia's subliminal quality control kicked in. She slept through the entire game, snug in her sling under my thick coat. An inquisitive Oxford supporter asked whether I was wearing a chest warmer. I admired his bravery. I might have been obese. I replied: 'Yes, the best kind.' 'What kind's that?' he persisted. 'The baby kind,' I said with a contented smile. The conversation ended there as he frequently twisted around in his seat, perhaps hoping to espy an NSPCC operative among the stewards.

Saturday, 6 December, was a tingling, cold day bathed in dazzling sunshine. The honeyed sunlight slanted low across the Manor Ground, refreshing the rustling foliage in the adjacent trees. Only patches of smudged high cloud disturbed the sky's milky blue hue. Burnley did their best to match the occasion. Playing composed, elegant football, they capped this impressive display with two goals of ferocious power. The first came in the 13th minute when midfielder Derek Scott was allowed unaccountable freedom to run at the Oxford goal. With the home defenders backing off, he let fly from around 25 yards. The ball screeched into the top right-hand corner of the net. Two minutes after the break, Burnley confirmed their superiority when fellow midfielder Kevin Young smashed home another long-range effort leaving Oxford goalkeeper Roy Burton helpless.

Oxford's fragile morale fragmented. Thereafter, they hardly figured. It was clear why they were in trouble. They were above the relegation zone on goal average only. Meanwhile, Burnley had managed to insert themselves among the promotion contenders, having recovered from a slow start. Little did we know that the fortunes of Oxford and Burnley would take unexpectedly divergent paths after Robert Maxwell came to the Us' aid, much like a Trojan horse or a bouncing Czech. After suggesting that they might mount a successful promotion challenge, Burnley had to settle for eighth place. Overson and Dobson forged a sound central defensive partnership. Laws was outstanding at right-back partnered by local signing Andy Warton. Scott scored nine goals from midfield, while Hamilton and Taylor combined well up front and Trevor Steven and Michael Phelan emerged as future stars. After the depressing 1979/80 season, there were reasons to feel cheerful. With the central defence featuring a new partnership, Jim Thomson was released, subsequently joining Morecambe, while Rodaway moved to Peterborough.

Bristol City 2 Burnley 3
28 November 1981
'Don't Stop Believin''

It was back to the sixties. The shadow of the bomb returned with US and USSR relations hawkish and edgy. With the

USSR moving SS-20 missiles into eastern Europe, Reagan retaliated by despatching cruise missiles to Britain, where Mrs Thatcher became the first European premier to accept them. Her action prompted strong protests not only from CND but also from the women's peace camp established outside the USAF base at Greenham Common. The eighties were characterised by a growth of protest and direct-action movements, which sought equality for disadvantaged and discriminated groups, promulgating the rights of women, people with disabilities, the LGBT community, and ethnic minorities. Other activists set up safeguards for vulnerable children, such as Childline, and defended the endangered environment, as exemplified by the actions of eco warriors such as 'Swampy'. There were those, too, who fought to uphold animal rights. What these activists had in common was a shared belief that direct action was more effective than placing faith in political democracy and established institutions, whether local or national.

This was also the time of the 'New Romantics' like Spandau Ballet, Human League, ABC, Culture Club, and Duran Duran, when pop prided itself on the diversity and creativity of its sounds and fashions, not merely providing banal opiates for starry-eyed young people. Artists like UB40 went further, releasing reproachful singles such as 'Food for Thought', a savage indictment of the inadequacies of western famine relief, and 'One in Ten', about the demoralising impact of rising unemployment. Meanwhile the Specials, also 2-tone artists, wrote 'Ghost Town' about the urban decay occurring in their home city of Coventry. Through their politicised messages and those of punk bands, such as the Clash, 'Rock Against Racism' had already made an impact in the mid-1970s, directly challenging the brutal discrimination perpetrated by right-wing movements and their repugnant ideologies. The multi-racial 2-tone bands such as the Specials took these anti-discriminative messages into the eighties.

2. A BRIEF REVIVAL 1980/82

The 1981/82 season began poorly with Burnley languishing in the Third Division relegation zone, and close to bankruptcy. Bob Lord retired, selling his controlling interest to a consortium of four directors for £52,000. This quartet included local barrister John Jackson, who had joined the Burnley board of directors in 1976. The shares were divvied out equally between the interested parties and Jackson was elected as the new club chairman. The low price paid reflected not only Burnley's calamitous financial state but also increasing public disenchantment with a game scarred with abhorrent hooliganism, crumbling stadia, and penal fencing. The new board quickly aroused the anger of Burnley supporters by raising the entrance fee from £1.35 to £1.90, a 41 per cent rise. With the acute financial pressures facing post-industrial towns of the north, it was not at all surprising that the first home game on 5 September attracted only 3,476 fans. There was a similar attendance for the Swindon game on 3 October.

A turning point was reached for Burnley while their manager, Brian Miller, was in hospital with appendicitis. His assistant manager, Frank Casper, took over and introduced a different-style formation in preparation for the league game at Portsmouth on 10 October, comprising two wing-backs, Laws and Wharton, and a sweeper, Martin Dobson. Both Laws and Wharton were comfortable bombing forward and tracking back when possession was lost, whereas Dobson adopted a Beckenbauer-like role with aplomb, solidifying the defence but also prompting counter attacks. Portsmouth were overrun although the 2-1 winning score did not reflect the extent of Burnley's superiority.

With Liz caring for Lydia, I went alone to Burnley's game with Bristol City at Ashton Gate on 28 November. The day was sunny but cold. There was a mood of chuffing dissent among the Bristolians. Their side had suffered successive relegations, having dropped out of the First Division in 1980 and the Second

Division a year later. City were in a mess. Their current poor team performances suggested a possibility of further demotion, while the catastrophic state of the club's finances threatened liquidation. Unsurprisingly home attendances had plummeted. So, when Burnley's young midfielder, Kevin Young, gave the Clarets a third minute lead the unrest among the City fans increased. But despite Burnley's success against Portsmouth and their subsequent unbeaten seven-match run, they were still in a dicey position – just four places off the bottom. Their precarious position was underlined eight minutes later when Bristol City's Jimmy Mann equalised from the penalty spot. Although half-time was reached with the scores still level, seven minutes after the break, Chris Garland put City in front. However, instead of incentivising the home side it was Burnley who sprang into action.

The instigator of this sudden revival was Burnley's eighteen-year-old midfielder, Trevor Steven. Oblivious of the frenetic tackling, he played with his socks bunched around his ankles. He seemed to be in the centre of everything, playing quick one-twos with his fellow midfielders, Kevin Young and Tommy Cassidy, as he probed for openings. Whether passing short or long, he executed his art with composed precision. He looked for runners on one side of him, before suddenly reversing direction to pick out an unmarked colleague elsewhere. Nothing seemed to trouble him. Unruffled by the bump and grind, he created space around himself with nonchalant ease. He seemed to have so much time on the ball. With a feint here, a drop of the shoulder there, he repeatedly slipped away from trouble. On a heavy, churned surface he played as if on a bowling green. It seemed clear to me that he was destined for stardom. With Steven continually wrong-footing the home defence, Bristol were forced to pull more men back. Burnley grasped the initiative. Posting their back four on the half-way line with their sweeper, Martin Dobson, reinforcing an advanced midfield, Burnley tucked into a turkey shoot. However, it took two late goals from Paul McGee for Burnley to snatch their just deserts. At the final whistle, the disgruntled Bristol players slouched off the field, heads down. A chilly mist drifted in from the River Avon, enveloping the ground in a damp shroud. In brighter circumstances the illuminated suspension bridge and the twinkling lights of Clifton might have suggested a festive event but there were no celebrations at Ashton Gate. It seemed as if both clubs were moving in opposite directions. Although Burnley were still in the relegation zone, thanks to their awful start to this season, I had a hunch that they could still achieve promotion.

Swindon Town 1 Burnley 2
13 February 1982
'The Model'

Despite the ravages of another severe winter wiping out almost all their December fixtures, Burnley had pushed on after their rampant victory at Ashton Gate. They won six out of seven of their next league games, drawing the other. With a friend looking after Lydia, Liz and I made for Swindon on a bright 13 February. Former chairman Bob Lord had died a week before. It seemed that he never recovered from the 1980 relegation. His ego might have had too much licence but there was no doubt that he truly cared about his club. Sadly, his final years were marred by an unseemly dispute over a land sale. Lord had sold the plot to the club for £11,000 and maintained he had the right to buy it back at the same price. This became a vexed dispute when the land's value soared once it became known that plans were being made to route a new motorway across this plot.

Despite having Paul Rideout, one of the best young centre-forwards in English football, Swindon had not prospered since their 2-0 victory at Turf Moor on 3 October. They looked a ragged side. Burnley had little difficulty in establishing their authority on a sticky surface. They opened the scoring in the 15th minute when Steve Taylor swept in Billy Hamilton's low right-wing cross. Irritatingly, Swindon fashioned a scruffy equaliser in the 40th minute with Rideout claiming the goal. Burnley were not shaken though and three minutes later Tommy Cassidy, a Northern Ireland international like Hamilton, restored Burnley's lead with a stupendous chipped shot, which alone was worth the entrance fee. The second half was a non-event as Burnley controlled possession superbly, keeping the shot-shy Robins at a safe distance. Sir Freddie Laker's cut-price airline had gone into a tailspin, and the DeLorean sports car business had stalled, leaving hundreds of Ulstermen without work. Meanwhile Kraftwerk's 'The Model' topped the singles chart, but on this day my focus was exclusively upon Burnley, who were up to fifth.

Burnley 3 Reading 0
3 April 1982

'Sweet Dreams (Are Made of This)'

A visit to relatives in Leeds conveniently coincided with Burnley's home fixture with Reading. Thankfully I was able to negotiate a trip to Turf Moor, my first since December 1978. It was a vital game as Burnley's form since Swindon had stuttered, with just two victories in nine fixtures, including an emphatic 3-0 win over Portsmouth on 27 February. Their unbeaten run, stretching back to 10 October, had finally been punctured by Exeter. Burnley had therefore slipped to sixth place.

Argentina had just invaded the Falkland Islands. Two days later the Royal Naval Task Force set sail for the South Atlantic. *The Sun* cat-called 'STICK IT UP YOUR JUNTA!' and 'GOTCHA!' We were at war. Or at least some of us were. Some cheered. Some jeered. Some treated it like a World Cup qualifier, notably the pub jingoists. *Private Eye* lampooned them and *The Sun* headliners with the quip, 'Kill an Argie and Win a

2. A BRIEF REVIVAL 1980/82

Metro'. Although many of us got on with our lives as if nothing extraordinary had happened, we jumped to attention when some of our warships were sunk with resulting losses of life.

The Reading side included Kerry Dixon, a powerful young centre-forward, and Neil Webb, a slender 18-year-old midfielder who was their leading goalscorer with 14 goals. But Burnley had bustling Billy Hamilton and precocious playmaker Trevor Steven. The Burnley boys would win this contest hands down. Hamilton should have scored five goals in the first half alone. As it was, he had to be content with two.

It took Hamilton just three minutes to open his account. Paul McGee chased down what seemed to be a lost ball near the right corner flag. Reading centre-half Hicks looked to shepherd the ball out of play but McGee was too quick and strong for him. Having snatched the ball from under Hicks's nose, McGee laid it back to right-winger Cavener, who punted in a low, curling cross. Hamilton was first to react, volleying the ball past goalie Fearon with the outside of his right boot. It was an exceptional goal because the ball reached Hamilton at an awkward height. Right-back Laws set up the second Burnley goal eight minutes later. After a powerful run down the right flank, Laws cleverly used Cavener as a decoy. This flummoxed the Reading defenders, giving Laws the space to whip over a high cross from the goal line, which Hamilton met with his forehead at the top of his leap. His cushioned header looped into the right-hand corner.

Three days before, Steven had secured a priceless point at promotion rivals Lincoln, with an 88th-minute equaliser. Here, he was in majestic form. He was everywhere, forever twisting and turning in central midfield, attempting to find a killer opening while also running directly at the Reading defenders with the ball confidently under his control. He also set up Hamilton for a sizzling shot that found Fearon's midriff. With both Burnley backs, Laws and Wharton, attacking at will, this game quickly became an arcade shoot-out. Reading were lucky to be only two goals in arrears at the break.

As is often the case, our opponents made a better fist of things after the interval. Dixon put himself about with greater menace, forcing several errors by the Burnley defenders. Nevertheless, Laws and Wharton continued to push forward on the flanks and the only goal of the second half went to Burnley in the final minute. Kevin Young dispossessed Reading full-back Lewis, cut inside and from the edge of the crowded goalmouth let fly with a low left-foot drive. It evaded Fearon and squeezed inside the goalie's left-hand post. This accomplished victory lifted Burnley back into fifth position, one point behind Reading but with five games in hand. Lincoln were top with 61 points from 37 games, followed by Carlisle with 59 points from 34 games and Fulham with 57 points from 34 games. Burnley had played 35 games but only 16 of these had been at home. Home form like this could well see them promoted.

Newport County 0 Burnley 0
1 May 1982

'Ghost Town'

Burnley's form had wavered before this game. On 10 April, table-topping Lincoln arrived at Turf Moor, attracting a 10,000-plus crowd. This was Burnley's highest home gate of the season. The home fans watched nervously in the Easter sunshine as Hamilton's 70th-minute goal gave his side a narrow victory. Two days later, at Chesterfield, Brian Laws's spectacular goal and Dobson's strike secured another three points. Burnley then took a point from their trip to sixth-placed Oxford on 17 April. But three days later they were surprisingly trounced 3-5 by visiting Southend, with former Bury striker Derek Spence the chief assassin. Nevertheless, they were back on track on 24 April when second-half goals from Laws and Dobson were sufficient to overcome hard-up Bristol City. There was little

2. A BRIEF REVIVAL 1980/82

doubt that Burnley's fixture congestion, a legacy of a harsh winter, was sapping their energy. The Newport game was of critical importance in a seven-horse race for a promotion berth. The introduction of three points for a win had helped Burnley make up lost ground after a poor start but it also made promotion more competitive.

Although Newport were ensconced in lower mid-table, they were no mugs. In the season before, they had narrowly failed to gain a semi-final place in the European Cup Winners' Cup, having won the Welsh Cup the previous season. They had three dangerous strikers: John Aldridge, who, fortuitously, was unavailable for this game; Tommy Tynan; and Dave Gwyther. In midfield they had several notable performers, such as Steve Lowndes and Nigel Vaughan, while in goal Newport had former Spurs goalkeeper Mark Kendall, who would later serve Burnley without distinction.

This game at Somerton Park was played in radiant spring sunshine but greater heat was generated on the pitch, where Burnley were largely on the back foot, with Newport's Tommy Tynan proving to be a real handful. For long periods, Burnley were pinned in their own half as shot after shot rained in on their goal. Without Alan Stevenson's phenomenal agility, we would have surely lost. The draw gained here kept Burnley well in the fight, but it was not enough to prevent them slipping one place to sixth. As proof of their resilience, though, they won their next four games, including a 1-0 victory over Carlisle who emerged as their greatest rival. The Newport game was played on the day that the RAF bombed the runway at Stanley in the Falkland Islands. BBC reporter Brian Hanrahan counted all the Harriers out from their aircraft carrier, and all of them returning, to assure listeners there had been no loss of our pilots' lives. But the war was about to become bloodier with the sinking of HMS *Sheffield*.

Southend United 1 Burnley 4
14 May 1982
'House of Fun'

The penultimate fixture of the season was at Southend on Friday, 14 May. Being in London on a work assignment, I agreed with Liz that I would return home via Roots Hall. Like many other Burnley fans, I was very nervous. So much hung on this game.

A victory would secure promotion and potentially the Third Division title. But Southend had already proved what damage they could inflict. Once at the ground among many expectant Burnley supporters, and jeering Southend fans, the stakes seemed to soar.

The opening half-hour was uneventful, with a rocky surface making ball-control problematic for both sides. Hamilton had one decent chance but volleyed over while Southend's Keith Mercer's two headers were also too high. It was reassuring, though, to see brawny Vince Overson dominating danger man Spence. Then in the 32nd minute the breakthrough came. Cassidy dispossessed a Southend midfielder, turned, and pinged the ball into the path of the sprinting Wharton on the left flank. Cassidy's long pass was superbly weighted, allowing Wharton to receive the ball without breaking stride. With no defenders to impede him, and seeing Keeley advancing, Wharton walloped the ball into the net from 15 yards. The roar from the away end was volcanic. Burnley-born Wharton was a fitting hero. He had spent his younger days as a Longsider and had BFC tattooed on his left hand. Eight minutes later, Hamilton headed on another long pass. McGee was on it in a flash, and seeing Keeley racing to intercept, McGee coolly lobbed the ball over him. Burnley's swift counter-attacking had been ruthless, but Southend were not beaten yet. Just before half-time Gary Nelson swung a corner high towards the far post. Stevenson slipped, allowing Mercer to score with a simple header.

2. A BRIEF REVIVAL 1980/82

This setback did not deter Burnley though, as they continued to take the game to their hosts at the resumption. Although Stevenson was tested a couple of times, most of the action was at the other end. Keeley did well to parry Hamilton's header and smartly blocked McGee's piledriver. McGee was not to be denied, though. With seven minutes left, and Southend pushing hard for a late equaliser, Burnley created another breakaway goal. With the Southend players camped in the Burnley half, McGee seized upon a long ball out of defence and hared off for goal, trailed by two Southend defenders. Having outpaced them and reached the Southend penalty area, McGee steadied himself before shooting underneath Keeley. A wave of joy and relief swept across the anxious Burnley fans. But their team were not finished. In the 88th minute Laws emulated his full-back partner by breaking down the right flank, evading all who attempted to tackle him. As soon as he reached the Southend box, he pulled the trigger. Keeley could only push away Laws's sizzling shot, leaving Laws to slam in the rebound. He had been outstanding, brilliantly tackling Phillips when the Southend player had a clear run at goal during the first half. I returned home woozy with beer and euphoria on an evening replete with the spring scents of chestnut and may. The icebound winter seemed so far away.

The final game at home to Chesterfield on 18 May was a farce, though. A cloudburst turned Turf Moor into a paddy field. To make matters worse, in front of 18,711 drenched fans, Burnley were a goal behind at the interval. Just as it seemed that the championship would evade Burnley, in their centenary season, Kevin Young put us back on track. Picking up Steven's pass he cut in from the left and unleashed a 25-yard skidding drive which found the far corner. Only a Carlisle victory by at least seven clear goals on the following evening would deprive Burnley of the title. This was beyond the Cumbrians. So, Burnley, bottom in October, were top in May. It was a rare moment of triumph in a decade which would be mired by plummeting fortunes and mounting debt, almost leading to the liquidation of our once proud club.

3. CUP FEVER/LEAGUE LAMENT 1982/83

'Hand in Glove'

Burnley manager Brian Miller was confident that his youthful squad did not need strengthening. Burnley director Derek Gill was equally confident that the club would never return to the Third Division. Sadly, both men were mistaken. By January 1983, Burnley had lost 24 league games including ten in succession away from home. Following a dismal 0-3 defeat at relegation-bound Bolton on 15 January, Miller was replaced as manager by his assistant Frank Casper, who was a better tactician. Casper took charge at a League Cup fifth-round tie at White Hart Lane on 19 January 1983. Helped by Spurs' calamitous errors, Burnley fought back splendidly to win 4-1! Burnley's brilliant cup runs comprised ten victories in only 16 games, overcoming several top-flight sides, enabling the Clarets to reach the League Cup semi-finals and the FA Cup sixth round, whereas their 42 league fixtures yielded only 12 wins, just five under Miller. It seemed that the Burnley board of directors should have changed their manager sooner.

Burnley 0 Bolton 0
28 August 1982

'No More Heroes'

And yet back in August all seemed well. I was still basking in the triumph of the previous season when I parked at Crown Point, Burnley, re-acquainting myself with the stark beauty of this once familiar landscape. Lying on the coarse grass I took in the dominant presence of Pendle Hill, somehow tamed in the warm sunlight, and the sprawling terraced housing surrounding the totemic floodlights of Turf Moor. Just a few scrambled clouds populated the sky, enough to impress a patchwork pattern on the valley below but insufficient to deplete the sun's strength. I then thought the club's prospects were as fair as the weather. Dexys Midnight Runners' 'Come On Eileen' was playing on my car radio, but Sting's 'Spread a Little Happiness' was on my mind. Little did I realise that the song accompanied a dark tale of abuse. And little did I realise the extent of Burnley's current vulnerability.

This opening game, which I had driven over from Leeds to see, ended as an anticlimactic goalless draw. Burnley's main attacking stratagem seemed to be a flicked-on header, at the near post. Bolton's central defenders, Paul Jones, and Mike Doyle, formerly of Manchester City, were equal to this. Neither goalkeeper had much to do. Bolton strikers Ian Moores and Jeff Chandler made little impact upon Burnley's tried and tested sweeper system. Much of the game was played in midfield where Young, Steven, and Scott sturdily contested the turf with Peter Reid, Tony Henry, and player/manager John McGovern. Philip Ray made his debut for Burnley at left-back. He did not seem ready for this promotion, but the others carried him through.

The 10,562 attendance was a little disappointing, too, for a 'new dawn' local derby, but it was a point gained and the sun shone throughout. While this disappointing game tempered my optimism, two emphatic 4-1 victories followed against Carlisle and Middlesbrough. These successes prompted me to flirt with the notion that a return to the top flight was not out of the question, but four successive defeats followed. Frustratingly Burnley squandered a two-goal lead at Queens Park Rangers on 2 October. A Hoops fan told me that Trevor Steven had been outstanding, scoring both of Burnley's first-half goals while impressing with his trickery and astute passing. Alas, the Hoops roared back in the second half, winning the game after a devastating 17-minute spell. It was then that I began to fear that Burnley might not survive at this higher level. Although they came back from a first-half deficit to beat Crystal Palace 2-1 a week later, with an 87th-minute winner from Hamilton, the next five games were lost, leaving Burnley perilously placed in 20th spot.

To my untutored eye, it seemed as if wing-backs Laws and Wharton were not tight enough defensively, leaving centre-backs Holt and Phelan too exposed. Not even Dobson, in his elegant sweeper role, could provide adequate cover. Burly centre-half Vince Overson was sorely missed, having been ruled out for most of the season with injury. Injuries to Tommy Cassidy and Paul McGee did not help either. Meanwhile, Burnley could not provide sufficient fire-power up front despite their goal rush in early September. Fresh from his World Cup heroics, Billy Hamilton was a highly effective target man but needed better support. Taylor scored 12 goals from 22 starts, a decent return, but his confidence was easily undermined. It seemed ironic, though, that he was replaced by Aston Villa striker Terry Donovan shortly after he and Hamilton had scored hat-tricks in a 7-1 demolition of nine-man Charlton on 26 February 1983. On the other hand, Donovan's six goals from 13 starts helped secure 11 points, suggesting that had he been recruited earlier Burnley might have escaped the drop. Yet Trevor Steven blossomed at this higher level, scoring eight league goals in addition to his shrewd playmaking. As Trevor demonstrated at Queens Park Rangers, he could mesmerise opponents with his range of skills. Clearly, this 19-year-old prodigy was earmarked for a glittering future at club and international level.

The delay in seeking reinforcements was a culpable error. By the time that remedial action was taken, Burnley had lost nine out of 13 league games. Former director Derek Gill told me around 30 years later that the board had been willing to make resources available for incoming moves, but Miller declined, believing his promotion-winning team was good enough. It took until November for Brian to change his mind. First to arrive was Scottish international left-back Willie Donachie, formerly with Manchester City and Portland Timbers. Next in was former Leeds, Burnley, and Welsh international midfielder Brian Flynn, but only after protracted negotiations with Leeds. Eventually a £60,000 payment sealed the deal. In his first game, on 13 November, Donachie helped Burnley achieve a narrow victory over Cambridge United. Flynn then made his debut, a week later, in a 1-1 draw at Hillsborough. However, Burnley lost five and drew one of their next six league games leading up to New Year. This dreadful run included a catastrophic 2-4 home defeat by promotion-bound Leicester City. The game was played in appalling conditions. Burnley had twice been in front, through Steven and Taylor, but Stevenson's dismissal turned the game. Missed penalties by Laws and McGee compounded their misery. At Grimsby, a week later, Burnley came back from a two-goal deficit. Yet Grimsby won with a 90th-minute goal.

Burnley 0 Blackburn Rovers 1
27 December 1982

'Relax'

An extended visit to relatives in Leeds enabled me to watch both home games over the festive period. Although bucked up by Burnley's cup form, the Clarets fans I spoke with were more concerned about their wretched league form. No fewer than 20,439 fans attended the derby clash on a blustery, showery afternoon. The atmosphere was combustible as both sides flew at one another from kick-off, but with everyone so pumped up, adrenalin triumphed over skill. The decisive goal came in the 33rd minute when Rovers' beanpole centre-forward Norman Bell won an aerial duel with Burnley debutant Mike Walsh.

Unluckily for Burnley the loose ball fell into the path of Simon Garner who belted it past Billy O'Rourke at point-blank range. O'Rourke performed heroics, though, with a succession of outstanding saves, keeping Burnley in the game. Alas, Taylor had a goal ruled out for offside and both he and Hamilton wasted splendid opportunities, Taylor when put through on goal, and Hamilton, when he directed his header straight at Rovers goalie, Gennoe.

Burnley 4 Sheffield Wednesday 1
1 January 1983
'Blue Monday'

The morning rain had cleared by midday, leaving a heavy pitch hissing with excessive moisture. Despite the ground staff's vigorous forking, the pitch remained saturated and prone to cut up. Although the Owls were promotion contenders, their recent form had been poor. Nevertheless, they started brightly with Gary Bannister leading his line with menacing energy. But it was Burnley who scored first, in the 19th minute. Willie Donachie found Hamilton in space deep inside Wednesday's territory. Billy turned on receiving the ball and shot more in hope than with conviction. It was a soft effort but goalie Bolder failed to hang on to the greasy ball, leaving Taylor with a tap-in. Sheffield Wednesday reacted quickly with a forceful run by Mel Sterland which resulted in a corner. Bannister took the flag kick, finding Pearson who redirected the flighted ball towards Mick Lyons. Thankfully Lyons's header clattered against a post.

Sensing it would be their day, Burnley pushed forward. Another defensive error gave them their second goal. Hamilton was consistently troubling Bolder in the air and, after another aerial duel, the ball ran loose to Derek Scott on the right flank. His swift cross deflected off an Owls defender, allowing Taylor all the time he needed to shoot between Bolder's outstretched legs with the goal gaping. The best Burnley goal came in the

59th minute. Hamilton had just had an effort disallowed for offside but Wednesday were helpless when he struck again. Having been put through on goal, following an exchange between Donachie and Taylor, Hamilton had sufficient speed to see off three defenders, round Bolder and smash the ball into the far corner. The Longside choir broke into 'Always Look on the Bright Side of Life'. Maurice Setters, deputising for the absent Jack Charlton, responded by sending on Andy McCulloch for Pearson and 11 minutes later he pulled one back, heading in from a short corner. With Wednesday over-reaching themselves, Taylor made a break down the inside-left channel, having been found by Flynn's quick ball out of defence. Taylor made no mistake, drawing Bolder towards him before knocking the ball into the roof of the net.

Welcome to 1983 we thought, but the new year was no better than the old! Despite plenty of exciting cup action, the Owls flattened Burnley 0-5 in an FA Cup sixth-round replay in March, after Taylor had fluffed a penalty in the home game. By then Liverpool had defeated Burnley in the Milk Cup semi-final, but the Clarets had put up a grand fight, troubling the Reds at Anfield and beating them 1-0 at Turf Moor. Casper's time in charge had begun encouragingly, after he had replaced Miller. He guided Burnley to seven league victories but a dreadful run in April, during which only four points were taken from seven games, left the Clarets with too much to do in their final five fixtures.

Leicester City 0 Burnley 0
14 May 1983
'Our Lips Are Sealed'

By the time I saw Burnley again, on 14 May 1983, their fate was almost sealed. With Leicester on the verge of promotion to the First Division, getting into Filbert Street was an alarming experience. Thousands pressed hard to reach the entrances,

3. CUP FEVER/LEAGUE LAMENT 1982/83

filling up the narrow streets and gangways in a heaving, rolling, sweaty tide. We seemed to be propelled through the turnstiles by the force of the throng. As expected, Leicester applied the early pressure. Their midfield starlet Robert Jones pulled back a smart cross from the goal line but Alan Smith headed over at the near post. Smith also reached a cross from Lynex, but his flicked header was just wide. Despite having greater possession, Leicester looked disjointed and edgy. Burnley did little to threaten Wallington in the Leicester goal, but they could justifiably claim the classiest moment of the first half. It came from imperious Martin Dobson. Having cut out a dangerous cross from Lynex, he surged down the left flank, combining the power of a Scania truck with the grace of a Rolls Royce. Three Leicester players lunged at him but with deft control and sharp acceleration he left them for dead. This run deserved more, but petered out in another blunt attack. The game remained goalless at half-time. It was clear though that Hamilton and Terry Donovan needed better support. A draw was no good. We needed to win to give us a slim chance of avoiding the drop.

This was the first time I had seen Lee Dixon play. During the second half he gave hints of his future pedigree. First, he made a perfectly weighted pass for Phelan to meet in full stride and advance at pace. Phelan immediately played in Donovan, but the striker's shot, taken on the turn, fizzed past the left-hand post with Wallington a spectator. Then, late in the game Dixon rescued a point when O'Rourke dashed from his goal after Smith was put through by Kevin McDonald's piercing pass. Smith lobbed the stranded O'Rourke but thanks to his keen anticipation, Dixon was able to scamper back and prevent the ball from crossing the line. In between these chances at either end, Billy Hamilton wasted Burnley's best chance to snatch the points. Put through by Flynn's astute pass, Billy had a clear run at goal in the inside-right channel. Alas, this was not the Billy that had wrapped up an amazing 4-1 Milk Cup victory at

White Hart Lane in January. There, his crashing drive, taken on the run, had flashed past Clemence's left hand and into the right-hand corner of the net. Here, the burden of carrying a struggling team had eroded his sharpness. All he could manage was a badly scuffed shot that dribbled wide of the Leicester goal. A draw suited Leicester. They were duly promoted to the top flight. Fulham had not won at Derby despite the misinformation perpetrated by the envious Burnley fans. A 0-0 draw against Leicester was an excellent achievement but it meant that Burnley would have to win at Palace in midweek to secure safety.

We expected a night of high passion and drama. It was nothing of the sort. The lights went out with barely a whimper, a colossal non-event. Burnley managed just one effort on goal. It came in the 80th minute from substitute Vince Overson, who had spent most of the season recovering from a serious injury. Burnley were already a goal down. It was a desperate way to leave the Second Division after just one season.

4. LOST HOPE 1983/84

'Money's Too Tight (to Mention)'

If relegation was deeply depressing, what happened next brought the club to the brink of oblivion. After Burnley's relegation in 1983, the Burnley board of directors decided to break with the club's 30-year reliance upon 'faithful retainers'. They chose an outsider as the new manager instead. Their choice was John Bond, a flamboyant, outspoken, and strongly opinionated man but one who possessed an impressive managerial record. He had transformed struggling Bournemouth's fortunes before steering modest Norwich back into the First Division in 1975. Under Bond's guidance, Norwich thrived in the higher division, reaching a League Cup Final in 1976. He also took Manchester City to an FA Cup Final in 1981. Much has been written about the club's reckless management during the John Bond era and its disastrous consequences. Suffice it to say I saw just two Burnley games under John Bond. Money was too tight to mention at home and Turf Moor.

Bristol Rovers 2 Burnley 1
12 November 1983

'Requiem'

The first was at Bristol Rovers on a damp, grey afternoon at Eastville on 12 November 1983. The travelling Clarets fans were buzzing after watching a rip-roaring home victory over the Blades in midweek. Given the acrimony new manager John Bond had aroused by his impulsive disposals of club favourites and ill-considered purchases of players who were crocked or no better, it was surprising to find that his team performed so well for him, at least at home. Seven out of eight home games had been won with 21 goals scored, whereas away from home only four points had been gained in eight fixtures with no victories. The Bristol Rovers game highlighted Bond's problems on the road. Rovers went ahead in the third minute and, despite some fine wing play from Hutchison and menacing forays by Hamilton and strike partner Kevin Reeves, Rovers doubled their lead with a 38th-minute penalty. Reeves, a former Norwich, Manchester City, and England striker, pulled one back four minutes later. However, as hard as Burnley tried, they could not find another way through Rovers' sturdy defence. It was a frustrating result but a fine game of football.

Newport County 1 Burnley 0
7 April 1984
'How Soon Is Now?'

The next and final time I saw Burnley play under Bond was at Newport. By then Reeves had sustained a career-ending injury, leaving Hamilton high and dry without his prolific strike partner. Bond unearthed a fine prospect in young striker Wayne Biggins, who had been playing non-league football with Matlock Town before moving to Burnley. But he and Hamilton were left firing blanks at Newport. There was no cohesion in this scruffy side and although Newport County were no better, they scored the only goal in the 84th minute with a rasping, rising drive.

The final nine fixtures garnered just two points. The proceeds of Trevor Steven's £300,000 sale to Everton had been utterly wasted not only by Bond but by the board of directors, who sanctioned his many careless purchases. Bond was sacked at the end of the 1983/84 season and replaced by his assistant, John Benson, who was unable to prevent Burnley slipping into the Fourth Division in May 1985, despite winning two of their

4. LOST HOPE 1983/84

final three games. Although John Bond's Swansea were beaten by Burnley at the Vetch Field on 4 May, Swansea ultimately survived at the expense of Burnley! It was a pain that just kept giving.

Bristol City 1 Burnley 0
29 December 1984
'What Is Love'

I saw Burnley only once in 1984/85. This was at Bristol City. It was a bitter, grey, misty afternoon. Burnley had not won in five leagues games, although they had thrashed Penrith (9-0) and beaten Halifax (3-1) in the FA Cup. I had hoped that consecutive victories over Brentford (3-1) and Bolton (3-2) in late October, and a stirring second-half comeback at Cambridge in November (3-2), heralded a bold upward momentum. But a 0-4 thrashing at York on Boxing Day proved this to be folly. I nearly did not go to Ashton Gate because of a sore back but I eventually decided I should. With Liz and me being cash-strapped and reliant upon lodgers to make ends meet, sightings of Burnley were rare for much of the eighties. Centre-forward Biggins and midfielder Kevin Hird were reliable strikers, sharing 34 league goals during this awful season. But here, they were squeezed out by a tight defence ably organised by manager Terry Cooper, formerly with Leeds, Middlesbrough, and England. Keith Curle and Rob Newman stood out. However, promotion-chasing Bristol City seemed equally as toothless until the 89th minute, when Howard Pritchard scrambled a winner. It was a depressing walk home. The game was awful, the pitch diabolical, the entertainment quotient zilch, and the state of my back stiff and sore. As I left, I thought of the game I had seen here three years before when I was minded to look upwards. What a waste!

5. SUPPING AT THE LAST-CHANCE SALOON: 1985 TO 1987

With the club's financial situation becoming ever more worrying, the Burnley board of directors had little choice other than to sell any player of value in cut-price deals. Hamilton left in 1984, subsequently followed by Phelan, Biggins, and Overson. When the 1986/87 season began, there were severe doubts whether the club could survive, as there had been a year before. Although Burnley battled on through both summer crises, it was only after chairman Frank Teasdale persuaded the club sponsors, Leyland, to pay their three-year sponsorship up front. Former director Clive Holt recalled: 'This was a major coup that just about kept us going, stopping the utility companies from turning off the water, the power, the heating and lighting. But the club's bank, the TSB, demanded stringent economies, including the release of our better players and the disbanding of the reserve side.' Loyal Miller's threadbare squad included returning Leighton James and Ian Britton but the threat of relegation remained. Had that happened, Burnley might have been liquidated, not only because of its mounting debt and significant weekly losses, but because it would have been inviable to subsist on a lower income in the Conference while bearing the costly upkeep of Turf Moor. As this crisis deepened, with a team carrying a crocked centre-half, and no reserves, gates for some midweek games fell below 2,000.

5. SUPPING AT THE LAST-CHANCE SALOON: 1985 TO 1987

Rochdale 0 Burnley 2
18 April 1987
'With or without You'

After moving to London in 1985, I made friends with Andrew, a work colleague who was a keen Burnley fan. With Burnley's demise becoming increasingly worrying we decided to drive north on Easter Saturday to watch their vital relegation battle against Rochdale at Spotland.

The 'Dale' were bottom, with the Clarets just one place above them. Rochdale had won the reverse fixture on New Year's Day with contemptuous ease, but had languished since, apart from a shock recent victory at Deepdale. The day was warm, and sunny, but we were tense and taciturn, fearing the worst. With so much at stake, a 3,000-strong Burnley contingent descended upon Spotland, determined to make their presence felt. Fired up by booze and derby bravado, they drowned the home vocal support with their incessant chanting and raucous invective. The away end shuddered under the weight of their furious defiance, reminiscent of better days in Burnley's distant past.

Brawny 18-year-old apprentice Phil Devaney, making only his second start, replaced the departed Derrick Parker. Watched proudly by his Merseyside family, he assumed instant hero status by hooking in Burnley's opening goal in the 13th minute. With Rochdale's goalie failing to deal with Ian Britton's flighted free kick, Devaney pounced. His shot was a bit of a shank, but it gave Burnley a priceless lead. With the exultant Claret choir baying them onwards, the Clarets began to play with unfamiliar confidence. Their defence, expertly marshalled by Ray Deakin, proved redoubtable in defying a side which had recently stunned promotion-bound Preston at Deepdale. Deakin, young Peter Leebrook, permanently crocked Joe Gallagher, and Peter Hampton were so commanding that our goalie, Joe Neenan, had little to do.

Ian Britton scurried around like an unruly terrier, forever snapping at his opponents' ankles, hustling them into errors, fiercely contesting the second balls, fetching, and carrying, urging his team forward wherever possible. But it was YTS lad Devaney who was Burnley's star turn, demonstrating the courage, brawn, and energetic persistence that had been lacking previously. And yet while Burnley were deservedly in front, their lead was agonisingly slender. Much to the relief of all in claret and blue, Burnley grabbed a second goal shortly after half-time. In the 53rd minute, pint-sized winger Ashley Hoskin received a short corner from Leighton James, and crossed for centre-half Gallagher to steal in at the near post and thump his header past Dale goalkeeper Welch. The roar from the Burnley fans was deafening. At the end, the younger Burnley supporters swarmed ecstatically on to the pitch, taunting their hosts. But the euphoria Andrew and I shared on our journey home did not last long.

After a desperate defeat at Crewe on 4 May, Burnley looked kippered. There was one game left, a home fixture with play-off-seeking Orient at Turf Moor on 9 May. Burnley needed to win and hope that either Torquay or Lincoln lost for our once venerable club to secure safety. Andrew and I could not go. We both had family commitments. All week I had a recurring image of Orient's Kevin Godfrey gently knocking the ball past our despairing goalkeeper, Joe Neenan, for the winning goal, with only minutes left. Our fans were seen burying their heads in their hands. Why I picked out Godfrey as our executioner I cannot say. The vision was so vivid, though, that I took this to be an accurate premonition.

I spent the afternoon in Savill Garden, Windsor Great Park, wheeling my disabled aunt around the blossoming flowers. My heart was thumping, my mouth felt lined with sand, my voice was croaking, my stomach was rumbling, and I was sweating profusely, not just because of the spring warmth. Eventually, we returned to the car minutes before *Sports Report*. My hand was

5. SUPPING AT THE LAST-CHANCE SALOON: 1985 TO 1987

trembling as I turned on the car radio. A game was being covered but it was difficult to make out what was happening because of the commotion engulfing the commentator. Then, a summariser cut in more audibly, saying, 'Burnley really need another goal.' My heart missed a beat. I muttered to myself: 'Christ, they must be winning but clearly not by much!' Throughout the 60-plus years I have watched football I have always felt more nervous when my side is defending a narrow lead. It was the same here in the most important game of my life. Unknown to me, our right-winger Neil Grewcock had scored with a brilliant left-foot drive, just before the break, and afterwards he had floated over a cross for pint-sized Ian Britton to head in the second. But back came Orient with a firm, angled shot from Alan Comfort that flew past Neenan.

I could not understand why there was no screeching for the final whistle. Then I was told. There were around 20 minutes left to play. My heart sank. Surely, they could not survive the bombardment which was being excitedly described. Just as I was preparing myself for this ordeal, the commentary ended abruptly. It was time for *Sports Report* with James Alexander Gordon's reading of the classified results. This was torture. There were no updates and an interminable wait for our relegation rivals' results: Lincoln at Swansea and Torquay at home. It took an eternity to reach Swansea but there was hope. Lincoln had lost! Burnley were safe if only they could cling on. The Torquay game was a late result, too, but this did not matter, if Burnley won.

To make the agony of not knowing even more brutal, *Sports Report* chose to go round the First Division grounds once the reading of the results was completed. Who cared about Everton and Manchester United? Oh, for God's sake not another bloody interview! I was chuntering as inaudibly as I could manage throughout the drive back to my aunt's home. Actually, the chores I needed to perform to settle her for the night were a helpful distraction. But once I left her, I dived for the car radio again, just in time to hear Burnley chairman Frank Teasdale say: 'I can't find the words to describe it. Put simply, we deserved it. The huge crowd were marvellous …' With that I welled up. WE WERE SAFE!! I had to pull over for a few minutes to compose myself.

I reflected that the club had been saved by 'the green' and 'the grey' – a pair of 18-year-old YTS youngsters on £25 per week, Devaney and full-back Peter Leebrook, and a quintet of former First Division players well into their twilight years, supported by a collection of journeymen, not forgetting the critical contribution of manager Brian Miller, who remained composed under extreme pressure.

Over 17,000 screaming fans drove Burnley on during this 'win or bust' finale, whereas just ten per cent of that number had turned up for several home games during this desolate season. The club and its town folk had re-found one another just in time. Despite the grinding austerity that had blighted so many post-industrial towns like Burnley threatening to keep the club and its local support apart, the Clarets had regained a future once more. The bank which supposedly 'likes to say yes' extended its help once more, encouraged by the massive turn-out for this defining game. Better players were recruited, including superb centre-half Steve Davis, nifty goalscorer George Oghani, and creative midfielder Paul Comstive. Helped by them and the remaining Orient-game survivors, such as James, Britton, and Grewcock, a promotion challenge was launched in the following season. Although that bid ultimately failed, Burnley reached the final of the Sherpa Van Cup at Wembley after a glorious smash-and-grab raid at Deepdale, where Burnley goalkeeper Chris Pearce was outstanding, despite suffering a painful injury during the game which prevented him from taking goal kicks.

PART 3

'THINGS CAN ONLY GET BETTER'

1988 to 1994

'Never Gonna Give You Up'

1. WEMBLEY WAY 1987/88

Burnley 0 Wolverhampton Wanderers 2
Sherpa Van Trophy Final, Wembley
29 May 1988

'Perfect'

All manner of transport was enlisted to ship 35,000 Burnley fans to Wembley for the Sherpa Van Trophy Final against Wolves. Every coach available had already been chartered, so some fans clubbed together to hire a furniture van. It was a day of warm, radiant sunshine. Andrew and I spent a pleasant lunchtime supping with a large contingent of Wolves fans in a Hampstead pub, trading good-natured jibes. They were wearing their 'Mind the Bull' T-shirts in homage to their prolific centre-forward Steve Bull, while the Clarets fans sported their ironic 'Burnley on Tour' wear, listing their Sherpa Van victims – Tranmere, Rochdale, Chester, Bury, Halifax, and Preston. This event had a strong reputation as a 'friendly final' and on this day there was no exception. After all, both clubs had endured existential crises. This was a day when fans of either side celebrated survival. On the day before, at Chelsea, 102 'supporters' had been arrested for violence. There was none of that nonsense here. After the game there was much shaking of hands and exchanging scarves, hats, and flags. This day remains fondly in the memory of those of us fortunate to be there. No one could have imagined that this final would draw 81,000 people, 30,000 more than at a recent England v Scotland game.

In an interview I conducted with Orient-game hero Ian Britton, shortly before his tragic death, he spoke at length about

1. WEMBLEY WAY 1987/88

his Wembley experience in 1988. He recalled, 'coming out in front of that huge Wembley crowd of 81,000 gave me goose bumps. It was a terrific day. Everyone enjoyed the occasion. There was no trouble at all. It was such a friendly affair. We were disappointed to lose, of course. Admittedly, Wolves were an especially strong side, far too good for the fourth tier. They scored a brilliant goal from a free kick, but we helped them by conceding a soft opening goal from a corner that should not have been given.

'We also missed some good chances in the second half, largely set up by Leighton James's brilliance. We were not downcast, though. A year before, the club was on the brink of extinction. We had come a long way in a short time. Burnley refused to lie down, though. On the hour, Steve Taylor had a good chance to open Burnley's account but his header, from McGrory's cross, cleared the bar. Shortly afterwards, Leighton James came on for McGrory and immediately turned the clock back with some sparkling wing play. Oghani provided a superb cross for Comstive on 62 minutes, but his header clipped the top of the bar. Then Andy Thompson cleared off the line in the 67th minute from Comstive after James had set him up. As the game reached its closing minutes, Oghani and Comstive had further opportunities but so did Wolves on the break with Mutch and Bull close to adding to their lead. Oghani ran valiantly and Comstive drove forward from midfield, but the killer touch was lacking. Looking back, Wolves were in a different class.'

The *Times* reporter wrote: 'Burnley's spirit was undimmed, and they played a full part in an enjoyable spectacle. They deserved better reward in the second half when Leighton James came on to offer a nostalgic reminder of happier days at Burnley.'

Brian Miller, a stoical and relentlessly loyal Burnley manager, deserved this day after the trials, tribulations, and traumas he had endured in his later years at the club. Sometime after, he was asked whether he would have preferred promotion from the Fourth Division to this day. He replied candidly, 'We were not quite good enough to go up. I thought that the Wembley experience might prove to be better for us in our pursuit of higher ambitions.'

On their return to Burnley, 5,000 people lined the streets in heavy rain to hail their team's efforts. Chants of 'We'll support you ever more' roared out from everywhere. The town's team had lost but the club had redeemed itself. Never has that chant been uttered with greater sincerity. Captain Ray Deakin said: 'I felt more emotional when we reached the Cat's Whiskers roundabout than when I stepped out at Wembley. With the rain and the fact we lost, I thought who would have blamed them if they hadn't turned up? But the fans are superb. They never cease to amaze us.'

Chairman Frank Teasdale remarked on it being a moving occasion. He added: 'The fans are unbelievable – we never thought they would turn out in such numbers. Their behaviour at Wembley was a credit to everyone and this is a wonderful way to round off a great weekend for the club.' John Gilbraith, the club's main sponsor, agreed, saying: 'The players did Burnley proud. This is once again a family club, and it wasn't for some time.'

The Sherpa Van competition netted over £150,000 for the club, helping to create an overall £210,000 profit for the season before tax. Director Clive Holt remarked: 'The money from that Wembley final helped keep the club going for several years after.'

Although Wolves went on quickly to bigger and better achievements, Burnley stalled in the two ensuing seasons. After an encouraging start to the 1988/89 season, Miller's side faltered, dropping from top at the end of October to 13th on 2 January, following a 1-2 defeat at Tranmere. In a re-run of 1983, Frank Casper took over team management in January 1989 while Brian Miller accepted the post of chief scout. But despite winning three of his first four games in charge, Casper was unable to halt the slide, with his team winning only one of their next 15 games. After a 1-3 defeat at Rotherham on 22 April, Burnley were perilously placed in 17th position. In the nick of time, though, Brendan O'Connell's brace and Paul Comstive's late strike brought them a 3-0 victory over relegation rivals Doncaster on 29 April, and much-needed breathing space. But the paltry 4,211 home crowd was almost half the figure that had watched Burnley seize top place after a 2-2 draw with Leyton Orient on 22 October. Burnley went on to beat Lincoln City 3-2, at Sincil Bank, on 1 May with two goals from midfielder Winston White, while a 2-2 draw at Hartlepool five days later confirmed their safety in 16th position. Notably, this game featured Leighton James's last goal for the club he had served so admirably. By then he had adopted a sweeper role, having lost his once electrifying pace.

The 1989/90 season was no better, although the addition of veteran striker Ron Futcher in November 1989 improved Burnley's ineffectual attack while the signing of John Francis from Sheffield United gave the side desperately needed pace.

During this barren period, Andrew and I went to as many Burnley away games as we could in and around London. Perhaps that restriction was a mercy, for almost every game we saw was dreadful. Two stood out. There was a bore draw at Aldershot on a sunny Friday evening in April 1990, where the Burnley faithful were too preoccupied with their zany motorway experiences to be bothered by a numbingly dull game that neither side cared much about. Worse still, was the fixture at Leyton Orient on 4 March 1990. The game was bad enough, but what remains burnt into my memory is the insanitary burger van parked inside Brisbane Road. Here we were confronted with a bubbling vat of what appeared to be crude oil possibly discharged by the holed *Amoco Cadiz*. It seemed feasible that there were oil-slickened seabirds within its murky depths. Incredibly, people were buying these abominable burgers while lambasting them. One guy quipped, 'It's a better idea to sit on your burger and eat your seat' while another conceded 'I guess it fills a hole but so does a landfill.' God knows what the impact was on Wandsworth A&E. Burnley lost 0-3 with a performance of monumental ineptitude. Leighton James played as sweeper, which was fitting given the rubbish produced by his side.

2. JIMMY MULLEN'S CLARET AND BLUE ARMY': 1991 TO 1994

'I Am the Resurrection'

The year 1990 was momentous. It was when Mrs Thatcher's luck ran out. For a time, she was the conquering heroine, the 'Iron Lady', and a courageous survivor of an IRA bombing, but her popularity waned thereafter, despite winning the 1987 general election. That antipathy was probably strongest among the dissolving mining communities following widespread pit closures. Some despised her for treating Orgreave as her Gettysburg and Scargill as another Galtieri. But it was the poll tax fiasco of 1989/90 and her enduring distrust of Europe which seriously undermined her. She had lost her three closest political allies: Cecil Parkinson, who resigned following public exposure of his affair with his secretary which had tragic and bitter consequences, with Parkinson lampooned mercilessly by *Private Eye* and *Spitting Image*; Willie Whitelaw, who resigned after suffering a stroke; and Nicholas Ridley, whose furious Eurosceptic rant, 'giving up sovereignty to the EU was as bad as giving it up to Adolf Hitler', compelled him to resign, too. With powerful, vengeful opponents, such as Michael Heseltine and Nigel Lawson, exposing her vulnerability, it was left to her once faithful servant, Geoffrey Howe, to strike the mortal blow. Meanwhile abroad, Baghdad had crumbled under relentless Allied bombing, and a Balkan war was stirring, that would be scarred indelibly with genocide, as was the ethnic conflict in Rwanda.

The British economy was receding, with a record number of bankruptcies, rising house repossessions and a national unemployment figure of 2.3 million, with 300,000 families placed on income support. Britain's increasing malady was reflected in the riots and illicit joyriding in Cardiff, Birmingham, Oxford, and Tyneside, after closure of their heavy industries.

Burnley 3 Stockport County 2
26 January 1991
'Which Way Should I Jump'

It was not until the 1990/91 season that Burnley mounted a convincing promotion bid. Coincidently, it was when Lydia, our daughter, became a Claret. At this time, we were travelling from London to Leeds most weekends to help care for a terminally ill relative. Lydia became increasingly distressed. One morning she asked if I would take her to a game, having shown no previous interest. Football would become a sanctuary for her just as it had for me all those years ago when my family fragmented. I was not sure that she had Burnley in mind when making her request, but she seemed OK with this.

It was a clear and ear-tinglingly crisp day. As we drove over Deerplay at noon, the tussocky grass remained clasped by the night's frost, easily resisting the weak winter sun. The surrounding moorland was etched with unusual clarity, with looming Pendle Hill silhouetted against a milky blue sky. Because of work and family ties, and cash shortages, I hadn't visited Turf Moor since 1983.

After two years of desolate disappointment, Frank Casper had begun to set things right. The defence had been strengthened by the addition of powerful centre-back John Pender to support an ever-reliable Steve Davis. Ian Measham and Ray 'Whooshy' Deakin were competent full-backs, while goalkeeper Chris Pearce enjoyed better protection. The midfield, led by combative John Deary and the versatile Andy Farrell, became more productive,

2. JIMMY MULLEN'S CLARET AND BLUE ARMY': 1991 TO 1994

assisted by Neil Grewcock's return to form and fitness. Winston White had pace and skill but tended to run around in circles, whereas Joe Jakub seemed better placed at full-back than in midfield. The main difference was up front where speedy 'Super' Johnny Francis, not-so-speedy 'Rocket' Ron Futcher, and Grace Jones hair-alike Roger Eli represented a formidable strike force, at least at home. By Christmas, Burnley were in sixth place, having achieved ten wins and four draws with eight losses in their 22 league games, scoring 35 goals. In the previous season Burnley had managed just 45 in a whole season, comprising 46 fixtures. Two weeks before Lydia's introduction, Burnley beat Darlington, Fourth Division champions-in-waiting, 3-1, with Davis, Futcher, and Francis their scorers.

Burnley's opponents on this perishingly cold afternoon were beefy Stockport, also promotion contenders. Stockport were first to draw blood. In the eighth minute Burnley's poor defence of a right-wing corner resulted in the unmarked Stockport centre-half volleying past Pearce, in front of us at the Bee Hole End. This did not look promising. The next 30 minutes featured an abundance of combative midfield skirmishes. Despite not knowing anything about football, Lydia was absorbed by the aggression shown by both sides. Play was repeatedly halted because of over-zealous challenges. Instead of recoiling at the sight of players writhing in pain, she warmed to the spectacle. Then out of nowhere, Burnley equalised. Five minutes before the break, John Deary used his powerful upper body strength to wriggle between two brawny Stockport centre-backs and find goal with a stabbed shot. Burnley were not finished though. Four minutes later 'Rocket' Ron despatched a blistering half-volley from outside the Stockport box. The visiting goalie was statuesque as the ball whizzed past him. I remembered Futcher in his teenage years when playing for Luton in the First Division. He not only had a ferocious shot with minimal back-lift, he also had uncanny accuracy. Throughout his long and varied career, he was a prolific goalscorer, averaging a goal per two and a half appearances. But he remained an acrimonious character.

Lydia appreciated the brutality of his shot as much as I, as we leapt together, my spare change spilling onto the terraces as if I was a demented fruit machine. At half-time a song was played that would become our signature track on our many football travels over the next ten years or more. Its jangling guitars were reminiscent of the Byrds and the Flaming Groovies. Lydia told me the song was called 'Which Way Should I Jump'. I later discovered that it was by some local young men called the Milltown Brothers. The PA guy or girl played it interminably, ostensibly in response to birthday requests, but it soon became obvious it was the only record they had. Talk about payola!

Standing at the Bee Hole End, we had a grandstand view of Roger Eli's deftly flicked header from Grewcock's splendid right-wing cross. That put us well in command with 27 minutes remaining. As the sun sank beneath the western fells, the already chilly temperature plummeted. Once the floodlights replaced the fading sunlight, an icy sheen spread insidiously across the pitch. Lydia's teeth started to chatter. I suggested that we should leave. She would not hear of it, determined to see the game through. As it happened, the game heated up. Ten minutes later Stockport reduced the deficit with a fierce shot, unleashing a late, frantic flurry. Having suffered a succession of ruthless challenges, Pearce's angry response resulted in his dismissal. Midfielder Andy Farrell once again demonstrated his estimable versatility by keeping goal with venerable composure, amid much bump and grind. As Lydia and I jogged back to the car, attempting to repel the penetrating cold, she remarked how the Burnley fans' screeching anxiety had got to her, signifying how much she had taken from this emotional fray. As the results came through, she used the table in the programme to calculate their impact. It took us to the end of *Sports Report*, though, before our shivering ceased. It is the song, however, which holds our remains of the

2. JIMMY MULLEN'S CLARET AND BLUE ARMY': 1991 TO 1994

day. You have only to play us the opening bars for those frozen memories to tumble forth.

Lydia and I managed to see two more games at Turf Moor during that season before we were no longer needed in Leeds. On a grey 23 February we watched Grewcock and Eli score the decisive second-half goals against unprepossessing Walsall in front of almost 8,000 fans, and we saw Ron Futcher's second-half penalty rescue Burnley from defeat against promotion rivals Torquay on 6 April, a day of wintry high wind and drenching rain. Having returned to London, we saw Roger Eli's brace defeat a spirited Aldershot side fortified by prolific striker David Puckett and future Claret midfielder Adrian Randall. Both were outstanding. This victory was the second of four consecutive wins which kept Burnley in sixth place, but with a good chance of securing automatic promotion.

But having disposed of Peterborough (4-1) and Blackpool (2-0) with goals from Eli and Futcher, the charge was brought to a shuddering halt at Dartford, where Maidstone were the tenants. To describe this game as execrable is outrageous flattery. The pitch was rutted and bone-hard, which made passing a lottery, but this did not excuse the lamentably lethargic performance Burnley produced. Petulant Futcher's short fuse was reignited, resulting in his immediate dismissal, thereby disqualifying him from three crucial fixtures. Maidstone took the lead with a penalty just before half-time and that was that. The sun shone maliciously and the weary Burnley fans, making their second 600-mile round journey inside a week, resorted to singing 'Always Look on the Bright Side of Life'. It was a rendition replete with bitter irony. Lydia asked, 'Is football often as bad as this?' With my nose elongating at pace, I answered, 'No, hardly ever.' Some truths are better withheld.

Futcher redeemed himself slightly, before his ban began, by heading a winning goal in the final seconds of the home game with Doncaster. But a subsequent 0-0 draw at Rochdale ended any hope of automatic promotion. The play-off semi-final with Torquay was disastrous, not helped by another exhausting, long journey, this time to Plainmoor, Devon. Frank Casper's apparent illness upset the players while his assistant, Jimmy Mullen, remained strangely distant. At least that was the view of injured striker Roger Eli, who attributed the team's poor showing to these factors. Certainly, the team performed feebly, losing 0-2. In the return leg Burnley bombarded the Torquay goal to no avail, as the visitors' centre-half Matt Elliott, and his industrious helpers, constructed an impenetrable wall barring Burnley's way to goal. Elliott would later play in the top flight and represent Scotland, too.

Burnley 3 Mansfield Town 2
9 November 1991

'Smells Like Teen Spirit'

Little did we know that Casper's resignation in October 1991 would bring about a huge change in fortune, led by his former assistant, Jimmy Mullen, initially in a caretaker capacity. But Frank Casper should be congratulated on his inspired summer signings which helped propel this upward trajectory. These recruits included centre-forward Mike Conroy, centre-half Steve Davis (the second), and left-winger Steve Harper. But his previous signings should not be forgotten, namely winger and centre-forward John Francis, centre-forward Roger Eli, centre-back John Pender, and midfielder John Deary who also played important parts in the renaissance led by Mullen.

Incredibly, Mullen won his first nine games in charge: Carlisle (2-0), Wrexham (6-2), Walsall (2-1), Lincoln (3-0), Halifax (2-0), York (3-1), Mansfield (3-2), Maidstone (1-0), and Northampton (2-1). How had he achieved this? The simple answer seemed to be that he capitalised on the greater pace of the team he inherited. They were briefed to attack at speed, adopting what often looked like a 4-2-4 formation. Their

2. JIMMY MULLEN'S CLARET AND BLUE ARMY': 1991 TO 1994

powerful assaults on their opponents' goal were irresistible as the goals flew in. This licence to race forward at will meant that the four Burnley forwards – Francis, Conroy, Eli or Lancashire, and Harper – were forever bearing down upon defences at their thinnest. But this tactic required the highest levels of fitness and placed a huge burden upon the two central midfielders, Farrell and Deary, who were repeatedly outnumbered. It also required tight defending at the back, organised and exercised superbly by centre-backs Davis and Pender, underpinned by full-backs Jakub and Measham.

Lydia and I drove up for this promotion clash against Mansfield, staying with relatives in Leeds overnight. It was a bright autumn day with the trees in the last throes of russet glory. Almost 12,000 turned up for what was an immaculate feast of attacking, combative football, expunging those dreadful memories of Maidstone. Driven on by a raucous home crowd, Burnley piled forward in the early stages, pinning Mansfield back, and shooting on sight. With Francis's speed and penetration causing mayhem in the Stags' box, Mansfield's goalie, Jason Pearcey, pulled him down. Conroy put away the penalty with customary aplomb. With only seven minutes gone, Burnley were ahead of the current table-toppers. How the Longside bellowed their approval.

But Mansfield were not here for a bit part. They began to exert pressure of their own. They deservedly equalised in the 29th minute when Steve Wilkinson and ex-SAS soldier Phil Stant combined superbly, allowing the former to beat loanee goalie Marriott with a vicious drive. By half-time Burnley were hanging on as Mansfield called the shots. The break helped Burnley because ten minutes after the resumption they snatched back the lead. Steve Davis's forceful header, from Jakub's corner, detonated an explosive roar on the Longside. Mansfield were not yet out of the race, though. On the hour, Wilkinson pounced upon a rare defensive muddle between

Pender and Davis and equalised crisply. With both teams intent upon winning, the play switched rapidly from end to end with several frantic blocks and clearances. It was heart-stopping, breathless stuff. But with seven minutes left Burnley struck the killer blow. Pender climbed higher than anyone else to head in another Jakub corner. The Burnley crowd went crazy. Lydia could not get the game out of her head on our long drive back to London, playing Nirvana's Album *Nevermind* at incinerating volume. This Fourth Division thriller remains one of my favourite games.

Northampton 1 Burnley 2
30 November 1991

'Give It Away'

After watching Burnley struggle to beat Maidstone at Dartford on 23 November, a game settled by Conroy's 28th-minute penalty, Lydia came with me to Northampton. It seemed an inhospitable place on a cold, damp, grey afternoon. As for the Cobblers' County Ground, it seemed little more than a shack, part of which had been destroyed by fire. It was also missing a flank on account of the club's obligations to county cricket. Nevertheless, the massed ranks of Burnley fans kicked up a mighty din throughout, making us feel as if we were at home. The travelling Burnley fans must have made up more than a quarter of the 4,000 people present. While the ground construction was decrepit, the pitch was a dream for the Burnley forwards, given the huge space it offered them. In the 20th minute Conroy belted down the left wing waiting for a long ball to drop into his path. Francis duly obliged, leaving Conroy with an unopposed run at goal. As he approached the apex of the Cobblers' box, he unleashed a searing cross-shot that sped into the top right-hand corner with the goalie still stuck on his line. This promised to be a cakewalk, as at Wrexham, where wunderkind Graham Lancashire scored a hat-trick in a 6-2 rout.

But Northampton were tougher than that. Inspired by their manager Theo Foley, a star of Northampton's incredible rise during the mid-sixties, they returned from the half-time break in a fighting mood. Burnley were forced to defend diligently. Just when it seemed as if the storm had passed, Northampton scored, with five minutes left. Bell clipped a ball high into the Burnley box. With Pender indisposed, Burnley lacked their customary aerial solidity. Adcock rose highest and headed down for Campbell to smash the ball against the underside of the Clarets' bar and in. The Northampton fans were delirious with delight, sensing a late winner. Their euphoria possibly led Northampton to overcommit themselves. A minute later Burnley repelled a Northampton attack, and with Steve Harper unmarked on the left wing, the unclaimed ball was rapidly relayed to him. Fleet-footed Harper quickly reached top speed. Seeing Conroy and Francis sprinting forward to his right, he chipped the ball over the remaining Cobblers defender, leaving Conroy to chest it down, take aim, and wallop it into the net. This was a perfect smash-and-grab raid and how we enjoyed this, leaping, jigging, and throwing our arms about with animal joy. It was Andy Marriott's last game for Burnley. He had been brought in on loan after Chris Pearce had lost form. He was given a splendid send-off with endless renditions of 'Swing low sweet Marriott'.

Aldershot 1 Burnley 2
21 December 1991
'You Were Always on My Mind'

The next game Lydia and I watched was at the Recreation Ground, Aldershot, in a howling gale. Aldershot were in dire straits and desperate for half-time donations made by Aldershot and Burnley fans alike while 'You Were Always on My Mind', previously covered by Elvis, competed gamely with the blustery conditions. Like Elvis, Aldershot were a goner, folding in March with all their season's records expunged. Steve Harper's wind-assisted 'Exocet' and Graham Lancashire's alert poaching had put Burnley firmly in control before a late riposte by Charlie Henry jangled our nerves. It was irrelevant of course. But we did not anticipate this then. Neither did Jimmy Mullen, having been congratulated by a Five Live presenter for taking his team to the top of the table. It was all too much for him as he immediately suffered a nosebleed.

Disappointingly, Burnley lost a craggy Boxing Day clash with Rotherham 1-2 in front of a Turf Moor crowd just short of 14,000. They also lost 2-5 at Blackpool, to another promotion-seeking side. Here Burnley's new loanee goalkeeper Mark Kendall was at fault for at least two of the goals. However, the defeats by Rotherham and Blackpool were quickly set aside as minor hiccups after Doncaster and Chesterfield were beaten and Gillingham were thrashed 4-1 on 18 January, with Conroy grabbing a hat-trick. A month later, Northampton suffered a worse fate as they were torn apart by Burnley's pace, power, and lethal finishing. Burnley won 5-0 with five different scorers.

The Clarets' resilience was put to the test at Walsall and Scunthorpe, where they recovered from two-goal deficits to claim draws. After holding Blackpool to a 1-1 home draw on 22 February, in a cracking contest watched by 18,183 fans, Burnley snatched a tough 2-0 win at Cardiff, although their pleasure was besmirched by the ugly scenes that followed after the game had ended.

Gillingham 3 Burnley 0
3 March 1992
'Killing in the Name'

Lydia and I then watched Burnley in a midweek fixture at Gillingham. She was then into Rage against the Machine, playing rap metal 'Killing in the Name' at ear-splitting volume on our outward road journey. As John Lydon declaimed,

'Anger is an energy'. Regrettably there was little energy from the Clarets on this chilly night. With Burnley ensconced in top position and mid-table Gillingham having been soundly beaten at Turf Moor, we had high hopes of another crushing win. We got a crushing victory, but from the wrong side. Nicky Walker, our third loanee goalie, had played a blinder at Ninian Park but he had little chance of preventing the three goals scored by David Crown and Steve Lovell. The Gills' opening goal came in the first minute. Meanwhile Burnley were left firing blanks. We drove home in morose silence, having heard that wins by Blackpool and Mansfield had enabled both clubs to overtake us. But our spirits were lifted a few days later as Barnet were blown away 3-0 at Turf Moor, putting Burnley back in top spot. Although Halifax put up more of a fight on their 14 March visit, John Pender's 70th-minute goal sent them home pointless.

Mansfield Town 0 Burnley 1
21 March 1992

'Crucify'

At promotion rivals Mansfield, we were treated to another howling gale. Unsurprisingly, the game was disjointed, with possession regularly won and lost. But in noble defiance of the difficult conditions, Conroy settled the game with a smart goal just before the break, following a slick exchange with Francis. It was not until the last quarter that Mansfield summoned the threat they had exhibited at Turf Moor. But commanding Davis led a bold defence, thwarting their late surge, backed by Nicky Walker's superb shot-stopping. Sadly, this was Walker's last game on loan with us, having solved Burnley's goalkeeping problem at a stroke. So, back came Chris Pearce to face Barnet in a return game on 24 March. Commendably, he kept a clean sheet as Burnley battled for a dull draw.

Burnley 2 Maidstone United 1
28 March 1992
'American Guitars'

Burnley spluttered and stuttered in their frustrated attempts at subduing plucky Maidstone United. Belying their perilous position, Maidstone were well organised and tenacious, drawing everyone behind the ball whenever possession was lost. They also employed a canny offside trap with exasperating precision, backed with blatant time-wasting. Their strapping but agile goalkeeper Iain Hesford, brother of rugby union star Bob, performed heroics, using his huge frame to block any incursion into his box, whereas Chris Pearce had not helped his misfiring team-mates by conceding a sloppy goal just after the interval. But adversity always brought out the best in Steve Davis and today was no exception. Levering himself above a melee of frenzied defenders at the far post, he headed emphatically past Hesford with 13 minutes left. But it took a wonder-goal from Roger Eli in the 87th minute to snatch all three points.

Burnley 3 Cardiff City 1
22 April 1992
'Sheela-Na-Gig'

Burnley's Robbie Painter had made his debut against Maidstone, the club he had just left. Here, he made his mark by scoring the opening goal, in the first minute, much to his delight and that of his team-mates. Cardiff were no pushovers, though. Their striker Nathan Blake was in superb form. He equalised in the 29th minute, cutting Burnley wide open with his destructive speed before finishing with a rasping drive that reserve goalkeeper David Williams had no hope of saving. But second-half goals from Farrell and Conroy brought victory at the end of a pulsating contest, in front of an excitable 12,408 crowd, bringing Burnley to the brink of automatic promotion. Three days later, thousands of Burnley fans made for Carlisle hoping to see their club win

2. JIMMY MULLEN'S CLARET AND BLUE ARMY': 1991 TO 1994

both promotion and the championship. Francis's scorching drive in the 43rd minute raised their hopes, only for these to be dashed by a 79th-minute equaliser. Burnley didn't have much longer to wait, though. On a balmy evening at York, at a jam-packed Bootham Crescent, John Francis bundled in the championship-winning goal in the 90th minute, capitalising upon Conroy's swift breakaway and precise cut-back. After seven barren and traumatic years Burnley were moving up again, having claimed championship titles in all four divisions, a distinction shared only with Wolves.

Lydia and I went to the Turf Moor festivities on 2 May when over 21,000 turned out to acclaim their team and manager. Although Wrexham turned out to be party poopers, coming from behind to snatch the points, nobody was too bothered. Besides, Burnley put the record straight at Rochdale three days later. After conceding a 15th-minute goal, they struck back quickly, winning 3-1. Conroy's 41st-minute goal was his 24th league goal of the season. Not bad for a former full-back!

The other memorable event of this glorious season was the passion exhibited by Burnley fans in an FA Cup fourth-round replay at Derby. Jon Sadler of *The Sun* reported: 'Burnley took 4,000 to the Midlands and they were sensational. They set up one of the loudest, sustained dins I've heard anywhere in the world. Their chants of 'Jimmy Mullen's Claret and Blue Army' totally drowned the home support. Over and over, they roared out the same message with no break and no reduction in volume. Clapping and stamping their feet and drumming on the advertising boards in perfect rhythm, they were the sole focus of attention over the final 20 minutes. Neither did it stop there, since this magnificent crowd sustained their defiant loyalty for over 15 minutes after the game had ended.' Jimmy Mullen added: 'In all of my 23 years in the game I've never witnessed anything like that. It left my players feeling they were prepared to die for these people.'

3. BACK AT WEMBLEY 1994

Burnley 2 West Bromwich Albion 1
3 October 1992
'Sleeping Satellite'

At the dawn of the Premier League, Burnley made a slow and uncertain start to life in Division Two. They were fortunate to win their first game 1-0 at home to Swansea. They also beat a pallid Mansfield side by the same score with reserve centre-half Mark Monington heading a 32nd-minute winner. He had also rescued Burnley on the previous Saturday by heading in a 90th-minute equaliser against Port Vale. Newly signed goalkeeper Marlon Beresford from Sheffield Wednesday, had performed magnificently against dominant Rotherham but it was Burnley midfielder John Deary who saved our bacon with an 85th-minute equaliser. He replicated this act of rescue at Wigan, too, this time with an 89th-minute leveller. As for star signing Adrian Heath, acquired from Stoke City during the summer, he scored a late goal at Stockport on debut, only for the hosts to win the game in the last minute. When high-flying West Bromwich Albion arrived at Turf Moor on 3 October, Burnley's undistinguished record read: played nine league games; won two, drawn four, and lost three, with ten points gained and placed in 18th spot.

Against powerful West Bromwich, though, Burnley displayed their capabilities. The road to Wembley and the second tier started here. Lydia and I drove up from London after a customary pit stop in Leeds. West Bromwich were among the early leaders, winning seven of their opening nine games and

3. BACK AT WEMBLEY 1994

racking up 20 goals. Their only loss had been against eventual Division Two winners Stoke City, by a 3-4 margin. The Baggies had two of the best strikers in the lower leagues in Bob Taylor, formerly with Bristol City, and Simon Garner, previously with Blackburn. Undeterred, Harper powered Burnley into a first-minute lead. The resulting roar from the Longside was incandescent. But West Bromwich retaliated mightily. For the rest of the half Burnley's defence was subjected to constant pressure, forcing their full-backs, Measham and Jakub, to stay close to central defenders Davis and Pender, who made countless headed clearances and blocks, while Beresford made many fine saves. But this did not silence the 14,000-plus Burnley fans. They bellowed their support throughout.

The second half was only eight minutes old when Conroy swept in Burnley's second goal, having been set up by the ingenuity and alertness of Heath. His relief at breaking his duck for the new season was palpable but the leaping Burnley fans were more relieved that Burnley had created a cushion. Yet, for the next ten minutes Burnley dominated, knocking the ball around with the fluency shown in the previous season. For this brief period the visitors seemed subdued. However, a weak back pass by Davis panicked Beresford into picking the ball up in his penalty area. An indirect free kick was awarded, with all Burnley players posted on the goal line and Beresford in front of them. The ball was passed quickly to the waiting Garner whose instant shot sent the ball hurtling high into the top-right corner. Albion immediately resumed their siege of the Burnley goal which was defended by all except marauding Conroy. As much as they huffed and puffed, the West Bromwich attackers could not find a way through Burnley's robust back line, with agile Beresford redeeming himself with some spectacular saves. Eventually the storm blew over and Burnley played out the final minutes with composed possession. As the final whistle was blown, the Longside derided Garner with the chant

'Garner, Garner, what's the score!' However, the largest cheer was reserved for Beresford, who contributed so much to this impressive victory.

For most of this season Burnley mixed pleasing victories, as against Fulham, Chester, and Blackpool, with abject defeats, as at Brighton, Port Vale, Bolton, and Fulham. However, while a mid-table finish was regarded by manager Mullen and chairman Teasdale as satisfactory consolidation, this was not acceptable to a contingent of Burnley fans who expected more. Even the successful 1993/94 season did not appease all Burnley fans. Rumours about Mullen's health issues and mood swings hardly helped. It seemed as if the strong bond established between the club management and its supporters in 1991/92 was showing signs of strain.

Burnley 2 Sheffield United 4
12 January 1993

'Animal Nitrate'

Burnley's best performance of the 1992/93 season was at Bramall Lane in the third round of the FA Cup. On an icy surface, Heath's brace threatened to eliminate the Premier League Blades before a late revival enabled the hosts to scramble a draw in the last ten minutes. The replay at Turf Moor attracted a 19,000 crowd, easily the highest home gate of this season. However, Burnley were overwhelmed by Brian Deane's decisive finishing. His hat-trick overturned Heath's opening goal and put his side out of reach, helped by Adrian Littlejohn's 59th-minute strike. However, the most alarming feature of this replay was the reckless surge by Longside fans which nearly brought about the death of an 11-year-old Burnley supporter. This charge followed Littlejohn's recriminatory celebrations after he had scored the Blades' fourth goal. Having suffered shameful racism during the game, he was understandably delighted to land the knock-out blow.

Burnley v Plymouth Argyle
Third Division Play-Off Semi-Final
15 and 18 May 1994
'Red Right Hand'

Before the 1993/94 season began there were several changes of personnel. Out went 1991/92 heroes Mike Conroy and Ian Measham and in came goalscoring wide man David Eyres, creative inside-forward Kevin Russell, and battling midfielder Warren Joyce, son of Clarets sixties stalwart Walter Joyce. Conroy was sad to leave, attributing the reduction in his goal tally to a change of position. With Adrian Heath allocated the centre-forward berth, Conroy undertook wide and target-man roles. Heath scored 20 league goals in his inaugural season at Turf Moor, a career-best return, apparently helped by Conroy's unselfish assistance.

While Burnley managed to clamber into the last play-off place, this was an exasperating season. At their best Burnley played eye-catching football as exemplified in a two-legged League Cup tie with Spurs. Their fluency of passing and twinkling ball skills were such that Spurs were fortunate to progress to the next round. London Claret Dave Parker summed up Burnley's schizoid performances, remarking: 'The contrast between home and away displays has been startling; at home, confidence abounds, the ball is played to feet, space is found with wonderful crosses and superb goals. Away, there is no space, long balls are hoofed out of defence to Kevin Russell, John Francis and "Inchy" Heath and the opposing strikers are allowed glaring gaps.' It seemed as if Jimmy Mullen was adopting similar tactics to those used in their 1991/92 triumph, which left the Burnley midfielders neutralised and often overrun, at least away from home, resulting in 'hoof ball'.

A week before the first play-off semi-final tie against Plymouth at Turf Moor, Lydia and I drove to Exeter to watch Burnley take on the already relegated Grecians. It was a car-crash display with Burnley losing 1-4, their 13th league defeat away from home during this season. Only one point was taken from their visits to four relegated clubs. While Burnley were subjecting us to another away-day humiliation, Plymouth were thrashing relegated Hartlepool 8-1 at the Victoria Ground.

Lydia and I drove to Burnley for the play-off first leg. It was a grey, cold Sunday afternoon but 18,794 fans turned out for this taut, jagged contest. The western end of the Longside was packed with Plymouth Argyle supporters who made an almighty noise before and during the game. Our Longside fans struggled to make themselves heard above the visitors' vocal artillery. This was an abrasive, attritional, ugly game which Burnley were fortunate to survive unscathed. Despite the dismissal of Plymouth's Adrian Burrows, the huge travelling support were convinced they would win, bellowing repeatedly, 'We'll score in a minute!' and 'We only need ten men!' Dwight Marshall had the opportunity to justify their faith after breaking through a less than robust Burnley defence, leaving him one-on-one with Beresford. Fortunately, Beresford's frantic dash from goal did enough to distract him and blight his aim. His scuffed shot was screwed wide. Certainly, depleted Plymouth were the stronger side, scrapping for everything and targeting Burnley's danger man Ted McMinn, an immaculate crosser of the ball. This ultra-physical tussle ended goalless. Lydia spent much of the return journey trying to persuade me to take her to the second leg three days later but I was not to be persuaded. After all, it was a school day.

At Home Park Jimmy Mullen had no need to motivate his team. Instead, he pinned up a page from a Plymouth local paper. It said that all 40,000 preliminary tickets for the Wembley final had been sold as had seats on the coaches to transport them. This arrogance was compounded by the presumptuous celebrations that greeted the Plymouth players as they came out to warm up. Everyone in this 17,000-strong crowd was convinced they would

3. BACK AT WEMBLEY 1994

win, save for the small, dedicated contingent of Clarets. The Burnley players' snarling indignation suddenly morphed into combustible anger after Burnley's flying winger John Francis was subjected to incessant monkey chants. Francis would make them pay, though. Despite seizing an early lead, Plymouth were undone by Francis's speed and strength. Midway through the first half, Francis twice burst through the ponderous Plymouth back line to slide the ball past the advancing Nicholls. After his first goal, Francis celebrated with recriminatory ape-like gestures before being engulfed by his exultant team-mates. His second, however, prompted a sinuous wiggle of his hips and a bark of delight. The Home Park racists had their bile stuffed down their throats. Burnley duly wrapped up the game shortly before the close. McMinn avenged his rough treatment at Turf Moor by sweeping past two defenders on their left flank and taking a pot shot, leaving Plymouth old boy Warren Joyce to tuck away Nicholls's spill. On a night where important scores were settled Joyce shook his fist at his detractors. Lydia and I listened to this on the radio, constantly interspersed with her grievance, 'We should have gone!'

The compensation was a date at the Wembley final. I took one of Lydia's friends with us, allowing both girls to cover their faces and mine in claret and blue paint. This exposed me to the withering scorn of the Stockport fans. I was taking an unaccustomed chance because this bold act signified a confidence about the result that I didn't hold. Quite rightly, for shortly after kick-off, Stockport took the lead. Eyres failed to pick up his man at a free kick on the left flank, and Stockport's Beaumont netted with a free header. Oh God! I muttered: 'We are in for another away-day embarrassment.' Our play was shabby. Possession was easily lost. We were lumping long, hopeless balls forward. It was mess. Then a nasty spat between Stockport's Wallace and Ted McMinn ended with the former spitting at 'Tin Man', bringing about his instant dismissal. Although John

Francis was carried off shortly afterwards with a nasty leg injury, this allowed Eyres more space in which to roam. How he made his unexpected freedom pay! With around 30 minutes gone he embarked upon a trademark winding run which dumbfounded his markers. Finding space on the edge of the Stockport box, he curled the ball into the unguarded corner of the net. Almost 40,000 Burnley fans erupted.

Burnley's task was made easier in the second half when Beaumont was sent off for violent conduct against the Burnley left-back, Thompson. Well, it should have been easier, but Burnley kept missing simple chances to wrap up the game. Eventually, an awkward toe poke by right-back Parkinson gave the ball just enough momentum to bobble over the diving goalie and find the net. The Burnley players and our fans went berserk. But while there was only a one-goal lead there was always the chance of a calamity. The tension was gut-wrenching with yet more chances wasted. Meanwhile Stockport began to mount a few attacks of their own. But after an interminable amount of added time, the whistle was finally blown. Burnley were back in the second tier! I asked my friend Andrew, who had resolutely refused to be painted: 'Do you really think we are good enough to stay there?' He replied wisely, 'That's for tomorrow, let's celebrate today.'

PART 4

ON A WILD ROLLERCOASTER

1994 to 2002

'Bang and Blame'

1. THE CALAMITOUS 1994/95 SEASON

Middlesbrough 2 Burnley 0
13 August 1994

'Black Hole Sun'

The sun shone brightly upon Ayresome Park as Lydia and I excitedly awaited second-tier football. The Boro mascot threw toffees at us while the Burnley kids threw back abuse. There was no reciprocity on the pitch, though. Powered by Bryan Robson's crunching strength in midfield, Alan Moore's speed and nimbleness on the wing, and Hendrie's bustling sharp shooting, Boro' had far too much firepower for labouring Burnley. The Clarets' underwhelming strike force comprised Adrian Heath and Liam Robinson, who was a record summer signing from Bristol City.

A Heath–Robinson pairing said it all. Neither Heath nor Robinson, both short in stature, made any impact upon Boro's hefty central defenders, Neil Cox and Nigel Pearson. To make matters worse, our idolised goalie, Marlon Beresford, had a stinker, conceding two soft goals, ensuring that Bryan Robson easily won his first game as Middlesbrough's player/manager. Despite some attractive approach play, prompted by McMinn's exemplary ball control, Burnley's few sorties upfield were rarely threatening, although Clarets left-back Vinnicombe was denied a penalty when felled by Blackmore's flailing boot. As Burnley played out time with respectful timidity, the home supporters taunted us with: 'What's it like to follow shit?' 'You mean you

1. THE CALAMITOUS 1994/95 SEASON

don't know?' was the obvious reply, for Middlesbrough had also been on the brink of folding a few years before.

Burnley 1 Stoke City 1
20 August 1994
'Hurt'

Before the game Lydia, Andrew, and I squeezed into the Park View pub to watch a ferociously quick Devon Malcolm blitz the South African tourists at the Oval. The atmosphere was febrile with the crammed gathering boisterously urging Malcolm on. It was an excellent pumped-up start to our first home game of the new season. Burnley had a strapping black guy on show too, in colossus John Gayle, making his Burnley debut, partnered by Liam Robinson. Adrian Heath had reverted to midfield. 'Big Bad John' put himself about with casual menace, feeding off McMinn's pinpoint crosses. One of these led to our goal three minutes before the break. Ex-Claret Vince Overson inadvertently flicked on McMinn's corner allowing Steve Davis to bury a header at the far post. Two minutes later we were awarded a penalty for handball. With Eyres out, Gary Parkinson took the kick, only to gently pass the ball into the Stoke goalie's midriff. Some idiots were moved to chant, 'Burnley, Burnley taking the piss' as Burnley dominated the second half, urged on by a baying 15,300 crowd. Predictably, Stoke equalised after some sloppy defending. On our 250-mile return journey we seethed with exasperation. We could not afford to throw away points as carelessly as this.

Luton Town 0 Burnley 1
10 September 1994
'Bring Me Sunshine'

Burnley went to Luton on the back of abject defeats by Oldham and Barnsley, having thrown away two more points in a home draw with Bristol City, after conceding another late goal.

Burnley were therefore in the relegation zone and desperately in need of a win. At Luton, Jimmy Mullen decided upon a novel innovation, picking two midfielders, Adrian Randall and Gerry Harrison, capable of playing there. His reward was a winning 44th-minute goal as Robinson tapped in after a rare breakaway. But oh, the agony of counting down those second-half minutes, with our rookie goalie, Russell, constantly barged and jostled by Luton's Welsh hulk, John Hartson! At the final whistle we joined the joyous acclamation before stumbling away from sun-drenched Kenilworth Road exhausted but exhilarated.

Millwall 2 Burnley 3
14 September 1994
'Heart-Shaped Box'

Millwall's New Den was a Premier League stadium in waiting. The Lions had not been defeated there in their last 25 games. Lydia, Andrew, and I were expecting the worst. Beresford was back in goal and John Deary replaced the injured Randall. In the first half, we battled well. Burnley centre-half Steve Davis was authoritative, exhibiting such self-assurance and potency. Every tackle was precise, every block was unyielding, every header firm and well directed. Yet, one minute after the break, Savage scored with a blistering shot having been set up by Kennedy's cross. We feared a deluge would follow. The Burnley vocal support was ear-splitting, though, lending us strength. Setting aside her natural reserve, Lydia joined in as lustily as Andrew and me.

Six minutes after going behind we were level. Robinson's cross from the right picked out Burnley centre-back Winstanley at the far post and his precise header sped past Millwall's American goalie, Casey Keller. Our roar boomed around the half-filled Den and 15 minutes later we were beside ourselves with joy after Winstanley doubled his account, this time deftly guiding in Heath's cross with his forehead.

1. THE CALAMITOUS 1994/95 SEASON

The lead lasted just five minutes. Millwall were awarded a controversial penalty. Alex Rae nonchalantly stroked the ball past Beresford. The doubts returned. 'We'll be lucky to hang on to a draw,' said a disappointed Claret next to us. However, with ten minutes remaining, Deary swung wildly at a loose ball on the edge of the Millwall box. His shot was going well wide before the ball hit a Millwall defender and looped high into the air. To our mounting excitement, it appeared to be dropping under Keller's crossbar. Wrong-footed Keller struggled to make his ground, managing a desperate overhead punch before the ball crossed the line. Unfortunately for him, Robinson's head was in the way. The ball ricocheted off our maligned striker, hit the underside of the bar and nestled in the net. We combusted. Having evaded the Millwall 'bushwhackers' on our way back to the car, we were still buzzing as we negotiated the South Circular. In keeping with this glorious evening, a full moon beamed down upon us. Burnley stayed in 21st place.

West Bromwich Albion 1 Burnley 0
24 September 1994
'Parklife'

It was a grey, greasy day. Not that the sun could redeem the wasteland upon which the Hawthorns sat. Its ground improvements were way behind schedule, meaning that this was their first home game of the season. The Baggies were stuck in the bottom places. It was only 24 September but already this game felt like a relegation six-pointer. As if to underline this, the first half was littered with nervous errors. Parkinson's back pass was woefully short allowing West Bromwich's Jeroen Boere to nip in and sidestep Beresford, but screw his shot wide. Boosted by this let-off, Burnley pressed forward with greater confidence. But Heath and McMinn spurned good opportunities while David Eyres missed a 35th-minute penalty. Having failed to capitalise on their first-half advantage, Burnley hardly showed after the break. Their sole effort on goal came from a Steve Davis header. Bob Taylor had an unfortunate habit of putting away his chances as he did here with a free header. We dropped one place into 22nd position.

Charlton Athletic 1 Burnley 2
22 October 1994

'Hallelujah'

Burnley came into this game in 21st place. They had pinched a home draw against Tranmere Rovers after Beresford had saved John Aldridge's spot kick at the death. While Wolves and Bolton were fortunate to avoid defeat at Turf Moor, Burnley took a point from a bore draw at Roker Park, Sunderland.

I began 22 October with an early-morning run in the Royal Parks. The dew-gorged grass glistened in the early sunlight while wisps of mist curled off the still surface of the Thames. The pallid blue sky was unblemished, but by lunchtime bloated clouds drifted across the South Circular, releasing sudden, tingling showers. Just as we reached The Valley, a shimmering rainbow appeared over the ground. If it was an omen whom did it concern? Having watched struggling teams for much of my life I was well versed in superstition.

The referee was suspiciously listed as M. Bailey. Surely this was not Mike Bailey the former Charlton stalwart? Whatever his allegiances, he seemed determined to spoil our day. He disallowed three goals seemingly without justification before half-time, two by Eyres and one by Robinson. Then we remembered this was the same referee who awarded Millwall an apparently dubious penalty and tried to send off Burnley winger McMinn for a second bookable offence when he had not shown an earlier yellow card. We were not amused.

Burnley were not to be denied, though. After the break, Davis side-footed a corner past Petterson while Robinson made

1. THE CALAMITOUS 1994/95 SEASON

the most of a rare route-one move by scooping in a second. It was fully deserved. The Clarets had performed brilliantly, exhibiting enthralling fluency and movement, not seen since the days of Dobson and James. Jimmy Mullen was sometimes berated for his tactical naivety. Today, he was spot on as endorsed by Addicks' striker Gary Nelson, who remarked that Charlton often had problems dealing with a diamond formation, as adopted by Jimmy Mullen here. It worked like a dream, albeit a wet one as the showers became extended downpours.

Everyone played their part, but the pick of this crop were Davis, recent signing Jamie Hoyland, Randall, and Eyres. Of course, Burnley have a proclivity for white-knuckle rides. This day was no exception. Charlton's Whyte scored a late goal to set up a tense finish, made more alarming by Hoyland's apparently soft dismissal. Burnley had to cling on, enduring a succession of fierce crosses that whizzed across our box. Among the appreciative Clarets was Neil Kinnock, guest of Alastair Campbell. Even the 'Welsh Windbag' was rendered speechless by the Burnley fans' chant: 'Kinnock is a Claret!' It was our third consecutive victory in the capital. As we left the ground, the dark, drenching clouds slid away to the east leaving a magnificent double rainbow in their wake. Even the glum South Circular appeared redeemed by the magnificent array of colour. This glorious result lifted us up to 21st.

Burnley 2 Notts County 1
29 October 1994
'Cut Your Hair'

This week, 'sleaze' entered the political lexicon with the resignation of Tory MP Neil Hamilton. Meanwhile, Wacko Jacko boasted about his three-month wedding anniversary: 'Just think, nobody thought this would last!' Today, we had the perfect opportunity to register our first league home win of the season and lift ourselves out of the relegation zone. Notts County were rock bottom despite having a talented squad, including England Under-21 centre-back Dean Yates and bright attackers Tony Agana, Gary McSwegan, and Paul Devlin. It was a murky, dank, dreary day as Lydia and I drove over from Leeds and so was much of this game. 'Ooh David Eyres' gave us a perfect start with a seventh-minute penalty, which clipped the inside of the post and went in. Burnley held this lead until the break although Beresford made several ill-judged but unpunished dashes from his goal. But on the resumption faultless Steve Davis diverted a right-wing cross past Beresford. Our hearts sank, knowing we had yet to create a single chance in open play. But much to our relief, one minute later, Jamie Hoyland buried an unstoppable header from a left-wing corner. This time Burnley held on, imposing their dull will on their easily bored opponents. Burnley's reward was 18th position, their highest placing this season. Oxygen masks, please!

Reading 0 Burnley 0
5 November 1994

'Glory Box'

By noon, the smudged early sun had given way to a curdling gruel-like greyness. Cold rain soon followed, persistent enough to spatter from Elm Park's dilapidated gutters, gurgle in their broken drains, and seep deep into our heavy winter clothing. Southern exposure!

This was the day when Ronald Reagan revealed he had early symptoms of dementia. Meanwhile, 45-year-old George Foreman continued to rage against the dying of the light, defeating Michael Moorer to regain the world heavyweight title he had lost to Muhammad Ali 20 years before. The light temporarily went out for poor Chris Vinnicombe, though, the victim of Bernal's late, reckless challenge, which shattered his jaw and left us without a specialist left-back for a crucial four-month period. It was a fiery, bloody end to what had been a fine

1. THE CALAMITOUS 1994/95 SEASON

contest, one which Burnley should have won, had their finishing been as good as their creativity.

We knew this was to be a tough game. Reading had made a fine start following their promotion as Second Division champions. Prior to this game they were in fourth spot having put some illustrious teams to the sword. They had deservedly defeated us twice in the previous season, exhibiting greater all-round strength and sharper tactical nous.

Heath was restored in midfield to replace suspended Hoyland, with John Francis returning to the bench having supposedly recovered from his Wembley injury. We thought we might be in for a battering as Reading flew at the Clarets from the off. But after Scott Taylor's amazing miss, Burnley took control of the game with Heath and Randall bossing central midfield and Eyres tormenting Reading's defence on both flanks. Robinson and a rejuvenated Alan Harper were close with good efforts, but we settled for half-time parity.

Watching games in incessant rain is like long-distance running: it discomforts us most when we stop. As the steaming players jogged off, the extent of my unease kicked in, having endured the dripping tendrils of hair, the squishy socks, the soggy jacket, the mildewing pullover, and the soaked underwear that clung to my buttocks. It was then when I noticed how smeared my glasses had become refracting the glare of the floodlights. Certainly, we could have done without the pre-pubescent girls twerking to the banality of Whigfield's 'Saturday Night' oblivious to the teeming rain. Wasn't this child abuse? Or perhaps parental abuse?

The rest of the game was a hit and miss affair: Eyres's and Deary's glaring misses and Bernal's grisly hit. Although a valuable point had been gained, it was difficult to appreciate this given Vinnicombe's horrific injury. Upon leaving the ground, our alarm increased as we saw the ambulance squeezing along the narrow perimeter street, its blue lights flickering and the paramedics frantically shouting at the milling crowd to disperse. This looked very bad indeed.

Burnley 4 Sheffield United 2
20 November 1994
'Live Forever'

We're on the tele!! This was the first time that an entire Burnley match had been covered live on terrestrial television since the 1962 FA Cup Final. What better proof was there that we had finally regained our place in the sun, although the heavy rain did not relent until kick-off, leaving just a smidgen of brightness before the heavy clouds returned bringing an early nightfall. Not that we needed trite metaphors, for Burnley produced a dazzling performance. Perhaps not for Elton Welsby and his 'expert summarisers', Lou Macari and Jim Beglin, who were stuffed together inside a Portakabin.

'Inchy' Heath set up the opening goal, taking on the dour Blades defenders single-handedly, outwitting them with pace and skill before pulling back a perfect cross for Robinson to squeeze in a 23rd-minute header. While the Longside celebrated wildly, the Granada 'experts' declared that Blades goalie Kelly had clawed the ball out before it had crossed the goal line. Macari pontificated: 'He's made the wrong decision. Unless there is something wrong with my eyes.' Fortunately, the match officials were immune to Granada's jurisprudence, and after a brief consultation awarded the goal. Oh, how we enjoyed the sight of humble pie being smeared across these pundits' faces as the Granada TV replay proved that the ball had crossed the goal line before Kelly pushed it out. Confronted with irrefutable evidence, Beglin managed a lame: 'Yeah, it probably crossed the line.'

For the remainder of the half, possession was shared equally although Burnley had the better chances. Eyres forced Kelly into a fine save and Robinson skied a close-range opportunity.

1. THE CALAMITOUS 1994/95 SEASON

It looked as if we would go into the break with our one-goal lead intact but in injury time Sheffield's Gage broke away on the right and, with Burnley's rookie left-back Dowell allowing him too much room, he was able to fire in a fierce, low cross, which centre-back Winstanley diverted past Beresford. Marlon's dejection was shared by all except the ecstatic Blades supporters.

At half-time, Granada TV's Rob McCaffrey tried to induce Jimmy Mullen into revealing his master plan for the remainder of the game. 'More of the same,' was his revealing reply. We needn't have worried. Everything was well under control. Just nine minutes into the second half, Randall's right-wing corner was laid off by Davis for Hoyland to crack home a vicious volley. No doubt about this one, Lou! Hoyland had not enjoyed his final months at Bramall Lane so he celebrated his goal lustily.

In the 65th minute Jimmy proved he could do shrewd, whatever McCaffrey might have thought. For Jimmy wheeled on 'Big Bad' John Gayle for the anonymous Alan Harper. Gayle is 6ft 4in and weighed in at 15 stone-plus. He was built like heavyweight boxer Audley Harrison but with the speed of Rex. 'Rolling Thunder' was the name of his game. Unimpressed with this show of power, Macari insisted Gayle was really a 'pussycat'. We thought that 'Your Highness' might be a wiser form of address. Anyway, this was Gayle's moment. Within six minutes of making his entry, Randall's pass found Robinson on the right who crossed high into the box. In lumbered Gayle, his clanking gears shifting up from 'dead slow' to 'you're dead'. Sheffield keeper Kelly and defender Brian Gayle stupidly stood in his way. This was no contest. 'Big Bad John' made some sort of contact with the ball – the TV replay showed that it was his shoulder – and it flew into the net, showered by bloody fragments of the Sheffield United defence. After that, Steve Davis's immaculate 78th-minute drive was mere garnish while Andy Scott's 84th-minute riposte was just irrelevant.

This impressive victory was achieved against a side which had been in the Premier League only a few months before. We had showcased ourselves on TV in the best way possible, whatever Welsby and his cronies might say. More importantly, we had breached the 20-point mark in our 17th game and had lifted ourselves up six places to 15th, well on course for survival. Alas, this was to be our high-water mark.

Swindon Town 1 Burnley 1
23 November 1994
'This Is a Call'

We're all friends now, aren't we? Tory MP Patrick Nicholls didn't seem to think so. In the *Western Morning News*, he wrote: 'France has the nerve to represent itself as a nation of resistance fighters when, in fact, it was a nation of collaborators. Germany's unique contribution has been to plunge Europe into two world wars and as for the lesser EU countries they insult us to the tune of their banging begging bowls.' Talk about 'Eva Braun cocktails' and 'Hors d'oeuvres will be obeyed'. It was a toss-up as to who merited the Basil Fawlty prize, Nicholls or Nicholas Ridley. It seemed appropriate that Nicholls's Ridleyesque rant should appear in this provincial western paper, sold in Swindon, as his career went west.

Tonight, we went west, too, except we prevailed, extending our unbeaten league run to nine games. To be honest, we were fortunate, for we were outplayed for long periods by yet another ex-Premier League side. Swindon's three strikers, Fjortoft, Mutch, and Scott frequently threatened to swamp our straining defence. Scott deservedly put the Robins in front after 17 minutes and thereafter Fjortoft did everything but score, hitting the bar, missing wildly from close range, having a stonewall penalty claim refused, and forcing Marlon into making two brilliant saves. This was particularly pleasing as Fjortoft had a real knack of winding up the opposition with his diving and 'Dambusters' goal celebrations. Now it was payback time.

But this was just a sideshow. There was too much danger in our box to mock Fjortoft's antics. All hands were at the pump, including midfielder Randall, who had reinvented himself as a street fighter. Perhaps it was because his family were watching? He grew up in nearby Amesbury. Or perhaps it was because Jimmy Mullen had threatened to brew his brains if he didn't show more industry. Whatever the reason for his makeover, Randall was up for this game in a big way, but it was his much-maligned midfield partner, Alan Harper, who helped rescue a point. With an hour gone the prospects were not good. It was time for Jimmy's worst-kept-not-very-secret weapon, 'Big Bad John'. Within six minutes of appearing in the unappealing yellow and claret stripes, he had levelled the score, sliding the ball home after Digby had parried a shot from 'Mooncat' aka Alan Harper. This was too much for the home crowd, who immediately launched into 'Sack the board!' and 'Where's the money gone?' Not wishing to be impolite we joined in lustily.

Grimsby Town 2 Burnley 2
26 November 1994
'Only Happy When It Rains'

Grimsby like Burnley seemed a forgotten town once its famous fishing industry declined. Levelling up here might be interpreted as levelling over. It seemed a despondent place on this wet, winter Saturday. Perhaps only zealots go to Grimsby or at least to Blundell Park, which is in Cleethorpes. On this day it was our turn to play the zealot, along with 3,000 Claret martyrs. Come 4.54pm we received our saintly blessing. It had been a tough contest. Twice we had gone behind. Woods put the home side one up just before the interval, but Davis then levelled 13 minutes into the second half, only for Gilbert to restore the Mariners' lead with 23 minutes to go. A second equaliser seemed unlikely. We were struggling against a better-organised, physically stronger side. Even with Gayle and Francis pushed on we were not making much headway. The Grimsby defence had us in their pockets.

Then with just 15 seconds left, Parkinson ventured forth from left-back, having picked up a square pass from Hoyland. Inexplicably, the Grimsby defenders backed off him. On and on he ran: ten yards, 20 yards, 30 yards, and finally 40 yards, reaching the edge of the Grimsby box but still no one challenged him. The home defenders were apparently content to cluster in front of their goal, denying him a clear target. Their wall appeared impregnable but Parky espied a chink. Transferring the ball to his favoured right foot he curled a shot around Grimsby's defensive wall. Crichton, who would later serve Burnley with distinction, clocked its direction but Parky's placement was too accurate. Crichton dived to his left, to no avail. We went berserk, ecstatically punching the air and screaming ourselves hoarse with joy and relief. Sometimes the bliss at snatching a late, unexpected equaliser is greater than the thrill of victory. Any preceding dross is instantly reframed. Hyperboles burst in where cynicism stagnated only minutes before. It is for those blinding, rapturous moments that we risk all, ignoring the bleak prospect of success, putting up with the discomfort of travelling so far, setting aside more pressing commitments. 'Bugger it,' we say, 'I'm going.'

Stoke City 2 Burnley 0
10 December 1994

'Slide Away'

Ironies don't come much bigger than this. Today, the onanistic supremo, Bill Clinton, sacked Joycelyn Elders, his highest-ranking health official, for advocating a place for masturbation within the national curriculum. This was in the interests of promoting safe sex, apparently. We were at the butt end of an irony today too. For most of this game we played superb, cultured football and yet we left empty-handed.

1. THE CALAMITOUS 1994/95 SEASON

It was a sour, grimy day with soiled clouds snagging on the tops of the Staffordshire hills. But the drizzle had ceased by the time we had parked in a soot-stained, terraced street adjacent to the Victoria Ground. It was not a place in which to dally. The over-officious police saw to it that we didn't, insisting that we enter the ground immediately upon arrival. Fortunately, the quality of the game exceeded the warmth of our welcome. The match was played at a bewildering pace with the ball zipping back and forth across the greasy surface. While Stoke City employed the direct route to goal, prompted by Peschisolido's pace and Örlygsson's vision, we played the more composed football, building patiently from the back with our defenders exchanging quick, precise passes with our midfielders and Gayle foraging dangerously down the middle. We oozed class and confidence in equal measure. A host of chances came and went at both ends but 'Big Bad John' missed the best of these. After half an hour Randall whipped over a sharp cross. Gaining improbable height, Heath headed down leaving Gayle with only Muggleton to beat. Alas, from just five yards' range, he could only prod the ball into the goalie's grateful hands. Marlon then had to be at his very best to palm away a thunderbolt from Carl Beeston to keep us level at the interval.

After the break, Stoke City became more dominant as we made the tactical error of trying to match them in the fast, direct stakes. However, the crucial 68th-minute goal proved to be an early Christmas gift from referee Wilkes. David Eyres was judged to have clipped Örlygsson's heels as the Icelandic midfielder powered into the area. The alleged offence was hardly clear-cut. But with advantage being played, Örlygsson still managed to evade Eyres's challenge and shoot, only for Marlon to make a comfortable, tumbling save. Referee Wilkes was not content with this and decided to double our punishment. Not only was a penalty awarded but Eyres was dismissed also.

Örlygsson gobbled down the offering, blasting the spot kick past Marlon. With ten-man Burnley fragmenting quickly in the face of this cruel adversity, Örlygsson added a second with just six minutes left. Still, it was a fine display. We returned home in hope even if we had fallen to 20th place.

Burnley 0 Middlesbrough 3
18 December 1994
'Play Dead'

Today was the 50th anniversary of the Battle of the Bulge. The Chechens recognised the occasion by furiously defying the Russian army in Grozny. Sadly, this afternoon we were unable to raise even a smidgen of resistance to the Middlesbrough steamroller, leaving us flattened in the Turf Moor mud and wishing we had spent the afternoon Christmas shopping.

The last time the Granada cameras came to Turf Moor, we were too sharp for Sheffield's Blades. On this bright Sunday afternoon, even our most partisan supporters could not deny that Bryan Robson's table-toppers trounced us. John Hendrie secured the man-of-the-match award on account of his hat-trick, but the guy who really filleted us was Alan Moore. For those who only saw his tepid performances in claret and blue, it might be difficult to grasp just how good Moore once was. In this game he was at the height of his considerable talent, shimmying this way and that, with a surge of acceleration here, a relaxed canter there, rarely losing possession, and always hunting for the killer pass, which he would deliver with pin-point accuracy and perfect weight. His mesmerising ball control was too much for our rookie left-back, Wayne Dowell. He had no idea how to track Moore let alone contain him, with the Irish winger ghosting past him on his right and slipping past him on his left. This humiliation could only end badly, and having received a soft early booking, Dowell was duly red-carded at the start of the second half, having done well to make any sort of contact with Moore. Jimmy Mullen should have substituted Dowell at the break. It must have been obvious that the youngster's frustration had him straining at the leash. Jimmy didn't and paid dearly for his poor judgement. Not that substitute left-back Parkinson had any more joy against the elusive Moore. Ex-Boro boss Lenny Lawrence had once lauded Moore as 'the new Ryan Giggs'. On today's showing this didn't seem to be slack hype. But as good as he was, this was not a one-man show. Boro had overwhelming pace and skill and with Robson pugnaciously controlling the midfield they had greater brute strength. After a few weeks' respite from relegation fears, the chill winds were returning. This defeat left us in 20th position, just one place above the drop zone. Four clubs were to be relegated this season to accommodate a reduction in the number of Premier League clubs. Burnley were in trouble.

Burnley v Port Vale (abandoned) 26 December 1994
'Unfinished Sympathy'

Weary with the blasphemous seasonal festivities, God trained his apocalyptic hose on the Boxing Day programme. Not that we had any cause to regret his petulance. Although McMinn had put us one up in the sixth minute with a swirling drive that skidded off the sodden surface, our visitors were better at aquaplaning, scoring twice in the 25th and 26th minutes with brutal shots that hissed past Beresford. To add to our woes, Dowell sustained a cruciate ligament injury, forcing us to revert to Parky as a makeshift left-back. Eventually the Canute-like referee Burns conceded defeat after Gerry Harrison had called for a life jacket to retrieve the ball from a Turf Moor lake the size of Coniston. The upshot of this no-show was that we fell into the relegation zone.

Derby County v Burnley (postponed)
27 December 1994
'Strawman'

After the Boxing Day deluge, the Baseball Ground was still awash. Postponement was inevitable. By 5pm we had dropped to third bottom, our lowest placing since mid-October.

Burnley 5 Southend United 1
31 December 1994
'Sparky's Dream'

The polar ice cap was creeping southward. The sun shone but spread little warmth. In the smarting northerly wind, there were whispers of snow. It was all too much for soft southerners Southend United. They took the briefest look at the proceedings before disappearing, gifting us our easiest and most comprehensive victory at this level in 11 years. Our cause was helped by a clash of colours, forcing the visitors to don our much-maligned jade and black kit. It was gratifying to see that it had lost none of its malevolent powers.

Jimmy had shored up his squad with two loan signings: much-travelled striker Andy Saville, from Birmingham City, and Nottingham Forest's young left-back Craig Armstrong. Both went straight into the team with Saville making an immediate impact. On the half-hour he latched on to Heath's superb through-ball and beat Southend keeper Sansome with a crisp drive. A few minutes later, 'Big Bad John' doubled our lead with a terrific scissor-kick. Heath was again the provider, clipping over a right-wing cross that Gayle converted with lithe perfection. It was as if he had been granted a Nureyev makeover.

If we had any fears that Southend would mount a stirring second-half recovery, we were quickly reassured. Gayle's shot was so far off target that an adjacent copper enquired whether it was lost. He needn't have bothered for Southend's defender Graham Brassington ushered the vagrant ball into the safety of

1. THE CALAMITOUS 1994/95 SEASON

the Southend net. So, with 50 minutes gone we were three up and surely home and dry. This was Jimmy Mullen's Burnley, though. We didn't do shut-outs. With 20 minutes left, 'Harry' Willis pulled a goal back and Hails should have added a second minutes later. But following the dismissals of Gerry Harrison and Gridelet for fighting, and Brassington for a professional foul on Saville, a Davis piledriver and a Robinson tap-in sealed an emphatic victory. We shot up to 19th place. Happy New Year!

Portsmouth 2 Burnley 0
2 January 1995
'The Narcotic Suite: 3 Kilos'

The Fratton sun shone from an unblemished sky, but merely mocked us with its ineptitude. I cannot remember ever feeling so cold at a game. We waddled onto the open terraces like stranded penguins on the edge of an ice floe, desperately in need of blubber infusions. We resorted to scalding plastic coffee cups as our hand-held braziers, while polar bears trundled by, growling about brass monkeys. Even with four layers of clothing on, the ice managed to penetrate our defences. It took a two-hour drive home with the car heating on full blast before our faces defrosted and we could shed a garment.

As we arrived at Fratton Park there was an icy sheen on half of the pitch shadowed by the main stand. Many fixtures had fallen victim to the merciless frost. Arguably, this game should have been postponed too. Referee Holbrook decided otherwise, causing Jimmy Mullen to lose it, just as we lost the game, a crucial six-pointer against one of our relegation rivals.

After half an hour Portsmouth's tricky midfielder, Preki, smacked in a sharp cross-shot that found goal via Marlon's far post. After 40 minutes we lost Marlon. Yet another kamikaze charge from goal was to blame. Having found himself well and truly stranded by his rush of blood he was forced to handle Gerry Creaney's lob while outside his area. Holbrook dismissed him.

Russell came on as substitute goalkeeper with Gerry Harrison making way. Craig Armstrong had to be replaced, too, following a clash of heads with Robbie Pethick. Burnley's number three shirt seemed jinxed.

We did put together a few attacking movements after the break and Pompey's veteran goalkeeper Alan Knight made excellent stops to thwart Saville, Eyres, and Davis. But we all knew the score, particularly Heath, who much to our embarrassment tried to persuade Holbrook to abandon the game. Whereas Jimmy had jumped up and down on the pitch like a demented cartoon character, to signify the lack of give in the surface, Heath went in for a grotesque imitation of figure skating. Holbrook remained unmoved, though. As for Portsmouth they experienced few problems with the slippery surface. As if to underline the point, Creaney finished us off four minutes before time when he turned in Pethick's low cross. Creaney nearly missed this game having been embroiled in a town-centre fight a few days before. Unfortunately for us, he recovered in the nick of time. A few years later he came to our aid as a loan signing from Manchester City, helping Chris Waddle's languishing side put a few vital points on the board. Here, he lifted Portsmouth above us, consigning us to 20th spot. For Burnley fans this was a perishing, pointless day carrying a salutary warning that global warming was not to be taken literally.

Notts County 3 Burnley 0
14 January 1995
'Basket Case'

Tuesday's home game against Charlton was washed out after a day of heavy rain so we resumed our league programme against bottom-placed County at a grey, soulless Meadow Lane. This time 3,000 Clarets travelled in good spirits, presuming that confidence had been restored after our spanking victory at Cambridge United in the FA Cup. As for the Magpies, they

1. THE CALAMITOUS 1994/95 SEASON

seemed entirely without hope despite appointing Howard Kendall as their new manager three days before our arrival. Normally, a change of manager lifts the mood of a struggling club but the home supporters I spoke with were not persuaded. One of them implored me: 'Please don't beat us. Everyone beats us. It's not nice. It makes us very, very unhappy.' Suddenly, I felt guilty, an absurd response given the paucity of our blessings. In any event I had no cause to fret for we tossed this match away with criminal negligence.

Marlon set us on the road to destruction after 50 minutes of dross. His error was to blast a back pass straight at the statuesque Devon White, whereupon the ball ricocheted over our goalkeeper's head and plopped into the net. It wasn't as if White had made himself a difficult target. Devlin and McSwegan then added to County's fortuitous lead by hanging around the Burnley defenders waiting for the next mistake. Had these Burnley players swapped places with 11 randomly selected fans, the result could not have been worse. At least there would have been commitment where there was none. Jimmy raged in his technical area, but he seemed as clueless as everyone else.

As we stuttered and spluttered to an inevitable defeat, Blackburn extended their lead at the top of the Premier League to five points, having put County's local rivals to the sword. Driving home, I could not bear to listen to the self-indulgent wailing and whining of *606*'s Premier League callers. As usual, they presumed they had a monopoly of suffering. We knew better. Today, we had been at Meadow Lane.

Burnley 1 Reading 2
21 January 1995
'On a Rope'

In Kobe, an earthquake measuring 7.2 on the Richter scale killed 2,700 people, nearly 20 per cent of the Japanese city's population.

Here, Labour leader Tony Blair yanked the tail of football's tiger economy, indicting Manchester United's new away strip as 'exploitation dressed as fashion'. Meanwhile, Portsmouth and Gillingham were the latest clubs to line up for handouts, having been put up for sale because of unsustainable debts. After today's sodden squib, we looked ready to join them. It had been a tempestuous journey up from London with the car buffeted by the gusting wind and relentless rain. Having arrived just before kick-off, we were given the worst possible welcome. In just ten minutes of play Burnley were two down, both goals the result of ruinous defensive errors. Parky's back pass to Wayne Russell left our reserve goalkeeper with a bit to do. With the ball bouncing awkwardly in the howling gale, and the muddy conditions causing slips, 'Rooster' made a hash of clearing the ball, allowing Nogan to intercept and score.

Just five minutes later, Winstanley gave the ball away in midfield. Mick Gooding instantly released Scott Taylor on the right. With no one to impede him, Taylor surged forward and smashed the ball in via the underside of the bar.

It took Jimmy Mullen 55 minutes to realise McMinn should replace inept Alan Harper. But having made the switch, the tide turned immediately. Reading's Viveash deflected a swirling Parkinson cross into his own net. McMinn and David Eyres spent the final 20 minutes tormenting Reading's full-backs, but the numerous chances they created were spurned. Winstanley's header crashed against the bar, Gooding scrambled Davis's effort off the line, and Gayle, on his last appearance for us, managed to miss an 'unmissable' opportunity. A pattern was set here to be stamped on each ensuing home game: soft, early goals would be conceded; heads would drop; Jimmy Mullen would angrily berate his players at half-time; a brief improvement, with a greater sense of urgency would follow, but always to no avail. Easy chances would be missed, and more soft goals conceded. A stirring home draw with Liverpool in the FA Cup temporarily defied this trend

1. THE CALAMITOUS 1994/95 SEASON

and lifted sunken spirits, but after playing courageously at Turf Moor and Anfield, the team reverted to type.

Burnley 1 Swindon 2
4 February 1995
'Black Star'

Jimmy Mullen thought that the brave performances against Liverpool signified that his side had turned a corner, remarking: 'We still have a very long way to go before the end of the season and I am sure that we are not going to have anything to worry about in the final analysis.' Oh really, Jimmy? Not even after this hapless, passionless defeat?

The sun shone but little else did. We managed to create just one scoring opportunity before half-time. Unfortunately, it fell to our loaned left-back Craig Armstrong, who blazed his hurried shot over the crossbar. Swindon had not caused us much anxiety, but with half-time almost upon us, ex-Blackburn striker Peter Thorne slid in Swindon's opening goal.

True to form, Jimmy had the team cranked up for an all-out assault after the break but with McMinn's dangerous crosses wasted, there was no breakthrough. And having soaked up almost continuous pressure for more than 20 minutes, Swindon suddenly broke quickly for Thorne to double his tally and seal the game. Gerry Harrison lashed in a goal with five minutes left, but despite some renewed biff and bosh, it was not enough. This was a disastrous defeat. Prior to this game, Swindon were one place and two points above us, while we occupied the final relegation slot. Not only did our loss leave us in 23rd place, we were also losing touch with our rivals. A week before, John Deary had been sold to Rochdale for £25,000. Gayle had also left after Jimmy agreed a £70,000 transfer fee with Stoke. Many of us felt that we could have done with him on this day. As for Saville, Jimmy declined to pay Barry Fry's absurd asking price of £200,000 and so the Birmingham striker returned to St Andrew's.

Watford 2 Burnley 0
11 February 1995
'Sorted for E's and Wizz'

If the stabbing, chilly rain wasn't bad enough, the enforced route-march around the allotments was bloody infuriating. Then there was the long queue at the few turnstiles still operating, but Burnley's limp performance was the final straw. This was yet another utterly feckless display. It was amazing that the score was still 0-0 at half-time, but thereafter Roeder's side seized control on the swampy surface with Ramage and Bazeley ramming home their advantage. They were so much in charge that they could afford to play the final 20 minutes with ten men – Payne was dismissed for two bookable offences. We had hoped that new loan signing Paul Stewart might give us greater strength up front, but we were told that he was not fit to play! It seemed incredible that we had shelled out big bucks for a loanee who was already injured. Watford's North Bank taunted us with: 'You're **** and you're going down!' We didn't bother to respond.

Burnley 0 Grimsby Town 2
18 February 1995
'Common People'

'No surrender to the IRA' hollered the Combat 18 hoodlums at Wednesday's 'friendly' football match between the Republic of Ireland and Northern Ireland in Dublin. Here these dissidents demolished both the Lansdowne Road seating and the match. No surrender to defeatism was Jimmy Mullen's cry in the *Lancashire Evening Telegraph*, urging the Burnley supporters to 'shout the house down' in our desperate search for salvation. Our catastrophic run had left us seven points adrift of safety. Only a victory today would do. Before the game, Lydia and I sat in a backstreet pub, mesmerised by the dust twirling in a shaft of pallid sunlight. Perhaps we had been hypnotised into coming. We had read Jimmy's impassioned pleas in the local press, knowing

1. THE CALAMITOUS 1994/95 SEASON

that repetitive messages seldom inspire, particularly in the face of relentless failure. Meanwhile the Prodigy's 'Firestarter' with its booming thunk-funk and whiplash 'yaaahs!' cranked up the volume on the pub juke box.

There was no need of stimulants, though. The fans were well pumped up for this one. As the teams appeared the roar was volcanic. The signature chants of 'No, Nay, Never' and 'Forever and Ever' boomed out, but the lack of reciprocity on the field quickly dissipated their intensity. The defence, deprived of the suspended Davis, was all over the place; the midfield was shackled and the attack toothless, although centre-forward Stewart denied any effective support from Eyres or McMinn, relied on his girth to put himself about. It came as no surprise when Grimsby's Mendonca rose unchallenged to meet a 25th-minute corner and bury his opportunity, leaving Marlon and Gerry Harrison to argue the toss. Instead of the impassioned war cry 'Jimmy Mullen's claret and blue army' there were hissed cries of 'Mullen out!'

Acrimonious arguments broke out between those fans still loyal to Mullen and his detractors. These heated arguments ran through the dregs of the first half and throughout an acerbic half-time, only interrupted by bouts of incensed booing of Jimmy as he left the field at the break and when he re-appeared 15 minutes later. One of the more reasonable critics argued: 'Mullen can't have it both ways. He accepts the praise for our promotions. Therefore, he must take the blame for our collapse. He's had funding. He's just wasted it. The board members need to get shot of him. The team is a shambles. He's a liability. We're going down 'cos of Mullen!'

What brought the argument to a halt was the team's renewed vigour. Despite his apparent failings, Jimmy Mullen was still capable of rousing his team. We proceeded to batter Grimsby with Eyres, Mullin and McMinn narrowly failing to find the target with good chances. Hoyland's goal-bound header was cleared off the line. But it was not enough. With just nine minutes remaining, Marlon fumbled Rodger's tame effort allowing Mendonca to steal a simple second. The euphoria we had experienced at Blundell Park was just a taunting memory.

Sheffield United 2 Burnley 0
21 February 1995
'Waking Up'

Tonight, Lydia and I listened to the updates from Bramall Lane. It was hard listening as Burnley equalled their worst run of league defeats in this century – seven, set a mere 90 years ago. In fairness, it seemed as if we had performed much better but were undone by two magnificent strikes from Nathan Blake – one just before half-time and the other in the final minute. However, a semblance of equality was just worthless consolation. We remained in 23rd spot.

Tranmere Rovers 4 Burnley 1
15 February 1995
'Sandpaper Kisses'

This game was a massive let-down after our board had sanctioned much-needed reinforcements. In came Kurt Nogan, a striker from Brighton, and Steve Thompson, a midfielder from Leicester. Their combined cost was £500,000. Not that the signings were greeted with universal joy. Nogan had a habit of scoring against us but had not scored for third-tier Brighton since October. And although Thompson was reputed to be a good passer, he seemed like a Ford Prefect in a Grand Prix. Both played at Tranmere but made so little impact they might have been better off sorting out their new homes. Tranmere pulverised Burnley in the Prenton Park mud. Even a 1-4 defeat did not adequately reflect their superiority or our wretchedness. Burnley's lack of a specialist left-back once again proved to be our undoing, with Tranmere's Thomas roasting the latest fall guy, Eyres. It was Thomas's 16th-

1. THE CALAMITOUS 1994/95 SEASON

minute right-wing cross that enabled a diving Ian Muir to head Tranmere into the lead, whereupon Tranmere found a myriad of holes in our suspect defence.

Miraculously, we staggered into half-time just one goal down. But within three minutes of the restart, Pat Nevin, in acres of space, slid in his side's second. Only Tranmere's profligacy saved us. Nevertheless, Muir and Aldridge added late goals while our solitary strike was a crazily deflected own goal. This time there was no chorus of disapproval. In fact, there was little response at all from our dazed supporters. Everyone was too deflated, too numb. We couldn't raise so much as a spark of anger, even at maligned loan signing Paul Stewart, who was, in fact, the last person to deserve it.

Many years later Stewart disclosed the traumatic abuse he had suffered as a young footballer, together with other victims. It was a stern message to me and hopefully to others that we need to be more thoughtful whenever tempted to damn others' failings. Admittedly, I have been a repeat offender in this respect. Thankfully, though, the impact of abuse is better understood now than it was 25 years ago, although there is still much room for improvement. Those like Paul Stewart who have bravely disclosed their abuse merit our understanding, compassion, and admiration.

Burnley 1 West Bromwich Albion 1
4 March 1995

'Screamager'

Barings Bank had collapsed and its rogue trader, Nick Leeson, had disappeared. But fortune made a sheepish return to Turf Moor this afternoon. With 89 minutes gone and hundreds of Baggies screeching for the final whistle, the less than predatory Robinson swivelled to meet Thompson's partially cleared corner. Catching the ball sweetly on the volley, he sent a sizzling shot into the top right corner of the net, helped by the slightest of deflections. We had seized a point at last – a deserved one, too, for we had pummelled

West Bromwich for most of the game. But what we couldn't escape was our familiar sloppiness. For this the Baggies made us pay. Andy Hunt had put his chance away earlier in the game, leaving us half an hour to salvage something from the wreckage. As we braved the blizzard on Manchester Road Station, urging our confounded, much-delayed train to appear, we could not take heart from the point saved. Given the extent of our deficit, we needed victories – lots of them. But Lydia and I were relieved we had chosen the train given the arctic weather on our return home.

Barnsley 2 Burnley 0
7 March 1995
'Melt'

Lydia and I followed this game on local radio. It was a disaster. Despite being well on top during the first half, our strikers, Nogan and Stewart, blew chance after chance. Worse still, by half-time we were not only a goal down, after referee Lynch awarded Barnsley a disputed goal, we were a man down, too, Stewart having been dismissed for his belligerent protest. Unusually, we didn't throw in the towel, with Adrian Randall surprisingly leading the charge. It was to no avail. David Eyres was denied a seemingly legitimate equaliser. Amid the ensuing protests, Parkinson 'lost it' pushing over ex-Claret Brendan O'Connell. Parkinson's dismissal followed. Barnsley's goalkeeper, Watson, then pulled down Burnley's Steve Davis as he rounded him, but there was no red card. It was clear we could not beat rough justice We were merely wasting time and energy, and who better than Andy Payton to rub that in with a minute to go. We felt cheated. At least our reinvigorated anger had flushed out our depression, but without any productive way of channelling this anger we were just left with a well-stoked engine that merely backfired. We were certainly not in the mood to appreciate the commentator's vivid description of Barnsley's supposed 'Tuscan hilltop'.

1. THE CALAMITOUS 1994/95 SEASON

Burnley 2 Oldham Athletic 1
11 March 1995
'You Oughta Know'

A relegation-haunted side may find wan solace in winter. Insulated by the cold with spring far away, there seems to be an abundance of time. But that first scent of rising sap, that first sniff of newly mown grass, reveals that the game is almost up. Shuffling through the park this afternoon that defining moment had arrived. It was now or never. We MUST beat Oldham.

John Major's run wasn't much better than ours. This week he lost his ninth minister since taking office in 1992. Five of them, including the latest casualty, Robert Hughes, had resigned because of personal indiscretions. Not a bad record for a government wedded to ethical cleansing.

At least Burnley made a better stab at 'back to basics' today. From the very start, they displayed desire, determination, and energy, and, from Hoyland, Randall, Thompson, and Vinnicombe, a measure of skill that had been absent since our December hibernation. We should have been out of sight by half-time. We had swarmed all over a bemused Oldham side. We even managed to secure an early lead when Nogan beat the offside trap, latching on to Steve Davis's long clearance. Despite being on the goal wagon for five months, Nogan showed considerable composure, outwitting Paul Gerrard before casually clipping the ball into the unguarded net. The roar that accompanied the goal was fed as much by disbelief as jubilation. We had scored first for the only time since New Year. It was good to know that we had finally renounced performance-retarding drugs.

Immediately after half-time, Oldham brought on Sean McCarthy, reminding us, as if we needed reminding, that there was unfinished business after his disgraceful antics in the away fixture. McCarthy was determined to inflict more pain, though, and within a minute of making his appearance he had successfully lobbed Marlon for an equaliser. The fact that

McCarthy appeared to be a mile offside added to our disgust, but heads didn't drop. Urged on by the increasingly shrill and frantic Longside, our lads pushed on relentlessly but chance after chance was spurned, with Nogan the worst culprit. Then, with 15 minutes left, Nogan broke free on the right and centred low for Eyres to push the ball into the path of inrushing Vinnicombe. Without hesitation, our belatedly restored left-back smacked the ball past Gerrard from 20 yards, the ball barely rising more than an inch or two as it crashed into the net. Turf Moor erupted in frenzied delight. 'Get me that league table, NOW!' It did little to assure us, though. We were still bottom.

Derby County 4 Burnley 0
15 March 1995
'Tonight, Tonight'

The Gang of Four declaimed, 'Please give us evenings and weekends!' After this fiasco, our fans should have settled for a warm fire. I pitied our faithful following, incarcerated in the decrepit Baseball Ground, three down in a blinding blizzard with 35 minutes of neuralgia still to endure, with the home fans bellowing 'You're sh** and you're going down!' Marco Gabbiadini then had the utter heartlessness to stick in a fourth just as the referee decided that our fans had had enough. Why can't football teams be allowed to declare? No, Gang of Four, 'Please give us unending workdays!' For once, Lydia and I decided we were better off at home.

Bristol City 1 Burnley 1
18 March 1995
'Shame about Ray'

Ronnie Kray died yesterday. The notorious East End gangster had been serving a life sentence for killing Jack 'the Hat' McVitie with his twin brother, Reggie. As for Reggie, he was treated to tea, biscuits, and sympathy with his old muckers, 'Mad'

1. THE CALAMITOUS 1994/95 SEASON

Frankie Fraser and Charlie Richardson, prompting *The Mirror* to headline 'I could murder a McVitie.'

Jimmy Mullen looked as if he could murder Kurt 'the Flounce' Nogan at Ashton Gate today. Nogan reacted to his substitution by having a public paddy before assistant manager Clive Middlemass ushered him into the dugout. A Burnley fan next to me remarked: 'It's alarming to find we have just shelled out £300,000 on a toddler.'

But it was easier to understand why Bristol were in the mire with us. Junior Bent apart, they were awful. Bent had spent a brief loan period with us when Frank Casper was in charge. His pace and skill sparkled amid the sun-drenched trash. Bent was too much for our bewildered Chris Vinnicombe, who hauled the winger down as he closed in on goal, earning an immediate dismissal. We even tossed Bristol a gift goal after just 12 minutes, when Russell, replacing the out-of-sorts Beresford, slammed a clearance against Scott Partridge's legs, causing the ball to ricochet into the Burnley goal. But Bristol's goalie, Keith Welch, returned the favour in the 65th minute when he spilled Randall's innocuous effort allowing Eyres to slam in the equaliser. It was Eyres's first goal in open play this season. How different to the previous year when time after time he would arrive at the near post on cue to smash in promotion-winning goals. The rest of the game petered out in a morass of mediocrity that even Bent could not evade. It was obvious why City's gates had fallen below 7,000 if this was what was on offer. Of course, it was good to grab our first away point since November but we couldn't get over the conviction that richer pickings had been missed.

Burnley 2 Luton Town 1
21 March 1995
'Release'

A Sunderland fan said on *Premier Passions*, a reality show about the Wearsiders' relegation season: 'Nothing hurts so much as lingering hope.' Perhaps that's why I refrain from such hope, never looking 'on the bright side of life'. I am an inveterate pessimist, believing that the best way to sucker an unwelcome fate is to imagine the worst outcome, given that so many awful experiences occur when they are least expected. Alice Walker wrote: 'Expect nothing. Live frugally on surprise.' Using her mantra, the unsuspected highs are all the more ecstatic while the predictable failures are less hurtful. With seven minutes left, Gerry Harrison lashed in what proved to be our winner, turning this incredibly tense game on its head. Gerry's effort came just ten minutes after John Mullin's cool equaliser. God knows, we'd done enough to win several games with the intensity of our second-half pressure, but it didn't look as if it would happen. Then out of the darkness, came not one but two shafts of light. But oh, the agony of counting down the bloody clock!

Wolverhampton Wanderers 2 Burnley 0
24 March 1995
'Won't Back Down'

Pushing his ever-intrusive microphone into the face of a startled Demi Moore, Dennis Pennis enquired: 'If it wasn't gratuitous in any way and tastefully done, would you ever consider keeping your clothes on in a movie?' We, too, were tired of our team's naked exposure, particularly on our travels. Having said that, the midweek home victory over Luton had lifted us off the bottom. But arriving at Molineux on this Friday night was like blundering bleary-eyed into an impossibly late re-showing of *The Stud*. Not that I had first-hand experience, of course. Similarly, with only a weary melancholy providing the anaesthetic, we were confined to sullen, slumped immobility as Wolves played out their usual script. Yes, Steve Bull blatantly handled the ball in the 11th minute before prodding it past Russell and yes, Stowell was lucky to deflect Eyres's shot against the post. But you can't beat predestination. Neil Emblen proved that when he thumped Wolves into an unassailable 2-0 lead on the hour. Paul Shaw, our new loan signing from Arsenal, defied the odds brightly after being introduced as a second-half substitute for the drooping Robinson, but, of course, it made no difference.

Burnley 4 Port Vale 3
28 March 1995
'Misty in Roots'

A nerve gas attack on the Tokyo subway had killed ten people and injured 5,500 others, Mike Tyson was released from jail having served three years for rape while Imelda Marcos, still on bail following her conviction for corruption, campaigned to be elected to the Filipino Congress presumably sponsored by Gucci. At home, Eric Cantona appealed successfully against his jail sentence having been convicted for his kung fu assault upon a Palace supporter. In full tilt *Being and Nothingness* mode, Cantona announced: 'When the seagulls follow the trawler, it is because they think sardines will be thrown into the sea.' Gordon Strachan retorted: 'If a Frenchman goes on about seagulls, trawlers and sardines, he's called a philosopher. I'd just be called a short Scottish bum talking crap.'

Tonight, we replayed the abandoned Boxing Day fixture with Port Vale. For 40 minutes we were treated to another washout. This time the victim was quality. The game was moribund, leaving the 10,000 or so supporters with little option but to talk among themselves. Then, out of the grey, Martin Foyle found enough space to crack in the opening goal for Port Vale. It was the catalyst we needed – on and off the pitch. With the Longside finding its collective voice, Gerry Harrison sallied forth on the right and, having cut inside his marker, he managed to slide a perfectly weighted pass into Nogan's path. This time 'Kurt the shirt' did not let us down. In his short stay with us, he had become better known for his sulky skills than for his finishing. But here he was positive, muscling in between the bruising Vale defenders and poking the ball past Musselwhite. With the half-time whistle about to be blown, we were unexpectedly back in the hunt.

We expected a rabid, raging second-half assault on the Vale goal. For 15 minutes we saw nothing of the sort. Then, out of the junk came a moment of sublime skill. Steve Thompson played Adie Randall in with the archetypical defence-splitting pass. Adie grasped the opportunity, waltzing around Musselwhite and clipping the ball home. Six minutes later we were, incredibly, 4-1 up. First Paul Shaw punished a poor clearance from Musselwhite and then Vale defender Bradley Sandeman slid Nogan's cross into his own net. However, instead of closing the game down, we went in search of further goals. The only beneficiaries were Port Vale as Martin Foyle and Joe Allon netted late goals giving us an almighty fright. Thankfully, we rode our luck and held on to the points, but it was too damn close for comfort.

Burnley 1 Millwall 2
1 April 1995
'Fuckin' Up'

How the hell did we lose this? We won 12 corners in the first half alone, while Millwall hardly managed a shot. Well, that's not strictly true. Ex-Manchester City striker David Oldroyd did get one shot away in the 38th minute and it counted. After the break, it was more of the same. We attacked. Millwall defended. Thanks to Millwall's US keeper, Kasey Keller, who was in breathtaking form, we continued to fire a succession of blanks, whereas Oldroyd had one more chance and again he tucked it in. Paul Shaw did finally breach the Lions' back line with 15 minutes to go but, despite throwing everything at the visitors' defence, we couldn't repeat the trick.

1. THE CALAMITOUS 1994/95 SEASON

Burnley 2 Charlton Athletic 0
4 April 1995
'Stupid Girl'

Heavy fighting had broken out once more near Tuzla in northern Bosnia. Meanwhile, baby Irma, the severely injured Bosnian child who symbolised Sarajevo's suffering, died in Great Ormond Street Hospital. Kenny Everett died today, too, having lost his fight against AIDS. But Charlton arrived at Turf Moor with no stomach for any fight. They simply laid down and mercifully capitulated, helped by two well-taken goals, the first from David Eyres in the 24th minute, with a towering header, and the second from Paul Shaw, in the 81st minute, with a poacher's special. Burnley immediately rose two places to 21st spot. We still had to play Portsmouth and Sunderland, two of our relegation rivals, at home and our next opponents, Southend, were the weakest side we had played this season. Not over yet? Not by a long chalk.

Southend United 3 Burnley 1
8 April 1995
'Back for Good'

Expectation was unaccountably high. What's more there was none of the customary pre-match churning and yearning. We felt relaxed and confident. Perhaps it was prompted by this warm day's hazy languor or the listless whisperings of a spring-scented breeze. More probably it was the product of the excellent lunchtime ale that we quaffed in immoderate quantities while seated underneath a gently swaying basket of polyanthus. The more we drank the more certain our conviction became. We were well overdue an away victory. But then the game started. Or at least Southend did. Within six minutes we were two down and almost certainly out. It was all too much for one of our drinking companions. With the Clarets' apoplectic anger subsiding into a brooding silence, he lurched to his feet, the ludicrously tight seating propping him up like a tottering El Cid. Taking a few seconds to recover a stray faculty or two, he broke into 'My Way', although his command of scale was less certain than his choice of verse. It went something like this, more Sid Vicious than Frank Sinatra, climaxing with: 'HE did it HIS way; the JIMMY MULLEN way; the F***ING relegation way.'

Jimmy Mullen's initial crime today was to ask young Chris Brass to man-mark Southend's Ronnie Whelan, the former Liverpool and Republic of Ireland international. Surely, the more experienced and highly industrious Robinson would have been a better choice? Two years later Brassy would cover himself in glory in nullifying Steve McManaman in an FA Cup tie. But on this day, he was still learning his craft and was well out of his depth. It was humiliating to watch Whelan give Brass the slip time and again. Of course, it was Jimmy's misfortune that he had lost Steve Thompson to a training-ground injury, particularly when Thompson was beginning to show some form, bringing the best out of fellow midfielder Adie Randall. Deprived of his mentor, Randall shrivelled. Consequently, we hardly managed a strike on goal during a thoroughly sour first half.

Within 11 minutes of the start of the second half, we were three down, having granted Southend's Tony Battersby space of prairie-like proportions. Jimmy Mullen responded by pulling off Paul Shaw, who had scored in each of the last three games, replacing him with the 'Incredible Sulk', who'd managed one goal in 11 starts. A cacophonous chorus of 'Mullen out' ensued. In fairness, Kurt doubled his tally with eight minutes to go, unleashing a rasping volley that fizzed past Simon Royce in the Southend goal. Kurt's effort probably owed as much to pique as technique, but it made no impact upon the result. We had lost … badly. The significance of the defeat was rammed home 15 minutes later. Stuck in a seafront traffic jam and staring dolefully at the sparkling sea, we received the news that all our rivals had triumphed. Not only had we dropped a place but also the gap between our position and safety had grown to a yawning six points.

1. THE CALAMITOUS 1994/95 SEASON

Burnley 3 Derby County 1
15 April 1995
'Where It's At'

Leftist teachers jostled David Blunkett, Labour's education spokesman, at the National Union of Teachers conference in Blackpool. Around 40 miles away, Burnley upset smug, well-heeled promotion contenders Derby County. Their sunny victory matched the balmy weather. This time Jimmy Mullen's tactics were on the money. Philliskirk was restored as target man, accompanied by Paul Shaw, and served by two wide-men, Eyres and McMinn. Philliskirk's selection caused initial consternation among the unforgiving Longsiders, but not for long. Within 12 minutes, Philly had made the most of McMinn's astute pass and pulled the ball back for Eyres to scramble home the opening goal. Seven minutes later we were two up with Philly again providing the decisive service. This time he nodded down Randall's cross for Paul Shaw to crack in his fourth goal for the club.

This irked the travelling Rams big time. They had come in their thousands for this Easter Saturday jolly, expecting a simple victory to boost their play-off challenge. With no booze to soften the blow they turned to sour grapes. 'You're s*** and you're going down,' they chanted. We retorted: 'We're s*** and we're beating you', which sealed the puerile argument. Not for Derby's Craig Short, though. Within minutes of scoring, Shaw was felled by Short's forearm smash. Short's stay was ... well, short.

Trollope did give us a momentary fright when, in the 68th minute, he pulled a goal back, but within two minutes Davis had restored our two-goal advantage when he headed in McMinn's free kick. Davis was outstanding, proving that his new skinhead look had not shorn him of his powers. A Samson in reverse, indeed. As perked as we were by this inspirational victory, we knew that we needed much more. The surreal half-time entertainment was a skirmish between a host of club mascots. As stupid as this contest was the mascots showed more fight than Burnley did when they visited Port Vale in their next fixture.

Port Vale 1 Burnley 0
17 April 1995
'Ready or Not'

Iran had banned the use of TV satellite dishes, announcing that American TV programme *Baywatch* was a corrupting influence. However, even watching the execrable *Baywatch* was preferable to watching this wretched defeat in the Burslem rain. It was yet another no-show on the road. We never came to grips with the Vale Park mud or our muscular hosts. When Robin van der Laan flicked his shot over Beresford's dive to give the Valiants a 40th-minute lead, none among us held any conviction that we would turn it around.

Burnley 1 Portsmouth 2
22 April 1995
'Down to Zero'

Jimmy Mullen had trotted out the tired catechisms about not accepting relegation until it was a mathematical certainty. Well, on this bitter day of swirling wind and rain, the speculation ended. Quite simply, Burnley had to beat struggling Portsmouth to give themselves the remotest chance of salvation. Ultimately, they went down fighting but that was immaterial. Eyres's 81st-minute effort was irrelevant. By that time, Portsmouth had already scored twice with a Durnin penalty nine minutes before the break and a Kit Symons breakaway 16 minutes after. The only fact that mattered was that we had lost, and that the damning R initial was placed against our inadequate points record. On the other hand, Portsmouth saved themselves with this hard-fought victory. Our punishment did not end there. Lydia, I, and many other London Clarets had to endure the drunken crowing of 'Pompey Chimes' all the way to Euston.

1. THE CALAMITOUS 1994/95 SEASON

Now that our fate was sealed, the all-too-brief promotion seemed to be just a huge, wasted opportunity.

The final two games were meaningless affairs: 1-1 draws against Sunderland and Bolton respectively. Not that our opponents saw them as such. Sunderland supporters turned up at Turf Moor in droves to celebrate their team's late escape from the drop, while Bolton's fans partied having secured a play-off place. This would ultimately lead to their promotion to the Premier League after a switchback victory over Reading at Wembley.

To add to our woes, our demise coincided with Blackburn's crowning success, their first and, so far, only Premier League title. The gnawing jealousy this provoked ensured that neither the board of directors nor Jimmy was left with any hiding place. In fairness, the board had made over £1.3m available for transfer fees; a considerable sum for a club that had survived a financial holocaust only eight years before. Moreover, Port Vale, Southend, Oldham, Luton, and Grimsby had survived without spending nearly as much. As for Reading, another club that did not splash the cash, they thrived, narrowly failing to win a Premier League place.

The problem was that Jimmy had not used his funds effectively. More prominent Burnley managers have also found difficulty in attracting targeted players to Turf Moor, but this did little to indemnify Jimmy against the increasingly hostile recriminations of Burnley supporters. His player selections and choice of tactics were frequently questioned too. The simple truth, though, was that his Burnley side were not good enough. Vinnicombe's enforced absence was not covered adequately. The midfield lacked pace, creativity, and bite while the attack did not have enough sting or power. Added to this, Beresford's errors probably lost Burnley almost as many games as he saved. Only Steve Davis stood out as our one consistent performer of pedigree and by the end of this campaign, the weight of responsibility began to hang heavily upon his considerable shoulders.

2. BACKS AGAINST THE WALL 1995 TO 1999

At the start of the 1995/96 season, club chairman Frank Teasdale had two priorities: ground reconstruction and a swift return to the First Division – now known as the Championship. The former entailed the demolition of both the beloved Longside and the Bee Hole End terracing, replacing both with all-seated stands. The Longside was the first to go, with demolition starting in October 1995. I went up alone to the 'Farewell to the Longside' ceremony as Lydia was understandably spending more time with her friends in London.

This was supposed to be a memorable afternoon. It wasn't. The game was awful, a ragged 2-1 victory over insipid Hull City. Mercifully, the sun shone brightly but most of us stood around feeling flat while the lunchtime beer soured in our bellies. The huge cost of ground reconstruction was partially offset by a Football League grant, earned by Burnley's one-year stay in the First Division.

Frank Teasdale still backed Jimmy Mullen. After Steve Davis departed to Luton for a fee of £750,000, Mullen was allowed to bring in Peter Swan from Plymouth for £200,000 to replace him. Hard man Swan had previously played for Leeds, Hull, and Port Vale. He could play up front or in central defence, which was his preferred position. He tackled with shuddering intensity and headed with visceral power but was often vulnerable against

2. BACKS AGAINST THE WALL 1995 TO 1999

swifter, more nimble opponents. He took his place as centre-half in Mullen's 5-3-2 formation in which Parkinson and Vinnicombe operated as wing-backs.

Despite Teasdale's continuing faith in Mullen, the Burnley manager was still a target for the boo boys, even after Burnley scrambled into fourth spot in early December. With Lydia no longer my regular travelling companion I went by train to several home games in late summer and autumn. Andrew and I even ventured west to Swansea in December to watch a crazy 4-2 victory, while Lydia and I went to Bournemouth (2-0), Stockport (0-0), and Peterborough (2-0) before all three of us met at a freezing Turf Moor just before Christmas, when Bristol City were the stunned visitors.

This game was as stultifying as the arctic weather and unsurprisingly ended as a 0-0 draw. While it was good to see Burnley win six out of the nine games I saw before New Year, losing none, it was apparent that this was a flawed team largely carried by Nogan's goals.

After a topsy-turvy 4-3 victory over Stockport on 13 January 1996, Burnley's precipitous fall began. By 2 March, a 0-1 home defeat by Blackpool reduced Burnley to 16th position. Jimmy had already resigned in February following a nasty confrontation with supposed fans in a local restaurant. Adrian Heath was the popular choice as his replacement, a preference which the Burnley board endorsed. By this time Burnley had parted with former stalwarts Pender, Deary, Davis, Randall, Philliskirk, and McMinn, while Francis, still troubled by his Wembley injury, had played his final game, as had Mullen's last signing, centre-forward Ian Helliwell. Among Burnley's promising young prospects were centre-forward Andy Cooke, wide midfielders Paul Weller and Paul Smith, plus full-back Chris Brass. But sadly, John Mullin elected to move to Sunderland for a £40,000 fee.

Bristol City 0 Burnley 1
9 March 1996
'Would'

Adrian Heath's first game in charge was at a sunny Ashton Gate. Fans' expectations of Heath seemed absurdly high. Many believed he would immediately turn around Burnley's flagging fortunes. His inaugural team selection comprised: Marlon Beresford in goal; Gary Parkinson and Chris Vinnicombe as full-backs; Mark Winstanley and Gerry Harrison in central defence; Warren Joyce and Steve Thompson in central midfield; Paul Weller and Paul Smith as wide midfielders; and Kurt Nogan and David Eyres in attacking roles, with Eyres having licence to roam.

Bristol City had been relegated from Division One along with Burnley and were also having difficulty in making an impact in the lower division. But here they sensed an opportunity to overturn the Clarets, given the parlous state of the club following Mullen's departure, as demonstrated by their barren New Year run. Bristol City began this game on the front foot, pressing Burnley into defending deeply. With the Clarets suffering a crisis of confidence, they had extreme difficulty in progressing beyond their half-way line. The Burnley faithful were alarmed at the sight of the Bristol City attackers repeatedly bearing down on Beresford's goal. With the Burnley defenders resorting to hoof ball, Bristol City found it easy to sustain this pressure, gobbling up the loose balls and launching further attacks. Nogan was utterly isolated up front, not helped by the absence of Eyres, who was preoccupied with troubleshooting at the other end. Incredibly, Burnley were still level at half-time.

Heath realised he needed to replace Smith, who had been nullified by City's greater experience and strength. On came Liam Robinson in his place, ostensibly to provide more beef in midfield and to lend support to the isolated Nogan. However, the second half was no better than the first. Only Bristol

City's wayward shooting prevented them from establishing an overwhelming lead. Somehow, Burnley survived, with a combination of agricultural defending and outrageous fortune.

Then, with six minutes left, Nogan was finally presented with a ball that he could profitably chase. With his predatory instincts undimmed by 84 minutes of frustrations, he homed in on the opportunity, only for his first touch to let him down, inducing him to handle the bouncing ball to bring it under his control. Benefitting from his illicit manoeuvre, he rounded the advancing goalie and slammed the ball into the net. Having had a clear view of what had happened, we expected the goal to be disallowed. So did the Bristol City fans. But amazingly the referee pointed to the centre spot. We were non-plussed, some beginning to doubt what they had seen. A spatter of uncertain cheers broke out, which were instantly drowned by the angry booing of the home fans. Their furious chants of 'Cheat! Cheat! Cheat!' were bellowed at the celebrating Nogan and the referee. Heath immediately replaced battling Gerry Harrison with Jamie Hoyland to see out the game. It was daylight robbery, causing Lydia and me to be shame-faced when we met our Bristol City-supporting friends after the game. One of them was so angry he could not bring himself to talk with us.

Burnley 2 Shrewsbury Town 1
4 May 1996

'Let Me Entertain You'

It seemed as if we had exhausted a season's worth of luck at Bristol, for six of the ensuing eight games ended in defeat. Promotion-bound Oxford thrashed us 0-5, after strapping substitute Paul Moody pulverised us with a nine-minute hat-trick. A week later Wycombe Wanderers hammered us 1-4, leaving Burnley stuck in 18th position. But possibly our worst humiliation was suffered at Brighton. The Seagulls were in disarray, faced with the prospect of extinction, with their Goldstone Ground sold from underneath them and no alternative in sight. And yet this financially ravaged, relegation-destined club proved too good for Burnley (0-1).

On 13 April, Heath finally won his second game in charge. He had good reason to feel grateful to restored Peter Swan, for it was his bullet header in the 66th minute that gave Burnley victory over visiting Peterborough. Swan also helped Burnley seize a point at Notts County, again with a firm header. Reinforced also by short-term signing Charlie Bishop, Burnley became harder to beat. This was evident in the 0-0 draw at champions elect Swindon on 17 April, a game watched by Lydia and me. Much to our surprise, the Clarets displayed outstanding tenacity in snatching this vital point. Although this was insufficient to lift them out of the relegation zone it seemed that this team could still save itself.

Despite suffering a disappointing 0-1 home defeat by Bristol Rovers on 23 April, Burnley claimed safety after they unexpectedly triumphed 2-0 at Wrexham. A spectacular goal from almost-forgotten Liam Robinson set up this victory, confirmed by Kurt Nogan's goal shortly after the interval. On the same day, relegation rivals Carlisle were crushed 0-4 at Wycombe, watched happily by me. Consequently, Carlisle slid into 20th position while we leapt over them.

Lydia and I had already booked a trip to Turf Moor on 4 May for what we had sensed would be a relegation decider. Although Burnley's safety had been assured, we still went, basking pleasantly in the spring sunshine seated in the newly opened Longside stand. Here, we had glorious views of the surrounding moors. For an end-of-season game with nothing at stake, this proved to be a worthy contest. Weller excelled with his twinkling footwork and penetrative pace, also scoring a fine opening goal in the 14th minute. Not to be outdone Winstanley secured 17th place with a sensational winner in the 77th minute.

2. BACKS AGAINST THE WALL 1995 TO 1999

Heath's first full season in charge was a more upbeat affair. The 1996/7 campaign began at scorching Luton, where first-half goals from Thompson and Nogan were sufficient to ensure a winning start, although we were indebted to a late penalty save by Beresford. Burnley then beat Walsall at home, also by 2-1, to claim top spot. Nogan was again on target. But subsequent results were frustratingly erratic. Heath was permitted to purchase another proven goalscorer, Paul Barnes of Birmingham City, for a club record fee of £400,000. Although Barnes remained goalless in his first eight games, on 5 October he scored all five goals in a 5-2 home victory over Stockport County. He became the first Burnley player to score five in one game since Andy Lochhead in the mid-sixties.

It seemed as if the Barnes–Nogan pairing was the best strike force in the division, and yet there was never a time when they both scored in the same match. The 22-year-old target man Andy Cooke, a bargain £40,000 signing from Newtown, appeared to be a better foil for either player. Nogan then became embroiled in a row with Heath over a new contract, believing he was worth more than he was being paid. After being demoted to the reserves, Nogan moved to Preston for a cut-price fee of £150,000, half his purchase value. Nogan had scored 33 goals in 87 league starts for Burnley. This seemed poor business. Liam Robinson and Steve Thompson also left at the end of this season as free agents. Neither Vinnicombe nor Winstanley attracted a fee either, when they left in the following seasons. This meant that only £150,000 was recovered from the £1.1m spent on these five players, an inexcusable waste of resources.

Nevertheless, Burnley maintained a play-off challenge for most of the 1996/97 campaign. Gillingham (5-1) and Peterborough (5-0) were put to the sword with Barnes and Cooke scoring freely. Impressive victories were achieved over champions elect Bury (3-1) and promotion-chasing Wrexham (2-0). But it was successive away victories at high-riding

Brentford (3-0) and Walsall (3-1) in March which suggested that Burnley might grab a play-off place. It was not to be. Four out of the next five games were lost, with the disgraceful 0-5 defeat at Wycombe the worst of these. Jamie Hoyland attributed the collapse in form to the departure of Heath's running mate John Ward, explaining: 'John was a superb coach. It was he who got us playing as well as we did that season. When he left towards the end of the season to take over the managerial position at Bristol City, we lost our main tactician and organiser. Adrian was a good man-manager, but it was Ward who had the ideas to make things tick on the field.'

A season which had promised much ultimately delivered little. Even a brave display against Liverpool in the FA Cup resulted in a 0-1 defeat, despite a fine performance from young Chris Brass as Steve McManaman's marker. Adrian Heath concluded: 'I honestly thought we could be looking at automatic promotion come April. But it's fallen far short of my expectations. Our lack of consistency has cost us all season. We probably have the worst record against the bottom five sides. The likes of Peterborough, Rotherham and York have been a thorn in our side. The top sides have managed maximum points against these sides, yet we have managed just four. I recognised we had a few problems in the make-up of the squad, and I thought I could work through them as the season progressed. But these re-surfaced and probably accounted for our inconsistency.'

What Heath was referring to here were the contractual disputes he had with Beresford and Nogan, which left him at loggerheads with both players. Heath admitted that this had been particularly difficult because they were former team-mates and, in Beresford's case, a previous roommate, too. He also felt compelled to drop Peter Swan for what he considered to be a 'poor attitude' although he later restored him after a successful heart-to-heart discussion.

Heath confessed to a national journalist that making the transition from player to manager was tougher than he envisaged, regretting the loss of dressing room banter and high jinks. He said, rather sadly, 'Whenever I enter the dressing room now it just goes quiet.' He also found just 'how bloody infuriating footballers can be', citing his frustration at their inexplicable inconsistency. He illustrated this by referring to a home defeat by York, saying: 'After having a great week of training, the players did not perform on the day. When it came to the match, I could have picked 11 people off the street who'd have given York a better game.'

Heath left at the end of the season to become Howard Kendall's assistant at Everton. Burnley were forced to find a replacement.

To our amazement, the club announced that Chris Waddle was to be the new boss. Waddle arrived at the club in a blaze of publicity. He brought with him ex-QPR and Newcastle centre-back Glenn Roeder as his assistant, plus former Aston Villa and England midfielder Gordon Cowans and ex-Norwich and England goalkeeper Chris Woods as coaches. Expectations soared. Many of us believed Waddle could emulate Bryan Robson's feats at Middlesbrough and restore Burnley to the top flight. Once again, those hopes were completely fallacious.

Although the club no longer had the resources Jimmy Mullen had benefitted from, chairman Teasdale provided Waddle with more than £700,000 for team strengthening. Regrettably, it was wasted on three players who did not improve the squad.

Burnley made a dreadful start to the 1997/98 season, failing to score in their first six league fixtures and not recording a league victory until their 11th game, in mid-October. Even Waddle's presence failed to provide the openings upon which Barnes and Cooke could thrive. The arrival of Gerry Creaney, on loan, prompted an immediate upturn in form. He scored eight goals in nine starts. However, the board were not prepared to offer the ex-Celtic, Portsmouth, and Manchester City striker a permanent contract. Chris Waddle was disappointed, recognising how much Creaney had improved his labouring side. But having blown his transfer budget on defenders Steve Blatherwick and Lee Howey, and midfielder Mark Ford, he was in no position to persuade the Burnley board to loosen their purse strings once more. He maintained, however, that the directors' aversion to Creaney was because of his alleged drinking habits. Whatever the truth was, once Creaney returned to Maine Road another barren spell followed.

Given the absence of creativity, it seemed perverse that Waddle should ignore the merits of 22-year-old right-winger Glen Little, for whom Heath had correctly predicted a bright future. Little recalled: 'I was totally bombed out. The only people who knew why were Waddle and Roeder. Waddle didn't even speak to me for three months. I never trained with the first team.' Eyres fell out with Waddle too and was transferred to Preston while Beresford's days were numbered, moving on to Middlesbrough in early March 1998 with coach Chris Woods taking over in goal.

Nevertheless, emerging youngsters Chris Brass and Paul Weller were given the opportunity to build upon the start that Heath had given them as first-team regulars. Paul Smith fared less well with the change of management, playing only sporadically.

After Creaney left, Burnley lost 1-2 at Millwall and 1-4 at Grimsby but their biggest humiliation was suffered in a 0-3 loss at home against Rotherham in an FA Cup replay. This dismal display was shown on national TV. Four days later, on 29 November, Andrew and I drove through fog and ice to watch Burnley come from behind to beat promotion contenders Northampton 2-1, thereby lifting themselves out of the relegation zone for the first time in 19 games.

2. BACKS AGAINST THE WALL 1995 TO 1999

Suitably re-invigorated, Andrew and I then travelled to Bristol City for a midweek fixture on 2 December. Barnes gave Burnley the lead on the half-hour with a blistering drive sending us into the half-time break buzzing. We should have known better. After the resumption, Shaun Goater led a series of ruthless counter-attacks with the Robins surging into a 3-1 lead. Burnley did not win any of the next four league games. The nadir was reached after a 0-2 defeat at Gillingham on 3 January. This loss left Waddle's men in bottom place. It was misfiring Paul Barnes's last game for the Clarets. Waddle transferred him to Huddersfield in exchange for excluded Andy Payton. This deal brought the Padiham-born striker back to the club he still loved despite being rejected by them as a youngster. It was an astute swap which benefitted Burnley much more than Huddersfield. Whereas Barnes netted twice in 30 league appearances for the Terriers, Payton scored 69 league goals in 115 starts for the Clarets. Not only did Payton help Burnley evade relegation in 1997/98 and 1998/99, his 27 goals in 1999/2000 powered them to automatic promotion.

The turning point in Burnley's fortunes came on 10 January when champions elect Watford were the visitors. On a bright afternoon and a heavy surface, Waddle decided to play himself, providing two inviting crosses which Cooke gleefully buried, to the delight of 9,000 Clarets fans. Despite a narrow loss at Bristol Rovers, the unexpected 2-0 victory over Watford inspired a brief run of success. Andy Payton scored on debut, enabling Burnley to defeat Southend 1-0. He also scored against York City, who were decimated 7-2 with Cooke claiming a hat-trick. Then, most satisfying of all, Preston were beaten 3-2 at Deepdale with maligned defender Neil Moore scoring the winner in the 90th minute.

These successes lifted Burnley out of the relegation zone. But then another seven-game barren run followed, dumping them back in the drop zone. Yet, in the final stretch, Burnley suddenly found their mojo, beating four promotion contenders – Grimsby, Northampton, Bristol City, and Fulham – with Payton scoring crucial goals in each game. But safety was not confirmed. On 2 May Burnley faced Plymouth Argyle at home in the last game of the season. The Clarets were in a perilous position. They needed to beat relegation rivals Plymouth, and hope that Bristol Rovers beat Brentford, otherwise they would return to the basement they had left under Jimmy Mullen six years before.

Burnley 2 Plymouth Argyle 1
2 May 1998
'High'

Andrew, Lydia, and I drove up from London to watch this dog-fight, which 18,811 fans attended, many from Plymouth. This attendance figure was almost twice the average home gate for that season. As the Plymouth manager Mick Jones rightly said: 'It was like a bear pit out there.' Gerry Harrison played in Burnley's defence on that nerve-shredding afternoon. His never-say-die attitude and willingness to give his all for the cause had played a critical part in Burnley's recovery during the second half of this season.

Gerry recalled when interviewed for a later match programme, 'It was out of our hands after we drew 3-3 at Oldham in midweek. We had been 3-1 up, against their ten men, but flunked it. So, we were left fighting for our lives on the final day, as were Plymouth and Brentford. Andy Cooke put us ahead in the 12th minute with a cracking header from Glen Little's wonderful right-wing cross. The roar from the Burnley fans was deafening!'

Plymouth equalised 13 minutes later through midfielder Mark Saunders, but Burnley took the lead again with a Cooke header before half-time.

Gerry continued: 'We had chances to put ourselves out of sight. Paul Weller hit the woodwork, but we couldn't get that crucial third goal, so it was a matter of hanging on. We had the

2. BACKS AGAINST THE WALL 1995 TO 1999

luck. The Plymouth centre-forward missed from six yards in the closing stages. He may have been put off by Mark Winstanley's air shot, but it was a huge relief when he prodded the loose ball gently into Chris Woods's midriff. From the fans' point of view, it was a great match to be at. [No, it wasn't, Gerry, it was utter torture! We expected a white-knuckle ride and that's what we got.]

'The atmosphere at the final whistle was incredible. I was on the floor, hurt, after blocking a shot but it didn't matter. It was such a relief to know we were safe, although the other key result didn't come through for five minutes or so.'

Gerry believed Burnley deserved to stay up, despite their 'dodgy' start to the season. 'Chris Waddle said before the game to go out and give it all we had. I think everyone did. I can't express how much that game meant to me, and everyone involved. It would have been hard for Burnley to come up again from the Third Division. I played in that division when I was on loan at Hull. It's a difficult one to get out of.'

We know, Gerry! At the final whistle, he was prostrate on the turf, utterly drained, both physically, and emotionally.

Throughout the game, the score at Bristol Rovers was passed around. We cheered wildly when we heard that Rovers had taken the lead, only for deflation to follow as we discovered that the goal had been disallowed. Then there was a further groan as Rovers' Penrice was sent off. It was still 0-0 at half-time. Shortly afterwards, Rovers went into the lead, only for Brentford to equalise. But the frowns rapidly turned to smiles again as Rovers regained the lead. It was bad enough coping with the Burnley game without this added pressure.

After minutes of screeching whistles at Turf Moor, imploring the referee to end the game, the final whistle was eventually blown, greeted by a roar that could have been heard in Blackburn. But we could not relax yet. We were told that there were still five minutes left to play in Bristol. It was OK though. We were safe.

As we trailed past the many Plymouth coaches, we were touched by their applause which we readily reciprocated. How impressive these travelling fans were to have come so far for this gut-wrenching defeat and yet managed this noble response. One young girl was shedding tears. A Burnley lad leapt to kiss her coach window before running off.

On the journey home we listened to a BBC interview with Chris Waddle. He sounded drained, relieved to have survived at the death but cagey about where he would go from here. It seemed as if he had decided football management was not for him, a surmise which was soon confirmed.

His replacement was Stan Ternent. It was to be another white-knuckle ride. Ternent had spent his formative years at Turf Moor but had established a reputation as a hard, combative midfielder at Carlisle. When his footballing career was ended by injury he moved into coaching and management, coaching a young Ian Wright at Crystal Palace and taking unfancied Bury into the second tier. His undying love of Burnley persuaded him to grasp the poisoned chalice which Turf Moor appeared to offer.

Stan started the 1998/99 season with a 2-1 home victory over a strong Bristol Rovers side with Payton scoring both goals, much against the run of play. But three subsequent defeats emphasised how much Stan needed to do to turn Burnley into a competitive side. His fury at a pathetic 0-1 home defeat by York led him to place four players on the free transfer list – Blatherwick, Howey, Williams, and Winstanley – exclaiming that they would not play for Burnley again. Chairman Frank Teasdale was understandably alarmed as Stan had effectively removed any possibility of gaining a fee for these players, two of whom had been bought by Waddle for £200,000 each. Although Chesterfield and Northampton ultimately stumped up £50,000 for Blatherwick and Howey respectively, Stan remained at loggerheads with the board until a club takeover took place at the end of the year. Burnley remained on the edge of the relegation zone throughout September. Ironically, they slid into the drop zone on 3 October after an impressive 2-2 draw at Maine Road, with goals from Payton and Cooke. Only a late goal saved high-riding City from defeat.

Colchester United 0 Burnley 4
9 October 1998
'Right Here, Right Now'

It was a diabolical, wet Friday night when Andrew and I drove to Colchester. The intensity of the rain and the dazzling, oncoming headlights frequently obscured the course of the road. I recall saying to Andrew, 'Why the f**k are we doing this?' Besides, Burnley had not won in six games, despite their uplifting draw at Maine Road. It seemed likely that this horrible night signified abject defeat.

It was not much better inside the decrepit ground, where we were allocated a shallow terrace behind the goal that Burnley were about to attack, with minimal protection against the penetrative rain. Within minutes we were soaked to the skin. Yet, shortly after kick-off Payton put us two up. This was too much to bear as we burst into 'What the f**k! What the f**k! What the f**k is going on?' to the tune of 'Bread of Heaven'. Vindheim and Cooke then took us out of sight in the second half. We could not believe what we had seen, even less so after Preston and Bournemouth rogered us 1-4 and 0-5 respectively in November. Although Payton's penalty enabled us to beat Blackpool in a dreadful home game on 28 November, Fulham, seven days later, would not be so obliging.

Fulham 4 Burnley 0
12 December 1998
'Teardrop'

This is what I wrote immediately after this resounding defeat. 'How can I begin to describe this shambles? I could say we were "outclassed", "outfought", and "outthought" but this would be mere flattery. Surely only Buddhists can contend with such indignity?

'Of course, Fulham are a good side. Given Al-Fayed's investment they bloody well should be, but that's no excuse. Hartlepool ran Fulham very close last weekend and even Leigh held them to a draw. From the beginning, Fulham denied us space, harassing our midfielders and closing down our defenders. With our midfield shackled, Cooke and Payton were left adrift, relying upon our goalie, Crichton, for any service. The only accurate passes were back to him, and all clearances ended up as high, hopeless punts. Our three at the back, Heywood, Brass and Reid worked hard enough trying to contend with Peschisolido's darting runs, Hayles's blistering pace and Horsefield's power. But three were not enough.

'Our wing-backs ended up playing as full-backs while midfielders Armstrong and Ford spent inordinate time in our box, mostly getting in the way. The only way that we could have hurt Fulham was on the ground, for Symons, Coleman and Morgan gobbled up our lofty, long balls. But we seemed incapable of mustering the quick one-twos and probing runs that might have opened up more space for counter-attacking.'

Stan claimed this was not his team. I had trouble with that because Burnley is always my team, whoever plays. But after Barry Kilby took over as chairman, he injected much-needed funds into the side while also clearing the debt incurred by the ground reconstruction. Hugely popular Steve Davis returned from Luton for a fee thought to be around £800,000. Scrapping midfielder Mickey Mellon was bought for £350,000. Utility player Graham Branch came in on a 'free' while 'muck and bullets' midfielder Lenny Johnrose, came in for £225,000 shortly afterwards, as did full-back Ally Pickering.

2. BACKS AGAINST THE WALL 1995 TO 1999

Bristol Rovers 3 Burnley 4
9 January 1999

'Firestarter'

A clutch of friends joined me for this 'new dawn' game. Because the Burnley allocation was sold out, we found space in the home end. It did not take Steve Davis long to show us what we had missed over the last four years. Muscling into the box he nudged in the opening goal in the 15th minute. I managed to keep a lid on my joy, confining myself to a whispered celebration. Besides, it was premature. Nippy Jamie Cureton and burly Jason Roberts represented a constant threat to our still-porous defence. It was no surprise when Cureton equalised with a snap-shot ten minutes later.

Branch's pace on the left flank was causing the Rovers defence no end of trouble. This was underlined when he dashed in to restore Burnley's lead on the half-hour. But six minutes later Roberts regained parity when he unleashed a powerful drive that was too good for Crichton. This was like a prize fight. Not to be left out, Payton then seized on a half-chance in his typical poacher mode to put Burnley 3-2 up just before the interval, only for hefty defender David Lee to let fly with a blistering 25-yard grubber that whizzed past Crichton! What a game this was! As the players left the muddy field, they were acclaimed ardently by both sets of supporters.

The second half was equally combative, making us thankful for Mellon's snarling presence in midfield instead of ineffectual Ford. The game could have gone either way even after Cooke gave Burnley the lead for the fourth time in the 54th minute. His pounding drive benefitted from a handy deflection as the ball zipped into the net. A chilly breeze wafted around the Memorial Ground as the sun dipped behind the Mendips, although the heat of battle never diminished. We stayed in Bristol for several hours after the game high on adrenalin. I did not even resent the awful non-alcoholic beer I was compelled to drink, being the driver.

We thought this game would immediately ignite a revival. How wrong we were! However, there was an away victory, at Millwall, on 23 January, to enjoy before the rot returned. Another powerful drive from Cooke and a beefy long-range effort from Davis helped seize the points at the Den with ten minutes left. But subsequent results were disappointing: two scrambled draws against Lincoln and Reading and two defeats by Luton and Wycombe. Then the sky fell in. On 27 February Burnley lost 0-5 at home to Gillingham with Robert Taylor scoring all five. It was to get worse. When Manchester City arrived on 9 March, we were torn apart 0-6. Burnley were in serious trouble and so was Stan. A subsequent defeat at home to Preston sent us tumbling into 21st place. But club chairman Barry Kilby held his nerve, backing Stan and agreeing to bring in Paul Cook, a tough midfielder with a left peg like a wand, together with energetic wing-back Tom Cowan. The Gordian knot was cut as Stan's side went on an amazing 11-match unbeaten run.

Burnley 4 Macclesfield 3
28 March 1999
'Letting Go'

Andrew and I drove up for this critical game on a bright and cold Sunday, still frail after the mauling by City. But with Burnley perilously positioned in 19th place we reasoned it was better to be there rather than fretting at home. Burnley made a disastrous start with Macclesfield's left-winger Durkan scoring twice in the first 14 minutes. This dual blow was administered by a side that had struggled to score all season. Much to our relief, Glen Little pulled one back three minutes later.

This was like a primary school game, with both sides neglecting to close their back door while piling forward. Steve Davis seemed to be the only cog in our defence that was working. So, when Cowan equalised with a spectacular scissor-kick in the 57th minute we were not reassured. Unsurprisingly, Macclesfield regained their lead six minutes later through their right-winger, Askey. Trust Payton to save our bacon, though, with only 11 minutes left. But a draw was not good enough. Burnley needed to win. As hard as they tried, this looked beyond them. Then, in the 90th minute Davis arrived at the far post to net a priceless winner. We and 10,000 other Clarets were ecstatic. Had that game been lost, Burnley's recovery plan might not have taken off. Andrew and I drove home basking in a magnificent sunset, content that Burnley were out of the drop zone.

Burnley 3 Colchester 1
5 April 1999
'Musette and Drums'

I drove up alone on a grey Easter Monday to cheer on Burnley against Colchester. Again, it was an unprepossessing start. Colchester's Lua Lua yanked our defence all over the place with his trickery, setting up Gregory for a brilliant long-range strike in the 26th minute. What with Burnley's insipid display and a weird half-time show of greyhounds in tutus, we were not amused. Neither was the dog handler, dogged with profanities. However, a different Burnley emerged after the break, eventually achieving a 3-1 lead helped by Johnrose's pugnacious leveller in the 57th minute and Payton's late brace which sent us home in good spirits. We were up to 17th place.

Stoke City 1 Burnley 4
24 April 1999
'Staring at the Rude Boys'

I nicked Liz's work car for this game. It was a last-minute impulse. She misunderstood my request, thinking I was going to a nearby game. When she rang to find out where I was, she shouted: 'STOKE! For Christ's sake! Whenever do you expect to be home?' I was lucky. Both journeys were unusually quick. I was fortunate with the game, too. Despite being under the cosh for substantial periods, with Irish international midfielder Graham Kavanagh dominant, Burnley counter-attacked with ruinous speed and power.

We were off to a great start against a team that had been top for most of this season. In the fifth minute Ally Pickering's 30-yard volley hit the back of the Stoke net at the speed of light. The Stoke crowd were stunned by their old boy's feat. Payton then added a second minutes later, only to limp off with a hamstring problem. Dean Crowe reduced the deficit with a half-hour gone, prompting an all-out assault on the Burnley goal. The Clarets remained resolute, though.

Having sucked up continuous pressure, Glen Little brought Stoke to their knees. With 24 minutes remaining, he claimed the ball in midfield. Sashaying along the right flank, he brushed aside each of his markers with nonchalant disdain. Suddenly he made a dash for goal, having rolled another bemused defender. Glen's finishing was still raw and erratic, but here he was composed and confident, slipping the ball past the Stoke goalie once he had committed himself. We went bananas at his audacious brilliance while Stoke boss Brian Little buried his face in his hands, realising Stoke's last chance of promotion had disappeared. Glen Little then added a derisive fourth in the 90th minute. How was it possible that a side that had been repeatedly battered and abused during this season could turn themselves into such a devastating killing machine? Our re-education would be completed a week later against all-conquering Fulham. I drove home from Stoke playing the Ruts' *The Peel Sessions* album at full blast on the car CD player.

Burnley 1 Fulham 0
1 May 1999
'This Perfect Day'

On the following Saturday, 'moneybags' Fulham, bankrolled by Al-Fayed's fortune, were outmuscled. At a balmy Turf Moor, in front of a basking 13,086 crowd, Ronnie Jepson's vicious strike secured the points and Division Two safety. This truculent display was the antithesis of what we had endured at Craven Cottage in December. A season which had begun in penury and angry recrimination ended in glorious delight. Burnley were about to rise once more. It was timely, for chairman Barry Kilby was a man in a hurry, reasoning: 'A Premier Two division will be created eventually. We must be in that division for there'll be serious money there. We need to push on. I expect us to mount a serious promotion campaign next season.' He would not be disappointed.

3. BACK AMONG THE BIG BOYS 1999 TO 2000

'Rise'

Stan pruned his squad radically. Out went 12 players, including the disappointing Mark Ford, and in came previous loan signing Paul Cook, 34-year-old central defender Mitchell Thomas, formerly with Luton and Spurs, and 26-year-old right-back Dean West from Bury. John Mullin also re-joined the club from Sunderland for a £150,000 fee.

Wycombe Wanderers 1 Burnley 1
7 August 1999
'You Get What You Give'

The new campaign started at a bright, clammy Adams Park. Stan packed the midfield, with only Cooke up front. But Burnley were rocked when Jermain McSporran – surely a *Carry On* film character? – put Wycombe ahead in the 27th minute with a searing strike. This blow left Burnley flat-footed. But not for long. For in the second half Stan strengthened his attack, bringing on bruising Irish target man Alan Lee, and predatory Payton. Lee's aerial strength soon paid off. He flicked on for Payton to find space on the left flank and from his pinpoint cross Cooke headed an equaliser. Burnley had enough chances to have won but Stan was satisfied with a point.

Although Manchester City dished out their customary punishment in the League Cup, winning the tie 0-6 on aggregate, business was resumed with an insipid 2-1 home

3. BACK AMONG THE BIG BOYS 1999 TO 2000

victory over woeful Chesterfield. Glen Little's exclusion made more of a splash. Stan's terse explanation was: 'If you are doing the business, you'll be in the side. If not, you won't.'

Lenny Johnrose, a midfield 'enforcer' under Ternent, reflected: 'Stan was incredibly tough and would hand out unbelievable abuse. Some players couldn't put up with him. He would destroy some people and they'd have to go. However, I stood up to Stan and ignored the abuse. I think he quite liked that.'

Lenny typified the 'hard as nails' competitor that Stan needed in his teams. As an ultra-tough midfielder, Stan was cast in the same mould. Payton said: 'Johnrose had real attitude and was one of the best at taking people out. Stan would say, "Sort f**king so and so out" and he would.'

After making hard work of beating a poor Oldham side at Boundary Park (1-0) Burnley travelled to Bristol Rovers on a scorching Bank Holiday Monday. There they found a trigger-happy referee who awarded 42 free kicks and booked ten players – six from Burnley. In a rare moment of unity, both sets of supporters chanted, 'You don't know what you're doing!' Fittingly the game turned on the controversial award of a penalty which Jamie Cureton duly despatched. Stan was fuming at the post-match press conference, exclaiming: 'The referee was not, repeat not, up to scratch. He has a responsibility not just to the players and managers but to Burnley's supporters who've travelled over 200 miles to watch a game of football that's been ruined by a shoddy, not-up-to-scratch performance.'

The Clarets took top spot, though, after beating Bournemouth 2-1 on 3 September. Graham Branch, who scored the opening goal, responded to criticism of him by explaining: 'I think sometimes the crowd believe I'm not trying, but I'm very laid back.' While prone to crises of confidence, Branch eventually attained a cult celebrity status. Dubbed 'Graham Di Branchio' after the Italian striker Paulo Di Canio, his name would be sung heartily, if with an ironic smirk, to the tune of 'O Sole Mio'. His willingness to play in any outfield position gained him deserved respect.

When Preston and Burnley met at Deepdale on 11 September they drew 0-0 for the first time in over 100 years. Burnley dropped to fourth place but re-took the summit a week later after a 3-0 drubbing of visiting Colchester with Payton notching his first Burnley hat-trick.

However, their form then dipped. There was a joyless 0-0 draw at Ashton Gate before squandering a two-goal lead against Brentford (2-2). Worse still they lost at home to relegation-bound Scunthorpe (1-2). Following a frustrating 1-1 draw at the New Den, Burnley slipped to sixth position. These disappointing results prompted Stan to abandon his preferred 3-5-2 formation. At Cambridge, on 19 October, Stan reverted to a 4-4-2 with Davis and Thomas as the centre-backs, West and Smith as conventional full-backs, Little on the right flank, Cook, Johnrose, and Mullin in central midfield, and Branch and Cooke up front. Payton was unavailable. On a chilly evening at the Abbey Stadium, Cooke vindicated his recall by netting an early winner in a dominant team display (1-0).

Ahead of the AGM, chairman Barry Kilby announced a record trading loss of £1.8m, largely brought about by a 30 per cent rise in the cost of playing contracts. Nevertheless, club debts were down by £1m to £3m helped by the £3.9m raised by a rights issue. Then on a showery 23 October, Burnley turned on a glittering display, beating Bristol City with a thunderous 30-yarder from Paul Cook and a brilliant curler from Andy Cooke.

Burnley's drab 1-0 FA Cup victory at Barnet was covered by Sky TV. A better result was in the offing, as Burnley went nap against Wrexham on a blustery, wet Turf Moor evening. Graham Branch completed the annihilation with a diving header (5-0). A narrow loss at Luton (1-2) was quickly corrected with a 1-0 home win against Blackpool in mid-November. Former 'Seasider' Mellon won the game with a vicious, rising 30-yard drive. Having endured a deluge of abuse from the Blackpool fans, Mellon milked the moment. The sponsors duly awarded him man of the match. Rotherham were comfortably despatched 2-0 in the FA Cup before Burnley attained a tedious 0-0 draw at the Madejski Stadium. Surreally, the disgruntled Reading fans threw underpants on to the pitch in a 'pants for pants' protest.

Wigan Athletic 1 Burnley 1
27 November 1999
'Ready to Go'

A pulsating contest ensued at sunny Wigan on 27 November. The Division Two leaders were managed by John Benson, with John Bond as his assistant. Wigan were fortunate to maintain their unbeaten record with a 1-1 draw. Burnley had bossed the first period, with Payton heading the Clarets into a 17th-minute lead. However, a rare moment of slackness allowed the home side to level minutes before half-time. Wigan threatened more in the second period, but Alan Lee missed a gilt-edged, late opportunity to win the game. A stubborn Wycombe side then parked the bus at Turf Moor a week later. They reckoned without Payton, though, as the Padiham predator squeezed in a 78th-minute winner (1-0).

Derby County 0 Burnley 1
FA Cup Third Round
11 December 1999
'Hey Jealousy'

The FA Cup tie at Premier League Derby resulted in a major shock. The pride in Pride Park belonged exclusively to us, the visitors. A Sunday-paper photographer captured Cooke in the act of scoring, rising a foot above his marker, a solitary, soaring Claret, frozen in mid-air, among a clutch of grounded Derby defenders. It was an apt metaphor. Having tackled harder, run faster, passed better and jumped higher, Burnley were literally head and shoulders above Derby. On *Match of the Day*, Alan Hansen said the Clarets were 'absolutely magnificent'.

The Promotion Push Gathers Pace after Two Festive Setbacks

'Lucky Man'

Cardiff were the next side to lose at Turf Moor, although the Bluebirds made the early running. Mitchell Johnson had been a colossus at Derby. But when he conceded a deflected own goal, Stan took remedial action, switching to a 3-5-2 formation, with Branch replacing West. Almost immediately Davis equalised with a power header, from Paul Cook's fizzing corner kick. The winner came in the 68th minute after Little had turned two Cardiff defenders inside out. His exquisite chip to the far post was stabbed in decisively by Johnrose (2-1).

There was not much festive joy at Gigg Lane, though, on 26 December. Bury flew into a 4-0 first-half lead. Burnley were depleted by injury and illness but this was a poor show. Once skipper Steve Davis was dismissed for a deliberate handball offence, his team crumpled (2-4). Stan griped: 'It would have to be Bury, again, wouldn't it? They were a mediocre, mid-table side, but of course they played like Real Madrid against me. At least Warnock wasn't around to gloat!'

Languishing Oxford United arrived at Turf Moor two days later and doggedly held on to a 2-1 lead until Payton struck twice in the closing minutes to seize a hat-trick and the points (3-2). Burnley rose one place to fifth, but that did not last long as Notts County inflicted their fifth league defeat of the season (0-2). Despite creating a host of chances, Stan damned his team's performance as 'unacceptable'.

Burnley then bade farewell to the FA Cup competition after being outgunned at Premier League Coventry (0-3). A seven-match unbeaten sequence followed, beginning with a 1-1 draw at Chesterfield, and including home victories over Oldham (3-0) and promotion rivals Bristol Rovers (1-0). Glen Little scored a scintillating solo winner against Rovers after Burnley were reduced to ten men, Payton having been red-carded for retaliation. Ian Cox, newly signed from debt-ridden Bournemouth for £500,000, played superbly in central defence alongside the redoubtable Davis.

Before serving his three-match suspension, Payton made sure Burnley grabbed all three points at sunny Bournemouth, heading Burnley into a 32nd-minute lead. Burnley's defence then barred the door (1-0). Cox was again outstanding against the club he had just left.

The home 0-0 draw with Wigan on 19 February was remarkable because it was Ian Wright's home debut for Burnley. Wright explained: 'I've known Stan since I turned professional, and he has been on at me for years to sign for him, so I've finally given in. I hope I can make some contribution to their promotion push, but the place has given me a really good feeling. I just want to play. It's a great place to end my career. Hopefully, I will be everything the fans want. It won't be for lack of trying. I've been slaughtered as some kind of football mercenary. That's rubbish! I hope this proves how much I want to play.'

Wright deserved a better introduction than the dour 0-0 draw between Burnley and Wigan. Not many in the Turf Moor crowd of 20,435 complained. Just as Stan predicted, the ticket office was besieged, while the club shop was hard-pressed to meet the febrile demand for Wright-related merchandise. Burnley suddenly became a 'boom town'. Ian Wright MBE – recast as 'Massive Burnley Enthusiast' – became the first serving Burnley player to appear on a TV chat show.

A week later, Burnley won 2-1 at Colchester, but Wright was unhappy. He was bewildered and angered by the abuse he and his wife received from some home fans. He was allegedly called a 'black bastard'. Wright hadn't scored yet and this troubled him too. While furious at Wright's abusive reception, Stan urged him to persevere. Wright complained, 'I have taken a lot of stick in my time which I can handle. But it's not on when fans aim it at my family. I want an apology from those fans.' He didn't get one. A Colchester spokesman stated: 'Wright is a superstar and he can expect a lot worse when he goes elsewhere with Burnley. The facts are that the chants are offensive but not racist.' Years later, Yorkshire County Cricket Club were widely condemned for such a complacent, racist response.

A shattering blow to Burnley's promotion prospects followed, as David Moyes's Preston outplayed the Clarets at Turf Moor, winning 3-0. Stan thought that the result flattered Preston. He was confident that his team would recover in the midweek home fixture with Luton. They didn't. On a night of heavy rain, Luton defied the squidgy surface and incessant Burnley pressure to win 0-2. Wright missed three good chances, including a one-on-one with the visiting goalkeeper, while the Hatters made the most of their fewer opportunities. During the second half, the home crowd implored Stan to bring on benched Andy Payton. After acceding to their wishes, Payton put the ball in the Luton net only to be ruled offside.

Payton was recalled for the game at Wrexham in place of Wright. At 32 years old, he was anxious about the prospect of a further contract. At Wrexham, he made his point. He wasted little time in scoring the decisive goal, then celebrated by revealing a T-shirt emblazoned with 'Natural Born Claret'. Burnley were back on track. While Wright commanded the headlines, in Payton Burnley had a rare jewel – loyal and lethal in equal measure. This was his 20th goal of the season and the 200th of his career.

Gillingham 2 Burnley 2
14 March 2000
'Kamikaze'

Promotion rivals Gillingham were one of six teams battling for a second automatic promotion place. Preston seemed unchallengeable in top spot. Driven forward by their belligerent central midfielders Hessenthaler and Smith, and fed by a marauding wing-back, Nosworthy, Gillingham tore into Burnley from the off, taking a fourth-minute lead through central-defender Guy Butters. With Burnley penned in their own half for much of the first period, Payton was isolated. Yet he made the most of a solitary chance to restore parity in the 31st minute. Home strikers Asaba and Onuora posed a greater threat, though. Only Crichton's agility and his defenders' tenacity kept them at bay. It came as no surprise when Asaba poked Gillingham into a 2-1 lead in the 68th minute, having evaded two Burnley defenders in a brilliant cross-field dribble. Burnley were under the cosh and losing.

Stan decided that it was time for 'Ian Wright, Wright, Wright!' Pent up with compressed adrenaline Wright shot off the bench, desperate to join the action. With muscular Ronnie Jepson also thrown into the fray, Burnley reverted to 3-5-2. Payton described Jepson as 'a big, hard, aggressive bastard who lifted the spirit in the dressing room. When he came on, he would rough up opponents, yelling: "Right I'm going to smash this c***!" The defenders were often scared of him which was great for me as I then got more chances.'

With Jepson and Johnrose putting themselves about, Gillingham's midfield dominance began to fracture. This allowed Little and Thomas more space to bomb forward. With only two minutes left, Thomas looped a centre into the Gills' box. In a split second, Wright stunned the ball with his chest and lashed it venomously into the roof of the net. Such was the velocity of his strike that Gills goalkeeper Bartram could only raise his arms in surrender. Wright then charged off to find Stan who embraced him like a long-lost son. The point stolen here would prove critical on the last day of the season.

A regulation 3-0 home win followed over unadventurous Reading, with Payton and Wright on target after Davis had outmuscled the visitors' defence to head Burnley into a 37th-minute lead. Branch rescued Burnley at Blackpool where Stan complained: 'We should have kicked off at nine because for the last half-hour we played OK.' And then Jepson saved Burnley with a last-gasp equaliser at home against Bury (2-2). Stan admitted it had been a mediocre display but added defiantly: 'We never jack it in, only that mob that I cleared out last season.' Jepson paid no regard to his goal saying: 'I don't give a monkey's about it. The goal belongs to the team not individuals.'

On April Fools' Day in rainy Cardiff, Payton scored again, after breaking away and nutmegging the advancing goalkeeper. It gave Burnley an unassailable 2-0 lead over the sinking Bluebirds. Cardiff did manage to reduce the arrears with an own goal, aided and abetted by Burnley's nemesis, Kurt Nogan, but it was scant consolation. Only Cardiff's 'Soul Crew' exhibited any hostility, recreating scenes reminiscent of the hateful eighties. Burnley remained in fifth spot.

On the following Saturday Burnley beat Notts County at home 2-1 thanks to Ian Wright's late strike. With time almost up and the referee consulting his watch, Steve Davis launched the ball upfield, Wright met it on the edge of the box, controlled it instantly, shimmied around a Notts County defender, and blasted an unstoppable drive into the top corner. His glee was uncontainable. Stan said: 'I think he kissed me, but I've tried to block that from my mind!'

At a wet, cold, and dreary Oxford on 15 April, Burnley again left it late to snatch the points. A remarkable long-range header from Davis and a straightforward one from substitute Weller turned the game on its head. It was a fitting moment of glory for Weller who had bravely survived a debilitating condition and a major operation. Here, Ian Wright was the provider, finding the unmarked Weller at the far post (2-1).

With an automatic promotion slot beckoning, Burnley stumbled at home against close rivals Gillingham, losing 0-3. Stan described it as 'a bad day at the office'. There were unwanted personal repercussions, too, as his contract talks were put on hold, pending the season's outcome. Gillingham seemed destined to accompany Preston into Division One. Gillingham boss Peter Taylor goaded Stan with the parting remark: 'Never mind Stan. Keep going. You'll get it right eventually.' Stan focused his fury on his preparations for Burnley's final four games.

Burnley 4 Millwall 3
22 April 2000
'This Corrosion'

First up was a feisty clash with Millwall. They were also promotion challengers with a huge, hostile away following. Burnley took a 4-0 lead, thanks to first-half goals from Cox, Cooke, and Davis, and a stunning long-range effort from Paul Cook shortly after the break. Incensed by their side's apparent capitulation, the Millwall miscreants took out their anger on the Cricket Field stand seating, slinging broken fragments into an adjoining enclosure populated by young Burnley fans, forcing their horrified parents to remove them to a safer place.

Meanwhile, on the pitch the Millwall Lions belatedly recovered their roar. With nothing left to lose, they began counter-attacking with startling energy and menace, led by their skilful centre-forward Neil Harris. Burnley reeled under the pressure, pulling everyone bar Wright back behind the ball. Stan raged at this, gesticulating wildly at his players, insisting they held a higher line. With only the isolated Wright offering his besieged defenders an out-ball, Millwall had acres of space in which to launch their attacks and pick their passes and crosses.

When Millwall scored their first goal on the hour it was met with only ironic cheers from the away end. When they scored their second, 18 minutes later, there was only a marginal increase in interest. But when they scored a third with three minutes still left, the roar from the visiting fans was explosive. Had the game gone on for another 15 minutes, Burnley might well have lost. Afterwards, Stan muttered acidly: 'that's what happens if you try to defend under your own crossbar.' This tense victory lifted Burnley out of fifth place and into fourth.

Brentford 2 Burnley 3
24 April 2000
'Crawling'

On Easter Monday at a bright Griffin Park, there was a similar mixture of exultation and relief when the final whistle sounded. Lowly Brentford produced a plucky performance, bossing the first period with the gangling Owusu snatching the lead shortly before half-time. Stan reacted by moving Little to the right flank and swapping Mullin to the left. But the masterstroke was the introduction of Wright for Payton. Wright proceeded to tear the Brentford defence to shreds with his powerful running and darting movement, creating gaps which he and Mullin (twice) could plunder. Had goalkeeper Crichton not played a blinder, though, Brentford would have taken something from this game (3-2). Burnley rose to third.

The Brentford game featured Ian Wright's final goal for Burnley. He had told Stan that he had been disappointed at making only eight starts. But Stan was concerned that Wright's initial scoreless run had put him under too much pressure. By benching him, Stan thought he had thrown those hacks who were eager to write his obituary off the scent. Wright admitted to Stan: 'I was gutted when I wasn't getting a start, but I suppose after I scored at Gillingham, it just kicked in. It was brilliant.'

3. BACK AMONG THE BIG BOYS 1999 TO 2000

Although Stan yearned for him to stay, Ian decided his future lay in the media. He joined the end-of-season team 'jolly' in Portugal, though. Wright said: 'Even in London, I've never met people like these Burnley fans before. If I walk down the High Street, they come from everywhere. They are really fanatical, but the thing I'll remember most is the amount of Burnley shirts I've seen on the streets. Everyone wears them. It must be part of the school uniform around here.'

The penultimate game at home against Cambridge resulted in a straightforward 2-0 win for Stan's men, with a brace of goals by Payton, one of which featured a magnificent 'Cruyff turn'. These were his 26th and 27th league goals of the season, a tremendous effort that deservedly won him the prestigious Golden Boot award. Elsewhere, Wigan lost at home to Wrexham (0-1), impeding their promotion prospects, while Preston ended Millwall's challenge at Deepdale (3-2).

Scunthorpe United 1 Burnley 2
6 May 2000
'Beautiful Day'

The season concluded on Saturday 6 May, a day of blue skies and hazy warmth. Andrew and I blagged our way in, purporting to be long-lost Scunthorpe fans. I was even prepared to sing the 'Lincolnshire Poacher'. A sceptical police officer looked directly at me, saying: 'For all I know you may not be a Scunthorpe supporter at all!' I just smiled. However, the PA announcer issued dire warnings about what would happen if any away fans were found in the home seats. We had to sit on our hands and restrain any impulse to cheer.

The calculation was simple. In order to claim the promotion spot, Burnley had to beat already relegated Scunthorpe, and hope that Gillingham did not win at Wrexham. But if both faltered then Wigan, or, more improbably, Stoke, could have stolen the prize.

Wrexham were managed by ex-Claret Brian Flynn. It was time to call in a favour.

After 11 minutes, there was wild cheering in the away end. Right-back Mark McGregor had put Wrexham in front with a 30-yard screamer. Stan would later reward him with a contract. This goal put Burnley ahead of Gillingham by one point. But ten minutes later the Clarets were in arrears, if only on goal difference. Scunthorpe's pint-sized midfielder Lee Hodges had cracked a vicious, rising drive against the underside of the crossbar and in. Belying their hopeless position, Scunthorpe immediately raised their game, forcing Burnley on to the back foot. However, almost upon the stroke of half-time, the Scunthorpe goalkeeper made a flailing clearance from a corner. His effort had neither distance nor power, reaching the unmarked Mellon on the edge of the box. Mellon unhesitatingly rifled in the equaliser through a thicket of legs. We bit our lips in delight.

Despite being pegged back, Scunthorpe continued to press hard. After the resumption, two good chances for Scunny went begging. There was no denying an irresistible force, though. With around 20 minutes left, Glen Little was sent on by Stan. It was an inspired substitution, for almost immediately Little struck a rising half-volley into the top left-hand corner of the Scunthorpe net. The goal had winner stamped on it. Ignoring the threat of removal, Andrew and I and hundreds more in the home end leapt to our feet in joy.

The Wrexham game had not finished when the final whistle was blown. With the Burnley fans streaming on to the field, few doubted Burnley were up. And so it proved. This time the fans sensed their team was good enough to stay. Burnley were on an upward march. The next day, Stan faxed Gills boss, Peter Taylor, with a consolatory message. It read: 'Dear Peter. Keep going son, you'll get it right eventually. Best regards, Stan.'

Andy Cooke's twin headers in the 'win or bust' final game against Plymouth in 1998 proved vital.

Ternent (far right) achieved promotion to the Championship in 2000 and almost achieved an EPL play off place twice.

Former Arsenal and England star Ian Wright (left) helped Burnley achieve promotion in 2000.

Steve Cotterill replaced Stan Ternent in June 2004 helping maintain hard-up Burnley's place in the Championship.

Robbie Blake (right) was Burnley's second £1m signing after Ian Moore. Blake helped Burnley to win promotion to the EPL in 2009.

Ade Akinbiyi hugged by his team-mates after a brilliant comeback victory at QPR in 2008. Andrew Cole, second right, scored a hat-trick.

Brian Jensen's penalty shoot-out save gave Burnley victory over Chelsea in the League Cup in 2008.

Owen Coyle (top left) replaced Cotterill in 2007 and guided Burnley into the EPL in 2009.

Burnley's Wade Elliott shaking off a Sheffield United defender at Wembley. His searing strike gave Burnley a deserved 1-0 victory.

Pensive Burnley chairman, Barry Kilby, introduced new manager, Brian Laws after Owen Coyle's sudden departure in December 2010. Relegation followed.

Rising star, Jay Rodriguez is congratulated on his winning goal by new manager, Eddie Howe who replaced Laws.

Charlie Austin was Howe's first significant signing. Austin scored 41 goals in 82 league games for Burnley.

Sean Dyche (right) with assistant Ian Woan (left) and first team coach Tony Loughlan.

Brilliant goalkeeper Tom Heaton played a major role in Burnley's returns to the Premier League in 2014 and 2016, also helping them to remain there.

Free-scoring Andre Gray equalising against Brighton in a tough promotion battle at the Amex Stadium.

Burnley won the 2015/16 Championship title at Charlton but had to wait for the trophy, making do with inflatable versions.

Resolute defender Ben Mee (second left) and versatile midfielder, Jack Cork, behind him.

James Tarkowski formed a combative and skilful central defensive partnership with Ben Mee.

From left to right: reserve striker Nahki Wells; scrapping central midfielder Dean Marney and attacking right-back Matthew Lowton

Burnley's pugnacious midfielder Ashley Westwood warming up watched by Wells.

Scott Arfield was a midfield lynchpin in the 2013/14 and 2015/16 promotion sides

Richard Chaplow was a product of Burnley's youth team. He was an under-21 international and was transferred to West Bromwich Albion in December 2004 for £1.5m.

Impressive Burnley centre-forward Sam Vokes (left) with right back Matthew Lowton at Old Trafford.

Burnley centre-forward Sam Vokes misses a gilt-edged chance with Burnley's Europa League campaign ended by Olympiacos in 2008.

Burnley centre-forward Chris Wood scoring against Norwich at Turf Moor in September 2019.

4. THE END OF THE NINETIES AND WHAT CAME AFTER

The nineties were book-ended by two major demolitions. The first was the fall of the Berlin Wall in 1989, while the second came in 2001 with the horrific assault upon Manhattan's 'Twin Towers'. The fall of the Berlin Wall led to the demise of the Iron Curtain, signalling the end of the Cold War. It also signified the beginning of greater freedoms. Repressive regimes were challenged and some overthrown. In Romania, the hated Ceausescu administration was ended. But in Beijing's Tiananmen Square, a protest movement was crushed with tragic consequences. The optimism aroused by the emancipations in 1989 was soon flouted by harsh realities. Soviet leader Mikhail Gorbachev, followed by Boris Yeltsin, carried out a policy of *perestroika* or reconstruction in the USSR, which led to a chaotic and rancorous dissolution of the Soviet states, the impact of which is horrifically reflected in Ukraine today.

However, it was the shocking attack on the World Trade Center in Manhattan which returned us to the politics of fear. Although US nuclear missiles had been withdrawn at Greenham Common in 1991, vociferously cheered by the women protesters encamped there, new threats to western security were being posed by religious fundamentalist regimes or bandit states that condoned, incubated, and sponsored world-wide terrorism.

Fundamentalist insurgency became the new global threat, stalking areas of political instability, notably those where collapsing oppressive regimes released toxic racial and religious animosities. At the end of 1988, Britain and the USA were reeling at the December downing of a Pan Am jetliner over Lockerbie. Author Salman Rushdie was threatened by an Iranian fatwa with Muslims at home and abroad vilifying his book *The Satanic Verses*. Genocidal atrocities in the Balkans, where 8,000 Muslims were murdered in Srebrenica and 2.1 million Bosnians displaced, flouted international peace-keeping. Similarly, in Rwanda 800,000 were murdered and 2.6 million displaced while the world averted its gaze.

In 1991, riots in British towns and cities revealed the extent of a snarling underclass, stripped of purpose, ambition, conscience, or inhibition. Canary Wharf seemed like a latter-day Babel, presiding over the disadvantaged communities around it, built in blind homage to the voracious demands of high finance. How ironic it was that this skyscraper should be constructed where working men and women once toiled, when commerce was measured in tangible commodities. Here, there, and everywhere, regeneration seemed to imply gentrification.

In 1999, Britain was largely sustained by a thriving global financial sector but its manufacturing base, the basis for its former world power, had largely withered. England's bottom place in the world's cricket hierarchy seemed a symbolic reflection of what had been lost since the end of World War Two: industrial might, military strength, and imperial power.

The new millennium arrived with pomp and angst. The Dome attracted relatively few customers, the river did not catch fire, and the Eye did not go around but at least the 'Bug' did not bite. Airliners did not crash to earth as had been feared, and we could still use the ATM the next day.

The 'noughties' were presaged with New Labour's politically abducted anthem 'Things Can Only Get Better'. For a while Blair's blarney held sway but his hubris quickly transformed 'better' into 'catastrophic'. The Afghanistan invasion cost around

176,000 lives while the dismantling of Saddam's brutal regime resulted in widespread cruelty and the loss of approximately 300,000 lives. Although these calculations vary, they represent a chilling indictment of the 'war on terror', a facile abstraction that had appalling tangibility.

Then came the banking crisis of 2008. This burst the complacent 'noughties bubble', exposing the harsh risks of maverick deregulation, with the global fiscal crisis causing the poorest members of our society particular hardship, notably those in post-industrial areas. During the resulting downturn of 2008 and 2009, hundreds of thousands of businesses shut down and more than a million people lost their jobs, while banks were propped up with government bail-outs valued at 25 per cent of Britain's GDP.

The immediate legacy of the fiscal damage perpetrated by reckless 'banksters' and irresponsible others was the government's policy of austerity. This saw our welfare safety net drastically reduced, leaving many on the breadline, forced to seek help from charitable organisations, such as foodbanks. These have now become the first ports of call for many without food or shelter. The anger of those dispossessed by the government's harsh and heartless policies had a direct bearing upon the 2016 Brexit referendum result. Many of these victims turned to populist leaders as varied as Nigel Farage, Boris Johnson, and Jeremy Corbyn, having lost faith in established senior government figures. This disaffection led to the abrupt resignation of Prime Minister David Cameron and the subsequent defeat of his successor, Theresa May.

But the signs of the times are often reflected in trivial preoccupations as much as momentous events. The noughties saw the emergence of TV reality stars. *Big Brother* premiered in July 2000, becoming an instant hit, with viewers taking sides in the participants' disputes, such as the supposed 'race war' between Jade Goody and Shilpa Shetty. This formula lives on, albeit with some twists, as in *Love Island*, a British dating game show.

Diana, Princess of Wales possibly contributed to this shift in our celebrity culture. While her heartfelt compassion for suffering people was rightly applauded, she brought together two separate notions of celebrity. In one sense she was a typical Hollywood movie star, with her royal remoteness and glamorous costumes. But her candid, tearful confessions smacked more of a reality TV celebrity.

And of course we have the exposés of the private lives of others such as the Osbournes and Khans. Are we becoming more voyeuristic? In my distant youth there were fewer opportunities, apart from ogling the saucy scandals in the 'News of the Screws'. As for today's interminable talent contests, dangling prospects of instant acclaim, why should anyone believe that fame and fortune can be won without unrelenting hard graft? Andy Warhol once claimed: 'In the future, everyone will be world-famous for 15 minutes.' Yeah right, Andy!

In these troubled times, scarred with the brutality of war and terrorism, pandemic and other diseases, with the threat of global warming reflected in increased famine, fires, and floods, the number of displaced people has reached 98 million globally: 13.7 million from Syria, 11.4 million from Ukraine, 4.1 million from Yemen and 1.7 million from Myanmar. This horrific reality tempts some to hide, maybe by shaping avatars, or by immersion in labyrinthine video games. However, football remains as my sanctuary. But unlike jungle celebrity Jordan North, Turf Moor is rarely my 'happy place'. It is too often a place of knuckle-gnawing pain.

PART 5

MISSED GLORY AND BEATING THE RETREAT

2000 to 2007

'Lose Yourself'

1. PREMIER AMBITIONS 2000 TO 2002

Stan strengthened his side during the summer of 2000, adding former Sheffield Wednesday full-back or midfielder Lee Briscoe. Stan described the former England Under-21 international as 'a determined left-sided player'. Fellow defender Mitchell Thomas quipped: 'Briscoe was the nicest man in the world until he has a beverage and then he turns into a monster.' Stan also signed Phil Gray, a 31-year-old striker from Luton. Gray had played for Northern Ireland and when he scored in a World Cup qualifier against Malta, in September, he became Burnley's first international goalscorer since Billy Hamilton.

However, Stan's prized signing was 'tough-nut midfielder' Kevin Ball. Stan believed Ball was his 'best signing', a kindred spirit, for Stan played with similar combative fire. Ball said: 'I had more arguments with Stan than with any manager I played for.' Not that this detracted from Ball's enjoyment of his two years at Burnley or his respect for Stan.

When Ball arrived at Turf Moor, he was 35 years old, but it was apparent that he had lost none of his trademark aggression with which he had intimidated so many opponents in his Sunderland and Portsmouth playing days. Ball explained: 'I hated losing. It didn't matter who we were playing. I just wanted to win and if it meant kicking your proverbial granny to do so, then that's just the way I was. I have no regrets.'

1. PREMIER AMBITIONS 2000 TO 2002

Against Blackburn in December 2000, Ball launched into a two-footed tackle on Rovers playmaker David Dunn, a reckless charge of juggernaut intensity. Ball recalled: 'Souness, the Blackburn manager, was going bonkers; Stan was going bonkers; the crowd was going bonkers; the referee was fumbling for his card, so I thought "bollocks to this!" and promptly marched off. My lad saw what happened on TV but stood up for me as always, claiming I got the ball. Not my wife though. She thought I should have been put inside. I saw David sometime after. We had a good laugh about it. I loved derby games. Just like the supporters do.' Mitchell Thomas told a *Lancashire Evening Telegraph* reporter: 'Kevin is always straight. Serious. Assertive in everything he does.' No kidding!

As if Stan didn't have enough steel at his disposal, he tried to entice his friend Vinnie Jones to join the Turf Moor throng. Although tempted, the former Wimbledon 'hit man' decided he was better off sticking with the movies.

A work colleague who moonlighted as a Preston scout had no doubt that Burnley would survive. He said that while Burnley's back three of Davis, Cox, and Thomas was sound, he thought that 'Davis's lack of pace might be targeted'. He thought that opponents might attempt to exploit his fondness for playing from the back, hoping to pick his pocket because Davis's recovery speed was allegedly 'not among the quickest'.

Burnley began the 2000/01 season confidently, holding promotion-bound Bolton to a 1-1 draw in the opening game at Horwich, with Phil Gray prodding in Little's inviting cross. Even more impressively, recently relegated Wimbledon were beaten 1-0 at Turf Moor with a goal from Paul Weller. According to Mitchell Thomas, Weller was known as 'Mr Angry, because of how easy it was to wind him up in training'.

Although Wolves inflicted yet another defeat on their favourite opponents, Burnley bounced back with an outrageous 'smash and grab' raid at Crystal Palace (1-0). The Eagles manager Alan Smith announced breezily: 'I've known Stan a long time. There won't be any surprises.' His rueful expression afterwards suggested otherwise, as his team spurned chance after chance, while the 'admirable' Crichton played a blinder in the Burnley goal.

A subsequent 1-0 win at Huddersfield featured another outstanding display by a Burnley goalkeeper. This time the hero was the lanky Greek international Nik Michopoulos, who took advantage of Crichton's late arrival to seize the number one position. Stan quipped to BBC presenter and die-hard Claret Tony Livesey: 'Nik was good. An expert at his drills. The problem was he could hardly speak a word of English … just "coffee" and "thank you". I left him with Jeppo [Ronnie Jepson] for two minutes and suddenly he knew five more, "It's f***ing freezing here, gaffer".' Mitchell Thomas said of 'Nik the Greek', 'He doesn't understand a lot but if he makes a noise when I'm in defence I know I have to get out of the way because he's so big.'

By the second week in November, Burnley were fourth, ahead of bitter rivals Blackburn Rovers. But Andy Payton, a hero of their 1999/2000 promotion campaign, was no longer an automatic choice, nor was his strike partner, Andy Cooke, who was transferred to Stoke in December for £300,000. Cooke parted with the gracious words: 'Over five and a half seasons, I have had a very good rapport with the crowd. I've got a lot of good things to take from Burnley. I wouldn't change a day of it.'

Payton was less sanguine about his loss of favour. He told his biographer, Gavin Roper: 'If I'd played the whole season, I'd have probably got at least 20, if not 30 goals. It was a crazy situation with the fans screaming "Get Payton on!" every game when I was on the bench. More often than not, Stan didn't want to play me for some reason.'

Stan wanted his front men to defend from the front in this more challenging division. Expensive recruit Ian Moore met that need, employing his lightning pace and phenomenal stamina to harry opposing defenders deep within their half, forcing errors and stemming their forward supply. Moore, a former England Under-21 international, was signed on 20 November 2000 from Stockport County for a club record fee, said to be £1m.

Chairman Barry Kilby said: 'It's a little scary but it's the right move and the right future. We must be careful with our cash despite a £2m increase in turnover during the 1999/2000 season, representing a 56 per cent rise. We didn't do it lightly, but we had to step up a gear and look to the future. We bargained down to the last penny.'

Stan added: 'Moore's young, 24-years-old, and we've signed him for this year and another four years so he will be the future of Burnley Football Club for the next five years. The chairman and the board have backed me on a £1m deal which is a lot of money for this club, and I thank them for that.'

Realising he was expected to graft for his new club, Moore said: 'It is an excellent move for me. Burnley is an impressive place, and the stadium is second to none. I can't wait to get started. I'll chase anything. I'm an honest player and I'll get on with it. If I'm up there, getting a few goals, I'll be a happy man. And if things aren't going well for me, I'll always work hard for the team.'

At the end of January 2001, 'headmaster' Gareth Taylor joined, initially on loan, from Manchester City, replacing the departed target man Andy Cooke. Taylor's aerial strength was also deployed effectively in defence, notably at set pieces. Like Ian Moore, Gareth Taylor was a hard grafter.

Payton remarked: 'Gareth Taylor would have been good to play with. He was good in the air. But I only got the chance to play with him once when he did his trademark flick-ons and I scored a couple. I didn't really get on with Ian Moore. He had pace – loads and loads of it – but I thought he was a soft git who wasn't good enough to replace me. He couldn't score regularly like I could.'

But if Payton felt jealous, unappreciated, and excluded, Mitchell Thomas commended him on his professionalism, saying: 'Andy keeps himself to himself and just gets on with it.' As for Payton's new rival, Ian Moore, Thomas described him as, 'Very quiet, very deep. Never get caught with him when he is having a deep moment, or you're trapped. It could be religion, football or home life, anything goes.' New recruit Phil Gray was also disenchanted with limited first-team opportunities and moved on to Division One Oxford in November.

While the competition for first-team places created some tensions, there was little doubt about the strength of team spirit as Burnley won four games on the bounce during October. Even a 0-5 battering at Nottingham Forest was quickly brushed aside with home victories over Crewe and Sheffield United, and a creditable draw at West Bromwich, where Burnley were denied a win after Jason Roberts's late equaliser.

The main jokers in this resilient pack were spellbinding winger Glen Little and elegant, yet combative, midfielder Paul Cook. Mitchell Thomas described the ultra-chatty Little as 'the life and soul of every party' and was convinced he 'could talk under water'. As for Scouse midfielder and 'dressing room bookie' Paul Cook, Thomas described him as 'a very funny lad, his accent making everything he says even funnier'. Thomas thought Lennie Johnrose was the most confrontational member of the group, claiming, 'He is constantly causing trouble. He loves winding people up, loves going against all the rules, like a naughty schoolboy.'

Before the Preston away game on 9 December, Burnley were strongly placed in sixth position, having won 11 and drawn five of their opening 20 league games. Home gates were averaging over 15,000, 15 per cent up on the previous season, and 12,300 season tickets had been sold, up from 6,800 in 1999/2000, an 81 per cent rise.

1. PREMIER AMBITIONS 2000 TO 2002

Burnley 0 Blackburn Rovers 2
17 December 2000

'Why Does My Heart Feel So Bad?'

Ian Moore finally opened his account at Deepdale with a princely, curling shot from outside the box, but Preston recovered in the second half winning 2-1. A greater disappointment came eight days later, when recently relegated Blackburn won 2-0 at Turf Moor in front of a febrile 21,369 crowd. Midfielder Jason McAteer scored the opening goal on the stroke of half-time, but Kevin Ball's X-rated tackle on David Dunn was the major talking point, exacerbating the game's vicious, gladiatorial emotions. These were also exhibited in an angry confrontation on the touchline late in the game when Burnley were frantically seeking an elusive equaliser. Their misery was compounded when Marcus Bent stole a second goal for Blackburn in the final minute.

Stan remembered how despondent his players were afterwards. Above their dressing room, in the Cricket Field stand, the ecstatic Rovers fans stomped and roared, while along the corridor there were raucous whoops from the triumphant Rovers dressing room. Andy Payton took this dispiriting defeat particularly badly. As a lifetime Clarets fan, he knew how keenly it would be felt by the Burnley faithful. Outside the ground the riot police had to battle to prevent the Blackburn coaches being attacked. Having had their violent intentions thwarted, a local contingent took out their frustrations in Burnley town centre, where, according to Stan, they smashed 'scores of windows'. Stan concluded: 'We had lost a football match. They had lost their minds.'

Three more league defeats followed in succession, including another 0-2 home loss, this time to Bolton, while Division Two Scunthorpe eliminated Burnley from the FA Cup at the first hurdle. A Boxing Day defeat at Barnsley (1-2) prompted Stan to lay into his players, ranting: 'It's not often I have a go at them, but I am now. The gloves are off. They might feel a little bit Billy Big Time, but we'll see.

'Our holiday period ended at quarter-to-five. We're training tomorrow and we'll be training right through the holiday period because I'm going to put this right for Burnley fans. They deserve better. Those players are having a laugh. I've stuck up for them, but they are having a jolly. That's not good enough. Everything's cancelled. There'll be no time off until I get better performances. When I see Paul Weller going to the line and whizzing balls across the box, and I see only one striker up, and no midfield players, and nobody from the other flank getting into the box, that tells me either they've eaten too much turkey and plum duff, or they don't have a desire. I don't want Glen Little back until he's right because he's no good to us as he is, and I've told the physio that.'

Rumours of Payton's alleged disaffection emerged. It was claimed that he and Moore were involved in a training-ground bust-up leading to their absence for the Bolton home game on 23 December. The truth was that both players were injured. Then speculation centred upon Andy Payton being transferred to Wigan or Notts County. Exasperated chairman Barry Kilby emphasised quickly that there was no truth in either account, adding: 'A lie gets out and is half-way around the world before the truth is reported.' Payton was dismissive: 'The rumours do not unsettle me at all because there is no truth in them. I don't know where they come from. I think there are only nine players in the history of the club who have scored 100 goals for them, so I want to do that.'

Taking umbrage at the modest clubs he was supposedly linked with, he sniped: 'It's never a decent club, is it?' Providing a timely reminder of his worth, Payton scored what proved to be the winning goal against Barnsley on 20 January, bringing Burnley's eight-game winless run to an end, only for three more dismal defeats to follow.

Burnley 2 Fulham 1
20 February 2001
'Gouge Away'

I took a day's holiday to drive up for this midweek game against putative champions, Fulham. I had a premonition we might win because Fulham seemed bound by a sacred command never to win at Turf Moor. They had not triumphed there since 1951 and they were pious as ever, ensuring this barren run continued. Two excellent goals in the final quarter gave Burnley a deserved victory in a tremendous all-action match.

In the first half Burnley were on top throughout, with Gareth Taylor and Moore causing constant problems for the normally resolute Fulham defence. With redoubtable Coleman injured, new loan signing Gareth Taylor won most of his aerial duals with Symons, wrong-footing the Fulham defenders with his flick-ons and excellent hold-up play. On three occasions he forced his namesake, Maik Taylor to make brave saves.

Fulham had few chances, the first falling to Lee Clark, whose snap-shot was kept out by an impressive diving save from Nik Michopoulos. Finnan also hit the post. A fine tackle by Steve Davis denied Clark for a second time. Clark had tarried on the ball for too long. Otherwise, the Fulham strikers Saha and Hayles did not unduly trouble Davis, Cox, and Thomas.

However, shortly after a goalless first half, Fulham unexpectedly scored. In the 49th minute, their full-back Steve Finnan dribbled neatly into the box and crossed to the far post where Barry Hayles headed Fulham into the lead in front of the Bee Hole stand. Burnley retaliated immediately, but it took them a further 24 minutes to penetrate the Fulham defence. A precise cross from Glen Little was met at the far post by Gareth Taylor who headed back across goal for Ian Moore to nod past Maik Taylor.

Inspired by this breakthrough, and egged on by a frenzied crowd of 15,737, Burnley poured forward. With only two minutes left they gained their due reward. Ian Moore sped through the

Fulham defence and laid the ball off to Little. The Burnley winger instantly created a smidgen of space before rifling in the winner.

It was only Fulham's fourth league defeat of the season. Gareth Taylor was constantly in the thick of the action. His new strike partnership with Moore augured well for the challenges ahead. A jubilant Stan Ternent gushed: 'The noise the fans made reminded me of the 1960s. It was fantastic, but to be fair we gave them a lot to shout about.' I returned to London excited by what I had seen, not giving a second thought about the heavy workload I faced on the following day.

Burnley 1 Huddersfield Town 0
24 February 2001
'Four Leaf Clover'

Four days later I drove up to Burnley again, this time with Andrew, to meet our Huddersfield-supporting friends before the Turf Moor game with the Terriers. This was a more attritional home win. To be fair the visitors deserved a share of the spoils but were undone by another powerful header from Steve Davis and by a series of brilliant saves by Michopoulos. Having come close to promotion to the Premier League in the previous season, Huddersfield were hurtling towards the third tier. During the game the sky darkened, resulting in a heavy snowfall. By the time we had reached Keele on our return journey, there were very few cars on the treacherous snow-covered motorway. Fortunately, the snow turned to rain by the time we had reached the Chilterns.

On the following Saturday, Lydia, Andrew, and I made the relatively short journey to Portsmouth. Pompey were no better off than Huddersfield but Burnley's ineptitude trumped their dockside opponents', and we lost lamentably to two second-half goals from Nightingale and Panopoulos. Lydia, Andrew, and I repeated this morose experience at Hillsborough on 17 March but at least the splendid roast pork and apple sauce teacakes brightened our day. Thankfully, four days before at Watford on 13 March, Gareth Taylor's goal gave us a 1-0 victory taking us to 52 points and safety. Gareth followed this up with another goal in a tough 2-1 home win over Queens Park Rangers for whom beanpole centre-forward Peter Crouch excelled.

Blackburn Rovers 5 Burnley 0
1 April 2001
'Break Down and Let It All Out'

The return game against Blackburn was played fittingly on April Fools' Day at Ewood Park. Burnley were torn apart, losing 0-5. Stan refused to shy away from the carnage, positioning himself defiantly at the front of his technical area, oblivious to the plethora of five-fingered gestures from the crowing Rovers fans. A savaging of this order requires a calm response from the man in charge, and to his great credit, Stan Ternent provided that.

He reflected: 'When we achieved First Division status, I knew we'd get our backsides tanned from time to time and that's happened today. But overall, the players have done very well. It's just a really bad day for our supporters. But the truth of the matter is that we're a million miles away, financially, from Blackburn Rovers, and that shows on the football field. If I have a Mini and you have a Ferrari, there's only one winner. If you go through the Blackburn side including the people who weren't even stripped, you're talking about an awful lot of money, probably seven years of my budget.

'Despite that, there wasn't much between the sides in the first half, apart from the two goals. And when the third went in, the players did remarkably well to keep it to five.'

Afterwards Stan had a drink with his longstanding friend Graeme Souness, the Blackburn manager, together with the Ewood coaching staff. He said: 'Everyone was on their best behaviour. No one mentioned the game. It was a bit like rowing away from the *Titanic* without mentioning the iceberg.'

As testament to what Stan Ternent described as his team's 'fantastic character and resilience', Burnley responded by pummelling Preston 3-0 at home and Wimbledon 2-0 away. A spirited comeback victory at Norwich (3-2) then put the Clarets in with a chance of securing a play-off place. Alas, they fell three points short. The two late equalisers they conceded against sixth-placed West Bromwich proved critical. Nevertheless, as Stan confirmed, seventh place was a fine achievement. He concluded: 'I think I'm close to having a good side. The players are fantastic professionals and all credit to them for a marvellous season.'

Paul Weller and Nik Micholpoulos deservedly won the lion's share of the supporters' clubs' player-of-the-year awards, although Stan picked out successful loan signing Gareth Taylor for special mention, confiding: 'He's done very well for us, and I certainly want to add Gareth to our squad.' Taylor, dubbed 'Golden Bonce' because of his aerial dominance, joined the end of season trip to Portugal. Stan was also mentioned in despatches, having guided his side to a lofty final position. At the player-of-the-year evening, he was presented with a special achievement award in recognition of his efforts. A final position of seventh exceeded most fans' expectations.

The feel-good factor swirling around Turf Moor was reflected in the 25 per cent rise in average home attendances which stood at 16,234 at the end of the 2000/01 season. Only 14 years before, this figure had been a meagre 3,342! It was small wonder that chairman Barry Kilby was so upbeat. At the AGM Barry said: 'Our club now stands in the top 30 clubs in the country. Once again great credit must go to Stan Ternent and all his staff in improving the standard of the first-team squad on what was an average budget for this division. On the commercial side, the new initiatives instigated by our chief executive Andrew Watson have started to bear fruit, with the commercial income rising again by 38 per cent to £3.4m, helping push our turnover up 28 per cent to £7.2m. Our desire is to maintain and improve our status in Division One. This led the board to authorise a trading loss of £2m as players' contracts were consolidated and additions made to our playing squad. This is imperative for the long-term progress of this club.'

Encouraged by the progress made during the 2000/01 season, by 9 May 2001, 10,000 season ticket holders had renewed their passes for the following season. But what should have been a time of celebration for Stan Ternent became a nightmare as he was rushed into Burnley hospital with a suspected heart attack. Much to his and his family's relief, it was a stomach ulcer. He was told very clearly that he needed to rest.

Stan was not idle for long, though. He had a team to build in pursuit of the Premier League dream. Having assembled most of his players on free transfers, Stan approached the board for a further £1m to purchase the gangling QPR centre-forward Peter Crouch, whom he described as 'sensational in the air and not too bad with his feet'. Ternent reckoned he had persuaded Crouch to join before Crouch and his wife were allegedly unnerved by a 'riot' in Burnley town centre. Burnley MP Peter Pike attributed this discord primarily to poverty, poor housing, and segregated schooling, rather than innate racism, blaming the local BNP for exploiting the community and economic tensions in perpetrating their racist policies.

Although believing his club could not help in reconciling local racial differences, Burnley chief executive Andrew Watson wanted to encourage young local people with minority ethnic backgrounds to attend Turf Moor matches and join club-run coaching, recreational or learning activities. Funded by a separate grant, Tunisian footballer Nourredine 'Dino' Maamria became the club's first part-time ethnic minorities development officer in April 2001. He had a remit to discuss racism in local schools, hoping to break down any aversion the Asian children might have had to joining coaching sessions. He also distributed free passes to encourage them to watch matches at Turf Moor.

He thought many Asian families were primarily interested in cricket, whereas another Burnley community worker, Mashuq Hussein, disputed this. He told *Independent* journalist David Conn: 'Asian people are passionate about their football. They watch it on TV, they play it, they talk it, the kids love it. But they won't go to Turf Moor. They fear the treatment they would get.'

Other potential moves collapsed during that summer, although Stan managed to sign free agent Alan Moore, a former Republic of Ireland international. Moore was once dubbed 'the Ryan Giggs of the northeast'. That was before his highly promising career was interrupted by injury. Ivorian-born French defender Arthur Gnohere was also offered a contract after a successful trial.

Sheffield Wednesday 0 Burnley 2
12 August 2001
'Hate to Say I Told You So'

On Sunday, 12 August, Lydia, Liz, and I dropped into Hillsborough after a weekend break in York. It was the first time all three of us had been to a game together since Lydia was a few weeks old. With new signings Alan Moore and brawny Arthur Gnohere on the bench, Burnley's starting XI comprised those who had completed the previous season. The 6.15pm start on a Sunday evening was decided by ITV Digital who covered the game. It was a dismal start for what became a doomed enterprise. The sullen atmosphere resembled evensong in a bare church.

The game began with little passion, although the Owls fans raised a stifled cheer in the second minute when the ball was put in the Burnley net. It was as if they expected it to be ruled out, as it was, for pushing. Although Weller and Taylor went close when well placed, the lethargic mood remained. Burnley's breakthrough goal came in the 57th minute. Little cut inside and fed the ball to Briscoe who backheeled it smartly into the path of Armstrong on the left flank. His first-time cross was headed

1. PREMIER AMBITIONS 2000 TO 2002

firmly past goalie Stringer by Taylor. This woke us up. It also prompted the Owls' boss to switch from a blunt 4-5-1 formation to a 4-4-2 one. This gave Wednesday more impetus, but when Paul Cook scored in the 79th minute from a twice-taken penalty, it seemed as if the game was up for Wednesday. However, their fans were finally aroused by what they thought was rough justice. The referee had ordered the spot kick to be re-taken because of encroachment. They disputed this angrily. Ugly scenes ensued.

Cook remarked a few days later: 'I can understand passions running high during games, but you can't have fans running onto the pitch and attacking players. I was grabbed and punched from behind. The assailant could have had a knife. Safety on the pitch should be paramount. He was on the pitch for quite a while. I would have liked to have seen the police or stewards trying to stop him. There were enough.'

Facing a possible FA censure for intervening, Stan retorted: 'If the police and the stewards are not protecting my players, I feel I have to do it.' While no action was taken against him, the fan who assaulted Cook was given a life ban. Others had season-long bans.

After Football League new boys Rushden and Diamonds eliminated Burnley from the League Cup, underlining the thinness of Stan's squad, he was permitted to buy Manchester City midfielder Tony Grant, for £250,000. Sunderland were said to have offered £3m for Burnley's ace winger Glen Little. But eying the prize of Premier League football, chairman Barry Kilby turned down the bid, believing that the ITV Digital money guaranteed solvency for the next three years. Little had suddenly discovered a talent for scoring as well as setting up vital goals. It was he who had tipped the balance in impressive league victories at Bradford (3-2), Birmingham (3-2), Coventry (2-0), and Preston (3-2). By Christmas, Burnley proudly led Division One having won 15 and drawn five of their opening 25 fixtures, scoring 48 goals. It was a remarkable feat from a side that Sheffield United manager Neil Warnock described as merely 'solid, with that extra bit of quality in Glen Little'. He added wryly: 'The sooner he's sold the better.'

Preston North End 2 Burnley 3
9 December 2001
'Freak Scene'

This was a breathtaking clash at a sunny Deepdale in front of a packed 20,370-strong crowd. The atmosphere was fevered with both sets of fans exchanging deafening insults, the Burnley fans mocking their adversaries with a festive rendition of 'Dingle Bells'. Preston manager David Moyes went for broke, deploying David Healy, Jon Macken, and Richard Cresswell up front. Healy came perilously close to giving North End the lead in the second minute when Ian Cox slipped while attempting to cut out Rob Edwards's cross. Thankfully Michopoluos was alert, pushing Healy's snap-shot aside with a firm hand. Burnley hard man Kevin Ball had been tasked with neutralising Sean Gregan, his roughhewn opposite number, but was unable to impose his customary authority. In the first 15 minutes Preston were quicker to the ball. However, in the 17th minute Burnley took the lead, much against the run of play. Lee Briscoe's curling free kick was prodded past Preston's goalie, David Lucas, by exultant centre-back Arthur Gnohere. Eight minutes later Burnley doubled their lead when Glen Little pounced upon a sloppy clearance to beat Lucas with a sublime shot that bent around him.

But Preston were not done yet. After Briscoe had pulled down David Healy on the edge of the Clarets' box, Nik the Greek found Graham Alexander's fierce free kick too hot to handle. Colin Murdock was first to the loose ball and laid it off for inrushing Paul McKenna to drill the ball high into the unguarded net.

Preston then turned up the heat on the back-pedalling Burnley defenders. Four minutes before half-time Preston were level when Alexander scored from the spot. Although Michopoluos got a hand to the ball he lacked sufficient strength to prevent the goal. There was still time for more first-half drama, though. Alan Moore's exquisite lob forced Lucas into hurling himself upwards to his right to deflect the ball on to the bar. Alas, there was no Burnley player on hand for a tap-in.

The second half was equally hot-blooded. Immediately after the resumption Michopoluos had to leap across his goal to palm away a bending shot from Healy that was destined for the top corner. On the hour, though, Burnley fashioned their winning goal. Gnohere collected a ball thrown to him by Lee Briscoe. Without hesitation he passed it to Alan Moore's feet. Crowded in by three Preston defenders, Moore eluded their clutches with a lithe twist and turn, back-heeling the ball into the path of Gnohere, who, at full pace, slipped it past advancing Lucas. The Burnley fans erupted in homage to a wonderfully created and finished goal.

The remainder of the game was hard fought, with Davis and Gnohere repelling a succession of Preston raids. North End's best chance fell to ex-Southampton striker Steve Basham, who poked wide at full stretch. Referee Pearson annoyed the Burnley fans by not penalising Murdock for two reckless fouls on Ian Moore and Little. They were also incensed when a linesman wrongly denied substitute Gareth Taylor a late lobbed goal, when it seemed that he was the victim of a foul by Lucketti, not the perpetrator. But none of this blighted our pleasure at seeing Burnley win a magnificent game of football, which put them four points ahead of Wolves at the top of the First Division.

This was as good as it got, as Kevin Keegan's Manchester City routed Burnley 1-5 at Maine Road on 29 December, a defeat which marked the beginning of Burnley's slump. Their final 21 league games yielded just six victories and seven draws with only 22 goals scored. Sadly, the Clarets' improbable, yet magnificent, pre-Christmas form became a rod with which to beat them. Their fans' expectations nosedived, notably after a wretched FA Cup defeat at fourth-tier Cheltenham Town (1-2), masterminded by future Burnley boss, Steve Cotterill.

In early March 2002, the fans' barracking of the Burnley players intensified. This caused Stan to angrily denounce the 'mindless few' detractors. He snapped: 'The fans here have got champagne tastes on beer money. This football club is fifth in the First Division, that means in the top 25 in England. We are going for the play-offs and yet still they moan, still they boo. They pay their money and are entitled to their opinion, but the booing has a completely adverse effect. These players have done magnificently. I am completely naffed off with the moaners. We've gone from the depths of despair to where we are now and still they are moaning, it is quite incredible.'

Stan was robustly supported by Barry Kilby and the players. Steve Davis, who had recently returned from a four-month injury, added: 'The booing is not fair. The chairman came in and, together with the manager, picked the club off its knees. When I came back, we were very close to going into the bottom division and now we are in a First Division play-off position. It is very easy to lose sight of that. I think the supporters have got to realise we want success as much as them.'

Leading goalscorer Gareth Taylor commented: 'I can't thank the gaffer enough. I have never had a regular run at any other club and hopefully I'm repaying him. It's nice to have 14 goals but there are still ten games to go. We do understand the fans' frustrations, but it is still disappointing. The players here are a great bunch, and we are all in this together. If one gets stick from the fans, it affects us all. If the fans get behind us it makes a hell of a difference and gives us such a lift. Until Christmas we had a great home record, when the pitch was in great condition. It's deteriorated a bit since.'

Phil Miller of Accrington Clarets remarked: 'I don't like fans getting on the players' backs. I understand the frustrations, but

1. PREMIER AMBITIONS 2000 TO 2002

it has been a great season so far. Expectation is so high because of the great start we had. I think some people have got to take a step back and look how far we have come. If you look at the sides at the top, they are bigger and stronger than us.'

The poor state of the Turf Moor pitch was a point of contention with Stan, too. He said: 'It is a difficult surface to play on. I have built a passing side and now we need to do something about the pitch. Even Pele couldn't pass on it.'

Sensing that top-flight football might elude them, the Burnley board backed Stan's request for reinforcements. After protracted negotiations with cash-strapped Bradford City, inside-forward Robbie Blake was signed for £1m with a £250,000 add-on should Burnley secure promotion. Alas, he was impeded by a hernia injury and made little contribution to the promotion push. Consequently, Stan was permitted to bring in David Johnson on loan from Nottingham Forest. Stan said at the time: 'Johnson is a class player, a genuine goal poacher. He will bring pace and the ability to hold up the ball. I took him from Manchester United on a "free", when I was in charge at Bury, and then sold him to Ipswich for £1.1m. From there he went to Nottingham Forest for £3.5m. With Gareth out for two games it is vital we have him in the side.'

Burnley 2 Preston North End 1
17 March 2002
'Take It or Leave It'

Burnley's comprehensive victory at bottom-placed Stockport eight days earlier was only their third in 13 league games. But if Burnley were to revive their hopes of promotion, albeit via the play-offs, they needed to beat visiting Preston too. In the first half Stan's men swarmed all over Preston. They should have been four or five up at the break, such was their total domination. It was Burnley's best performance since their scintillating victory at Deepdale in December.

Burnley's new pairing of livewire debutant David Johnson and electric Ian Moore was breathtaking at times as Burnley rushed Preston off their feet. The game began in a frenzied manner and never relented. Oddly enough, Preston might have taken an early lead when Lucketti's downward header from Alexander's free kick required a fine save from loanee Marlon Beresford, replacing injured Michopoluos. Seconds later Ian Moore opened the scoring having taken advantage of a poor clearance and successfully chipped goalie Lucas from long range. The accompanying roar was one of relief as well as glee. It was Moore's 12th league goal of the season but only his first in 2002, although he scored a hat-trick against Canvey Island in an FA Cup tie in January. He quipped afterwards: 'I was watching David Beckham yesterday and I thought I'll have a bit of that!'

Midfielder Tony Grant, who was in top form, almost added another, forcing Lucas to push his shot away. Alan Moore seemed back at his best, too, putting Johnson through on goal only for Lucketti to deny him with a goal-line clearance. Johnson had not long to wait, though. In the 25th minute he made no mistake when Alan Moore's perfectly weighted pass allowed him to outpace Lucketti and slot the ball past Lucas. Ian Moore then had the opportunity to seal the game when Johnson set him up for a one-on-one duel with Lucas. But the rapidly advancing Preston goalkeeper managed to block his shot. His namesake was not amused, believing that he should have squared the ball to him for a tap-in. Johnson also failed with another one-on-one chance, with Alan Moore again the provider.

Preston no longer had David Moyes to rouse them at the break, after their former boss had moved to Everton, but they turned the tide at the resumption of play. With thousands of North End fans hollering them on, they laid siege to the Burnley goal. But for Beresford's string of brilliant saves, Burnley might have succumbed. As it was, Anderson's 84th-minute

1. PREMIER AMBITIONS 2000 TO 2002

goal came too late to inflict serious damage. It was a close-run thing, though.

Stan wanted to buy Johnson from Forest. The tearaway striker was apparently keen to make his stay permanent. Forest were desperate to reduce their wage bill, with Johnson one of their highest earners on £10k a week. Stan thought he might be available on a free transfer. Despite Johnson's high wage at Forest, Stan reckoned that Johnson would not have cost the club much more than £1m for a two-year deal. But the Burnley board rejected this proposal, fearing the consequences of the ITV Digital collapse. Johnson scored five goals in Burnley's final eight games. But it was not enough. After the Preston victory, Burnley won only two of their remaining seven games, losing three. Their hapless defeats at Sheffield United (0-3), where Gazza was a liability, and at Grimsby (1-3), where former tennis star Michael Boulding tore them apart, proved very costly.

It was hoped that the short-term signing of stellar international superstar Paul Gascoigne from Everton would help Burnley achieve promotion to the Premier League in 2002, just as the signing of star striker Ian Wright had done in helping Burnley reach the First Division in 2000. Sadly, Gazza was beset with a serious drink problem. But Gascoigne's presence raised home attendances and club shop sales, while his wickedly curling free kick, in the final minutes of the Coventry game, almost grasped a play-off place. He was denied, though, by a magnificent save by Swedish international goalie Magnus Hedman.

Again, Burnley had failed to win a play-off place, this time by just one goal. Stan cursed the wrongful decision that ruled out Gareth Taylor's 'goal' against Wolves (2-3). The consequences were ruinous, for Burnley needed Premier League riches to avert the financial wreckage caused by the ITV Digital fiasco.

ITV Digital was founded upon an agreement struck between the Football League and Granada and Carlton TV companies, granting them exclusive TV rights to cover live matches, principally involving Division One clubs. The deal was worth around £90m a year to the Football League. Burnley's share was almost £3m. The club had budgeted for a receipt of £12m from the TV companies, representing the full value of its four-year contract, before it was revealed that the contract was not worth the paper it was written on. The financial impact upon First Division clubs was devastating. Meanwhile Carlton and Granada, collectively worth around £5bn, walked away unscathed.

Unfortunately, the legal case was not as strong as Barry Kilby had hoped. Carlton and Granada were subsequently sued by the Football League, but the case was lost, after the judge ruled that the Football League had 'failed to extract sufficient written guarantees'. The Football League filed a negligence claim against its lawyers, resulting in a paltry award, far less than the £150m damages it had sought. Consequently, around 600 professional footballers were put out of work while the transfer market values nose-dived.

Immediately after the last game, at home with Coventry, Stan released Kevin Ball, Mitchell Thomas, Lenny Johnrose, reserve striker Tony Ellis, and deputy goalkeeper Luigi Cennamo. This reduced the annual wage bill from £5m to around £4.5m. Barry Kilby announced that the wage bill needed to be reduced to £2.7m, warning that the club could not afford to turn down a £3m bid for prime asset, Glen Little. But there was no chance of such a lucrative deal being struck in this depressed market. The ITV Digital collapse not only stripped Football League clubs of essential revenue, it curtailed their capacity to make up the shortfall with player sales.

As galling as it was, in October 2002 the Football League clubs reluctantly acceded to a £5m bid made by Carlton and Granada to screen match highlights. While some Burnley supporters decried the deal as shameful, Barry Kilby retorted: 'At the end of the day we had to go along with the decision. It was a case of either getting the £88,000 or nothing. All clubs must face their bank managers! As part of the two-year deal, Carlton and Granada agreed to relinquish their claims to £1m legal fees incurred by the Football League's failed court action against them.'

2. ON THE BACK FOOT
2002 TO 2007

Derby County 1 Burnley 2
7 September 2002
'Rehab'

Burnley's 2002/03 season began with a feeble 1-3 home defeat by newly promoted Brighton. Ensuing ineffectual 0-3 losses at Wolves and Reading were separated by a dismal 0-1 Turf Moor defeat by Sheffield United, watched by a crowd of only 12,868. This figure was almost 20 per cent below the previous season's average home gate. It was Burnley's worst start to a new campaign in 25 years. With former favourite Marlon Beresford back in goal, after agreeing another short-term deal, and Robbie Blake demonstrating his pedigree up front at last, Burnley finally came good.

At the start of this game, Derby were in tenth place and Burnley were rock bottom. When Derby's Adam Bolder opened the scoring in the eighth minute, my fragile hope collapsed. There seemed little prospect of a revival. Derby were all over us during the first half. Burnley's three centre-backs, Cox, Gnohere, and McGregor, performed as if they were strangers. Wing-backs West and Briscoe were confined to defensive duties. A midfield of Weller, Grant, and Johnrose hardly created a thing, while Ian Moore dashed around pursuing lost causes, with Blake anonymous.

Stan obviously had a go at his players during the break for they returned to the field prepared to do battle. Crucially, Glen

2. ON THE BACK FOOT 2002 TO 2007

Little replaced Johnrose. With Little bolstering Burnley's attack, Derby came under increasing pressure. Just six minutes after the resumption Burnley were awarded a penalty. I watched the spot kick through shuttered fingers. Robbie was more resolute, ramming the ball past Poom. It was as if a switch had been flicked, for the Clarets seized control, with Blake at the centre of almost everything. Derby buckled. It seemed only a matter of time before Burnley would take the lead, which came about four minutes later, thanks to an own goal by Warren Barton. Burnley should have put the game to bed, but no, we had to endure an agonising 30 minutes before we could scream with relief.

It was indeed the turning point. On the following Saturday, Burnley came from behind to beat Stoke 2-1 at sunny Turf Moor, with a diving header from Greek Under-21 international Papadopoulos sealing victory. Thereafter, Burnley's season fluctuated wildly. Impressive victories over Premier League Spurs (2-1) and Fulham (3-0) in cup competitions stood in stark contrast with the shameful capitulations at home against Rotherham (2-6), Reading (2-5), Watford (4-7), and already-relegated Sheffield Wednesday (2-7). Burnley also discarded a good opportunity to progress to the FA Cup semi-finals they were beaten 0-2 by Watford after a depressingly defensive display at Vicarage Road. Following a bewildering 5-6 loss at 'Blunder' Park, Grimsby, on 'fright night', Stan Ternent was asked whether Burnley's under-performing centre-back, Arthur Gnohere, had been substituted because of injury. Ternent snapped: 'If he was injured it was only between his ears.' The collapse in Gnohere's form led to the signing of Mauritanian free agent Drissa Diallo from defunct Belgian club KV Mechelen. He provided much-needed stability at the back where Davis was struggling with injury and waning form.

As poor as some of Burnley's league performances were, the lowest point of their season was reached on 7 December when a visiting Nottingham Forest fan was killed before the game.

After the 2-7 humiliation exacted by Sheffield Wednesday, Stan Ternent fumed: 'It's back to five years ago and I can't wait for the summer now so I can build a new team, because I have to.' It was inevitable that there would be major changes. Among the former stalwarts released were Ian Cox, Steve Davis, Gordon Armstrong, Lee Briscoe, Nik Michopoluos, Marlon Beresford, Paul Cook, and Andy Payton. But Stan's plight was made even worse during the following 2003/04 season. Although the club escaped administration by a very slender margin, Stan had to survive with a threadbare squad augmented by eight loanees.

On 31 May 2003, Barry Kilby told a *Lancashire Evening Telegraph* reporter that he was expecting to bring in nine or ten players during the summer but insisted: 'We are not going to be paying any transfer fees. The team ran out of steam last season. We need an influx of younger players. I am quite bullish about it.' It seemed that he and his manager were not on the same page in placing a greater accent upon youth. Sensing this, perhaps, Barry added: 'My relationship with Stan is pretty sound. We have had our disagreements for sure, but we have always sorted them and continue to work well together. He is very loyal to me, and I hope I am to him.'

Clarifying his intentions, Kilby stated: 'The board has decided to try to improve our youth scheme. You must accept that it is not as it was in the sixties when I played in the Burnley 'A' team. We had schoolboy internationals then. We know we can't get academy status yet, although it is an objective for sure. We know, too, that an academy is not a cheap option and that you are not guaranteed success.'

He pointed out that talented midfielder David Dunn had been in the Burnley youth set-up as a 14-year-old before Premier League Blackburn enticed him to Ewood Park, with a much larger budget. Stan was dubious about the efficacy of such ambitions because Burnley no longer had the pulling power to attract the most talented youngsters as it did in the 1950s and

2. ON THE BACK FOOT 2002 TO 2007

1960s, and 'it did not have the infrastructure to support such an enterprise'.

Stan later reflected upon the unremarkable conversion of youth team players into first-team regulars with a strong sell-on value. He said: 'Today there's just the £1m we received for home-grown midfielder Richard Chaplow, and possibly £3–5m for young striker Kyle Lafferty to swell the coffers. Whereas Andy Lochhead and Willie Irvine, at their peak in the sixties, would have brought in over £20m each today. Get the club into the Premiership then the best young players will want to come. It only makes sense to think of an academy once the club is in the Premiership. So, what I'm saying is, if the money is tight then the best thing is to use seasoned pros and track the progress of young academy players and use them if there is enough finance to find the quality players.'

Barry explained: 'Taking account of wages and other outgoings, this translates into a possible £2m loss for the 2003/04 season. I have put in £3m in capital into the club which I don't expect to see again. We managed to get a suspension of capital payments, we got a commercial loan that we have been able to pay back, and the directors have loaned money. Vice-chairman Ray Ingleby has been a great support to me, particularly, last year. When doing deals with creditors he was fabulous.'

Meanwhile Stan was telling the local press that he hoped to be competitive despite being reduced to 18 professionals, six of whom were injured, namely Alan Moore, Robbie Blake, Arthur Gnohere, Mark McGregor, Gareth Taylor, and loan signing Luke Chadwick, while Ian Moore faced a three-match suspension for his indiscretion during the 2-7 debacle against Sheffield Wednesday. Stan told a *Lancashire Evening Telegraph* reporter: 'It's very difficult, without a doubt, as hard as I've had it. It has been a hectic summer and I've hardly had any time off. The players on big pre-ITV Digital wages have one or two years left of their original three- or four-year contracts. It will gradually work its way out. I've moved a lot out, including Greek Under-21 striker Dimi Papadopoulos for a £250,000 fee, and I might have to move on some more to bring some in.

'Realistically, as things stand, we are looking to stay in the First Division. That would be massive with what I have got now.'

To add to Stan's woes, 2002/03 player of the year, Gareth Taylor, was sold to Nottingham Forest for £500,000. He wasn't keen to leave but Burnley could no longer afford him.

The 2003/04 season began, like the previous one, with three consecutive defeats. The Clarets lost 2-3 to visiting Crystal Palace in an error-strewn display. On a blistering hot day, Burnley were undone by their suspect defence in which Graham Branch deputised at centre-back, alongside an increasingly erratic Arthur Gnohere. But it was debutant full-back, Lee Roche, a loan signing from Manchester United, who was at fault for Palace's opening goal, while newly recruited goalkeeper Brian Jensen was culpable for the second and third goals. Despite a sparkling debut by Luke Chadwick, on loan from Manchester United, Palace were gifted the points. A heavy defeat at West Bromwich followed (1-4), where Robbie Blake opened the scoring in the 27th minute with a magnificent strike. Further defensive calamities in the home game against Wigan resulted in a third successive loss (0-2).

Gillingham 0 Burnley 3
25 August 2003
'Gasoline'

But at Gillingham on a bright, warm 25 August, Burnley thrashed their hosts on a ground that had largely been a graveyard for them during the noughties. Ian Moore began the rout in the 27th minute. His swift breakaway on the left flank concluded with a sharp shot on the run that beat goalie Brown at his near post. Right wing-back Dean West then rifled in the second on the half-hour, having outstripped his markers and cut

2. ON THE BACK FOOT 2002 TO 2007

inside, letting fly with his unfavoured left foot. Robbie Blake capped this impressive performance by curling in the third in the 77th minute. It was a bravura display of perceptive passing, dashing movement, and clinical finishing, buttressed by robust defending. New signing David May, formerly with Manchester United and Blackburn, was a pillar of strength at centre-back.

On the following Saturday, Crewe were overcome 1-0 thanks to an outstanding performance by youth team graduate Richard Chaplow. Stan was delighted, crowing: 'It was a fantastic three points for us, and we created a lot of chances again. Richard Chaplow was fantastic today. The goal was marvellous for him. He's a player, if he can keep his feet on the ground.' Stan also praised the passing of Chaplow's fellow midfielder, Tony Grant.

With 800 out-of-contract players seeking employment around the country, club chairman Barry Kilby claimed: 'The negotiations concerning potential incoming moves are now all about wages. I will be extremely surprised if there are any transfer fees paid outside the Premiership.' Meanwhile, Burnley's once prized asset, Glen Little, was in limbo. Having been loaned to Reading at the end of the previous season to reduce Burnley's wage bill, his hopes of securing a permanent contract there evaporated once the Royals were eliminated in the play-offs. It seemed unlikely that any team outside the Premier League could afford to match his wages, which were then thought to be around £8,000 per week.

Stan Ternent's problem was bringing in essential replacements on his reduced budget of £3.5m. That budget was £1.5m down on the 2001/02 figure. Besides, 90 per cent of the budget was already committed in meeting the pre-ITV Digital contracts. It was no surprise that Little was loaned out again, this time to Premier League Bolton. In return the Trotters' Republic of Ireland midfielder Gareth Farrelly and centre-forward Delroy Facey joined Burnley in short-term loan deals. Combative centre-back Andy Todd was also loaned from Blackburn. Stan was permitted three permanent acquisitions, all on free transfers: flying Guinean left wing-back Mo Camara from Wolves; ex-Manchester United and Blackburn centre-half David May; and imposing goalkeeper Brian Jensen from West Bromwich, known affectionately as 'the beast'. Of the newcomers, only Lee Roche failed to distinguish himself. He quickly relinquished the right wing-back berth to Dean West.

Stoke City 1 Burnley 2
6 September 2003
'Somewhere Where I Belong'

Lydia joined me on the road trip to the Britannia Stadium on a grey, squally Saturday, 6 September. Here we were treated to one of Burnley's finest displays of the season. Stoke City were blown away. We were amazed how well Stan's patched-up team performed. While May and Todd were rock-like in central defence, halting Stoke's erratic attacks with ease, Camara and West bombed forward with menace, tracking back quickly when possession was lost. Gareth Farrelly was composed and incisive in midfield, fanning out penetrative passes for wide men Chadwick and Branch to exploit. Meanwhile, Blake pulled the strings in advanced positions. Burly Delroy Facey had made little impact at Bolton, but here he led the line with verve and punch. Far from seeming like a scratch side, Stan's bargain boys seemed like the real deal.

In the first half Burnley constantly attacked their hosts, taking the lead when May converted from a set play in the 18th minute. May's powerful physique was put to good use at both ends. Nine minutes later Chadwick danced through the Stoke back line to score Burnley's second goal. Although Asaba reduced the arrears in the 53rd minute, Burnley held out with few alarms. This third consecutive victory lifted the Clarets from the bottom up to tenth place. After enduring five successive defeats at the Victoria Ground, the Britannia Stadium seemed

2. ON THE BACK FOOT 2002 TO 2007

a luckier place. The return journey flew by as we played Linkin Park and Primal Scream at high volume.

Bradford were crushed 4-0 at Turf Moor on 20 September, with another top-drawer performance from two-goal Luke Chadwick. Paul Merson's Walsall were also brushed aside at home, two weeks later, featuring Facey's powerful hat-trick (3-1). Although a depleted, flu-stricken Burnley side lost 1-6 at Ipswich a few days later, they then achieved a creditable 2-2 draw at West Ham where they were denied a prestigious victory by a late equaliser. However, a disappointing run followed, comprising four draws and two defeats. The sequence was broken when nemesis side Reading were surprisingly routed 3-0 on 25 November. Sheffield United were subsequently beaten 3-2 in a switchback game on 6 December but it was a brief respite as four successive defeats ensued.

After a gutless display of defending at Preston, five days before Christmas, it was rumoured on Sky Sports News that Stan had been sacked or resigned, whereupon Ternent retorted angrily: 'Under no circumstances will I resign. I would not let this football club down. I wouldn't let the chairman down, who has been brilliant, or the board of directors. I have never turned in anything during my life and I don't intend to start now.'

The club's AGM, held a few days later, provided little cheer. The 2001/02 wage bill of £7.4m had been reduced to £3.6m in 2002/03 but that figure needed to be trimmed further to £3m. During the 2002/03 season there was a loss of £2.6m with the estimated figure for 2003/04 about the same. New chief executive Dave Edmundson confirmed it was Barry Kilby who was keeping the club afloat. Kilby said: 'The problem will get worse before it gets better. There's enough money to last until February, but if we don't have a good cup run, the bills or staff will need to be restructured.'

Burnley progressed to the fifth round of the FA Cup before being eliminated in a toxic tie at Millwall, mired with mutual accusations of racial abuse. Had Alan Moore not missed a sitter, Burnley might have reached the quarter-finals where they would have faced Tranmere. Fortunately, Barry Kilby had agreed with Millwall's owner, Theo Paphitis, to share the proceeds, whatever the result. He had struck a similar deal with Watford's chairman before the execrable sixth-round tie at Vicarage Road in 2003.

On 16 February, chief executive Dave Edmundson revealed that the Clarets had avoided administration for this season, at least. The club needed to raise £500,000 by the end of that month and 'thanks to a brilliant response from the fans, plus the proceeds from the FA Cup run, Burnley FC would remain in business for now'. There was no discussion of players deferring their wages, as was considered at Leeds. Some Burnley fans were irritated by this, feeling that the players were contributing less to the cause than themselves.

The club was granted a temporary respite, but the team hovered alarmingly just above the relegation zone. Luke Chadwick, who began the season well, had faded as injury impaired his form, fitness, and confidence. The mercurial Jensen was brilliant in some games, as at Sunderland, West Ham, and Bradford, but was a liability against Palace and at Preston. Lee Roche arrived with a high recommendation but struggled to assert himself in the bump and grind of Division One. Meanwhile his partner, Mo Camara, flattered to deceive. When he bombed forward, he represented a threat to opposing defences, but too often his crossing was woeful. Troubled by a recurrent Achilles problem, Glen Little failed to make his customary impact, leaving Burnley short creatively, despite Tony Grant's and Richard Chaplow's best efforts. Little had returned to Burnley for the start of the 2003/04 before being loaned to Premier League Bolton in September 2003. Little's short loan period was unsuccessful and he came back to Turf Moor after making only four appearances at Horwich. This was Little's last season at Burnley. Alan Moore was again hamstrung by injury while Ian Moore felt his striking potency was reduced by playing wide. Nevertheless, he chipped in with important goals, none more vital than his late headed winner at Bradford on 27 March.

Of the eight loan signings, only centre-forward Delroy Facey, and centre-back Andy Todd, made much impact during their brief stays. Although decried by some supporters, Lenny Johnrose's return during an anxious run-in proved invaluable. In short, Burnley were too reliant upon 19-goal Blake, Grant, Chaplow, May, and Branch, with Branch filling in wherever he was needed, at full-back, centre-half, wide midfield, and centre-forward. It was small wonder that Burnley laboured. Priceless victories at relegation rivals Walsall (1-0) and Bradford (2-1) kept Burnley narrowly the right side of the line. But ultimately, they were indebted to wrongly maligned Graham Branch in scrambling to safety. His goals in successive home games against 'franchise' Wimbledon, and Derby, in late April, garnered the six points needed to avoid relegation.

Barry Kilby then dropped a bombshell, announcing that Stan's contract was not to be renewed. A dire 0-3 defeat at Rotherham in the penultimate game probably sealed his fate. An additional concern to this cash-strapped club was a further ten per cent fall in Turf Moor attendances. The average gate for the 2003/04 season was 12,541, 3,693 or 23 per cent lower than it had been in 2000/01.

Barry explained his decision thus: 'Stan has done a fantastic job for this club, including a promotion, and keeping us in the First Division for five seasons. I'm looking to the long-term future of Burnley. Managerial changes are inevitable. Stan and I have enjoyed a close working relationship, he has always been passionate about Burnley and has been one of the best Burnley managers of all time. I would like to thank him for his devotion and dedication to Burnley. He will always be revered at Turf Moor. I sincerely wish him well with his future plans.'

Stan's last game was a home fixture with Sunderland, the club he had supported as a boy. The sun shone and 18,000 turned up, including nine committed cyclists who had completed their 500-mile bike ride, raising £13,000 for the club, a magnificent effort. After the game, a tearful Stan received the rapturous applause of the Burnley supporters with a large Sunderland contingent joining in.

In his farewell message Stan said. 'I can't quite believe I'm about to take my last walk out of the tunnel as Burnley manager today. I will take a last look at a few familiar places. I will try to take in the amazing atmosphere generated by you, fantastic fans. I will fight – but can't promise – to keep my emotions in check.

'As a kid, I dreamed of playing for Burnley in the top division. Lately, I thought I could take us there as manager. You know how close we came. Now, for me, at least, it is over. We have had some wonderful times together during the past six years. I will remember the scenes of sheer joy when we won promotion at Scunthorpe. I won't forget the hangover suffered by half the town the next day either.

'My players throughout these times have all worked fantastically hard. Like me, I'm sure you'll never forget the moment you saw Ian Wright and Gazza walk out at Turf Moor in our famous claret and blue. Lately our financial problems, which meant losing some of our best players, have made life tougher. Because of the budgets imposed upon me, I stand by the claim that keeping us in the First Division this season has been my greatest achievement so far in management.'

After making 300 appearances for Burnley, the Sunderland game was Glen Little's last, too, after he agreed to sign for Reading. He was equally complimentary about his time at Turf Moor, stating he was 'privileged to play for the club and proud to be part of a club with such a great history'. About Stan's managerial style, Glen said: 'You must be mentally strong, and I've always been that. I've had my run-ins with Stan, but that

2. ON THE BACK FOOT 2002 TO 2007

is part and parcel of football. He's swung for me a few times and you have your rows and square-up, but if you don't take it to heart that's the important thing. I've been hit with a bottle, called everything under the sun and even had a right hook, but the day Stan stops shouting in your ear, that's the day you get worried. He might not be everyone's cup of tea and people might not like the way he does things but that's the way it is with him.'

Stan Ternent was replaced with Steve Cotterill, an ambitious young manager who had lifted Cheltenham Town out of Southern League obscurity and into the third tier of English football in a handful of seasons. It was a remarkable achievement given the paucity of resources at this humble Gloucestershire club. Cotterill's move to third-tier Stoke City, in the summer of 2002, ended abruptly and acrimoniously, for shortly after his appointment, he deserted the Potters to become the right-hand man of veteran manager Howard Wilkinson at Premier League Sunderland. Cotterill believed that he had been chosen as Wilkinson's heir apparent but became bitterly disappointed. Wilkinson was unwilling to delegate, and with Sunderland careering towards relegation in March 2003, Wilkinson and Cotterill were sacked. Cotterill was without a management post for over a year.

On 3 June 2004, Barry Kilby announced Cotterill's appointment as Burnley manager, saying: 'All the applicants, including Ronnie Moore (father of Ian) and ex-Claret Brian Flynn, had impressed, but Cotterill, who has signed a three-year deal, was the outstanding candidate to take us forward.'

Cotterill added: 'I turned down eight offers since I left Sunderland, but this Burnley job is the right one. There's something about this north-west corridor. Burnley have the tradition and the chairman is a man I can work with. Everyone here, including the famous old players, has been very supportive and I've been reminded there are wonderful people in our game.'

Cotterill was even more impressed by the local benefactors who freely offered their time and money in a period of continuing financial hardship for the club. He enthused: 'We have someone who has donated new showers, toilets and wash basins and we have someone who is going to come in and fit them for nothing. How terrific is that? I want it to be a nice place, comfortable, clean, and tidy. I want things to be proud of.'

Cotterill was delighted to find the community and club pulling together. He told Alastair Campbell: 'If you walk down the road you don't see Manchester United or Arsenal shirts, they'll be claret and blue. If I was to achieve half here of what I achieved in Cheltenham, I'd get the key to the town.'

A Cheltenham Town supporter posted the following testimonial on the popular Clarets Mad website: 'Cotterill's attributes: incredibly hardworking and focused; excellent knowledge of other teams and players; gets his players very fit and engages with them well; intolerant of prima donnas; meticulous; top coaching qualifications; self-confident and single-minded; good contacts; gets the best out of moderate players. His greatest skill is inspiring and motivating a team.'

The fan said Cotterill had inherited a squad of 'talented (by Southern League standards), but flippant, under-achievers' at Cheltenham. He had transformed their form, using the same first-choice back four between 1996/97 (when Cheltenham were Southern League runners-up) and 1999/2000 (when they finished eighth in Division Three).

Among Cotterill's weaknesses, the fan listed, 'has obvious "favourite" players – showing excessive loyalty to them during long dips in form; can revert to long-ball game too easily; can create unnecessary difficulty by being uncooperative with the media'. He also pointed out that although Stoke fans would criticise him, the 'Potters' headed rapidly downwards after he left.

'His move to Sunderland was foolish, motivated by over-ambition, and he himself has publicly regretted it. I would

2. ON THE BACK FOOT 2002 TO 2007

suggest he is too bright to make the same mistake again. He won't be an overnight success, but he will do a good job for you in time.'

Derek Goddard of the *Gloucestershire Echo* described Cotterill as 'a very emotional coach and very sensitive bloke. I first knew him at Cheltenham as an 18-year-old player. He was always a bit tetchy and cocky then. He left to go to Wimbledon where he was plagued with injury. He is not one to get on with the press. If you ask him his name, he will want to know why you were asking.'

Upon his appointment Cotterill told the press: 'The first plan is to get three players, because we have only eight.' He did not offer new terms to the four out-of-contract players, May, McGregor, Weller, and West, but he quickly signed imperious 32-year-old centre-back John McGreal, from Ipswich, on a three-year deal. Cotterill remarked: 'The hardest thing is trying to bring players in because the chances are that three or four clubs want to talk with the good ones. We won't be bringing in a lot. That's a sure fact. We've got to put a team together before we can put together a squad. I don't want to be changing the team every five minutes. If we had a budget double what we have then I could bring in more players, but we haven't. What happens when you don't have a lot of money is you end up with team players rather than star individuals.'

As part of a team-building exercise, Cotterill took his players on a short pre-season trip to Austria where they played two Bundesliga Division Two sides. He commented: 'Trips like Austria are important, otherwise the players come in and go home and you don't get to know them. There is so much more to it, they are people, not just footballers.' Cotterill's strength as a team-builder was illustrated following a 1-2 FA Cup defeat at Premier League Blackburn, in March 2005. At the final whistle, Cotterill drew his deeply disappointed players into an on-pitch huddle, rousing their spirits before presenting them to their fans who gave them the ovation they deserved.

Most Burnley fans were pleased with Cotterill's appointment. But season ticket sales were sluggish with only 8,000 sold by the end of June, just 100 up on the 2003 figure. Knowing that money was very tight, Cotterill played the transfer market astutely, acquiring five quality players at little or no cost. In addition to McGreal, he signed Watford's pugnacious midfielder Micah Hyde, Cheltenham's right-back or centre-half, Michael Duff, who had already been capped by Northern Ireland, pacey ex-Chelsea and Leicester defender Frank Sinclair, and accomplished Welsh international goalie Danny Coyne, also from Leicester. Only the transfers of Coyne (£25,000) and Duff (£30,000) required a fee, and both were modest payments given the players' calibre. Coyne had represented Wales on 16 occasions having proved himself at struggling Grimsby, where he had been the fans' player of the year in successive seasons. Unfortunately, his Burnley career was stunted by a serious injury, whereas Michael Duff's prospects soared. Duff would play in 383 league and cup games at Burnley. Despite sustaining a cruciate injury during the 2007/08 season, Duff recovered to help Burnley seize a hat-trick of Premier League promotions in 2009, 2014, and 2016. He also represented the senior Northern Ireland side on 24 occasions, playing a key role in their memorable victories over England in 2005 and Spain in 2006.

In September, Cotterill added French winger Jean-Louis Valois to the ranks, initially on a 30-day contract. The free agent was unkindly dubbed 'a poor man's Ginola', by one of my work colleagues, who scouted for Preston. He told me: 'Valois has some skill but little bottle.' Nevertheless, Valois remained for the entire season, playing a prominent part in the League Cup victory over Aston Villa in October.

Cotterill was equally adept in the loan market, signing Aston Villa's fledgling centre-back Gary Cahill during November 2004, on a season-long loan deal. At the outset of his Burnley career, Cotterill seemed as sceptical as Ternent about selecting

2. ON THE BACK FOOT 2002 TO 2007

youth players, although he, too, considered Chaplow to be an exception. Cotterill questioned: 'Some of the youngsters might be good enough technically but are they tough enough mentally to go out in front of the crowd, and do it?'

And yet he had no qualms about blooding the inexperienced Cahill, playing him in all but one of the 28 league games remaining. Cotterill's trust was richly rewarded. It was readily apparent that Cahill had the necessary maturity, might, technique, and mentality to go far. He starred in a debut 1-0 home win over Nottingham Forest, helping Burnley keep seven clean sheets in his first nine games. Such was his commanding presence, that he and his centre-back partner, John McGreal, snaffled most of the player-of-the-year awards at the season's end.

With Cotterill's already small squad shrinking to unsustainable levels, because of injuries and departures, several other loan deals were struck. Combative midfielder James O'Connor spent two spells with the club, the first on a short loan, the second as a prelude to a £175,000 transfer, having lost his way at West Bromwich. Ipswich reserve striker Dean Bowditch also came in during March on a month-long loan, scoring the opening goal in a 3-1 home win over Watford. Cotterill described him as 'a good, young, exciting player'.

Aston Villa's Peter Whittingham and Portsmouth's Richard Duffy performed filling-in turns, as well. While Whittingham showed little of the attacking verve and set-play acumen that marked his later displays for Cardiff, the latter distinguished himself in a brief stay by scoring the winning goal at Leeds in early November 2004. That unexpected 2-1 victory, with a heavily patched-up side, epitomised the fierce battling spirit and defensive nous which Cotterill instilled in his players. Cotterill seemed at his best when the odds were onerous, as was the case when his side overcame Premier League teams Aston Villa (3-1) and Liverpool (1-0) during this season's cup competitions. Lest it be forgotten, he had also orchestrated Cheltenham's FA Cup victory over Premier League-chasing Burnley, in 2002.

In a *Times* article in September 2004, Cotterill made a rare disclosure of his chosen methods. He said: 'When defending corners and free kicks against taller players, I ask my players to stay on their feet and not give away more set-plays than necessary. If you keep the ball better than the other team, you will tend to concede fewer corners than you earn. Against set-plays, there are two ways of defending: zonal, which I'm not keen on, and man-to-man. I also have a spare man who is free to chase the ball. If the opposition have a player who is head and shoulders their best header, then we'll have done our scouting and get our spare man to lock up the area where he is most likely to attack.'

While Cotterill remained alert to bargain deals, skill improvement was his priority. The fruits of this were realised in the better performances of Mo Camara and Frank Sinclair. The poor quality of Camara's crossing had been a source of exasperation to Stan Ternent throughout the 2003/04 season. With his playing resources so limited, Steve Cotterill could ill afford such wastage. During pre-season, he had Camara repeatedly practising crosses, not letting up until the left-back could routinely attack with intensity and accuracy. Similarly, he tasked his coaches with removing the careless aberrations in Frank Sinclair's game. The result was equally impressive as Sinclair was transformed into a rock-solid centre-half or full-back, given a re-birth as 'the Power'.

After extending his one-year contract in December 2004, Frank Sinclair said: 'Initially I came because of the gaffer, because I needed to play for someone I trusted.' Reflecting upon the stringent demands of his personal training plan, he added with a beaming smile: 'I had a hard summer, but it was an opportunity to start afresh. I've enjoyed it so much here that I had no hesitation in signing for a further two years.'

2. ON THE BACK FOOT 2002 TO 2007

Steve Cotterill's first competitive game was at home to Sheffield United in the newly re-branded Coca Cola Championship. Although Micah Hyde deservedly snatched a first-half lead, Burnley had to scrap thereafter to remain on terms. On an afternoon of scorching heat, a 1-1 draw was a commendable return.

Adopting a tightly disciplined 4-5-1 formation, Cotterill's Burnley were equally hard to beat in the games which followed. Despite their slender resources, Cotterill's Clarets reached 11th position by early December, well in sight of a play-off place. Of their first 23 league games, eight were won and nine drawn. While only 20 goals were scored, just 19 were conceded. Lone striker Blake contributed 50 per cent of his side's goals.

While Blake lacked pace, he had consummate skill. His first touch was deft and sure. His nimble dexterity, his quick feet and sudden twists and turns often confounded the tightest of markers, creating space where there seemed to be none. Although he offered little in an aerial contest, he was rarely overpowered on the deck. With his strong back and muscular legs, he regularly held off burly defenders pressing from behind. In addition, he had a fine array of penetrative passes. And as Preston found in a 2-0 defeat at Turf Moor in December 2004, Blake had a ferocious shot, too. Cotterill took little time in choosing Blake as first-team captain, arguing: 'Robbie came back for pre-season leaner and fitter than ever before.'

Reading 0 Burnley 0
2 October 2004

'Novocaine for the Soul'

On this dazzling autumn day next to the M4 we prepared for another dose of beautiful frugality. A London Claret told me: 'I should really hate these ultra-defensive tactics, but I don't, I love watching how we squeeze the life out of our opponents' game. I no longer worry about the result either. I trust Cotterill's team to grab a result.'

Today was a case in point. Reading had considerable firepower with three goal-hungry forwards, Dave Kitson, Nicky Forster, and Shaun Goater, supported by attacking midfielder Steven Sidwell. But time and again their forward forays were blunted by McGreal, Sinclair, and Duff, with Branch, Hyde, and Chaplow battling in midfield. A Sky reporter wrote. 'Steve Cotterill has assembled a superb rear guard in a summer of wheeling and dealing. While Reading had two goals disallowed, it could have been Burnley that stole the points, especially in a second half that saw them sit back, soak up the pressure and counter-attack superbly, led by Blake and Ian Moore. If Burnley can find a natural goalscorer to play off the sublime Blake, they may well have a shot at the top six.'

What followed, though, became an unwelcome annual pattern. A promising pre-Christmas promotion tilt degenerated into a New Year slump, occasioned by the loss of Burnley's premier striker. On 5 January Robbie Blake signed for Premier League Birmingham City for £1.5m. 'Crown jewel' Richard Chaplow departed soon after, signing for West Bromwich, also for £1.5m.

Undaunted, Steve Cotterill congratulated chairman Barry Kilby on achieving an 'excellent deal' with these sales, 'having held his nerve right until the last minute'. Even when confronted by the temporary losses of Branch and Duff through injury, Cotterill wasn't inclined to complain. He asserted: 'I know we won't be buying anyone. A lot of the Blake transfer fee is going towards the Turf Moor pitch, to prevent waterlogging in front of the Bob Lord stand. The pitches at Gawthorpe training ground need improvement, too.'

With Burnley reduced to 14 fit senior professionals, Cotterill was permitted to sign 26-year-old midfielder John Oster, who had a loan deal with Leeds terminated for his off-field behaviour.

2. ON THE BACK FOOT 2002 TO 2007

Oster had played 40 Premier League games for Everton and 59 first-team matches for Sunderland, as well as representing Wales in 11 full internationals. Cotterill described Oster as: 'Very good technically. With his play-making ability he will help restore some of what we lost with Robbie Blake's departure.' But Oster did not make the impact Cotterill was hoping for and left in April 2005 after only 14 senior appearances.

A much bigger surprise came on 24 February when Burnley beat Sheffield United in the race to sign 30-year-old Stoke striker Ade Akinbiyi. Because of a thigh injury and a three-match suspension, Akinbiyi had only nine games in which to make an impact. His four goals garnered four points, but this came far too late for Burnley to revive their pre-Christmas momentum.

Nevertheless, Steve Cotterill and Barry Kilby were delighted with the overall progress made. Cotterill said: 'This has been a remarkable season. We have more than cemented ourselves in the division and yet sold £2.75m worth of players, while bringing in over £1m from the FA Cup run, which included a 1-0 victory over Liverpool, and over £250,000 from the Carling Cup competition, in which we beat Aston Villa.

'Barry Kilby told me my brief was to keep Burnley up but said if we got relegated, I wouldn't get the sack. I have found this area to be very hard-working. It's very, very working class which I warmed to, having grown up on a council estate. The only thing against it is the constant bloody rain. If we had better pitches at the training ground and the ball rolled in the right direction, the weather might not bother me so much.'

At the end-of-season awards night, Steve Cotterill was rightly awarded an outstanding achievement commendation for helping his team achieve two prestigious cup victories, and for guiding them to a respectable position of 13th, despite losing two key players and having to juggle with a small first-team squad. Barry Kilby said: 'Steve's established himself here very well, and I'm not claiming credit for that. We have had a bumper year, making a profit this time, but what that money is going on is to fund wages for the next two years. It is getting tougher and tougher for a club like Burnley in the Championship with its revenues. We're about 18th in the table of revenue. You have got to remember that we're playing clubs that take £250,000 more than we do at every home game.'

Chief executive Dave Edmundson stated that the club had survived the financial storm caused by ITV Digital's collapse, thanks to ruthless cost-cutting. While the average gate remained almost static at 12,466, Edmundson maintained that 'one of the greatest performances off the field was getting 8,500 season ticket holders, a phenomenal achievement when there was no optimism'.

Given the welcome cup booty, and the savings accruing from the departures of three high earners – Blake, Grant, and Ian Moore – Cotterill was given a £500,000 war chest for the 2005/06 season. Cotterill commented: 'I think the situation has got worse from the last year. There's only so many good free transfers out there, and you can't get every one of them.'

The departing Camara, Grant, and Ian Moore saved the club around £100,000 in wages. Goalkeeper Brian Jensen and Graham Branch became the only survivors from the Ternent era. Brian had covered Coyne's five-month absence capably, inducing Cotterill to award him three more years.

Having only nine first-team players at his disposal, Cotterill returned to his former club, Bournemouth, to bring in winger Wade Elliott and midfielder Garreth O'Connor. Elliott had excelled in Bournemouth's luckless 0-2 FA Cup defeat at Turf Moor in 2005, having roasted Mo Camara. Cotterill also signed Stoke striker Gifton Noel-Williams on a free transfer. Cotterill explained: 'Gifton will be a good asset in both boxes. He is a good lad, an intelligent footballer, and comes in on the right pay structure, as all the players have. He's not always easy on the eye but he will do what he is very good at – holding the ball up and heading it. He won't outrun centre-backs, but he will help us keep the ball and bring midfielders into play. If he gets the right service from Wade Elliott, he will score a lot of headed goals. He is a big, strong, physical presence, and you need that.'

Cotterill made a further swoop at Bournemouth, signing their 22-year-old former Arsenal midfielder John Spicer for £35,000. He then flew to Florida to persuade Wayne Thomas to sign. Thomas was a burly central defender, previously with Stoke. Former Chelsea left-back Jon Harley was also signed from Sheffield United for £75,000 to plug the gap left by the departed Camara.

The 2005/06 season began badly, though. Only one victory, a 4-0 home drubbing of Coventry, was recorded in Burnley's first ten games, which included five defeats. Thomas incurred a serious knee injury in the 1-2 defeat at Reading on 29 August, ruling him out of the next 17 league games. Jensen also suffered a nasty injury at Watford, culpably ignored by the referee, who allowed the Hornets to score a match-clinching third goal despite Jensen remaining prostrate in pain. Following a 1-0 reverse at Plymouth on 17 September, Burnley were second from bottom.

However, Cotterill's men suddenly turned the corner on 27 September with a 3-0 home victory over Ipswich. Former trainee Chris McCann, a Republic of Ireland midfielder, netted late in the game. A rare victory was then achieved at Molineux, thanks to dogged defending and Garreth O'Connor's brilliant long-range free kick. Despite losses at home to Leeds (1-2) and at Crystal Palace (0-2), Burnley's subsequent four-match winning run lifted them into a play-off place in mid-November.

Luton Town 2 Burnley 3
5 November 2005

'American Idiot'

On the brink of Guy Fawkes Night came an explosive victory at Kenilworth Road, one that lives long in the memory. Akinbiyi was on fire, twice bursting through the Luton defence to blast Burnley into a two-goal lead with only 30 minutes gone. His second was a 20-yarder, that veered past ex-Claret Marlon Beresford at blistering speed. But our elation turned to concern when Jensen was dismissed for handling outside his box. Burnley had to play for an hour without a recognised goalkeeper, having no reserve goalie on the bench. Unabashed, midfielder John Spicer put on the gloves. He had no previous experience but performed heroically behind his gritty defenders. But two minutes before the break, Steve Howard reduced the arears in front of us, the dismayed Burnley supporters.

With Luton having recovered from their first-half mauling by Akinbiyi and exerting greater pressure, we had serious doubts about our capacity to hang on. This was Ade's day, though. For in the 54th minute, besieged Burnley were awarded a penalty. Ade grabbed the ball and beat Beresford's dive with a measured shot right in front of us. Cue raucous pandemonium! Luton were not finished though. On the hour Warren Feeney's effort was too good for Spicer and once more we were biting our knuckles.

Burnley's back-to-the-wall efforts were incredible, given they were without McGreal and Duff. Everyone pitched in, though, attempting to build an impenetrable wall around Spicer. The minutes ticked by so slowly. At the other end the Luton fans were hollering on their increasingly frenetic side. Shots rained in on the Burnley goal. Block after block defied the Hatters. Crosses fizzed across the box. There were countless near misses. It was heart-stopping stuff.

Curiously, the coolest man on the pitch seemed to be Spicer. He appeared so calm, unfazed by the fierce battle taking place before him. Finally, the full-time whistle sounded. We and the exhausted Burnley players shared a hoarse, euphoric celebration with Akinbiyi holding his hat-trick ball aloft. Even the Luton fans applauded. Cotterill hailed the win as the greatest of his career, enthusing: 'It was fantastic character by the boys. I'm

2. ON THE BACK FOOT 2002 TO 2007

proud of them. Luton are a good side. Ade is a gem. There were a few eyebrows raised when I signed him. I told him at half-time to make sure he got the match ball. I love him to bits and so do the players.'

Akinbiyi's 12th league goal of the season was sufficient to defeat his former club, Stoke, on Boxing Day, lifting Burnley into fifth spot, their highest position under Cotterill. Ade was indeed a gem, coveted by others, notably Neil Warnock, manager of promotion-bound Sheffield United. The Blades' £1.75m bid was too good to ignore. Akinbiyi moved to Sheffield on the 25 January 2006, bringing about another post-Christmas slump. Akinbiyi told the press at his departure: 'I am definitely sad to leave. I will always remember Burnley as a great time in my career.'

Barry Kilby explained: 'The truth is we made a profit of £1.8m last year and after spending around £800,000 on Akinbiyi and James O'Connor and £100,000 on agents' fees, what was left enabled us to keep the wage bill at £3.5m, the fifth lowest in the division. Steve will get well over £1m of the money from Ade's sale to rebuild, while the arrears are being met by the profits we made last year. Eventually that will run out. We are fortunate to have directors who, between them, have put something like £8m into the club in the past four or five years. I have put £5m of my own money in and have pledges to put in another £750,000 to cover us until February of next season. That's when the money runs out again unless we have money from cup runs or try to get someone to put capital in or trade players. The only alternative is cutting our wage bill.'

At the November 2005 AGM, Kilby confirmed that the sale and lease-back of Turf Moor and Gawthorpe training ground was imminent. It transpired that Longside Properties, a company in which Barry Kilby owned 51 per cent of the shares, was the purchaser. This £3m deal arranged by him in 2006 was crucial. Without this, Burnley's future would have been grim.

The sale of Turf Moor and Gawthorpe was expected to clear all external debt, although £1.6m of directors' loans remained. The affordability of football in Burnley had been called into question. While the unemployment rate in Burnley had fallen to four per cent, lower than the national rate of five per cent, and much lower than its mid-eighties figure of 15 per cent, local wage levels in 2004 were well below the national average. More than half the local population had an average annual income of less than £15,000 compared with a national average of £25,000, with only 6.5 per cent of local households earning more than £40,000 per year. A quarter of Burnley's population lived in the most deprived neighbourhoods in the country.

Former England and Bolton striker Michael Ricketts then arrived from Leeds on a loan deal just as Ade was departing. Cotterill had been a great admirer of Ricketts, alongside many others, when the ex-Bolton striker had been in his prime. At Bolton, Ricketts had initially impressed. Tall and muscular, he was a target man with thunderous power and speed. However, a dismal debut for the senior England side in February 2002 appeared to derail him. Thereafter, his career unravelled at breakneck speed. Cotterill argued: 'He wants to do well, having been in the wilderness for a couple of years. We'll try our best to help him.'

Ricketts began promisingly. On debut, he scored the goal which defeated Plymouth 1-0 on 4 February 2006. Having neatly averted a challenge at the edge of the Pilgrims' box, he despatched a low drive into the left-hand corner with the nonchalance of a master craftsman. His nimble winner ended a seven-game winless sequence. There was brief hope that he would fill the gap left by the departed Akinbiyi. But apart from finishing clinically at Portman Road a week later, Ricketts contributed little thereafter as Burnley racked up six successive losses, imperilling their Championship status. His 12 league games at Burnley had produced only two goals.

2. ON THE BACK FOOT 2002 TO 2007

Just in the nick of time, Sunderland striker Andy Gray and Wigan's Irish playmaker Alan Mahon were signed on loan deals, both with a view to permanent transfers. Gray was signed for a £750,000 fee while Mahon cost £200,000. Burnley accrued 11 points from the final eight games, securing safety with ease, but four places down on the previous season. Gray opened his account in a debut victory over Norwich and seized the match-winner against Queens Park Rangers. Gangling Northern Ireland striker Kyle Lafferty, a former Burnley trainee, like Chris McCann, scored his first goal for Burnley with a late equaliser against Luton. Ex-Burnley captain and talismanic centre-half Steve Davis Mark II was appointed as first-team coach after another former Claret, Mark Yates, moved to Shrewsbury. Cotterill and Davis were delighted with the signings of Gray and Mahon, with Cotterill stating: 'They're two quality players. Mahon will make us play more football than we play and that is vital.'

Burnley's 2006/07 season started well, with victories over Queens Park Rangers and Leicester, only for them to stutter, losing successive home matches against Wolves, a longstanding habit, Hartlepool, in the League Cup, and newly promoted Colchester. Just when a slip was turning into an embarrassing slide, Barnsley were beaten 4-2 after the visitors had taken an early two-goal lead. The unlikely hero in this impressive turnaround was Gifton Noel-Williams who recorded his first Football League hat-trick. A self-deprecating Gifton admitted: 'I can't really blame the fans for not fancying me. But I have broad shoulders. Hopefully, I've shown the Burnley fans what I can do and it's up to me to continue that and to kick on and score a few more.' Gifton was immediately taken off the transfer list.

With Gray's first-minute goal proving sufficient to defeat Stoke at the Britannia Stadium, Burnley rose to third place. Disappointingly, on 23 September Burnley failed to beat Southampton in a winnable home game. Shortly after Jones had given Burnley a fourth-minute lead, captain Wayne Thomas was sent off for violent conduct. Cotterill fumed: 'A moment of unthinkable stupidity has cost us three points. We were the better team, and they knew it.'

Norwich City 1 Burnley 4
1 October 2006

'I Bet You Look Good on the Dancefloor'

October began with renewed hope as Burnley crushed Norwich 4-1 at Carrow Road, captured live on Sky TV. Having received a boardroom ultimatum, Norwich manager Nigel Worthington was under extreme pressure, not helped by this hapless performance. Norwich failed lamentably to crack Burnley's solidity at the back or cope with their devastating counter-attacks. The outstanding features of Burnley's victory were Wade Elliott's dazzling wing play and Steve Jones's bustling approach work. A scurrying James O'Connor set the ball rolling with a smart shot in the 32nd minute. Then Gray scored twice, his first goal coming just before half-time, assisted by Elliott, and his second arriving shortly after the resumption, set up by Jones. Substitute Alan Mahon finished the game off in style with a screamer from the edge of the box. Enjoying their Sunday schadenfreude, the large Burnley contingent chanted 'Worthington out'. Burnley moved up into third place while the dignified Worthington stepped down.

Hull were then despatched 2-0 in an unremarkable home win on the following Saturday. Steve Cotterill commended his new centre-back partnership of Duff and Sinclair for the 'immaculate way they dealt with Hull's constant stream of crosses'. Duff also chipped in with a headed goal. Burnley rose to second spot, causing chief executive Dave Edmundson to appeal for more support. The 11,530 attendance figure for the Hull game was the third lowest in the division. Edmundson revealed that while Burnley's home attendances remained around this level, the club

2. ON THE BACK FOOT 2002 TO 2007

would continue to lose £30,000 per week. He urged more local people to attend,

Two hard-fought, goalless draws with Southend and Plymouth followed, causing Burnley to slip a couple of places. Steve Jones told a *Lancashire Evening Telegraph* reporter: 'I think there's a lot of managers in the division that must feel we shouldn't be up there, but we feel we should be, with the results we've got. We're quietly confident.'

Burnley 3 Preston North End 2
27 October 2006
'Blood'

The Preston game was a scorcher, watched by a raucous crowd of 14,871. After a ferocious start, man of the match James O'Connor gave Burnley the lead on the stroke of half-time with a smart shot from inside a crowded box. But second-placed Preston were not subdued, pressing Burnley back strongly after the break. Burnley were hanging on desperately. Helped by two key substitutions, the game was turned on its head. Substitute midfielder Simon Whaley slammed in a 77th-minute equaliser, causing much grumbling among the home support. Urged on by their baying fans, Preston mounted attack after attack. Burnley were toppling. It was no surprise when Preston's second substitute, Brett Ormerod, a former Seasider, gave North End the lead with only ten minutes left. While the home fans were silenced, the visiting supporters were exultant.

But Burnley were not finished. Irrepressible Frank Sinclair stepped up to the plate. Rediscovering an elixir of youth, Frank zipped down the right flank, producing a sizzling, low cross which Preston's central defender Sean St Ledger could only divert into his own net. Back on terms with eight minutes left, Burnley smelt blood. Pouring forward, they won the game in the final minute, when an exquisitely flighted left-wing cross from Jones deftly glanced off Gray's forehead past flailing

Preston goalie Carlo Nash. Bedlam broke out on three sides of the ground.

A relieved, hoarse, and exhausted Steve Cotterill croaked: 'God shone down on us today because we deserved that!' I was not so sure about that, for Preston had dominated this game for long periods. But this had been a superb contest garlanded with topsy-turvy drama. Gray's predatory instincts then enabled ten-man Burnley to snatch all three points at Luton, too. His deft lob left Beresford helpless while his powerful back-post header, from Wade Elliott's accurate cross, took the points and the plaudits. Burnley were third, but the clouds were gathering.

McGreal and Thomas were out with knee injuries, Noel-Williams and Garreth O'Connor had succumbed to illness, and Foster faced suspension for his dismissal at Kenilworth Road. An exasperated Cotterill demanded more reinforcements, stating: 'We need these before we get to Christmas because by the time we get there, we'll have only 11 players and no sub at all. Everyone knows we have got the smallest squad and I'm sick and tired of saying it. Tonight, at Luton we were down to our last 16 players. If we want to stay there or thereabouts, we need to strengthen. The boys have given their all again and they are really first class.'

Having received the Championship manager of the month award for October, Cotterill dedicated it to his team, stating: 'I take the little personal pat on the back, but it is very much a collective effort.'

Although Chris McCann's last-minute header, from Mahon's pinpoint cross, was sufficient for Burnley to overcome Ipswich, three defeats on the bounce followed, inflicted by Cardiff, West Bromwich, and Birmingham. Winning ways were restored on 28 November 2006 when lowly Leeds were beaten 2-1 at Turf Moor. Gray was once again on target against his family's club. However, he sustained a metatarsal injury in this game, ruling him out for at least ten weeks.

2. ON THE BACK FOOT 2002 TO 2007

Steve Cotterill put on a typically brave face for the press, announcing: 'There are opportunities now for others, namely Kyle Lafferty. That's the only way we can look at it.' Lafferty made an immediate impact, curling a beauty into the bottom corner to give Burnley an 86th-minute lead at Ipswich on 2 December. Annoyingly, Burnley then conceded a soft equaliser four minutes later. The error was repeated in the following home game against Sunderland. Lafferty's brace of goals had given Burnley a two-goal advantage but in the final ten minutes the Black Cats struck back twice to earn a draw. A loss at Coventry on 9 December was followed by others at Barnsley and Hull during a cheerless festive period. By New Year, Burnley were 11th and falling. Between 28 November 2006 and 31 March 2007, Burnley failed to win a single league game in 18 fixtures, also losing a third-round FA Cup tie at Reading. This slump left Burnley just three places above the drop zone.

When Burnley began this slide in December, Steve Cotterill turned to new Burnley director Brendan Flood for help. Flood responded by funding the return of Ade Akinbiyi for £750,000 during the January window. All but £100,000 of the fee was paid up front. A grateful Steve Cotterill stated: 'I don't think we would have been able to bring Ade back without Brendan coming on board. He's not only a fan, but a big fan of Ade's. With the loss of Andy Gray, we have struggled to win a game, as hard as we have tried. Another striker was therefore a must. The prices quoted for younger strikers were unbelievable and certainly not something we could get into. We have got someone who is 30-plus, but Ade didn't do too badly the last time he was here, and he was 30-plus then. Only the pessimists will say you shouldn't go back. The optimists will be delighted.'

However, Ade had bulked up at Bramall Lane, spending excessive time weight-training while sidelined. This had impaired his speed and dexterity. Despite scoring an immaculate FA Cup goal in a losing cause at Reading, it took him nine league games before he scored again, when he equalised against Palace on 3 March. By then Burnley were 18th.

Flood invested £2m in the club, most of which was made available for transfers. Steve Cotterill told Flood that the first team could not be successful without more experienced players, although he continued to select Lafferty and McCann. Flood then funded the signings of two battling midfielders, Cameroon international Eric Djemba-Djemba, on loan from Aston Villa, and Icelandic international Joey Gudjonsson, from AZ Alkmaar, for £150,000. Flood also bought Sunderland's Scottish international centre-half Steven Caldwell, with half of the £400,000 fee paid up front. Reserve goalkeeper Mike Pollitt was brought in too, from Wigan, as cover for Jensen. Before wages were reckoned with, Flood had shelled out a further £1.3m in these four deals, £1m of which was paid immediately.

This was a bold measure. It was anticipated that Caldwell's firm leadership and organisational ability might tighten the defence. Before his arrival, there had been discontinuity, with the club captaincy passed quickly from Thomas to McGreal and on to Sinclair. These incoming transfers gave Cotterill the scope to release Frank Sinclair, Micah Hyde, and Noel-Williams.

Despite the deeply disappointing results, John Harley told a local journalist: 'We're a good team. Steve Cotterill has got together the best team ethic I have come across. Once we get one win, we'll be OK.'

This offered scant solace while Burnley remained precariously placed above the drop zone. Barry Kilby then sanctioned two emergency loan signings: Graham Coughlan, an intimidating centre-half, from Sheffield Wednesday; and Paul McVeigh, a striker or winger from Norwich who had previously played for Spurs and Northern Ireland.

On the eve of a crucial midweek home game against Plymouth on 3 April, Steve Cotterill gave a pumped-up

2. ON THE BACK FOOT 2002 TO 2007

interview to the local press asserting: 'As regards the chairman and the board, I think the job I've done here in two-and-a-half years, and what it's been done on, probably earns myself time and credit with them. There have been three or four occasions when I could have left the club, but I didn't. I think there have been several good managers who have been on uncomfortable runs this season. You just have to get on with it.'

Burnley 4 Plymouth Argyle 0
3 April 2007
'Herculean'

Against Plymouth, Burnley turned the corner. Urged on by a slim but stoked-up crowd of 9,793, Burnley roared into action against back-pedalling Plymouth. Duff put Burnley ahead in the 13th minute while loanee McVeigh found his feet quickly, adding a second seven minutes later. Not to be outdone, Jones found the net, too, in the 38th minute. After firing blanks for months, Burnley were tearing Plymouth apart. Argyle could not cope with the Clarets' aggression and intensity. Burnley eventually won the game 4-0, after Elliott had cracked in a fourth on the hour.

Cotterill told the waiting press: 'The lads played angry, stirred by the stick they received at the weekend after their 0-0 draw with Luton. I suppose the key now is to keep angry! They wanted that result for a long time. We have had a big cross to bear. I'm delighted for the players, for the chairman and the directors and the supporters who have stood beside me, because it's probably been the toughest time I have had to face.'

As glib as Harley had sounded in his press interview, he was right. Following that emphatic victory over Plymouth, Burnley proceeded to beat promotion-bound Birmingham at St Andrew's four days later, winning 1-0 after a wonderfully cool finish from John Spicer. Cotterill dedicated the victory to recently deceased Brian Miller, forever a Burnley hero. Cardiff, Norwich, and high-riding West Bromwich were also overcome, lifting Burnley well clear of the relegation places. A final position of 15th represented an improvement of three points and two places on the previous season.

A relieved Steve Cotterill showered his players with plaudits, notably goalkeeper Jensen, Wayne Thomas, and Andy Gray. The latter pair had struggled to recover their form following injury. Cotterill said: 'Thommo's ended up being the player I signed him for. He's defended first and foremost and earned rave reviews, while Andy Gray is one of the top strikers in this league. Anybody can play with him. He's intelligent and does all the horrible work, holding the ball up, the aerial stuff and the fighting with the centre-halves. Paul McVeigh has helped here, allowing us to play a bit differently, and taking some of the weight off Andy.'

He complimented Djemba-Djemba, too, describing him as 'mightily impressive in the heart of midfield'. The previously muscle-bound Ade Akinbiyi was mentioned in despatches as well. Cotterill said: 'I had to take him out of the side, but he doesn't sulk, and he was the first one to his feet when we scored against Plymouth. He's a good man and deserved his headed goal in the 3-0 win over Norwich.' A Burnley star of the future was unveiled in May when local youth player, Jay Rodriguez, signed his first professional contract with the club.

Cotterill's squad for the 2007/08 season was enhanced by several notable signings. Robbie Blake returned from relegated Leeds for a £250,000 fee. A Kosovan Albanian forward, Besart Berisha, was signed from Hamburg for £340,000 following a brilliant display at Turf Moor in a 'B' international, and Manchester City's left-back Stephen Jordan arrived on a free transfer, providing competition for Jon Harley. As for the other full-back berth, Cotterill was permitted to spend a further £200,000 on Preston's highly competitive right-back Graham Alexander. This seemed a lot to pay for a 35-year-old player, but

2. ON THE BACK FOOT 2002 TO 2007

Cotterill argued: 'We've got probably the best right-back in the Championship over the last eight years.'

With injury-prone keeper Danny Coyne released, Cotterill found an apparently worthy replacement in Hungarian international Gabor Kiraly, formerly with Crystal Palace, although his trademark jogging bottoms seemed to belong to *Shameless*. But Cotterill's best deal of the summer was selling Wayne Thomas to Southampton for £1.2m, and replacing him with Watford's elegant, quick, and doughty centre-back Clarke Carlisle, for £200,000. Although Cotterill would not remain in post long enough to witness the fruits of his recruitments, he had assembled the nucleus of a side which would win promotion to the Premier League in May 2009, under his successor, Owen Coyle.

Among the others leaving the club were centre-half Stephen Foster, midfielder Garreth O'Connor, and utility player Graham Branch, who had served Burnley well in a stay of nearly eight years in which he had made 232 senior appearances. There were changes behind the scenes, too, with former chief executive Dave Edmundson moving to a new role as head of strategic development, focusing upon the club's community activities. Chairman Barry Kilby and operational director Brendan Flood took on more hands-on responsibility for the everyday running of the club, jointly sharing the functions previously held by the chief executive. Barry Kilby pointed to the need to 'drive up the club's revenue streams'.

Meanwhile, the club had to prove its worth on the pitch. Steve Cotterill remarked on the eve of the 2007/08 season: 'We've had a tough two or three years with injuries to players at important times and hopefully we won't get that situation anymore. The one thing we have got is a bit more strength in depth.' With the club allegedly turning down a £2m bid from Fulham for young striker Kyle Lafferty, Cotterill added: 'We're delighted we've got four strikers now.' Sadly, new signing Besart

Berisha would not make an appearance for Burnley after he sustained a serious injury

Although stronger up front, Cotterill fretted over his back four, particularly after Michael Duff suffered a cruciate knee injury. Nevertheless, Burnley made a flying start, defeating West Bromwich in the opening home game in front of a healthy 15,337 crowd, but as autumn arrived that early momentum became lost. With the team spluttering once more, Turf Moor attendances began to decline. Only 9,978 turned up on a chilly November evening for an awful home game against Hull. Abject Burnley allowed the toothless Tigers to win the game with a late, scuffed effort. It remains as one of the worst games I have seen at Turf Moor. Ironically, Hull feature in three of these.

The club was about to announce an annual loss of £4.3m to the end of June 2007, almost double that of the previous financial year. The wage bill had risen to £7.1m against a £6.7m turnover. This deficit would have been higher had Brendan Flood not bought more than £3m worth of shares, making him the club's second largest shareholder. Other directors had made loans to the club as well. Flood was not only worried that the new investment was foundering. He was convinced that it was time for a change of manager.

Barry Kilby agreed, telling the assembled press: 'Let me first say that Steve Cotterill has all the capabilities to be a Premiership manager. However, what has happened in the last ten games and the slide down the table, maybe the directors thought it was time for a change. We played poorly against Hull and bad home defeats never help. That was a defining moment. I think we are the fourth lowest in the division in terms of attendances, and last Tuesday we had a gate lower than 10,000. It's not necessarily about performances but people want winning teams, and we still have ambitions to get into the top six.'

PART 6

CAPITAL PUNISHMENT

2008 to 2009

'In for the Kill'

1. 'FAKE IT TO MAKE IT': THE COYLE WAY

After considering several candidates, Brendan Flood's interest turned to St Johnstone manager Owen Coyle. Sports journalist Alan Nixon and Bolton chairman Phil Gartside backed his candidacy enthusiastically. Having sounded Coyle out, Flood was instantly impressed, persuading Barry Kilby that this was the man the club were looking for. On 22 November 2007, Coyle was confirmed as Burnley's new manager.

At Coyle's inaugural press conference at Burnley, he stressed: 'We are only one step away from the Premier League, and that's where we want to be.'

In his first game in charge, against Stoke, Burnley played with fluency and verve, but were unable to break down the visitors' robust defence (0-0). Three days later, Burnley won 2-1 at table-topping Watford with goals from Gray and Gudjonsson. Burnley then won 3-1 at fourth-placed Charlton with Blake and Elliott in devastating form. Coyle commented: 'Our sense of spirit and camaraderie was evident for everyone to see. Even when we were under pressure, each player knew that there was a colleague at their shoulder giving everything for him, and that augurs well.'

After a frustrating 1-1 home draw with Leicester, Burnley turned in another impressive performance on the road, defeating their bogey team, Wolves, 3-2 and lifting themselves into seventh place. Here ended the Coyle bounce, though, as Burnley lost four

1. 'FAKE IT TO MAKE IT': THE COYLE WAY

and drew two of their next six league games, reducing them to 12th place.

Worse still, on 18 January leading goalscorer Andy Gray was transferred to Charlton for an initial fee of £1.5m, having had his head turned by his father, Frankie. Taking account of potential additions, the total fee was possibly £2m. Coyle expressed his disappointment with Gray. But Ade Akinbiyi performed well as Gray's replacement, scoring the opening goal in a 2-1 victory at Coventry, causing Coyle to exclaim: 'Ade led the line brilliantly. I can't speak highly enough about him as a man. He is still prepared to knuckle down and await his chance.'

Flood promised Coyle he would have the £2m for summer deals. In the meantime, former Celtic centre-back Stanislav Varga and fellow Sunderland 'exile' Andrew Cole were signed on loan. Cole was a free-scoring former Newcastle and Manchester United centre-forward, also capped for England. An exultant Coyle said: 'I'm absolutely delighted to have a player of his calibre at the football club. It gives the whole club a lift.'

Queens Park Rangers 2 Burnley 4
12 February 2008

'Eyes on the Prize'

On a chilly February evening at Loftus Road, Cole treated us to a masterclass of finishing. His performance here emphatically vindicated Coyle's assessment of him. Not that he was conspicuous during the first 30 minutes, when newly enriched QPR burst into a two-goal lead with midfielder Gavin Mahon and ex-Preston striker Patrick Agyemang on target. Cole was subjected to merciless derision by the smug home fans. However, four minutes before the interval, Cole expertly flicked in Gudjonsson's fiercely struck, if wayward, free kick. Burnley were back in the game. At half-time Coyle astutely replaced tricky Blake with barnstorming Akinbiyi, rightly believing that Ade could punch bigger holes in QPR's hesitant defence.

Within six minutes of the restart, Burnley were level. Cole located a pounding Akinbiyi on the right with a defence-splitting pass. Akinbiyi's instant cross found Cole in space, who volleyed home with unstoppable power, the ball clattering against the underside of the bar before rippling the net. Burnley were in the ascendancy, swarming all over their reeling hosts. On the flanks, Elliott and Lafferty tormented their markers with pace, power, and trickery. An Elliott drive smacked against the woodwork, but Coyle's men were not to be denied. In the 77th minute Akinbiyi headed home from Caldwell's flick-on, to put Burnley in front.

But Burnley were not finished. With four minutes remaining Cole seized the game and his hat-trick, sweeping in Alexander's zipping free kick at the near post. At the final whistle, Cole held the ball aloft for all four sides of the ground to admire. It was a perfect riposte.

A delighted Coyle said: 'I thought Andrew Cole was superb, and Ade Akinbiyi again. Ade was unfortunate to be left out of the starting XI but came on at half-time and summed up the spirit in the whole football club. Tonight, was about our spirit and sense of togetherness. It would have been very easy at 0-2 down to fold and end up getting a hiding, but nothing could be further from the truth.'

Cole was equally buoyant, exclaiming: 'I am very pleased, not just by the hat-trick, but by the way the lads came back from 0-2 down to win. That gave me great pleasure because when QPR went two-up, they were giving it the big "Ole". Every goal feels good. I have not played too many games this season, but to score goals now gives me the same feeling as it did when I was a kid. I still have the same appetite to play and win games. The manager played a big part in getting me to the club. He said he thought I could bring a lot to the club, playing week in and week out, helping others. When managers have that belief, it makes you feel really good, and he has that belief in me. We are all playing for the manager. He gives us the enthusiasm to want to carry on playing and he makes me feel as if I am 21 again.'

Off the field, the redevelopment plans for Turf Moor and Gawthorpe were underpinned by the appointment of former Burnley centre-forward Paul Fletcher as development director.

On 5 February, Fletcher announced that the projected costs for the redevelopment programme would rise to £30m. He explained: 'The building needs to be a community building which is not just owned by the football club. The new facilities can regenerate the area and help increase the value of people's houses. We are clearly not sitting back and waiting for the future to happen – we are creating one.'

With the global economy engulfed by a growing fiscal crisis, many supporters were concerned about the viability of this project, fearing that the scale of borrowing involved exposed the club to potentially ruinous risks.

Burnley 2 Barnsley 1
29 March 2008
'Daft Punk Is Playing at My House'

The stunning victory at Loftus Road raised hopes of winning a play-off place. But this optimism was dashed quickly. Only four of the remaining 14 games were won, with seven lost. The solitary bright spot in this dismal sequence came at a sodden Turf Moor on 29 March when Kyle Lafferty performed superbly as a spearhead striker. His capability in this role should have been apparent from his Northern Ireland displays. Sure-footed on the saturated surface and ruthlessly dominant in the air, he bullied the Barnsley defenders from start to finish. He also scored a memorable acute-angle goal, smacking the ball into the far top corner. His stunning strike put Burnley two goals ahead in the 36th minute after Elliott had opened Burnley's account on the half-hour. Under Coyle, Lafferty had played mainly on the left flank. Despite this awakening, little more was seen of his prowess as a central striker, at least at Burnley, after Rangers bid an astonishing £4m to take him to Ibrox, £3m of which was paid up front.

The season came to a calamitous end with a 0-5 defeat at Crystal Palace. A dejected Coyle told the press: 'It reinforces what I knew we needed in terms of personnel, and we will endeavour to rectify that in the summer. Defensively, we've not been good enough. Albeit with ten men today, we've given away really soft goals. I thought young Alex MacDonald did well. If there's anything positive we can take from today's shambles, Alex's display was probably the only thing. I'll speak to the players on Tuesday. There will be some we make offers to and some we won't.'

Brendan Flood was true to his word. Owen Coyle was given the financial backing to bring in significant reinforcements: striker Martin Paterson from Scunthorpe, for a fee around £1.3m inclusive of additions; versatile midfielder Chris Eagles from Manchester United, for £1.5m; midfielder Kevin McDonald from Dundee United, for £500,000; Chilean goalkeeper Diego Penny; Dutch holding midfielder Remco van der Schaaf; and craggy Norwegian left-back, Christian Kalvenes. However, Coyle's £500,000 bid for Hearts left-winger Andrew Driver was rejected. Also, Andrew Cole turned down a permanent deal, presumably because of the wages offered, and David Unsworth rejected a player-coach role at the club, having expressed the wish to extend his playing career. Meanwhile, midfielder James O'Connor departed for Sheffield Wednesday, left-back Jon Harley joined Watford, and midfielder John Spicer, the goalkeeping hero at Luton, went to Doncaster.

Coyle said of Paterson: 'There is a premium you pay for goalscorers. Last season he played 36 games, scoring at just under a goal every two games. There is no doubt we are getting a player who is hungry and scored 15 goals in the Championship for a relegated side. He's lightning quick and has a great work-

1. 'FAKE IT TO MAKE IT': THE COYLE WAY

rate. He's 20 and is a Northern Ireland international. He can only get better. We want younger types to boost the team.'

Coyle said of strapping 19-year-old McDonald: 'I have known Kevin since he made his debut at 16. I couldn't have been more impressed by a young man who has developed each year into a fine footballer. He has progressed to such an extent that we felt we wouldn't get him at one point. There were some big clubs courting his services – Celtic, Liverpool and West Bromwich. Last year he took his game on and scored plenty of goals from midfield. He's 6ft 3in, mobile, and has a great physique. We feel we can make him even better in a good Burnley team for years to come.' McDonald confirmed there may have been bigger, better offers but he valued the link he already had with Coyle.

And of Eagles, Coyle said: 'To get a player of this stature shows what we are trying to do. He can play anywhere but I see him playing in a very attacking role for us, to get forward at every opportunity. He's a creative player, scores goals and capable of taking players on. He has an array of talents, and we are delighted to get him.'

As for youth development, Flood thought that there needed to be a re-think after Manchester United's successful raid on their 14-year-old starlet, John Cofie. He said: 'Our best prospect is to focus on the 16-upwards age group, both here and abroad, because with under-16s we are always going to get them stolen from us. The John Cofie thing certainly made me aware of what the risks are in relying on that pipeline.'

The 2008/09 season kicked off at Hillsborough, not that the Burnley defenders seemed aware of this as they found themselves two down after only four minutes' play. Wednesday eventually won at a canter 4-1. An aggravated Coyle told the press conference: 'The defending was nothing short of naïve. I can accept being beaten and I can accept somebody working really hard to score a goal against us, but I don't think Sheffield

Wednesday had to work particularly hard for any of their goals and I left the players in no uncertain terms about that. Clarke Carlisle was a big miss at the back. I thought Martin Paterson did well, Stephen Jordan did well, and Wade Elliott played well. But you are not going to win games with three players doing well.'

Jensen was recalled in goal with Gudjonsson becoming the holding midfielder before Alexander was chosen for the part. But these changes did not plug the leaks. On the following Saturday, suspect travellers Ipswich plundered the gifts offered by their hospitable hosts, winning 3-0. A Red Devils parachutist failed to deliver the match ball, having landed by mistake on the fragile Cricket Field stand roof. His rescue team struggled to retrieve him, at risk themselves. Therefore, the game had to be postponed for 45 minutes before the parachutist could be rescued from his lofty perch. It was as if Fred Karno's Army was in charge. The upshot was that Burnley were bottom with a minus-six goal difference. One supporter drew a parallel with the Waddle era, remarking: 'Again, we have vastly inflated expectations alongside much laudable talk of creative, attacking football, undermined by insufficient attention to the workaday detail of sound defence.'

Speaking with surprising candour, Burnley winger Wade Elliott told a *Lancashire Telegraph* reporter: 'When we played Inverness in a pre-season game, it went too well for us. We were knocking the ball about so easily. I don't know whether we thought the same would happen for us at Sheffield Wednesday. It was a completely different game, though, shocking everyone. Maybe the Inverness game lulled us into complacency. Before we knew it, we were getting steamrollered. It was a horrible start to the season. We went back to basics at Palace and at home to Plymouth, both 0-0 draws. To come off the back of a 1-4 and 0-3 beating, you're never going to stroll around playing brilliant football, getting a big win and have things suddenly drop for

1. 'FAKE IT TO MAKE IT': THE COYLE WAY

you. You do it in small steps, and we've done that in the last couple of games.'

Nottingham Forest 1 Burnley 2
13 September 2008
'Rock El Casbah'

After this shocking start, Coyle realised that he needed a more redoubtable formation, led by an uncompromising, combative target man. He addressed this deficit by signing Cardiff City's Scottish international centre-forward Steve Thompson, who had become surplus to the Bluebirds' needs. Coyle's baby steps suddenly morphed into huge strides at the City Ground, Nottingham, where his 4-1-4-1 formation worked like a dream. With Alexander robustly protecting the back four and Thompson holding up the ball in advanced positions, Burnley were transformed. Coyle earned his win bonus by taking off disappointing Paterson and tiring Thompson, re-uniting Blake and Akinbiyi up front. Armed with destructive speed and power, Akinbiyi created havoc, continually pulling the Forest defence around. Blake was superb, too, exploiting the gaps his partner created while providing a deft and perceptive link between defence and attack. Burnley won 2-1, helped by Alexander's brace of goals. The first came in the 25th minute, and although Robert Earnshaw levelled shortly after the break, Burnley were unruffled, winning with a spot kick 20 minutes before the final whistle.

This impressive victory moved the Clarets up to 19th place. Owen Coyle was quick to praise Alexander in his new bolt-like role in front of the back four. He said: 'I felt "Grezza" was nicked twice in possession in the first ten minutes. But as an experienced pro, he knew he had to move the ball quicker. After losing the first two games he's acted well as a defensive screen. We know when he gets the ball he's capable of passing it well, helping relieve danger and initiate dangerous counter-attacks.'

Further victories over Blackpool (2-0), Watford (3-2), Preston (3-1) and a draw at Swansea (1-1) took Burnley up to eighth place by the end of September. Premier League Fulham were also beaten 1-0 at Turf Moor in the Carling (League) Cup. There was little doubt that Coyle was a deserved winner of the Championship's manager of the month award for September.

Burnley 1 Fulham 0
Carling Cup Third Round
23 September 2008

'Kids'

Fulham were the first top London side to suffer the Clarets' 'capital punishment', meted out to four Premier League heavyweights during this glorious season. Against Fulham, Burnley's surprising executioner was rising home-grown star Jay Rodriguez. With only two minutes remaining, Eagles produced a defence-splitting pass, putting the alert young Rodriguez through on goal. Instead of snatching at the opportunity, Jay coolly shimmied past the flailing Fulham goalie and planted the ball in the back of the Cottagers' net. Coyle said: 'I'm just delighted for young Jay to come on and show that level of composure. We do that in training but to replicate that in a game against a Premier League team is magnificent.'

Jay's coaches, Geoff Smith and Vince Overson, were impressed, too. Three years later Smith observed: 'He always had something – good touch and movement and the willingness to work so hard, too hard perhaps. There was a time when he got very anxious about his finishing, causing him to break into tears when he rounded the Bradford goalkeeper and missed the target. There was some doubt then whether he would succeed because he got so down. But he managed to come through this setback, which was brilliant, because he has such a great appreciation of players around him. That's what the pros want.'

1. 'FAKE IT TO MAKE IT': THE COYLE WAY

Former Burnley centre-half Overson added: 'Jay isn't a natural finisher. He's had to work particularly hard at it. But he's got a fantastic attitude. He's such a down-to-earth lad, respectful of his coaches, colleagues, family and roots. Despite winning an England Under-21 cap, he knows he's not yet the finished article but remains determined to succeed. He was later deservedly awarded the Burnley players' player-of-the-year at the end of the 2010/11 season after scoring 15 league goals, but that didn't turn his head either.'

Meanwhile, Paul Fletcher in his new role of chief executive admitted that the ever-escalating fiscal crisis was affecting the club's ability to borrow money to fund the proposed Turf Moor redevelopment. A more cautious progression on a down-sized project was proposed with the assurance given that 'we won't press the button on the project until we have the funding'.

On the eve of the home clash with top-of-the-table Birmingham City on 18 October, which resulted in a 1-1 draw, Robbie Blake gave a forthright opinion of Burnley's prospects: 'The games coming up at home against Reading, and at Wolves and Coventry, could determine our season. If we've got aspirations of being in the top six, we've got to take points off these teams. I'm not getting any younger. I'm frustrated that I'm not playing but I must knuckle down and get on with it. There's a lot of quality players who aren't even in the 16. I think I'm good enough to take the chance when it comes. I've just got to be patient.'

Blake was given his chance at Coventry on 21 October when he came off the bench to score a late winner, adroitly lifting the ball over Westwood, the Coventry goalkeeper. Then, against Reading, Blake again came on as a late substitute, striking the decisive goal with a moment of magic. It allowed a patched-up and besieged Burnley side to escape with the points, thanks also to Jensen's heroic performance between the sticks. Having been restored to the starting XI at QPR, Blake scored the crucial opening goal with a shot so powerful and precise that Rangers' goalkeeper Cerny was left rooted to the spot. Blake then retained his first-team place for the rest of the season.

Up until the end of November 2008, results were mixed. There were comfortable home wins against Norwich (2-0) and Derby (3-0) but disappointing losses at Wolves (0-2) and Barnsley (2-3). However, the outstanding result was the defeat of Chelsea in the Carling Cup after a penalty shoot-out.

Chelsea 1 Burnley 1
(*Burnley won 5-4 on penalties aet*)
Carling Cup Fourth Round
13 September 2008

'One Day Like This'

More than 6,000 Clarets turned up at Stamford Bridge to bawl Burnley on. Drogba's goal shortly before half-time only served to crank up their volume. Undaunted by this deficit, Coyle had the prescience to replace hard-working, but neutralised, Paterson with bounding Akinbiyi. Ade immediately put himself about, giving McCann and Gudjonsson more passing options and treading on a few Chelsea toes to boot.

In the 69th minute, Eagles and Blake connived an opening with a flash of brilliance. Eagles darted along the inside-left channel. Anticipating his break, Blake located him with a perfectly weighted pass. Eagles latched on to it, turned quickly, wrong-footing his marker, and unleashed a stinging shot that Cudicini could only parry into the path of the onrushing Akinbiyi. The Burnley fans clustered at the Shed End held their breath as Akinbiyi steadied himself before calmly poking the loose ball into the unguarded net to spark a cacophony of unhinged celebration. Akinbiyi tore off his shirt in exultation, roaring his defiance as his delirious team-mates engulfed him. Thereafter, the game became an attritional battle with the rattled Chelsea players resorting to pumping unproductive

1. 'FAKE IT TO MAKE IT': THE COYLE WAY

high balls into the Burnley box. While Chelsea fashioned a few openings that fortunately fell to the profligate Di Santo, Burnley held firm.

This hard-fought contest went to penalties, Jensen making the crucial save at the death to seize the tie. A tabloid paper captured that moment of triumph as the great Dane hurled himself to his left to push away a goal-bound spot kick. 'Jensen Interceptor!' read the caption. 'Capital Punishment' Two had been administered. Burnley were in the quarter-finals.

An ecstatic Owen Coyle picked out Jensen and Akinbiyi for a special tribute. He declared: 'Brian has been outstanding all season and we said if it got to a penalty shootout, we felt he'd save a minimum of one. I'm delighted for him because it's a reward for how hard he's been working in the games and training. Aside from scoring the goal, Ade led the line, brought us up the park to get others on the ball, and that was a big turning point in the game. The backing we got from 6,100, suggested there were 30,000 there! Hopefully it gives everyone in the town a lift!'

But, as exciting as this cup run was, promotion was of greater importance. The club's latest accounts underlined this. The annual operating loss was down from £4m to £1.8m, but this hid a 24 per cent rise in the wage bill, which had increased to £8.8m. The club partly bridged the gap with a £1.6m increase in match income and other commercial activities, but the most substantial income came from player sales. Lafferty's transfer contributed the lion's share of the £5m sales profit. Chairman Barry Kilby told the shareholders: 'It was particularly pleasing to see Owen Coyle step in and make a positive impact on and off the pitch. Under his stewardship, the club is actively pursuing a policy of investment in younger players and developing our youth system, thanks to the sterling work of Vince Overson, Terry Pashley, Jeff Taylor and their backroom team, now under Martin Dobson, director of youth development.'

Burnley 2 Arsenal 0
Carling Cup Fifth Round
2 December 2008
'North American Scum'

Back at Turf Moor, the Burnley players were flexing their muscles in readiness for Arsenal's December visit in the quarter-final of the Carling Cup. Martin Paterson said: 'Going away to somewhere as massive as Chelsea was a wonderful experience, but we weren't there to enjoy it and rub shoulders with them, we were there to beat them, and it will be the same tomorrow. We're not there to take people's shirts and be glad to have played against them – we are aiming to get into the semi-finals of the Carling Cup.'

Ade Akinbiyi added: 'Arsenal have probably the best kids that most people have ever seen, but they are not going to like coming to Turf Moor on a cold Tuesday night. We've come this far, we have nothing to lose, and everyone has confidence in themselves. When we went to Chelsea we didn't lie back, and we are not going to do that against Arsenal.'

The Burnley players were as good as their word, as Kevin McDonald plundered two goals in a brilliant display of sprightly skills and hefty power, while the Arsenal players, particularly Bendtner, squandered chance after chance, with Jensen once again magnificent in the Burnley goal. A triumphant Coyle said: 'The last thing I said to the players before they went out for the second half was to come in with no regrets. If we got to our maximum and were beaten by a better team, then we could accept that. We just didn't want to feel we had let ourselves down, but with this group of players there was no chance of that happening.' A crowd of 19,045 created a febrile atmosphere for Burnley's third successive cup triumph, admired by all except the silent Arsenal fans and a sulking Wenger.

Four days later, Burnley faced a tough contest against promotion rivals Sheffield United, at Bramall Lane. It was crisis time. Michael Duff was injured in the warm-up, Chris McCann had already succumbed to sickness and Carlisle was suspended. Coyle was forced to play left-back Jordan at centre-half, winger Elliott at right-back, and right-footed Alexander at left-back. However, Coyle's makeshift team did him proud, winning 3-2 with Eagles scoring a terrific goal to seal the game.

Against Cardiff at home on 9 December, Burnley looked understandably 'leggy' and were fortunate to escape with the 2-2 draw earned by Thompson's late equaliser. Four days later, visiting Southampton appeared to be an easier proposition as Burnley racked up a 3-0 interval lead, but they were left hanging on anxiously as the Saints retaliated strongly in the second half (3-2). Burnley remained in fourth place. With Christmas only five days away, the Clarets celebrated by coming from behind at Ashton Gate to win 2-1, with goals from Paterson and Thompson. At this point Burnley appeared odds-on to secure at least a play-off place. Then the wheels fell off. The next five league games were lost. The downward spiral was finally halted on 31 January when Thompson's 90th-minute goal was just enough to defeat visiting Charlton (2-1). Burnley rose to eighth.

Burnley 3 Tottenham Hotspur 2
Carling Cup Semi-Final Second Leg (*aet*)
21 January 2009
'Hit the North'

Despite Burnley's spluttering league form, they put on a scintillating first-half display in the Carling Cup semi-final first leg at White Hart Lane, leading 1-0 at the interval thanks to Paterson's 15th-minute goal. Spurs were reeling from the crispness of Burnley's passing and the intensity of their attacks. Sadly, a calamitous second-half performance gifted Tottenham four avoidable goals, all scored within 23 minutes of the resumption (1-4). The semi-final tie seemed dead and buried but Coyle's indefatigable men thought differently.

Spurs arrived in Burnley two weeks later. It was a cold, squally, dog of a night. Sheeting rain swirled in the glare of the floodlights, saturating thousands of fans queuing at the turnstiles, while above them the howling gale rattled the stand roofs ominously. In the 34th minute Burnley were awarded a free kick 30 yards from the Spurs goal. Novice Spurs goalkeeper, Ben Alnwick, took up a position right of centre in anticipation of a cross to the far post. Blake espied the gap to the goalie's left, took aim, and curled a vicious shot into the unguarded top right-hand corner. Turf Moor erupted. Alnwick hung his dripping head in shame.

Burnley pressed forward relentlessly, to no avail, until the 73rd minute. Blake embarked upon a twisting, turning run on the left, bamboozling Gunter and Bentley, before whipping in a low cross which McCann stabbed in at the far post. Hope turned instantly to belief. The roar from a crowd of 19,500 had shuddering intensity. Rodriguez was brought on for Gudjonsson. Akinbiyi replaced the exhausted Paterson.

Burnley piled forward. With just two minutes left, Alnwick tried to claim a high cross but failed, the greasy ball slipping from his grasp. Rodriguez instantly volleyed the loose ball home. Rarely has Turf Moor seen such a tumult. It was all square, but with Burnley now in the ascendancy. Regrettably, a gilt-edged chance to finish off faltering Spurs was missed by Rodriguez in a moment of indecision. It proved fatal. With Burnley almost played out, first Pavlyuchenko, then Defoe scored the late extra-time goals which took Spurs to Wembley. While Spurs lost on penalties to Manchester United in the final, the Burnley players doubled their resolve to win promotion. That night of disappointment would ultimately lead to a triumphant Wembley appearance in May 2009.

Before that, there was an FA Cup campaign to contest. Following victories over QPR and West Bromwich, both after replays, Burnley were paired again with Arsenal. This time it

1. 'FAKE IT TO MAKE IT': THE COYLE WAY

was at the Emirates. It was a round too far, as the Gunners ruthlessly took their revenge with a 3-0 win.

In readiness for the Clarets' promotion push, Coyle sought to bolster his suspect defence. But the well had dried up. Flood's chain of perfume shops had gone into administration and Modus, his property development company, was in grave trouble, forcing him to reduce its commitments. It was little surprise when Coyle's request for more cash was rejected.

Coyle's impatience was palpable, stating: 'We can't stand still. We must keep striving to improve.' In late February, a Sunday tabloid speculated that Coyle was about to return to Bolton as their manager. On 28 February, Sheffield Wednesday crushed Burnley 2-4 at Turf Moor. Once again, the case for the defence was found wanting. No one managed to shackle Leon Clarke, Wednesday's powerful, marauding centre-forward, or their probing playmaker, Tudgay. Burnley dropped two places to ninth. Returning to his broken record, Coyle exclaimed: 'We cannot keep shooting ourselves in the foot. We were really poor in defence.'

On another squally night on 3 March, Burnley put their promotion bid back on track at Blackpool. The conditions were atrocious, with a whistling gale and slanting rain. There was considerable doubt whether the game would be played. But with the endorsement of the Blackpool management, it was. Christian Kalvenes decided the outcome with a late, winning goal of high quality. Venturing down the left flank, Kalvenes reached the edge of the Blackpool box, exchanging a sharp one-two with McCann before calmly slotting the ball past Rachubka. Burnley rose to seventh. A relieved Owen Coyle said: 'The goal was a fantastic move and such a cool finish, but the biggest thing that summed us up was character. The desire to come back from Saturday was immense.'

Burnley's results continued to improve. Crystal Palace were defeated 4-2 at Turf Moor on 11 March, with the Clarets recovering from a two-goal deficit. Neil Warnock was apoplectic at the award of an 83rd-minute penalty from which Burnley equalised, setting up their late victory. A relieved Coyle exclaimed: 'Again the lads have shown real courage and bravery, to go with physical fitness and mental strength to see it through. I don't want to be chasing games every week, but we know that when we do, we're still in every game we play. It's a tremendous thing to have in your armoury.'

Three days later, on 14 March 2009, Burnley thrashed Nottingham Forest 5-0, lifting themselves into fifth place. A bubbling Owen Coyle said: 'Some of the finishes were exquisite, fit to grace any game. A few of them deserved to win a match on their own. It doesn't happen very often that your left-back's the man of the match when you have won 5-0, but Christian Kalvenes was outstanding, as was right-back Rhys Williams [a loan signing from Middlesbrough] and Carlisle and Caldwell, because Forest's McSheffrey, Tyson and Earnshaw are very good strikers. It's very much a team effort.'

Burnley were frustrated at Ipswich, having led for much of the game (1-1), but they won 2-1 at Plymouth with another magical goal from Blake. It was time up for Ade Akinbiyi, though, who completed a move to Houston Dynamo in the USA. Coyle said: 'Ade has had a massive impact at this club, and I cannot speak highly enough about him. He has been a model professional and a big part in what we are doing, on and off the park. He is going to America for a lot less money than he earns here. He is going for a lifestyle change, and I just wish people would be aware of the facts before commenting on them.' Some fans wrongly believed he had been pushed out.

Burnley reached the play-offs having squeezed past QPR and Sheffield United, and thrashed Bristol City 4-0 in their final game at home on a scorching 3 May. Their semi-final opponents were Reading, strongly tipped for automatic promotion at Christmas. However, the Royals side which arrived at Turf Moor was a pale shadow of the free-scoring outfit that had terrorised Championship defences earlier in the season. Their leading scorer, Kevin Doyle, started the game but was clearly unfit.

2. WEMBLEY TRIUMPH 2009

Burnley's Play-Off Victories
May 2009
'Up for Sale'

It was a typical play-off contest, taut and tight, with few chances, seemingly destined to end in stalemate. But with six minutes left, Reading's sturdy centre-back Andre Bikey unaccountably tugged at Thompson inside his box. A penalty was awarded which Alexander despatched curtly, whereupon Bikey 'lost it', histrionically haranguing referee Atkinson and stamping upon Robbie Blake. The errant defender was dismissed immediately. Although Burnley had only a slender lead to take into the second leg, the melancholic demeanour of Steve Coppell, the Reading manager, suggested that the tie was already won.

And so it proved. In the return game, Coppell blooded 20-year-old Simon Church, while inexplicably leaving his experienced strikers, Dave Kitson and Noel Hunt, on the bench. Although Reading had the better of the first half, both Paterson and Thompson hit spectacular goals after the break to take Burnley to Wembley. However, the wild celebrations in the away end were not replicated by the Burnley players or their manager. Coyle insisted: 'We acknowledged the fans' tremendous support, but we haven't yet achieved our goal. There's so much work to be done. Sheffield United are a quality side.' Grizzly Graham Alexander growled: 'We've won nothing yet.'

The Blades manager, Kevin Blackwell, was a Sky TV pundit for the second leg at the Madejski Stadium. His mood darkened as Burnley took control, first with Paterson curling a 30-yarder into the top left-hand corner, and then Thompson finding goal with a volley that clipped the underside of the bar. As the Sky camera focused on Blackwell for his post-match reaction, he looked ghastly. Clearly, Burnley represented the greater threat to him, having already beaten his side twice this season. Blackwell later rebuked the Football League for choosing Mike Dean as the play-off final referee, citing his shortcomings in a recent Sheffield derby. Blackwell's consternation was very encouraging.

Burnley chairman Barry Kilby believed that one season in the Premier League would clear his club's considerable debt. And with the prize so agonisingly close, the pressure was ramped up enormously. Meanwhile, the pessimists on social media predicted administration and a fire-sale of Burnley's top earners if their team failed to win. Barry made light of this, assuring Burnley fans: 'I'm fine. I'm quietly confident. Everything is in order, and we are ready for the big game. It has been one of the best seasons ever and we want to cap it off on Monday.'

As it happened, the Blades' performance at Wembley was as dismal as Blackwell's mood. Burnley should have won more comfortably, having squandered several good chances to add to their narrow lead. Only Sheffield United's wing-backs, Kyle Naughton and Kyle Walker, distinguished themselves in their side's plodding display. It was left to Burnley's midfielder Wade Elliott to win the game with an eye-catching goal, a superb, curling, 25-yard effort that goalkeeper Paddy Kenny hadn't a hope of stopping. Sheffield United might have saved themselves had Mike Dean not waved away an apparently just claim for a late penalty, when Kalvenes shoulder-charged Walker clumsily inside the Burnley box. Otherwise, the Blades seemed utterly blunt. Burnley fully deserved their victory, which returned them to the top flight after a 33-year absence, during which the club almost expired.

Afterwards, a surprisingly restrained Coyle commented: 'We were worthy winners. From start to finish we got the ball down and played. We knew we would come under some pressure when Sheffield United put the ball into our box, but we stood up to that. Caldwell and man-of-the-match Carlisle were imperious in central defence, limiting them to very few goal-scoring opportunities. We have used the fewest players and don't have quantity, we know that, but I believe we have real quality.

'Our goal typified the way we play, the passing and movement, culminating in a great finish. We looked dangerous on the counter-attack. We have had around seven ties with Premier League clubs this season and we have shown that we can stand up to the best, although it's easier to play in one-off cup ties than it is to play weekly in the Premier League. There's no doubt we'll need to add to the squad, but we do have terrific spirit and that will never go away.'

Coyle was credited by his players for helping them to remain confident and relaxed, enabling them to play at their best when under pressure. Robbie Blake said: 'Owen was so relaxed around the players and made the place so relaxed, you'd think you were just going out into the car park for a kick-about. He was so enthusiastic and positive. He never brought anything negative to the club. He improved my game, too. I had always been a striker, never having to track back much, but he got me playing wide on the left in a three-man attack, tracking back to help the full-back, when needed. He deserves massive credit for believing I could do this. I never thought I was capable of making tackles in my own box.'

The play-off final man of the match, Clarke Carlisle, added: 'Owen told us week in, week out, that it didn't matter what other teams were doing or who they'd got in their side. It was all about what we did and how we performed, because he believed – and this filtered through the club and the squad – that if we played to the best of our ability, we'd be more than a match for anyone. There was a freedom to go and express ourself and play the game in the right manner. It was instilled into us that if we,

2. WEMBLEY TRIUMPH 2009

as a team, played to our strengths and abilities, we could win the game. On the other hand, Steve Cotterill was a set-play man. He'd instil in us the routines, the disciplines, the ruses. He told you exactly what he wanted you to do. There were no grey areas. If you didn't comply, he'd give you grief. He was in total control. Owen didn't bother much with positional-play practice, set plays, and corner routines, so much so that when it did happen, we would look at one another in amazement. What he encouraged was spontaneity, thinking on your feet, ad-libbing whenever the opportunity arose.'

3. THE DREAM SOARS

Away from the rejoicing Burnley fans, many sporting Owen Coyle masks, it was rumoured that their 'messiah' was about to join Celtic. Barry Kilby commented: 'I heard in the post-match press conference that Strachan had gone at Celtic and that Owen was mentioned. It is a big distraction and we've lost valuable time that we should have been putting into other matters. The Glasgow press have been stoking this up and both Owen and I have been annoyed with it all. Owen is adamant that he's happy here.'

And yet Coyle seemed to equivocate about his future when Alastair Campbell publicly questioned him on the subject while on the Burnley town hall balcony, during the promotion celebrations. Coyle's unease was palpable. Burnley fans were holding their breath for several weeks, until the club announced on 19 June that Owen Coyle had extended his contract with Burnley until July 2013.

With business as usual resuming, Brendan Flood told the local press that he was seeking other clubs' advice in managing the Premier League money. He indicated that wages would be kept low in Premier League terms. A figure of around £15m per year was mentioned, nearly doubling Burnley's existing wage levels. But with income set to soar to £40m, £30m of which was TV money, the ratio of Burnley's wages to income would be reduced to much healthier levels than hitherto.

On 1 June it was announced that Modus Ventures Ltd, Brendan Flood's commercial property company, was in

3. THE DREAM SOARS

administration, reviving speculation about whether the football club would have suffered a similar fate had promotion not been won. At the end of July, the local press reported that KPMG administrators had reclaimed a £3.7m loan made to the club while Modus was a going concern. Burnley FC made a statement denying that the repayment would adversely affect the football side of operations.

Steve Jones, Gabor Kiraly, and Alan Mahon were released by the club, while van der Schaaf and injury-plagued Berisha were deemed surplus to requirements. This allowed Coyle to splash out a club record fee of £3m to capture Hibernian's Scottish international centre-forward Steven Fletcher. He also signed Derby's pacey attacking right-back Tyrone Mears for £500,000 and Newcastle's Canadian centre-back David Edgar, who was a free agent, having rejected a new contract with the relegated Magpies. The 20-year-old Manchester United right-back Richard Eckersley joined too, for a £500,000 fee, determined by tribunal. Hamilton were also persuaded to part with their promising Scottish Under-21 international left-back Brian Easton, for an initial fee of £350,000. Extending his search to South America, Coyle acquired, on loan, Fernando Guerrero, a 19-year-old Ecuador international winger with blistering pace.

Unfortunately, Coyle's pre-season preparations were interrupted by some strangely timed international fixtures which robbed him of seven members of his first-team squad for several days just prior to the opening game. Coyle's irritation was magnified once he learnt that Caldwell had sustained a groin injury while representing Scotland, ruling him out of first-team action until early October. Coyle reacted quickly, bringing in the muscular Andre Bikey who was a Cameroon international central defender, signed from Reading for a £2.8m fee. Despite Bikey's indiscretion in the play-off semi-final, he had been a physically imposing presence in Coppell's side, totalling 62 appearances at Premier League and Championship levels. Coyle said: 'He has loads of pace and power – he is a very good player.'

Burnley's season started at Stoke where they lost 0-2, not helped by a makeshift centre-back partnership of Carlisle and left-back Jordan. Brian Jensen said: 'We played quite well at Stoke at the weekend but conceded two poor goals, quite unlike ourselves.' But then came successive 1-0 home victories over Manchester United and Everton, with Blake scoring with a ferocious volley against United and Wade Elliott netting against a subdued Everton side.

Burnley 1 Manchester United 0
19 August 2009
'Underdog (Save Me)'

Robbie Blake recalled: 'With Park, Carrick, and Wayne Rooney finding space, it seemed only a matter of time before United broke the deadlock. We were under pressure. Michael Owen should have done better when Patrice Evra's left-wing cross whistled past him at the near post. Yet their opening goal did not come and, as time ticked by, we visibly gained in confidence.'

Martin Paterson and Fletcher started to create problems for United. Ben Foster blocked a shot from Paterson and Carrick did the same when Blake tried to score from the rebound. Blake continued: 'United could not relieve the pressure. When our full-back Stephen Jordan crossed to the far post, I was on hand to pounce on the second ball, letting fly with a fierce volley that sped past Foster before he could react. Having watched that goal umpteen times, I still can't believe it.

'What a tremendous atmosphere there was that night. You are not conscious of it when you are playing, you're too involved in the game, but at the end you are! The gaffer won't let us get our feet off the ground, though. We need to press other teams like we did against Man U to have a chance. We know we must

3. THE DREAM SOARS

play at our best and hope that the other teams don't. The gaffer is so upbeat. It is very infectious.'

Brian Jensen, who saved a penalty from Carrick, added: 'It was pure instinct. Last season Ronaldo took the penalties so we didn't have a clue which way Carrick would hit it. We squeezed Manchester United in the centre, pushing them out to the wings. Our work-rate was magnificent, with everyone pulling back behind the ball when possession was lost. However, they didn't pressurise us as much as I thought they would. It was a brilliant atmosphere, the best it's been since I've been here. The stands were vibrating with the force of our fans' roar. We need this support in every single game whether winning or losing and we need the team to work so hard in every game. In our favour, we have an unbelievable work ethic.'

Coyle reflected: 'Our movement and passing were good against Manchester United. We got our blocks in. I wasn't surprised by our goal. I know what Robbie Blake is capable of. Against Everton we started the game at a terrific pace. They didn't cut us open too often. I thought we were the better team. We've had a great week but that's all it is. We have a long way to go. We train at high intensity and that shows on the pitch. We have honest, hard-working players: 35 more cup finals ahead.'

Just as the transfer window was about to close, Portsmouth and former Preston and Bury striker David Nugent was signed on loan. Upon arrival, he expressed the hope that he would be deployed in a spearhead role, saying: 'I'm looking to play as a striker here. At Portsmouth, I was playing mainly as a winger. I didn't get much opportunity to play – ten minutes here, 20 minutes there. It wasn't enough time to get into the game.'

Nugent did not have to wait long to make an impact. Against Sunderland at home, he met Elliott's perfect cross with a bullet header, restoring Burnley's lead in the 67th minute. Then nine minutes later, he danced around the Sunderland central-defenders on the edge of their box, before curling the ball into the top left-hand corner. It was a stupendous finish. Up until Christmas he was used as an impact substitute but having headed Burnley level in the Boxing Day derby with Bolton, he started in 17 of the remaining 20 league fixtures, scoring four more goals.

PART 7

DECLINE AND FALL

2010 to 2012

'Bruise Pristine'

1. THE DREAM SOURS AND DIES 2010

Burnley made a good start to life in the Premier League, winning their first four home games against Manchester United, Everton, Sunderland, and Birmingham, beating Hull at home in late October and drawing with Arsenal (1-1) and Aston Villa (1-1) at home before the festive season began. Despite being heavily beaten on the road, notably at Spurs (0-5) and Liverpool (0-4), after the Boxing Day game Burnley had 19 points from as many games.

Nugent's goal against Bolton enabled Burnley to climb one place into 13th position, comfortably above the relegation zone. However, the manager who helped them rise so spectacularly was about to desert them for the club they had just played.

Five years after Owen Coyle's sudden departure from Turf Moor, Barry Kilby reflected: 'If we could have maintained our form, I knew we had a realistic chance of survival. Then Owen shocked us by leaving early in the January transfer window, after pledging he was committed to completing his work with Burnley. The players had bought into his upbeat message. We all had. But he thought Bolton offered a better prospect of survival, believing them to be five or ten years in advance of ourselves, despite their lower position then.

'I thought I had persuaded him to stay but by the next day he was gone. His departure had a devastating effect upon the players he had inspired with his spirit and drive.'

1. THE DREAM SOURS AND DIES 2010

Kilby wanted Coyle's assistant Sandy Stewart and first-team coach Steve Davis to stay on, but they both left with him, as did Phil Hughes the goalkeeping coach, and chief scout Cliff Roberts. New signings that Coyle had lined up, such as Arsenal midfielder Jack Wilshere on loan, and American winger Stuart Holden, went with them too.

Contrary to what some fans thought or what Burnley director Brendan Flood hoped, there was not a legion of eligible candidates eager to replace Coyle. Neither Alan Curbishley nor Steve Coppell seemed interested. If Paul Lambert was, Norwich soon scrubbed that by offering him a new, presumably better, contract. Burnley chief executive Paul Fletcher said he was keen on Iain Dowie, but nothing came of that. In the end, it seemed to be a choice between free agent Brian Laws and Doncaster boss Sean O'Driscoll, although it wasn't entirely clear whether O'Driscoll was really interested in the post or whether anyone on the Burnley board was captivated by his candidacy. Finally, Barry Kilby announced to the local press that Brian Laws had been appointed as manager.

Kilby said, 'The team was down because of Owen's abrupt departure. I thought Brian Laws was a decent call, but he had an invidious task trying to fill Owen's shoes. He had little time to strengthen the team because of the timing of Owen's departure. The crowd got on his back, particularly when the results deteriorated. When Owen jumped ship, he probably sealed our fate. We never recovered the verve we had shown at the start of the season.'

Immediately after Coyle's departure, Barry Kilby lamented: 'Obviously, it is a trauma for the football club to lose our manager and our entire coaching staff within a week. Anybody would have had a rough time coping with that. We have had little time to negotiate the appointment of a new manager, particularly if he was already with a club, and try to bring in the players to keep us in the Premiership. We fully expected that he would move on eventually, but upwards not sideways. He was very emotional about leaving the club, claiming that only an offer from Celtic or Bolton would have induced him to depart. It's come at a bad time for us. We have now got to get going again.'

Club captain, Steven Caldwell, was equally upset at Coyle's departure, commenting to Burnley author Dave Thomas: 'To us, as players, it was a huge moment in our season. I always felt it was a possibility, but when you are such a tight-knit group any major change hits you much harder. I don't blame him for that in the slightest, but it had a huge bearing on our season. All of Cliff's scouting knowledge disappeared as well. That shocked us. Usually, some staff are left behind.'

Caldwell said because new manager Laws had to bring in all new staff, the disruption damaged the players' confidence and they stopped playing to their strengths.

He continued: 'I had it in mind that I'd be leaving. I suppose I felt that way since Owen left. I had a fantastic relationship with him. He is a top-class manager, and we would have stayed up if he had remained in charge. That's how good Owen was. He got the best out of players and built a great dressing room spirit so he's second to none. But I totally understand why he left. The transfer kitty he had at Bolton was much bigger than what was on offer at Burnley. Burnley could or should have backed him more to get to the next level. I suspect that is why he left. I was bitterly upset. It took the sting out of us. The team was in shock. Everybody was gutted.'

Players' meetings were held to try to resolve the issues but the instability continued. 'Maybe people started to think about themselves, not the club,' said Caldwell.

'I'm better for working with Owen. He brought a lightness and enjoyment. He brought over-achievement, changed the way I thought about football. For 18 months we over-achieved.

'Brian Laws wasn't impossible to work with. I'd hoped we would have a good relationship. A few things happened with

1. THE DREAM SOURS AND DIES 2010

that relationship that caused problems. I wasn't fit for a start and was sitting on the sidelines. There were no run-ins, it was just unfortunate I wasn't fit and wanted to play. I felt Laws should have pushed me into the team to help them even though I wasn't fully fit. Nevertheless, the best decision I ever made was coming to Burnley.'

Clarke Carlisle recalled: 'Stevie Caldwell said to me that when he moved to Wigan, the players there couldn't believe some of the stuff Owen had said to us. It was simply the power of positive thinking. It's a confidence thing. You fake it to make it. You give people confidence, and they play better. From that comes more confidence leading to further improvement. He could make an average player good, and a good player excellent. If he had a secret, this was it.'

Laws immediately faced the small matter of a return league game at Manchester United, although club elder statesman Martin Dobson and youth team boss Terry Pashley were entrusted with the team preparations. Nevertheless, Burnley acquitted themselves well in the first half, during which they should have taken a two-goal lead.

With Burnley losing their first five games under Laws, including a toxic relegation tussle at Bolton, the pressure mounted on him.

Burnley 2 West Ham United 1
6 February 2010
'Please Read the Letter'

When West Ham arrived at Turf Moor on a bright 6 February, Burnley were occupying the final relegation place. Brian Laws realised this was a must-win game. His new signings, centre-back Leon Cort, a £1.5m acquisition from Stoke, and Danny Fox, reputedly a £1.8m buy from Celtic, were in his starting XI. Much to the relief of the club and its fans, Burnley won – just!

Laws concluded: 'The players were magnificent in dealing with that pressure. They were assured, competitive and creative. A terrific goal from David Nugent put us ahead. Danny Fox had a fantastic debut, setting up Nugent's goal, with a long, raking pass, and scoring with a cracking free kick. He stopped one as well. New signing Leon Cort showed composure and firmness at centre-back. He showed no sign of panic. However, it was a very nervy last ten minutes. We lost a bit of shape and dropped too deep but managed to hang on to win.'

The corner was not turned, though. An abject 0-3 defeat at Fulham followed. Worse still, relegation rivals Portsmouth, and Wolves, snatched maximum points on their visits to Turf Moor. Only a home draw with Stoke on 10 March interrupted an eight-match losing sequence. Nevertheless, player/coach Graham Alexander was upbeat about the point gained here, insisting: 'Stoke are a hard team to play against. We forgot to play our own passing game in the first period but were happy to get something out of the game with a good second-half performance. It showed how well we are coping with the pressure of relegation.'

The Easter home losses just about sealed Burnley's fate, though – a controversial 0-1 loss to Blackburn and a 1-6 humiliation by a rampant Manchester City. Despite winning 4-1 at Hull a week later, helping ensure the Tigers accompanied them down, Burnley returned to the Championship. They had won three, drawn one, and lost 14 of the 18 Premier League games played under Laws's management. Under Coyle, Burnley had won five, drawn five, and lost ten of their first 20 league games.

As relegation loomed, Barry Kilby put on a brave face, claiming: 'We kept to our plan with our budget. We are going down strong. The Owen Coyle factor had a big impact upon our season. We go down in a healthier state than Hull and Portsmouth. It's given us the chance to bring through younger players. We have sold 10,000 season tickets for next year. This is way above many clubs in the Championship. We still want to

1. THE DREAM SOURS AND DIES 2010

end up above Hull because this will give us £800k more that we can spend very well.'

A remarkable 4-2 home victory over Spurs in the final game of the season ensured that this consolatory prize was gained. Burnley bravely recovered from an early two-goal deficit. Barry concluded: 'The final game against Spurs was on the 23rd anniversary of the Orient game. It provides a timely reality check, demonstrating how far we have come.' It was also the 50th anniversary of Burnley's top-flight championship-winning season.

One of the few bright elements in Burnley's catastrophic collapse was the energetic and skilful play of loan signing Jack Cork, the son of Wimbledon's FA Cup-winning striker Alan Cork. Chelsea's young midfielder enjoyed his stay at Turf Moor, saying: 'The fans were brilliant and the players great despite the results. I've loved it here. It's very easy to settle, one of the best places I've been at.' Brian Laws added: 'Jack is such a popular player. He's been a big plus after the bad news we've had about Chris McCann's injury.'

With McCann still sidelined, Jack Cork returned for another season-long loan in 2010/11. He was joined by tall, burly Scottish international striker Chris Iwelumo, who arrived from Wolves, with Steven Fletcher moving in the opposite direction for a £7.5m fee. Preston's Scottish winger Ross Wallace joined for an undisclosed figure, as did Hull's combative midfielder, Dean Marney.

Marney told a local reporter: 'I was getting a bit stale at Hull. Burnley is a club on the up. I want to get back in the Premiership. It's a strong squad here. I like to get the ball down and play. I've a good engine but need to work on my goal-scoring.' Laws also signed the Owls' goalkeeper, Lee Grant, for around £1m. He was expected to challenge strongly for the number one slot.

Although Robbie Blake left for Bolton, Chris Eagles and Tyrone Mears remained, as did Jensen, Bikey, Fox, Cort,

Easton, Edgar, Duff, Carlisle, Alexander, Rodriguez, Paterson, Thompson, and Elliott. On paper, this seemed to be a team good enough to challenge for promotion. The pressure was on Laws to bring about a swift revival. He acknowledged this, stating: 'This is my team. I'd like to think I'd be judged on that, more so than last season. The summer has given me a clean slate and the time to enforce what we want to do and how we want to do it. That's given me a huge lift because the players have been so responsive.'

2. WHAT GOES UP ...

The 2010/11 season began well, with Chris Iwelumo's header defeating Nottingham Forest in the opening game at home. A satisfactory point was gained at Ipswich before an out-of-sorts Leicester side were beaten 3-0 at Turf Moor. However, this encouraging start was undermined by a poor first-half display at Swansea, where Burnley were undone by Scott Sinclair's eighth-minute goal (0-1).

Burnley 4 Preston North End 3
11 September 2010
'Harder Than You Think'

A pulsating home derby with Preston followed, covered live on BBC TV. A switchback contest ended in a Burnley win. Brian Laws exclaimed: 'What a derby! It had everything. Seven goals. Tackles going in with a passion. Both sides giving it a real go. The sending-off of Preston's Billy Jones was possibly the turning point, though. I was very disappointed with our first-half display. Preston went man-to-man. They didn't give us an inch of space and every time we lost the ball they counter-attacked us.

'The introduction of Jay Rodriguez and Chris Eagles later in the second half gave us more impetus. We became sharper and quicker in our passing too, penning them in for longer periods. The crowd then got behind us. In the end, we won the game because of this. It was a great hat-trick by recent recruit Chris Iwelumo. It showed he's not only good with his head but with his feet too. There were many mistakes, though. We got away with it, a bit. It showed us how hard this division will be. I sensed we would get a third to put us back on terms, but it was Jay Rod who got us off the hook with that late headed winner.'

Laws was commendably honest, for Preston had looked the better side for much of this game, with their marauding Republic of Ireland winger Keith Treacy creating havoc on the left flank.

At Middlesbrough, Burnley had no such luck, losing 1-2. Laws was critical of central defender Carlisle, for his defensive lapses, stating: 'We went with a positive approach at Boro but Carlisle was too gung-ho and it cost us. Instead of capitalising on our set pieces we gave away too many soft free kicks. It was very disappointing, particularly to get within three minutes of a decent result.'

However, this setback was quickly forgotten after Burnley came out on top in the grudge match with Bolton in a home, third-round Carling Cup tie. Brian Laws reflected: 'The pleasing thing was we focused on the game not what surrounded it. It was nice to put to bed the acrimony concerning Owen Coyle's sudden departure last January, and to focus on the future. The atmosphere was terrific. It drove the players on from the first whistle. The momentum never dropped. There was no holding back. Chris Eagles was outstanding, working hard in defence too. Despite facing an experienced Bolton team, we were the better side.'

The ill feeling felt by many Burnley fans towards Coyle enticed an extraordinary 17,602 attendance for an early-round League Cup fixture. After the game, a delighted Jay Rodriguez commented: 'I learnt a lot while on loan at Barnsley. Their manager, Mark Robins, was very helpful, staying behind with me after training, helping me with my game. Now I am playing on the flank in a front three with Chris Iwelumo as the central striker and Chris Eagles on the opposite wing. I'm happy with this role as it extends my learning. The team are playing well away but have yet to get that first win. I'm sure it's not far off, though.'

2. WHAT GOES UP ...

However, Burnley would not record their first league away win until Boxing Day. Frustratingly they surrendered two-goal leads at Sheffield United (3-3) and Norwich (2-2) during October and November. Nevertheless, young Rodriguez proved to be the real deal, fully vindicating Laws's faith in his ability, troubling defences with his pace and nifty footwork, packing a powerful shot, and possessing impressive aerial strength. Laws deserved great credit not only for sticking with Rodriguez, but also for recognising that his starlet was much more effective facing goal, having the opportunity to run at defenders with the ball at his feet, rather than having his back to goal as a target man. In Rodriguez's inaugural season as a first-team regular he became Burnley's 'top gun', scoring 14 goals in 37 Championship starts. It was just as well, given that Paterson remained plagued with injury. Brendan Flood commented: 'We want to get the Academy up to scratch, so we can produce another Jay Rod. It may not be like the sixties, but we should grow our own talent.'

What caused Laws most grief was the fragility of his defence. After Sheffield United snatched a 94th-minute equaliser, Laws griped: 'We're not looking to get plaudits for being an attractive side, we want to be professional and organised. We were sitting so deep that I thought our defence was behind our goalkeeper.'

While Laws complained about his players' lack of discipline, many fans blamed Laws's tactics. A 3-0 home win over Barnsley on 19 October 2010 only briefly subdued the discontent. Afterwards, a relieved Brian Laws praised Chris Eagles, Brian Easton, and Leon Cort, who was awarded man of the match for his two critical tackles when the game was in the balance.

But four days later, Burnley were thrashed 0-4 at home by tenth-placed Reading. Shell-shocked Laws said: 'We lost our unbeaten home record today with our poorest display of the season. Half the team weren't with it. Our key players were snuffed out. After Cort was dismissed for two rash tackles, we tried to be positive, but conceded two more sloppy goals. We missed Carlisle – his organising ability and leadership. Hopefully this is just a blip.' Centre-back Leon Cort was often left alone in marking fleet-footed Shane Long. As in Burnley's wretched 1-6 home defeat by Manchester City in April, Burnley's swifter visitors were allowed too much acceleration room.

New Burnley director John Banaszkiewicz, from Nelson, told the local press: 'Like the other directors, I'm passionate about this club. The club needs to be more global if it is to grow. I can help here with my international business experience. One of my early objectives is to get Gawthorpe and the academy up to scratch. We can't afford a £35m player, but we can find a new Jay Rodriguez.'

While plans for the redevelopment of Turf Moor were put on hold because of the possibility of a double-dip recession, Philip Wilson was appointed as chief executive of the proposed university of football at Burnley, focusing on football finance, stadium management, commercial matters, accounting, and law. Burnley FC chief executive Paul Fletcher stated that the university would attract students from across the world emphasising, 'I think this is a first for a British football club.'

The club reported a £14.4m pre-tax profit for 2009/10. Income rose from £11.2m in 2008/09 to over £44m, with TV and matchday revenue comprising £40m. Retail turnover was up by 43 per cent, ground advertising revenue up by 40 per cent, and corporate hospitality income doubled. On the debit side, the wage bill continued to soar. In the 2007/08 season, £9.76m was spent on wages. In 2008/09 that figure rose to £13.4m because of the promotion drive, while in the club's solitary Premier League season, there was a further 60 per cent rise as wages totalled £22.37m. This figure was much higher than Brendan Flood's estimated £16m. Nevertheless, the cost of wages as a proportion of turnover reduced to a more sustainable level. In 2008/09, this figure was an alarming 119 per cent. By 2009/10 it had been reduced to 51 per cent, well

2. WHAT GOES UP ...

within the Financial Fair Play limits. The club also settled all but £1m of its debts, repaying its directors' loans and settling the outstanding bills from the 2008/09 promotion season. The bottom line was that the club emerged from its one season of Premier League sun with all debts cleared and £14m in the bank. Moreover, the club's average home attendance in the Premier League was 20,654, its best since its glory days in the early sixties.

Yet, on 11 December 2010, visiting Leeds overturned a first-half two-goal deficit to beat Burnley 2-3 with a crushing second-half display. Although Easton's poked effort had put Burnley in front with Rodriguez doubling that lead with a fine breakaway goal, the Clarets had ridden their luck. Leeds's left-winger Max Gradel burst through Burnley's flimsy defence twice, only to fluff his lines when one-on-one.

Having strengthened their midfield at the break and adopted a higher defensive line, Leeds overran Burnley. Brian Easton was roasted by tricky Snodgrass, while Gradel continued to run riot on the opposite flank. Leeds poured forward at will, with their Argentinian striker Becchio leading the line with darting menace. It seemed as if Laws had no response to Leeds's change of game plan.

Laws was baffled and angry at the post-match press conference. He said: 'A few words have been said, and rightly so, because that's not acceptable. We should be winning that. It's about being professional. It's about being switched on and organised. The manager will always take the rap, but the players must also take some blame because of the way they went out in the second half. I'm disappointed that we didn't continue to do what we did in the first half when we were 2-0 ahead. Their winning third goal came from our corner! Howson was allowed to run the length of the field. In the first period, we troubled their centre-halves with our attacking formation but after the break they had it easy. That's not good enough!'

Although Burnley won well at Barnsley on Boxing Day (2-1), recording their first victory at Oakwell in over a generation, it seemed as if Laws was on borrowed time. Sure enough, after another dismal home defeat, this time to languishing Scunthorpe (0-2), Laws's unhappy period in charge came to an end. As in previous press conferences following a defeat, Laws seemed bewildered, blaming his players' attitude. Here he said: 'It is difficult to understand how the same players who turned in such a good performance at Barnsley on Boxing Day should be so below par against Scunthorpe. It is difficult to put my finger on it. It must be complacency, expecting Scunthorpe to be an easy ride. Our passing skills were off. I can understand the supporters' frustration.' Possibly, it was because the 'band of brothers' mentality which had served them so well under Coyle had been lost.

3. NEW BROOM AND SWEEPING CHANGES 2011/12

Barry Kilby was generally cautious about ditching his helmsman after a run of poor results but here he felt bound to take decisive action if his club were to return to the Premier League before the parachute payments ran out. Bournemouth's 33-year-old manager, Eddie Howe, was selected in Laws's place after a £300,000 compensation package was agreed for him and his assistant, Jason Tindall.

Howe's candidacy rested upon his impressive feat in helping Bournemouth achieve an astonishing recovery in the face of chaotic bankruptcy.

Eddie Howe told the Burnley local press: 'The ambition of the club matched mine. I'm very impressed with the stadium, crowd, and players. The players are good technically, skilful with flair. We have already enjoyed a good, sharp training session. That's what I enjoy being involved in – games and training. I'm a coach, more of an enabler, an encourager rather than a shouter or screamer.

'I don't relish having the spotlight on me. I would much rather the focus was on the club and the players rather than on any one individual. I am part of the coaching team. It is not about me. It is about the team behind the team. I know I must do the media side, but football is what excites me. I'm here to build not just for now but for the future. I have goals but these are best kept for myself and the players.'

Howe wasted little time in bringing in speedy 25-year-old central midfielder Marvin Bartley, from Bournemouth, in January, for around £350,000. He also signed Swindon's prolific goalscorer Charlie Austin, for a reported £1m fee. Howe said of Austin: 'Charlie learnt his trade at Poole Town. He didn't lose hope after being released by Reading as a 15-year-old. He has always had a knack of scoring goals. He is a very good finisher but works hard, both on and off the ball. He is strong in the air. Importantly, he wants to improve. There was a lot of competition, but he wanted to come here.'

A delighted Barry Kilby commented: 'Eddie Howe is a breath of fresh air. We needed a new broom and with Eddie we believe we have a very thoughtful and intelligent manager. Austin is an excellent signing – exactly what we need; younger players like Austin and Bartley whose value will appreciate.' Unfortunately, Austin sustained a shoulder injury at the end of January 2011, ruling him out for the rest of the season. While Howe's Burnley flirted with play-off ambitions, prompted by a six-match unbeaten run, they were undone by barren spells, notably during mid-March and early April when six fixtures yielded just one point.

New director John Banaszkiewicz addressed the London Clarets' AGM in July 2011. He was candid and forthright, admitting that the club had made the mistake of 'resting upon the laurels of Premier League money, rather than re-doubling its efforts at generating more income'. With new Financial Fair Play rules due to come into force for the 2012/13 season, he expected the wage bill to drop substantially. He pointed out this would place a tight curb on all Championship clubs, given that they were currently spending, on average, 88 per cent of their annual turnover figure on wages. Such expenditure was said to fall foul of the new rules. With former loan signing Jack Cork expected to move to Southampton, Banaszkiewicz thought, with hindsight, that the club should have attempted to buy him in

3. NEW BROOM AND SWEEPING CHANGES 2011/12

January 2011 when his wage demands were more manageable. The young Chelsea midfielder had played superbly in an erratic Burnley side for a season and a half.

After completion of the 2010/11 season, Barry Kilby described the club's financial situation in these terms: 'In 2008/09, we made an £11m loss; in 2009/10, we made a £14m profit; in 2010/11, we made a £4m loss, when we were in the top quarter of Championship clubs for wages. This was covered by the £17m parachute payment we received following our relegation from the Premier League. Our one-year stay in the Premier League enabled us to clear the £10m debt incurred by loans made to the club by the Burnley directors during the 2008/09 season.'

Barry continued: 'In a normal Championship season, without the cushion of a parachute payment, we would expect to achieve a £10–12m turnover. With the Football League Financial Fair Play regulations now in place we need to ensure that wages amount to no more than 60 per cent of our turnover. So, after the parachute payments expire, we will be looking at a maximum wage bill of £6–7m.'

He pointed out there was a lot of foreign money coming into the Championship, with only seven clubs now not owned by foreigners.

'The Championship is attracting more foreign money because of the potential financial incentives given by the Premier League. We always need to be aware of our size. We are planning on having an £11m wage bill in 2011/12, taking account of the continuing parachute payment.'

He added that they were committed to developing Gawthorpe training centre and expanding the scouting network and bringing in more younger players, as they were generally on lower wages.

As for John Banaszkiewicz's regret at not offering Jack Cork a permanent contract earlier, Barry Kilby commented: 'We wanted to sign Jack Cork permanently at the end of the 2010/11 season, but his wages had become unaffordable. We took the £3m offered by Bolton for both Mears and Eagles because there was only one year left on their contracts, and both wanted to play in the Premier League. Chris Iwelumo also moved to Watford for around £50,000 during the summer of 2011.'

The average home gate in 2010/11 was just under 15,000. This represented an annual fall of 28 per cent, placing additional pressure upon manager Eddie Howe to divest his team of their higher earners and place a greater accent upon youth. Therefore, Clarke Carlisle also left, on loan to Preston, as did Leon Cort, who was moved to Charlton, ultimately in a permanent deal. Meanwhile, Graham Alexander, Steven Thompson, and Kevin McDonald were released. Much to his chagrin, Howe was compelled to accede to Danny Fox's transfer to big-spending Southampton. The deal was apparently worth £1.8m, which the Burnley board said 'was too good to turn down'. Finally, Wembley hero Wade Elliott moved to Birmingham for an undisclosed sum.

Howe then brought in England Under-21 internationals Junior Stanislas and Zavon Hines from West Ham, the latter having his £250,000 transfer fee set by tribunal. Preston's 22-year-old Republic of Ireland international winger, Keith Treacy, was signed, too, for a fee around £750,000, while young Manchester City defenders Kieran Trippier and Ben Mee were signed on season-long loans. Both players had represented the England Under-21 side and had experience of playing in the Championship, Trippier with Barnsley, and Mee with Leicester.

Howe introduced Mee thus: 'Ben is a fantastic young player. He has a fantastic attitude, a winner who is an England Under-21 international. He is rated highly at Manchester City. He is a left-sided centre-half but can play at left-back. He is comfortable on the ball. He is very aggressive.' As for Trippier, he was described as an attacking right-back with an impressive crossing ability

3. NEW BROOM AND SWEEPING CHANGES 2011/12

and a fearsome shot. He seemed an ideal replacement for the departed Mears.

In addition, midfielder Chris McCann was persuaded to sign a further two-year deal while Portsmouth's £2.5m offer for Martin Paterson, and a separate unnamed bid for Rodriguez, apparently worth £4.5m, were both rejected.

Howe also placed his stamp upon youth development, appointing Jason Blake, another former Bournemouth colleague, as head coach for the younger professionals and reserves. Blake had never played football professionally, but he was a UEFA A-licence holder. Howe told the local press: 'He's someone I'm delighted to bring to the club. He will bring enthusiasm and dedication to the job. He has had experience of running the centre of excellence at Bournemouth and was a big part of the team down there. Jason's main strengths are working with and developing young players.'

In late October 2011, Martin Dobson left his role as director of youth development, having fulfilled his contract, while Vince Overson, head of the club's centre of excellence, left with immediate effect. Estimable youth coach Ashley Hoskin left, too. Their loss dismayed many Burnley supporters, notably those with an active interest in Burnley's youth development. They were concerned that well-regarded and experienced Burnley coaches were being replaced by Howe's former Bournemouth colleagues, allegedly without good reason. Doubts were expressed, too, about the dismantling of an apparently successful recruitment network.

The 2011/12 season began disappointingly as visiting Watford, under the management of future Burnley boss Sean Dyche, coasted into a two-goal lead, helped by an unfortunate error by Ben Mee. Hornets striker Marvin Sordell ran Burnley's newly assembled defence ragged with his pace and power. However, thanks to Howe's late introduction of Austin and Treacy, the game was saved with two goals in the last 13 minutes. Howe said: 'I feel frustrated more than relieved after pulling back a two-goal deficit. New signing Keith Treacy was excellent. He gave us real impetus providing an indication of what he is about. Regarding the interest being shown in Jay Rod and Danny Fox, it's not ideal.' With a lucrative deal with Southampton in the offing, Fox made it clear that his ambitions lay southwards.

With Charlie Austin still finding his feet and Paterson injured again – he would be out of action until December 2011 – Howe was permitted to buy Bournemouth's highly promising 19-year-old striker, Danny Ings. Howe's assistant Jason Tindall told the local press: 'Danny Ings is a fantastic talent. He had a very good season with Bournemouth last year, prompting various Premier League sides and three Championship clubs to show a keen interest in him. He's a 110 per cent player, a very intelligent young man, who scores and makes goals. I have worked with him for some time. He works hard and listens well.'

Regrettably, Ings sustained a knee injury in his second training session, ruling him out of action for five months. Tindall remarked: 'It is a great blow to lose Ings to injury in only his second training session at the club. We are a bit thin on the ground at present, with Paterson injured once more. But Danny's attitude is fantastic. He's in every day at 8.30am ready to work on other parts of his body, increasing his upper body strength.' Burnley's injury woes were compounded when Michael Duff suffered damage to his knee ligaments in a League Cup victory over Barnet. He was expected to be sidelined for six weeks.

Tindall added: 'We have a nice bunch of lads here; 21-year-old Junior Stanislas has joined from West Ham, encouraging his friend, Zavon Hines, to join him. Junior had been at West Ham since he was ten, so it was quite an upheaval for him to move so far away, but he arrived with a positive attitude, wanting to do well here. He likes to attack and score goals, but he has the

3. NEW BROOM AND SWEEPING CHANGES 2011/12

versatility to play on the left, with good crossing ability, or just behind the main striker. We have high hopes of him.'

Austin and Rodriguez quickly established a formidable striking partnership. Nottingham Forest found out the hard way on Tuesday 27 September 2011, when Burnley thrashed them 5-2, Rodriguez scoring with two headers and Austin nabbing the fifth. Stanislas was the architect of this impressive victory, supplying a succession of devastating crosses that the Forest defenders struggled to combat. Blackpool were also beaten 3-1 at Turf Moor, while Derby (2-1), Millwall (1-0), and Coventry (2-1) were overcome away. Austin and Rodriguez seemed to be monopolising the goalscoring.

However, as autumn turned into winter, Howe's men were struggling on the brink of the relegation zone. Howe stated: 'We need to improve in all departments, but particularly at the back.' He suggested that he had extracted all he could from the current players and needed to bring in fresh legs. Howe's plea did not fall on deaf ears. During the January window, the club allowed him to shell out £150,000 on Derry City's left-back Daniel Lafferty, and to sign ex-Cherries striker Josh McQuoid, on a three-month loan from Millwall. In addition, permanent deals were agreed for Trippier and Mee, the former costing around £400,000 and the latter a little more.

Hull City 2 Burnley 3
26 November 2011

'Racing Rats'

On a wet, glowering November Saturday, Burnley were at the KC Stadium. Hull were in sixth place, looking up optimistically, whereas Burnley, in 21st spot, were peering down nervously at the gaping trap door. Burnley had just lost four games on the bounce. Goalscoring had become problematic despite having one of the Championship's most potent striking partnerships with Austin and Rodriguez. Burnley's defence was inadequate with only one clean sheet in 17 league fixtures during this season.

Nevertheless, Burnley started brightly, but were frustrated when Stanislas missed two enticing chances in the opening minutes. Hull's Matty Fryatt was less wasteful, though, tapping in Cameron Stewart's low cross in the 11th minute. This was Fryatt's fifth goal in eight games. Hull then seized control, with Fryatt only inches away from doubling Hull's lead from Brady's free kick, seconds before the break.

Sam Vokes came on for Stanislas at the resumption as Howe looked to pep Burnley's attacking potency. Rodriguez almost obliged his manager when he turned to strike a ferocious volley at goal, which Peter Gulacsi did well to push on to the bar. But Hull once again struck against the run of play. In the 55th minute Robert Koren found Fryatt unmarked in the Clarets' box. Without hesitating he beat Burnley goalkeeper Lee Grant with a rising drive. Fryatt then missed an inviting opportunity to complete his hat-trick, aiming his shot straight at Grant.

Hull looked comfortably in charge with their two-goal lead but were caught napping with only 12 minutes left. Burnley defender Edgar nipped in behind Andy Dawson to nod home Ross Wallace's pinpoint cross. Moments later, full-back Kieran Trippier found sprinting Edgar with a sharp, right-wing cross. Without breaking stride, Edgar volleyed the ball high into the Hull net at scorching speed. Sensing victory, Burnley poured forward and, with time almost up, Rodriguez's composed cross-shot found goal to end his side's barren run.

While the Burnley players wildly celebrated their remarkable victory, Hull boss Nick Barmby furiously berated his sloppy side. It was his first defeat as Hull's manager.

This game proved to be a turning point for Howe and his team. Five of the next six league games were won, including a prestigious 2-1 victory at West Ham on 3 December, clinched with a powerful header from loan signing Sam Vokes. After a

3. NEW BROOM AND SWEEPING CHANGES 2011/12

fortuitous 1-0 home win over Hull on New Year's Eve, sealed by newly returned Paterson, Burnley were in seventh place and eyeing a play-off spot. However, just six of the final 22 games were won, meaning that Burnley slumped into 13th position, five places lower than in the season before. Home form was particularly frustrating – seven wins, nine draws, and seven defeats.

On 18 November 2011 chief executive Paul Fletcher announced that he was leaving the club. He explained: 'I thought I couldn't contribute anymore, apart from making Burnley's University College of Football Business a success. Hopefully, the new chief executive will have more success.'

American Lee Hoos was chosen as Fletcher's replacement as Burnley's chief executive, having served Fulham, Southampton, and Leicester in a similar capacity. While at Leicester, Hoos oversaw the purchase of the club by a consortium from Thailand, and the subsequent appointments of Sven-Göran Eriksson and Nigel Pearson as their successive team managers.

But not long after Hoos's arrival at the club, Burnley's estimable chairman, Barry Kilby, announced he was standing down in May 2012 because of ill health. His place was taken by John Banaszkiewicz and Mike Garlick who agreed to share the chairman role.

Banaszkiewicz said: 'Mike and I will chair board meetings alternately with the casting vote alternating, too. Because of the Financial Fair Play regulations, youth development has become more important here. We can't stop talented young players like Jay Rod moving on. Incidentally, he has been an excellent ambassador for this club. What we need to do is find and bring on more young players like him.

'The Championship is probably the most competitive league in the world with around 15 teams vying for a place in the Premier League. According to an analysis conducted by Deloitte, during the 2011/12 season, Championship clubs incurred a combined loss of £189m contributing to an overall debt of £720m. The clubs with the greatest debts were said to be Middlesbrough with £98m, Nottingham Forest with £75m, Leicester with £48m and Preston with £38m. In all, Championship wages represented about 90 per cent of its clubs' collective income. We don't have to bet the ranch, though, if we continue to invest in young talent to sustain us, acquiring and developing young, up-and-coming players like Austin and Ings. As for the transfer fees we obtain from sales, most of the revenue has to be put into the club to sustain its continued running.'

Mike Garlick added: 'In 2011/12 we made a loss of £4m. We need more non-matchday revenue and to do this we need to become more proactive in seeking commercial sponsorship. This is of paramount importance. Both John and I have international businesses, giving us the opportunity to promote Burnley FC abroad. We must be ambitious on and off the field. If we're not, we will go backwards. If we remain competitive in the Championship, we'll get another shot at the Premier League.'

As expected, Jay Rodriguez was transferred to Southampton in June 2012 for a fee of around £7m. He represented the Burnley youth system's most lucrative product. This year was a time of celebration as the Burnley youth team progressed to the semi-final of the FA Youth Cup before being eliminated by Blackburn. Yet, despite Eddie Howe's reforms of youth development, not one member of this talented squad became a first-team player in the top half of English football.

With the 2012/13 season just one month away, Eddie Howe reflected: 'It's been a very busy summer. We've signed centre-back Jason Shackell from Derby for £1.1m. I've admired him for some time. He will fit in as a leader. In fact, he has everything you want in a modern centre-half. We had to be patient, though, in negotiating his transfer. We have also brought in George Porter, a very quick young winger from Leyton Orient who brings exciting promise to our development squad. We have added right-back Luke O'Neill, from Mansfield, as cover for Trippier, and acquired Reading left-back Joseph Mills on a season-long loan. We have paid £500,000 to Wolves, too, for their centre-forward, Sam Vokes. The board have also been very receptive to my ideas about what improvements we need in training. Here, we do very little running without the ball. As far as training facilities are concerned, it is important to keep on the move as a club.' Shortly after his arrival, Jason Shackell commented: 'I like training here. It's based upon attacking football which I enjoy. It's a massive honour to be awarded the captaincy.'

The 2012/13 season began well with an emphatic 2-0 win over Owen Coyle's recently relegated Bolton side. Eddie Howe concluded: 'It doesn't get much better than this. It was pretty much the perfect performance. I thought we were well on top for most of the game. The decision-making was good throughout. We knew we needed to improve our defensiveness after last year.'

Owen Coyle had to endure an unpleasant afternoon. His team played dreadfully and he was constantly jeered by the Burnley fans, notably when a small plane trailing a recriminatory banner circled overhead. The banner read: 'Judas Coyle you reap what you sow.' In his post-match press interview, Coyle preposterously claimed credit for assembling the victorious Burnley team when only two of its players had served under him! Having scored the opening goal, injury-jinxed Martin Paterson exclaimed to the press: 'I always said that when I'm fully fit, I'll score goals and work defences.'

But the euphoria of this impressive victory soon dissipated. A 3-2 defeat at Middlesbrough followed, causing Howe to say: 'In the first half we were excellent, passing and moving well and getting a lot of balls into their box. However, we scored twice only to concede almost immediately. Stanislas was excellent – his best game for the club. But Boro played well between our lines as we defended a bit too deep.'

Another defeat at Huddersfield followed. An increasingly exasperated Howe said: 'We didn't keep it tight at the beginning as planned. We never really opened them up either. It was a disappointing display. We gave Jordan Rhodes too much time in the box for the second goal. Pato is out again as well, having sustained a tiny tear in his hamstring, and leaving us thin on the ground with strikers.'

Brighton then rammed home Burnley's shortcomings in a crushing 1-3 victory at Turf Moor on 1 September 2012. Howe conceded: 'Brighton dominated the first half. We gave away three goals from set plays which was particularly disappointing. There were two great finishes, but we should not have allowed Mackail-Smith the space to produce an overhead kick in our box. Because of injuries, we were forced to play one up front, so it was difficult to make an impact. We need Pato back.'

With Burnley then languishing in 22nd position, Howe was grateful to play a side without a point thus far. Peterborough packed a surprising punch, though. Howe commented: 'Peterborough at home was a crazy game. After scoring first and being well on top, suddenly we were 1-2 down. Although we eventually won 5-2, we could have scored more for we created enough chances to win three games. Once again there were defensive lapses, with our midfielders letting runners go. But Junior was excellent again – very positive, showing pace and running at people. This ability has been evident in training for a year, but he hasn't shown it enough in games. Technically and athletically, he's got the lot. Now he needs to be more ruthless.'

Although Charlie Austin embarked upon a prolific goal spree, notching hat-tricks against Peterborough and Sheffield Wednesday, and producing a winning brace at Derby (2-1), Burnley continued to concede too easily. A first-half lead at Leicester was frittered away by poor defending. Swindon were gifted three avoidable goals in a League Cup defeat. Then both Millwall (2-2) and Sheffield Wednesday (3-3) grabbed late goals

3. NEW BROOM AND SWEEPING CHANGES 2011/12

to deny Burnley victory in games which should have been won. Charlie Austin fumed that his goal rush was not reaping better rewards.

Then to cap it all, Burnley blew a two-goal lead at Crystal Palace to lose 3-4. Howe's post-match comments were becoming repetitive. After the Palace fiasco, he said: 'We had a plan to cope with Palace's wide men but once Zaha switched wings we couldn't cope with it. This performance was nowhere near good enough. We defended well for 30 minutes. We were two up but then fell apart. When we concede we appear nervous. We don't look as good in the second half of games as we do in the first. Charlie's goals are fantastic, but the ones we are conceding are not.'

Club captain Jason Shackell added: 'We're doing a lot of talking but there's not enough action. There is a lack of discipline. Collectively, we are not defending well enough.'

Shortly afterwards, Howe and Tindall left Turf Moor at their request, returning to their former club, Bournemouth. It was reported in some national papers that Bournemouth chairman Eddie Mitchell had offered Burnley £1.4m in compensation.

Co-chairman Mike Garlick told the local press: 'John B and I are surprised and disappointed that Eddie is leaving a great club like Burnley so soon in the season. However, we understand that his decision reflects his personal circumstances rather than any matters at Burnley Football Club, be that the supporters, the players, or the board. We agreed with Eddie that quite a lot of things have gone well. The infrastructure has been improved and that remains as we move forward. He left for valid family reasons. There's 80 per cent of the season left so there's plenty of time in which to turn things around.'

Eddie Howe said: 'I'm pleased Burnley have been well compensated for our services. That was important from my respect. Hopefully that will help them make the right appointment. Burnley treated me very well. I can't speak highly enough of the club, the people who work for it, the players, and the supporters, who have all been brilliant to us since we walked through the door. Hopefully we've played our part in a rosy future for the club.

'We've done our best to try to promote a long-term plan for the club. But it's for other people to judge our time in charge. There's stability in the boardroom, and they have been fantastic with me and my team and helped us to implement what we wanted to do. To leave is incredibly difficult, but it is a decision I must make for my family and for personal reasons, which I can't go into detail on. There is only one club I would contemplate leaving Burnley for and that is Bournemouth. Whoever takes the job of manager here will be taking over a fantastic football club.'

In reviewing the interest shown in the managerial vacancy, co-chairman John Banaszkiewicz said: 'There have been 15 to 20 applicants for the vacant manager post so far. We want someone like Eddie but with a bit more aggression with the players. Mike and I are going to take our time. It's a massive appointment. We need to get it right for the long term. In the meantime, youth team manager Terry Pashley will take over the running of the first team.'

Various contenders were mentioned, including Mick McCarthy, Ian Holloway, Michael Appleton, Billy Davies, and, surprisingly, Owen Coyle. At least Lee Hoos was quick to scotch that rumour, stating: 'I just couldn't see how that one would happen. Obviously, I wasn't there when the whole Owen Coyle saga happened, but I got enough feedback to know that there was a very bitter aftertaste and I just couldn't see a way back for that one.'

On the pitch, Charlie Austin extended his purple patch by nodding in the winner against Blackpool. He said: 'I've been told that my goal today means that I've equalled Willie Irvine's 1966 club record, having scored in seven successive games. This is nice but a win counts for more. Lee Grant made two great saves

3. NEW BROOM AND SWEEPING CHANGES 2011/12

to make sure we got all three points. Pash has been brilliant for us in training, leaving smiles on all the players' faces. He's so enthusiastic. It rubs off on all of us.'

Recent signing Brian Stock added, 'Pash deserves a lot of credit. He's got us to be more professional on the pitch, alongside Faz and Blakey. It's been a good atmosphere since Eddie and Jason left. It's also given me the opportunity to play in my favoured midfield holding role.'

Terry Pashley won both of his initial games as caretaker. After netting a brace of goals in the midweek 4-3 win at Bristol City, Austin trumped Ray Pointer's 1958/59 club record by scoring 12 goals in eight successive games. Just as fans' thoughts were turning to Pashley as an eligible managerial candidate, Burnley were tonked 0-4 by promotion-bound Cardiff.

PART 8

THE DYCHE FACTOR

2012 to 2022

'Times Like These'

1. 'TO SUCCEED YOU MUST START AT THE BACK'

On 30 October 2012, co-chairman John Banaszkiewicz announced: 'After two weeks of interviews we have decided to appoint Sean Dyche as Burnley's new manager. He impressed us with his pride, passion, motivation, and hunger. He is a strong character who, as a player, won four promotions with four different clubs. He is a leader, who is extremely ambitious, more so, we thought, than any of the other candidates we considered. He came across as very good on the technical aspects of the game, who has the qualities needed for bringing club and community close together. Sean has loyally served Watford for eight years whereas we have had three managers in as many seasons. We need greater continuity and stability if we are to move forward. Consequently, we will do our best to hold onto Charlie Austin in the January window.'

Sean Dyche chose ex-Nottingham Forest midfielder Ian Woan as his assistant, while Tony Loughlan was appointed as first-team coach. Dyche commented: 'The players were immediately very responsive, receptive to realigning with the way things need doing. We want to be flexible in our thinking. It's a case of adding to the defence not taking away the scoring. All players have the will to win. But sometimes it needs re-igniting.'

Dyche explained he gave each player a questionnaire, asking for their ideas for improvement. 'This enabled me to gauge

1. 'TO SUCCEED YOU MUST START AT THE BACK'

how clear they all were about what needed to be done. What I emphasise is the framework, the shape of the team, rather than the individuals, although I try to develop the players as much as the framework.

'My emphasis is upon how the *club* can move forward. We need to develop the connection with the people of Burnley. A Burnley supporter told me that Burnley people support the club. That's music to my ears. It's a fantastic club. If they phone you, you take notice. My background has been in youth development. I want to see this club being as successful as Watford were in that regard.

'As manager, I'm at the front of the club, no more.' As for his unusual, rasping voice, Dyche said, 'It's a family thing. My boy has it, so did my dad. It does have its uses, mind!'

The players soon found out how determined their new boss was, insisting upon a culture of 'minimum requirement: maximum effort'. Dyche demanded a higher level of fitness stating: 'I want to see honesty, integrity, pride and passion. I want to see a team who puts sweat on their shirts. As a supporter, I wanted to see a team which gave everything for the club.'

Midfielder Dean Marney was enthusiastic about the regime Dyche had introduced, saying: 'Sean Dyche's training is intense. His game plans are good.'

Co-chairman Mike Garlick outlined to the local press the board's ambition for the rest of the season, stating: 'Ultimately, we want to try to get promotion, but we don't need to go up this season. Sean has just over a two-and-a-half-year deal, so we'd like to think he's got time to improve things. The target we set Sean for this season is to get above 13th position, which we achieved the season before, and to stop shipping goals and improve home performances which have not been good enough over the last two years.'

Burnley 2 Wolverhampton Wanderers 0
3 November 2012
'Work That'

Sean Dyche made a perfect start to his managerial career at Burnley with a resounding win over lethargic Wolves, formerly a Burnley nemesis. The Clarets were on top from the start. In the fifth minute centre-back Michael Duff swept the ball forward and, after some neat interplay, Ross Wallace fizzed a left-footed effort over from the edge of the box. Wallace was fortunate though to avoid a red card shortly after, for he clipped the heels of Kevin Doyle as the Wolves forward was breaking clear.

The Clarets went ahead in the 18th minute. Burnley left-back Ben Mee found Paterson on the left flank with a clever pass that curled around the back of the Wolves defensive line. Paterson was not a reliable finisher when one-on-one, but here he gathered the ball neatly in his stride, made for goal, and, without delay, fired past visiting goalkeeper Ikeme. Burnley were well on top and Dean Marney should have doubled their lead shortly before half-time. But we were not kept waiting long for the decisive second goal, for in the 53rd minute prolific striker Charlie Austin was left unmarked as he headed in his 19th goal of the season. Burnley's momentum was briefly interrupted when Wallace went down following an aerial collision with Jermaine Pennant. Alarmingly, Wallace required oxygen on the pitch before leaving on a stretcher, to be replaced by Danny Ings.

Bakary Sako was the only Wolves player to threaten the Burnley defence. He almost set up Sylvan Ebanks-Blake for a tap-in, and rattled the post later, but Burnley saw out time comfortably. In fact, Clarets substitute Sam Vokes almost increased their lead in stoppage time.

This was a second clean sheet at home for the Clarets, offering further encouragement to Dyche as he and his team attempted to make Burnley more defensively sound. Dyche's verdict was: 'It was a fantastic start. I spoke about bringing about

1. 'TO SUCCEED YOU MUST START AT THE BACK'

a one-club mentality and that's a good way to start when a big club like Wolves comes to town and you get a nice win and a clean sheet. The players have been very honest, they know there is still work to be done but it was more a case of realigning them. They're good people and are very honest, and they know what they can do and some of the things they haven't been doing well.'

There were few positives though for Wolves manager Stale Solbakken as his side dropped to ninth in the Championship table, one point above Burnley in 13th. He said: 'It was a bad performance overall until there were 15 or 20 minutes left. When Burnley scored their first goal they were on top, so I changed it around at half-time. At the end we had chances to score but it was one of those days. I must say that I probably picked the wrong team. All the players tried hard, but they didn't have a good day and it is down to me.'

In midweek, Burnley beat Leeds 1-0. A delighted Charlie Austin remarked: 'We kept it tight. Everyone put in a real shift. We deserved the points. Chris McCann provided Tripps with a superb ball which enabled him to produce a great cross that I nodded in.'

Dyche's tactics succeeded in bolting the back door, halving the number of goals conceded. In his first match in charge, against Wolves, Dyche set out his stall, playing Marney and Edgar in central midfield, with Stock operating in a holding role in front of a back four of Trippier, Shackell, Duff, and Mee. Wide men Paterson and Wallace were instructed to support Austin as the solitary striker when in possession, but to track back swiftly to cover the full-backs when not. With Burnley playing an energetic pressing game, both Wolves and Leeds were squeezed, and restricted to few chances.

Dyche experienced his first setback in a 2-1 defeat at Ipswich. He observed: 'Against Ipswich we deserved something, but we gave it away by attacking with gusto without making sure we had enough balance behind. We will be working on that. We didn't create as I hoped either. We need to shift the ball quicker because teams bank up swiftly.'

Burnley 1 Blackburn Rovers 1
2 December 2012
'Read All about It'

Dyche's first high-profile challenge came on a sparkling, bitterly cold Sunday lunchtime on 2 December. This was the feisty home derby with arch-rivals Blackburn. A crowd of 21,341 watched a pulsating, no-holds-barred physical contest. It began with Burnley pushing forward energetically and ended with Sam Vokes's late headed equaliser in front of the Jimmy McIlroy stand. Vokes's goal created bedlam among the feverish Burnley fans.

Dyche said: 'We came across two fine centre-halves and a goalkeeper on form. I really enjoyed the impact the subs made though. To give the fans that goal at the end is important because it would have been a travesty had we come away from that game with nothing.' He quipped with a smile: 'It also showed up that chap who shouted out "What's Vokesy going to do in five minutes?"'

Rhodes had put Blackburn ahead in the 68th minute with a trademark poacher's goal, leaving Burnley to hammer unproductively upon a closed door. Or so I thought, until the 89th minute when Vokes leapt higher than his markers, precisely glancing the ball into the right-hand corner. It was a delicious moment having endured 20 minutes of the Blackburn chant, 'Same old Rovers beating Burnley.' What goes around, comes around, eh?

The annual accounts for the year ending 30 June 2012 revealed a profit of £3.16m, which would have been an operating loss had it not been for Rodriguez's transfer fee of £7m. In a statement smacking of the past 'sell to survive' policy, the co-chairmen pointed out that 'player trading remains a cornerstone of how the club balances its books'.

1. 'TO SUCCEED YOU MUST START AT THE BACK'

One surprise, however, was the size of the wage bill. Despite the strict economies introduced at the start of the 2011/12 season, wages remained high at £16.9m. Given the impending new Financial Fair Play regulations, this was a cause for concern, particularly with the parachute payment having halved to £8m.

Howe's restructuring of Burnley's youth development system had raised staffing costs. The impact of the Elite Player Performance Plan (EPPP) was a factor here, but with Jason Blake replaced as development coach by Simon Weatherstone a year after his appointment, there were further doubts raised about the success of Howe's reforms. Lee Darnbrough, another Howe signing, joined the club in November 2012 as head of recruitment and analytics. He had previously served West Bromwich in a similar capacity. Burnley's chief executive Lee Hoos confirmed that Darnbrough would not dictate which players Dyche should sign, but would assist 'in terms of tracking and landing those players, helping myself and the board ensure we are getting value for money'.

Dyche was positive about Darnbrough's appointment stating: 'It's a similar model to what I had at Watford. It's the way a lot of clubs are looking now because as manager you are very time-bound. We do DVD analysis, pre-hab programmes, weights programmes and all different things. We want as much information on targets as we can. It's still not an exact science but the more you can put into the process, the better chance you have of a better outcome.'

While Dyche made Burnley harder to beat, the goals dried up at both ends. Nevertheless, the defensive disciplines Dyche instilled served Burnley well in their subsequent upward surge.

In January 2013, the board decided to re-purchase Turf Moor and Gawthorpe training centre via a new company, Turf Moor Properties Ltd, by means of a bond issue. Co-chairman John Banaszkiewicz explained: 'This arrangement enables us to protect Turf Moor and Gawthorpe from the uncertainties of the football industry and its finances. Having examined all the options, the board is confident that a bond issue represents the most cost-effective finance option and enables a section of our fans to play a part in bringing our spiritual home back under the control of the club. Additionally, buying both Turf Moor and Gawthorpe back makes sense financially and operationally for our long-term future. It will eventually see an end to rental payments and put the club on a firmer financial footing.' On 5 July 2013, the club proudly announced that its ground and training complex were once again back in its ownership following the completion of a buy-back campaign developed by the co-chairmen. Banaszkiewicz said: 'Despite concerns that it would be tough to raise the funds we needed, this innovative scheme has been very successful, bringing us £3.5m.'

During February and March 2013, Burnley struggled. Dismal home displays against Middlesbrough (0-0), Huddersfield (0-1), Barnsley (1-1), and Hull (0-1) caused dismay in the stands and on the websites. However, a spirited performance at Ewood Park helped allay relegation worries. Here, Burnley were robbed of victory by a poor refereeing decision, late in the game. Nevertheless, a subsequent 3-1 home win over relegation rivals Bristol City appeared to signal safety, only for lacklustre defeats at Blackpool (0-1) and Leeds (0-1) to suggest otherwise.

Relegation was ultimately averted, thanks to Edgar's late headed equaliser against champions elect Cardiff, on 20 April, and to winning strikes by Ings and Paterson at Molineux (2-1), a week later. While the victory at Wolves removed the threat of relegation for Burnley, it sealed Wolves's successive drop. A spectacular shot from Stanislas and a tap-in from Paterson were then sufficient to beat Ipswich in the final game of the season.

Burnley rose to 11th place, ensuring Dyche met the board's immediate objective of achieving a higher position than in the season before. Dyche concluded: 'We have finished 11th in arguably the toughest ever Championship, certainly in my

1. 'TO SUCCEED YOU MUST START AT THE BACK'

lifetime. Next season will be even tougher given the profusion of cash-rich opponents. But as Burnley has done in years before, we'll punch above our weight and come together as a community and a team.' And how!

2. 'ROOM AT THE TOP'

Having secured safety by a comfortable margin, Sean Dyche's next headache was to form a competitive team for the 2013/14 season. To complicate matters the contracts of six members of his first-team squad were due to expire in June 2013.

Dyche had already told the press that the club must play hardball with new contracts. He said: 'There are players – who were deemed to be good players – on contracts that were agreed when we were trying to get back into the Premier League immediately. That doesn't mean we aren't trying to do that now, but those contracts must now come down because the cost base must come down. So, the negotiation process becomes obviously more difficult. We can't just give them what they want. It's not perfect, but it is what it is.

'I don't think as a club there will be massive investment. Burnley is a club that pulls together and that's important because if there's money for investment it won't be millions. Burnley wants to be a club that is solvent, it wants to be a club that moves forward, it still wants to be competitive. But if competitive means rolling out millions of pounds and then a year later finding it is in absolute trouble, I'm not sure that Burnley fans really want that.'

Four high-profile squad members left the club before the start of the 2013/14 season. Former prized asset Chris McCann was surprisingly not offered a new contract. Martin Paterson, the £1m-plus striker, left the club having dismissed a new deal as 'derisory'. Goalkeeper Lee Grant elected to return to Derby,

2. 'ROOM AT THE TOP'

nearer to his family, and Charlie Austin transferred to Queens Park Rangers for around £4m, after his proposed move to Hull collapsed, allegedly because of a suspect knee.

However, midfielder Dean Marney and centre-back Kevin Long signed new contracts, while Dyche moved quickly to plug the gap left by departing Grant by signing Bristol City goalkeeper Tom Heaton on a free transfer. Heaton had begun his career at Manchester United, as had creative midfielder David Jones, whom Dyche also signed on a free transfer. Jones had previously helped Derby and Wolves win promotion to the Premier League. He seemed to be an ideal replacement for departed McCann. Versatile Scottish midfielder Scott Arfield was added to the squad too, having impressed during a trial period. He had been mystifyingly released by Huddersfield. The Terriers' negligent loss would become the Clarets' enormous gain.

With Austin moving on just before the new season started, Burnley were left with only two recognised strikers, Vokes and Ings. Ings had already suffered two serious knee injuries. In the previous season he had managed only three goals in 32 league appearances, albeit 17 as a substitute. Vokes had scored only four goals in 46 appearances, although 33 of these were as a substitute. It was small wonder that Burnley were listed among the bookies' favourites for relegation. I was certain that Burnley would struggle to avoid the drop.

Yet by tea-time on 21 September, Burnley had won five, drawn two and lost just one of their opening eight league fixtures. Sheffield Wednesday had been ruthlessly cut open then stubbornly resisted at Hillsborough (2-1), while Derby were overrun at Pride Park with Ings in devastating form (3-0). At Turf Moor, Birmingham were easily brushed aside (3-0) and plucky Yeovil were eventually shrugged off (2-0), although both Bolton (1-1) and Blackburn (1-1) came from behind at Turf Moor to share the spoils. Only Brighton had dented Burnley's flying start, not helped by the dismissal of goalkeeper Heaton (0-2).

On a dazzling afternoon at Elland Road, on 21 September, Burnley swarmed all over Leeds, leading by two goals at the break, thanks to Arfield and Vokes. As at Hillsborough, Burnley then stood firm in the second half, defying Leeds's attempts at recovery, although Smith's towering header in the 79th minute caused some discomfort.

An elated Sean Dyche reflected: 'At Leeds we created many chances in the first half. We looked like we had that real air of confidence. In the second half, we started brightly, and Paddy Kenny made a fantastic save from Danny Ings. Had it been 3-0, that would have been job done, but they settled and in the last 20 minutes we had to hang on. I would say that was controlled, but of course Tom Heaton deserves massive credit. The two saves he made here were worth two goals. Although we have kept him quiet so far this season, when he's needed to, he has made big, big saves.

'It's not easy to get things to work immediately, but we have galvanised a group of people who want to play for Burnley Football Club, and I think that is a massively important thing. The fans can see their will to win a football match and it's hard not to gush about them at the minute because they have been terrific. They are delivering every week and that is a fantastic feeling for everyone connected with the club.'

Burnley 2 Reading 1
5 October 2013

'Alternative Ulster'

Burnley seemed unstoppable, flattening Charlton 3-0 at home and outplaying Doncaster away (2-0). But the star performance came in a home win over Reading on a radiant autumn afternoon on 5 October. Burnley flew at Reading from kick-off, pressing them hard all over the pitch, not giving them any time to settle or pick their passes, repeatedly catching them in possession and forcing a litany of distributional errors. From front to back,

2. 'ROOM AT THE TOP'

Burnley were ruthless and relentless while also playing beautiful, fluent football.

Dyche was understandably euphoric after the game, hailing his team's performance as a brilliant display. He enthused: 'I think that is one of our best performances since I've been at the club. Reading are a big club, just out of the Premier League and highly fancied, with a very good manager and good, experienced players. But I thought some of our football was terrific. We opened them up at will at times in the second half, and to me deserved to win more comfortably. It got a bit nervy in the final five minutes, with the mayhem that can sometimes happen from putting balls in the box, but we thoroughly deserved to hang on to win.'

Dyche said he cited the example of 400m runner Ed Moses to inspire his players to keep up their winning form.

'Ed Moses was not beaten over ten years in 122 races,' said Dyche. 'I said, imagine getting to 50, then 70, then 90. What were his thoughts about the challenges, his opposition and all the science allowing everyone to get better and stronger? But he just kept winning. Now I'm not suggesting it's a given and I am not suggesting we will win forever, but you must be open-minded and push away that thought that we're due a defeat because we're not. If you think about it statistically, you can win every game. It's not a probability, but the mindset has to be to forget the past and look to the future.'

On the following Saturday, the Ipswich hoodoo was put to bed with a ragged 1-0 victory, thanks to a late header from Arfield. Once again Dyche warned his players not to be distracted by their club's poor record at Portman Road – Burnley had not won there since January 1970. Dyche insisted that what happens in the past has no impact upon the present or the future.

He told the waiting press: 'All credit to everyone. The players put so much effort into that performance again today, and although there were quiet moments in our display, we still found the wherewithal to go and win it 1-0. Within all that, I am really pleased that we have turned around what could have been a negative situation.

'There were people questioning why we sold Charlie Austin, and then about the funds and all of that, so I am so pleased. The board came out and were very honest, and we came out and said we were believers in the people we work with. So, I am really pleased for the players and the supporters who looked beyond that.'

Dyche praised the positive energy among the players, saying the club was ready to provide any support 'within the finances that are available'.

'The challenge of football is not to say you can't do this or that. You can do anything you wish, and I have made that clear to the players. We have good players in a tight group, and it will need support at some point, but we can only do that one step at a time, and today was another big step forward in what we are trying to achieve here.'

So was the next game against moneybags QPR!

Burnley 2 Queens Park Rangers 0
26 October 2013

'Jetliner'

On another scintillating autumn day, we were treated to another dazzling victory, this time over promotion rivals QPR. Sean Dyche said: 'I think you have to say that the QPR result is the best of our season, given the quality in their ranks, the manager and the resources they have. To come to Turf Moor and for us to give a performance like that, to win, was terrific and I am so pleased so many were here to see it [16,074 attended].

'I thought we were fantastic from the first whistle to the last. I thought the energy, discipline, application and, most of all, the quality was excellent, culminating in a great result. QPR had only conceded four goals before today and were unbeaten.'

2. 'ROOM AT THE TOP'

Danny Ings scored the two goals, one an excellent finish to a great move and the other a late penalty. Dyche continued: 'I spoke to Danny on Thursday and said he looked like a young man enjoying his training and his performances. He said he was and that will do for me, but credit to all the players. We have spoken to the lads about having a freedom to play, no matter who that is against. The players have a framework, but within that they have immense freedom to express themselves. I believe in them and trust them to deliver performances.'

Ings complimented his strike partner, Sam Vokes, telling former Burnley media manager Darren Bentley: 'My first goal against QPR gave me satisfaction, because of the preceding passage of play, which included the sharp one-two with Big Sam, that put me through on goal. I'm not sure people realise how good he is. He is not just a big, typical English striker who can head it; he can slide other people in as well. He's done that on many occasions this season.'

Full-back Kieran Trippier also gave his perspective on this crucial victory: 'We have no fear of any team in the league. Our spirit this year is unbelievably high. The difference comes from our superior fitness. We ran non-stop for 98 minutes against QPR. The gaffer's first pre-season training laid the foundations for this.'

Centre-forward Sam Vokes and goalkeeper Tom Heaton then gave their opinions on why Burnley were then topping the table. Vokes said: 'Dyche is the reason that Burnley are currently doing so well. He is very high on different types of psychology. He is a good motivator off the pitch and in the changing rooms. Coming here with his extensive playing experience has helped, as has his relatively youthful age. He understands the lads and gets on with them off the pitch. We know how good we are as individuals and what a great team spirit we have. It's why we are able to keep up with those clubs that have spent millions.'

Goalkeeper Tom Heaton agreed: 'I think most of the credit can be put Dyche's way. He sets the standard, the expectation, the format of what he wants. He simplifies it for players. We knew from pre-season there was something special and we managed to keep it going. He's been fantastic to play for and he should be very proud.'

Heaton also highlighted the importance of the team's improved physical fitness derived from an immensely challenging pre-season programme. 'We know we've got the quality, so if you can put in the work ethic and application as we have done in every game this season, you are already giving yourself a chance, especially in the Championship where fine margins can make big differences. There are some great sides in the Championship this year and we're one of them.

'It helps that the manager is so approachable. There's a great camaraderie with him but there's also an authoritative line that you don't cross. The ground rules are simply his expectations: smartness is one – being in club tracksuits and club-issued trainers when we are in public. Forget that, and it's a fineable offence. He likes smart haircuts. He doesn't want people slouching around with headphones on when in public. We don't wander around texting either.'

Republic of Ireland international Keith Treacy credited Dyche for helping him with his personal issues, saying: 'There have been a few ups and downs since I came to the club, but I'm trying to put everything behind me now. Everything off the field is starting to fall into place, and my football is hopefully going to see the benefits of that. That's mainly down to the gaffer, to be honest. He cares, that's the bottom line! Football isn't the be-all and end-all with the gaffer. He actually cares about the players as individuals and their off-field problems and tries to help as best he can. I can't speak highly enough of him.'

In reflecting upon his apprenticeship at Nottingham Forest, Dyche said that his manager Brian Clough ensured that each player understood how a Forest team should play and behave, irrespective of their position, status, or experience. Dyche recalled Clough telling him and his fellow centre-halves to 'head it; kick it; pass to someone better'. Dyche maintained that once the Forest players had grasped Clough's basic instructions, they had a freedom to play.

In turn, Clough attributed his managerial success to the example set by Alan Brown, his former boss at Sunderland, whom he regarded as royalty. Brown had once been a morally strict and uncompromising centre-half, captain, and manager at Burnley. Former Burnley wing-half Bob Seith regarded him as the true architect of Burnley's league triumph in 1960, achieved under Harry Potts. As a player at Turf Moor, Brown had served under the ascetic, demanding, and shrewd manager Cliff Britton. Like Britton, Brown insisted upon the highest standards of conduct on and off the pitch. Brown also focused on the details of how his teams should play, being a brilliant coach, strategist, and innovator, who devised a vast array of mesmerising set-play ruses. With Dyche arriving at Turf Moor, exhorting the Brown/Clough mantra, it was as if the wheel of time had turned full circle.

Dyche's pressing game, which had been employed so decisively against Reading and QPR, was derived from Barcelona, whom he regarded as the finest exemplar of this method. Dyche remarked that while it was Barcelona's passing skills which garnered the plaudits, it was their pressing game which impressed him most of all. He said that when he took over at Burnley, he and his players looked at replicating their approach. Dyche said that at Burnley the tactic starts with forwards Sam Vokes and Danny Ings, who harry the opposing defenders and goalkeeper, and then extends through the midfielders to the back four. He expected everyone to do their bit to deny their opponents time and space and continually strive to get the ball back.

Dyche's influences extended beyond football. He referred to his interest in leadership styles formed outside the game, and winners in other sports. He cited the huge impression made upon him by the dedication, determination, fitness levels, and collective spirit of the Oxford University rowing team, with whom he spent some time while completing his pro-licence coaching qualification. He said: 'There is no confusion in their journey. They focus fiercely upon the Boat Race they are driving to win. Within the boat you have the reserves, who train as hard, if not harder, than the elite crew, even though they know they might not get in the boat for the big event. There was also a simplicity, a rawness of vision, just a blackboard with a date and a time when the Boat Race is going to be. I took a lot from that. The coach, Sean Bowden, was brilliant. He took me on the water in the launch boat at six in the morning and I was with them right the way through until they were on the rowing machines at eight at night. It's still a team game, but they work six months for one event – we, of course, do it every week.'

Although Burnley's subsequent results up until New Year were less impressive – two victories, six draws, and two losses – they still went into Christmas in pole position, following a 2-1 home win over Blackpool. Dyche wryly reproached his detractors, saying if this had been a mini slump, as was claimed by some, it was a remarkably productive one.

But the club's financial situation was less healthy than their mid-season points tally. A £7.6m loss was announced for the year ending 30 June 2013. This comprised a sobering £146,000 loss per week. The fall in turnover from £23m to £15.2m was a direct result of a £7.4m reduction in the FA parachute payment. It meant that core turnover – money generated outside of the Sky TV contributions – had dipped below the £10m that had been the norm before promotion in 2009. Co-chairman Mike Garlick indicated that the £8m shortfall had been covered for this year but drew attention to the much-reduced turnover expected in the following year, with the FA parachute payments ceasing.

Better news came with the appointment of Terry Crabb to the board. He was the founder of Dorset Cereals and, like other Burnley directors, was locally born and bred. He stated his willingness to contribute to the club's unexpected tilt at promotion, saying: 'It was the homespun culture of the Burnley board that swung the deal. That's probably the most important thing, alongside the fact that the club is run properly by people who are either born in Burnley or who are local to it now.'

Despite the hugely impressive start made by Dyche's men, the case for reinforcement had become overwhelming by Christmas, particularly given the small size of Sean Dyche's first-team squad – just 19 players – and the mounting risk of injuries to key players derailing the team's upward momentum. Michael Kightly had already been brought in from Stoke on a season-long loan, but there were no obvious replacements for Vokes or Ings should either or both become injured. Consequently, Dyche was permitted to sign a belligerently industrious Brighton striker, Ashley Barnes, for a fee of around £750,000.

Barnes said shortly after arrival: 'I have never had such a welcoming feeling before at any club. From the moment I walked through the door, it was just brilliant. This is a club unlike any other that I have been at. The training is so intense. You must be sharp every single day. I love that intensity. It can only help you on a match day.'

Meanwhile the Clarets pressed onwards and upwards. Despite a 1-0 defeat at Middlesbrough on Boxing Day, they embarked upon a 16-match unbeaten run in the Championship, which featured ten wins, the most important of which were probably those against promotion-chasing rivals Nottingham Forest and Derby County.

Burnley 3 Nottingham Forest 1
22 February 2014
'Desire'

In reflecting upon his side's 3-1 defeat, Forest manager, Billy Davies, said: 'In the first half, we played against a side that looked like promotion contenders. They bossed us all over the pitch and we gave away three soft goals with some silly mistakes at the back. We didn't play anywhere near well enough to contend with them in the first half and we got what we deserved. The second half was much better and much more like us. We hit the bar, had two efforts cleared off the line and scored late on. We were more aggressive, more energetic, but it was too little, too late. Burnley play a very direct game that puts you under pressure and quite simply we never handled it.'

Dyche responded: 'As a manager you never get that perfect half, but that first 45 minutes is certainly as good as I've seen from our group. Some of the football was absolutely first class. We have a belief in the team, and you saw today we were majestic in the first half. We scored three and it could have had more. I thought it was total domination in the first half. Our passing and movement were exceptional, we played through the units quickly and we hurt them in so many ways.'

Dyche felt the high quality of the opposition made Burnley's performance all the more impressive. 'To dominate so powerfully for 45 minutes is rare in any game. Goalscorers often get the headlines, but everyone delivered today.

'Once you are 3-0 up, it turns into a different game and in the second half, as teams with nothing to lose do, they rained balls into our box from every area of the pitch. Tom had to make one big save but I never really thought we looked in trouble and could have had more on the break.

'We have set that mantra of one game at a time, so now we prepare for next week's game against Derby. At this stage of the season, points from wherever you can get them are valuable, but we are on another good run and are looking forward to the next one.'

Burnley 2 Derby County 0
1 March 2014
'Get Out'

Burnley's victory against Derby gave them a five-point lead over their dangerous rivals in third place. When asked about the crucial dismissal of Derby's Chris Martin, Dyche said: 'There are fine lines, but we've had seven penalties not given this season, including one today. I must say, I felt they should have had one in the second half, but so should we for the foul on Ashley Barnes. What put Martin in trouble was the previous incidents. He had been lively, let's say, and he got away with one with Jason Shackell, and another with Ben Mee. He then got booked with the third one and the referee is then under pressure. In the incident, I think he lost his footing, but once he does that he appeals very quickly. If you do that, it's hard for the referee to decide. In a tough call, he felt it was a second yellow and Martin went.'

David Jones and Dean Marney scored Burnley's goals and Dyche commented, 'It's always pleasing for the players and staff when a set play comes off. I am pleased for them because they have been in the right area several times and it's just not fallen to them, but it's a group effort and we were outstanding again today.

'Sometimes the toughest fight you have is against someone with nothing to lose. They were 1-0 down and with ten men, so in the second half they had four at the back, one in front and the rest running everywhere. That can be awkward to play against, as it was in pockets, but overall, I felt we deserved the win. I thought the football in the first half was terrific.'

Dyche said the way the players work hard day-to-day makes it easier for them to deliver on matchdays.

'Individually, you just go and deliver, and I thought in the first half, after a slow start, we soon started to play. Some of our movement and the way we shifted the ball through the units was excellent. Several teams have come here and have looked to contain us this year and I'm pleased to say they haven't fared that well. There was another sign of that today, but that's great respect to our players.'

Blackburn Rovers 1 Burnley 2
9 March 2014

'Rosettes'

Probably the most important result, though, for long-suffering Burnley fans, was the victory at Ewood Park on Sunday 9 March. For a generation, we had endured the haughty derision of our local rivals, whose club had been consistently richer and stronger thanks to Jack Walker's millions. Here, the wheel turned completely. I had a strong sense this was going to be our day. Rovers were not the force they had been in the mid-nineties. They were in ninth position and had just lost at Bolton.

But in the 24th minute Rhodes scored the opening goal and that certainty instantly disappeared. Once again came the bellowed chant: 'Same old Rovers beating Burnley!' But this was merely blind bravado. Burnley were now the stronger team.

We were made to wait, but in the 73rd minute our centre-half, Jason Shackell, scored with a brave, powerful header, like that which had brought about his equaliser in the previous season's derby. His snarling fist pump celebration was one of entitlement not merely a growl of the underdog. Six minutes later, Ings rammed home that sentiment. OK, it was a scuffed effort but one that wrong-footed goalkeeper Robinson, allowing the ball to bobble into the unguarded net. The booming roar emitted from the Darwen End was one of jubilation and vindication.

Afterwards, Dyche proclaimed: 'Today is about the supporters. I'm delighted for them because before today Burnley

2. 'ROOM AT THE TOP'

had not defeated Blackburn in the past 35 years. The players and staff were desperate for things to change, so I am really pleased for them and for the board, as well.

'All the board members have been Burnley fans since they were boys. It is certainly an enjoyable feeling to win, particularly after coming from behind. I think the mentality has been there for all to see.

'I said to the lads at half-time that they were on the cusp of making history and that we should keep going forward. I told them that the marker is one goal, score that goal and the game will change. And it did. After we scored, they found it difficult. We were always on the front foot and always looking to nick another.'

Dyche praised his team's physicality and said he had confidence in their ability and their understanding of how they needed to play.

'The physicality today was again exceptional. They'll go hard this group, for however long it takes to achieve what we can achieve.

'Shacks has done brilliant for the equaliser. He's thrown his head in where it hurts, and he's got his reward for the team. He got one here last year and that was a very brave header too, just his natural reaction. I must say it was a fantastic cross from Ross Wallace. We know he's got that quality. The cross is a horrible one for keepers because it is one that just sucks them off their line.

'As for the winner, I thought Ingsy was exceptional with his work ethic today, he just kept going and going and going. The demand that he's placed on himself, and for us as a group, is absolutely first class. Some strikers, if it's not quite happening for them, will switch off, but he doesn't. He keeps going and I thought he got his rewards today. He is a fantastic person as well as a player.'

Burnley 2 Wigan Athletic 0
21 April 2014
'Adore'

Despite losing at home to champions elect Leicester on 29 March, a game in which Sam Vokes was carried off with a cruciate injury, Burnley built up an unassailable lead over the chasing pack in the race for automatic promotion. On Monday 21 April, it was duly achieved with a fluent victory over Wigan. Fittingly, the game was won with two goals of sublime quality. In the 22nd minute, centre-back Duff pinged a long, lofted pass to Kightly on the left flank. The former Wolves and Stoke winger immediately found Arfield who, in turn, fed Jones. Jones then chipped the ball to Ings who unhesitatingly flicked it over his head into the vacant space within the inside-right channel. Anticipating Ings's intention, Marney fastened on to the ball, and instantly crossed into the box for Barnes to race forward and smash home the opener. Turf Moor shuddered with the resulting roar, while Barnes, berserk with elation, slipped and fell on the adjacent advertising hoardings as he hurled himself at the adulatory crowd.

The game was sewn up 20 minutes later as Kightly rifled a left-wing free kick inside the far post. At the final whistle, most of those in the 19,125 crowd charged on to the pitch to acclaim their heroes.

The Clarets' triumph comprised a string of new records: it was Burnley's best start to a season since 1897/98; their first victory over Blackburn Rovers in 35 years; their first win at Bolton in 29 years; and their first double over Leeds in 87 years. The 89 points they gained in finishing second to Leicester was the most the club had achieved since 1981, when three points were first awarded for a win. The 35 goals Burnley conceded during this season were the fewest in the Championship, making them the meanest defence in the division, with 20 clean sheets maintained in all competitions. Burnley lost only five league games, the lowest number of defeats since the club's Second Division championship-winning season of 1972/73. Before being beaten by Leicester in March, Burnley had maintained an unbeaten home record in the league for 23 matches. Right-back Kieran Trippier was credited with an incredible 14 assists. Vokes and Ings clearly benefitted from Trippier's prowess at crossing. Having managed just seven league goals between them in the season before, Vokes and Ings shared 41 this time around. It was a phenomenal transformation.

Dyche attributed his side's success to three factors: meticulous planning, a team always willing to go that extra yard or mile, and a highly dedicated backroom team. He explained to a *Burnley Express* reporter: 'My backroom team comprises my assistant Ian Woan, first-team coach Tony Loughlan, goalkeeping coach Billy Mercer, medical physiotherapist Alasdair Beattie and sports scientist Mark Howard. They are all different. This works well because if you have only "yes men" then you will never achieve a better outcome. We often come up with different ideas and opinions, whether it is about training, team preparation, planning or players. It's up to me to make the final decision, but it is good to have their support.

'Alasdair and Mark are vital workers behind the scenes. Mark learnt his craft with Sam Allardyce at Bolton. It was Mark who advised me that although only Walsall and Morecambe had used fewer players than Burnley, in this season's league games, we were still outrunning our opponents, even after 30 games. Moreover, his statistics also proved we were then still full of energy and quality. So, added to the players' obvious belief in themselves and one another, these statistics underlined the advantage we had gained over our closest rivals.

'Helped by Alasdair's considerable expertise we have tried to guard against soft tissue injuries. The game is changing in terms of severe contact injuries. So now, it is more about building muscular strength. We think we have good support from our science and physiotherapy staff members, but their work depends upon the players taking responsibility for the sessions they lay on. The players have grasped that here, and long may it continue.'

Dyche said there was more work to do in improving analysis, the players' diets, strength and conditioning, and so on.

'We're not yet the finished article. I didn't get carried away when promotion was won despite having that pent-up anxiety of getting over the line when you're so close. I don't get too high with the highs nor too low with the lows. It's an internal celebration for me, though. I can assure you I'm more delighted than you will ever know. I'm extremely proud. The players have achieved so much this season,' Dyche continued.

'There are words we've used a lot: relentless, limitless. It's just a mindset. The hardest thing is to contend with all the noise on the outside. But it's only noise if you stay focused on what you do. Real achievers, I believe, stay focused on the job in hand, whatever job that might be. They don't get caught up in all the noise around them. They stay focused on that role and responsibility. The players have been exceptional. Next season, all we can do is what we can do. I'm always reality-bound.'

Right-back Kieran Trippier was less cautious, remarking with unreserved joy: 'I want to play against the best teams and the best players. I'm looking forward to playing at the Etihad. City let me go without me having the opportunity to prove myself, but I came here and enjoyed myself.

'This season has been unbelievable. What a set of lads! Look at Tom Heaton. Last year he was relegated with Bristol City and now he's part of the defence with the best record in the Championship. You must cherish these moments. I've always said to myself, my dad and mum, I'll never make a better decision in my career than signing for Burnley.'

Goalkeeper Tom Heaton believed the rudiments of success were set before the season started, maintaining: 'It was the pre-season period in Cork that was critical. The time when we knew

2. 'ROOM AT THE TOP'

it had all come together was after a day of incredibly strenuous work, hard labour in fact, which ended with us split into three teams. Each team had to complete a lap of the pitch in less than 60 seconds. If one team member failed, then the whole team had to do it again. Not one person from any team failed. It was then when we knew we had something special going. It left us feeling really fit and ready to go, fresh and energised.'

Heaton said the club's use of sports science was very thorough, in terms of nutrition and prehabilitation programmes to help prevent injury. 'The chef at Gawthorpe makes sure that food selections are of the right kind. Breakfast is optional. Lunch is not. And let's say you won't get bacon, sausages, a full English. Salads, soups, fruit are the norm at lunchtime along with varied hot food, different options of meat, vegetables, and potatoes.

'Lunch is an example of where the manager's little ground rules come in. If anyone sits there texting, that's a "no" and a fine. Fines aren't always money and Friday is the day when they are imposed in a fun kind of way. Anyone can nominate someone for a fine whether it's being late or using a phone when we shouldn't. A fine can sometimes be a forfeit, having to sing or dance.

'The daily training depends on whether there is a Tuesday game, but it is always high tempo and the application from everyone has been incredible. At some clubs, you get slackers but not here. No one has tailed off. In fact, everyone has put even more into it as the season has gone on. All of us have pulled in the same direction and that's rare. It's been a pleasure to come in every day.'

Captain and centre-half, Jason Shackell, remarked: 'I've played in every game this season. It's been my biggest involvement, so for me this is the best promotion by far. You see some of the clubs and the money they've spent, so to do it with such a small squad is an incredible achievement. I can't give the gaffer and his staff enough credit. We stay together. People doubted us from the outside and maybe that galvanised us more. The lads will always have one another's backs and that's shone on several occasions. From day one we knew we were a good team and a good squad and when the results started coming that just bred confidence. The gaffer gets us working day in, day out and the lads have really bought into what he wanted and believes. We've been a real tight-knit group from the start. The gaffer wouldn't let us lose focus, whatever happens. From being fourth favourites to go down and then getting automatic promotion with the likes of cash-rich QPR and Wigan below us just makes it an incredible achievement.'

Mike Garlick, the club's largest shareholder, became the sole chairman of the club on 28 May 2015, following three years as co-chairman alongside John Banaszkiewicz, who had stepped down to devote more time to his family and his diverse international business interests. Barry Kilby became Mike Garlick's vice-chairman.

Mike Garlick and Dyche were equally committed to redeveloping the Gawthorpe training facilities to support the club's quest for category one status. They recognised that if they were to realise their ambitions it was necessary to set aside much of the 2014/15 Premier League booty for this radical upgrade. Mike Garlick explained that such improvements were also necessary to attract higher-grade established players not solely promising apprentices. Dyche neatly summarised this shared objective with the words 'We are intent upon building a club not just a team.'

The upshot was that Sean Dyche was unable to keep Burnley in the Premier League in the 2014/15 season, despite strengthening the defence with the addition of young Manchester United centre-half Michael Keane.

However, Burnley took four points from reigning champions Manchester City, assisted by George Boyd's fizzing half-volley in front of the Jimmy McIlroy stand on 14 March 2015, which secured a dramatic victory. Much to Mourinho's chagrin,

2. 'ROOM AT THE TOP'

Burnley also snatched a courageous draw at champions elect Chelsea.

Dyche's unshakeable belief persisted, despite the departures of the outstanding Ings, Trippier, and Shackell. Once back in the Championship for 2015/16, Burnley thrived. Joey Barton, James Tarkowski, and Andre Gray were drafted in, the last of these for a club record fee of £6m-plus. After a Boxing Day defeat at soggy Hull, Burnley remained unbeaten in their final 23 league games to take the title in front of stiff opposition. It was a truly remarkable achievement.

When asked about how he managed Joey Barton, Sean Dyche replied: 'One of the first questions I was asked, when I signed Joey Barton, was "How are you going to handle him?" And I told them exactly what I told Joey, that I wasn't going to handle him. He's a man not a boy and he's enjoyed that openness. We have respect, we have honesty, and he thrives on that. Sometimes you must interview someone to know how they are feeling. With Joey, you just look at him and you know he's in a good place. His conduct, the way he's been around people in Burnley. He's been a credit to the club.'

Barton responded: 'The staff and players have made me feel part of the group from day one. It's been easy for me, playing in such a good team with good people, and I'm enjoying every minute of it.'

Barton's contribution was crucial: his astute reading of the game, his fierce competitiveness, his composure, the range and vision of his passing, his remarkable stamina, his sharp anticipation of 'second balls', and his keenness in grasping them. Dyche recognised and utilised his leadership strengths, too. At Milton Keynes and Charlton, Dyche allowed him to berate his team-mates after sloppy first-half performances. Barton's angry interventions prompted immediate improvements after the break. MK Dons were thrashed 5-0 while Charlton were thumped 3-0. During half-time at The Valley, Barton demanded that his team-mates tell him who came second when Usain Bolt won his first Olympic gold medal. Not one of them knew. Barton snapped, 'See! No one remembers those who come second. To make history we must take the title! Promotion is not enough.' Soon after the resumption, George Boyd and Andre Gray scored the goals that deservedly secured the Championship title for Burnley.

Dyche continued: 'I don't do screaming at players. I don't do names. If I use expletives, it's to enhance a moment. It's not directed at anyone. And despite how I look, I don't do teacups either. Why would I do that? Everybody is just trying to do a job. A footballer's job is to learn. In helping players to improve, first, you should work out how they learn: visual, kinaesthetic, written or discussion. With footballers, the usual three are kinaesthetic – that's showing them things out on the grass – discussion and visual. Very rarely do footballers write things down. Not because they're thick, but they're not in school anymore.

'People put a lot of stock in what managers say in moments before you go out onto the pitch, but that's not where the real work is done. If the players don't know what they're doing by that stage, then, trust me, you haven't had a good week. It's just about reminding and prompting. We focus on ourselves not anybody else. The key core values are respect, good manners, good timekeeping, pride, passion, hard work, belief, and integrity. This is the glue that holds everything together.'

Andre Gray and Sam Vokes led the charge to the Championship title, sharing 38 goals, with pacey Gray winning the Championship player of the year for his 27 league goals. Vokes and Gray formed a solid partnership both on and off the field, although their regular car-sharing arrangement failed to bring about a convergence in their musical tastes. Sam Vokes said: 'We have an argument every morning because Andre's not having my music at all. He calls it "hillbilly music" and I'm not having his, to be honest, as you can't understand a word of what is going on.'

2. 'ROOM AT THE TOP'

Brentford 1 Burnley 3
15 January 2016

No Epiphany

As this unforgettable game against Brentford proved, Burnley's Championship-winning goals weren't just left to Gray and Vokes. A midfield fortified by pugnacious yet polished Joey Barton added 21 league goals. Arfield contributed eight of these while the tireless Boyd scored five.

At Griffin Park, Burnley burst into a three-goal lead. It began when Arfield's sumptuous curling shot found the top-right corner. A cheeky free kick from Barton followed, before a stinging 20-yard volley from flitting Boyd seemed to take rampant Burnley out of reach. The Clarets should have doubled that 3-0 first-half lead given the number of other clear chances which went begging.

A local reporter summed up thus: 'The Bees were put to the sword by an incredibly impressive Burnley team in the first half at Griffin Park. The visitors, playing some of the most incisive football seen at Griffin Park in recent memory, made the most of a poor Brentford performance. They scored three first-half goals and could have had a couple more.

'The visitors set up in a traditional 4-4-2 system that was anything but. Wide players George Boyd and Scott Arfield drifted all over the pitch, linking with strikers Andre Gray and Sam Vokes. That left space for Matthew Lowton and Stephen Ward to get forward from full-back. With the visitors trusting Joey Barton and Jones to control the middle of the pitch, Lowton and Ward poured forward.

'Burnley were happy to mix it up, knowing they had the pace and strength in attack as an outlet, but playing through the centre of the park when they could. Although Brentford provided stiffer opposition in the second half, pulling back a goal in the 57th minute, scored by impressive Alan Judge, Burnley might have added to their lead.'

This victory ranks as one of the best I have seen during a half-century of following Burnley. Before the game I met a carping London Claret moaning at Dyche's supposed negativity. Afterwards I caught up with him on a returning train. Maintaining a poker expression, I exclaimed: 'Rubbish, wasn't it!' It was enough to prompt a sheepish smile.

It wasn't as if the Burnley goals were just coming from their strikers and midfielders. Even the defence managed ten. Two critical late strikes were landed by imperious centre-half Michael Keane, denying hot rivals Brighton and Middlesbrough vital victories. Meanwhile, the meagre number of goals conceded (35), and their 20 clean sheets, identified Burnley's defence as one of the tightest in the division.

Keane commented: 'This club has helped me massively. At United they make you a technical player but coming here you must defend. I learnt a lot in that first season in the Premier League because there was a lot of defending to do. I've gone from strength to strength, helped by the consistency of playing in the same back four and the reminders from the manager each week in training – he just drills it into you, so when it comes to matchdays it all comes naturally. My centre-back partner, Ben Mee, has been brilliant, going from strength to strength like I have. It's dead easy playing with him. He talks to you all the time and puts his body on the line for you. He likes to play as well, but the first thing for Ben is to defend, and he's brilliant at it.'

Republic of Ireland left-back Stephen Ward added: 'I feel I have improved a lot here. The manager's attention to detail, especially with the back four, is something I have not always had at other clubs. Here, the detail is brilliant. It might be the smallest thing, a yard here or there, but it makes a big difference in a game. I don't think I've been at a club where we have worked so hard.'

Once again, the watchwords were: 'framework', 'discipline', 'togetherness', 'resilience', and 'relentless' plus a new one, 'strong

2. 'ROOM AT THE TOP'

jaw'. Some names had changed but the mantra remained the same: 'Minimum requirement: maximum effort.'

Sadly, Ian Britton, one of the heroes of 1987, succumbed to prostate cancer shortly before his former club were crowned as Championship winners in May 2016. However, this is a football club that respects and celebrates its past and honours its heroes. Ian will never be forgotten. His goal against Orient in 1987 helped keep the club alive. Without that goal, this incredible journey would not have started.

Back in the Premier League for a third time in seven years, Burnley finally had the resources to strengthen in depth. Turf Moor was improved. State-of-the-art training facilities were created at the Barnfield Training Centre, Gawthorpe. All remaining debts were cleared. It was, therefore, time to develop a team capable of holding its own in the top flight.

Icelandic international winger Johann Berg Gudmundsson was the first to arrive, in July 2016, alongside Charlton teammate, goalkeeper Nick Pope. However, it was the £8m club record signing of Steven Defour, Anderlecht's Belgian international midfielder, which underlined Burnley's new intent. Defour made an instant impact, setting up match-winning goals against Liverpool and Watford and scoring with a blistering long-range strike against Hull.

Steven said: 'I've scored a few nice goals in my career, but I think the whole action of the Hull goal makes this the nicest for me. I still have to fully adapt to the Premier League. I am used to playing with a lot of possession, whereas here there are games when you do not have so much possession. Here, the game never stops! There is no pause in play, so you can be 2-0 up and the game is never finished. In Belgium, the intensity is a bit lower.'

Sadly, this bright beginning was not sustained, not helped by niggling injuries. There was little doubt about Defour's class, though. His disappointing experience seemed to underline how physically demanding it is to play in Dyche's Burnley side.

The club's record transfer fee was then broken twice more with the signings of Republic of Ireland internationals Jeff Hendrick and Robbie Brady. The acquisition of central midfielder Ashley Westwood took the club's total spending on new players up to an astonishing £40m for the season.

With Tom Heaton and Michael Keane winning senior England caps, the number of full internationals in the Burnley squad rose to eight, the highest figure since the early sixties. There was certainly no lack of ambition here. Turf Moor became a fortress as Burnley took more than 30 points from their home games. Sean Dyche reflected: 'Only once this season, following the opening day defeat, have we been in the bottom three, so nobody can argue that we haven't deserved to retain our Premier League status.'

Burnley 2 Liverpool 0
20 August 2016
'Mountain at my Gates'

Burnley's most impressive victory this season was at home against Liverpool on 20 August. This game was won despite the Clarets having the lowest percentage of possession (19.6 per cent) attained by any winning side in a Premier League game over the previous ten years. It was a model, counter-attacking display, combining energetic pressing from front to back, disciplined defending in depth, and swift, decisive raids, which yielded two fine goals. Whenever possession was lost, Burnley's two wide midfielders reinforced the back four. Burnley consistently squeezed the space between their lines, ensuring Liverpool's gifted playmakers had little room in which to operate, forcing their attackers into wider positions where their movement and passing became largely lateral. Having barred their direct route to goal, the visitors resorted to unproductive long-range shooting.

Champions Chelsea were held, too, at a snowy Turf Moor on 12 February, thanks to Robbie Brady's stupendous free kick, on debut. Burnley confounded Chelsea with their resolute and tireless defending in depth, while their probing long balls interrupted the Londoners' pressing game. Although visiting Manchester City and Arsenal teams were victorious, Burnley deserved at least a share of the spoils. Only Manchester United and Spurs, after inspired tactical changes, merited their wins at Turf Moor.

Burnley showed, too, that they had the mental and physical strength to win games while under the cosh. Their home victories over Everton and Crystal Palace illustrated this, both games being decided by last-minute goals. Although Dyche successfully employed a 4-5-1 formation in several games, he mostly favoured a 4-4-2 or 4-4-1-1 set-up that had yielded previous success. Despite operating in a much more challenging league, his three strikers, Gray, Vokes, and Barnes, did him proud, sharing 25 goals, while the defence remained largely redoubtable, as recognised by the international selections of Heaton, Keane, and Ward.

A 2-0 win at balmy Selhurst Park on 29 April took Burnley to the brink of safety. Barnes steadied jangling nerves with a seventh-minute goal while Gray's breakaway dash and scorching shot eliminated any lingering doubt. This was Gray's ninth and final league goal of the season, a significant tally which included a hat-trick against languishing Sunderland on New Year's Eve. Although sometimes criticised for his heavy first touch, Gray had served Burnley well. During the summer he moved to Watford for a reputed fee of around £18m.

A subsequent 2-2 home draw with West Bromwich Albion on 6 May 2017 gave Burnley their 40th point, thereby securing their Premier League status for a further season. The key to their success was their home form: 33 of their 40 points were won at Turf Moor. The Crystal Palace victory was their only league win away from home. The club's 30-year journey from rags to riches had reached an incredible, lofty milestone.

3. BOARDING THE ORIENT EXPRESS

Chelsea 2 Burnley 3
12 August 2017
'Marks to Prove It'

My dad took me to my first top-flight game at Stamford Bridge in August 1958. It was a scalding afternoon like this one. But here all similarities disappeared. For in 1958, Chelsea were a struggling First Division team reliant upon Jimmy Greaves's goals to keep them up. Their mighty opponents on that day were Football League champions, Wolves. Almost 60 years later, opulent Chelsea were the Premier League champions. Here, Burnley were their modest opponents.

But by half-time there had been a bewildering reversal of roles, for Burnley were 3-0 ahead. Admittedly, Chelsea's centre-half, Gary Cahill – a former Claret – had been dismissed for a reckless tackle, but this did not adequately explain why Chelsea were so poor and Burnley so accomplished.

Vokes opened the scoring in the 24th minute when he swivelled to meet Lowton's right-wing cross, caressing the ball past diving Courtois's right hand. Burnley full-backs Lowton and Ward were not confined to barracks, frequently pushing forward in support of midfielders Brady and Gudmundsson. In the 39th minute Ward bombed down the left flank before releasing the ball to Cork, positioned just outside the Chelsea box. Cork instantly returned the pass by flicking the ball over an adjacent defender. Ward seized upon it without breaking stride

3. BOARDING THE ORIENT EXPRESS

and, after bulldozing past a marker, let fly with a ferocious cross-shot that whizzed past Courtois before he could move.

The restive Chelsea fans began to berate their heroes. This was not in the script. Burnley were expected to lie down meekly in homage to their superiority. Burnley weren't finished, though. Two minutes before the break a free kick was awarded on the left flank. The Chelsea players positioned themselves at the edge of their box, expecting the kick to be aimed at the far right-hand post. Instead, Defour was picked out on the opposite flank. He took a couple of strides before crossing venomously towards the left-hand post. Leaping higher than his marking defenders, Vokes propelled a bullet header past Courtois.

The downcast Chelsea players left the field to bitter booing. Chelsea manager, Conte, was apoplectic. Despite being 0-3 down and reduced to ten men, Chelsea returned to the field in a more determined mood. Helped by Burnley's defensive errors, Chelsea turned up the heat. Morata's diving header pulled one goal back in the 69th minute before David Luiz powered through Burnley's sleeping defence to lash home a second with two minutes remaining. By this time Chelsea were down to nine men following the dismissal of Fabregas. Burnley were not without sting, though, for Brady's grubbing free kick slapped against a post.

Burnley boss Sean Dyche reflected: 'We are learning and building an assured view of the Premier League. The first half pleased me because although Chelsea went to ten men, we kept going, kept probing. Winning away from home on the first day quietens down some stories. We're written off at the start of every season. It kills off a few things early doors and it allows the players that space for growth. Chelsea have players of such calibre and to see the game through is so pleasing. Not many gave Burnley a chance.'

Sam Vokes added: 'We were sloppy at times, but we ground out the result and we're delighted. That's a huge result – a lot was made of our away form, last season. It was always going to be tough here, but we got our heads down and put in a performance.'

As for Conte, he said: 'Chelsea lost their heads too easily. I don't want to comment on the referee, absolutely not.'

Burnley sprang several surprises during this season: drawing 1-1 at Spurs with a 90th-minute goal from debutant Chris Wood; drawing 1-1 at Anfield, helped by Scott Arfield's opener; winning 1-0 at Everton, thanks to Jeff Hendrick's goal, following an elaborate build-up comprising 20 passes; a 2-2 draw at Old Trafford, having led until the 90th minute; and five consecutive victories in early spring against Everton at home (2-1), West Ham away (3-0) amid ugly home unrest, West Bromwich away (2-1), Watford away (2-1), and Leicester at home (2-1). It all helped Burnley clinch a prestigious place in the Europa League competition.

Deputy goalie Nick Pope performed admirably, having replaced injured Tom Heaton in September. Pope was well supported by a redoubtable central defence headed by Mee and Tarkowski and backed by loyal Kevin Long. Chris Wood scored ten goals in his first full Premier League season, ably assisted by Ashley Barnes with nine, but Sam Vokes failed to make his customary impact, scoring only two more league goals after his brace at Chelsea.

Summer signing Steven Defour was an outstanding success in midfield, developing a productive partnership with Jack Cork, before injury sadly curtailed his short yet illustrious career at Turf Moor. Jonathan Walters suffered a similar fate as did Robbie Brady, who had just hit top form when he was injured at Leicester in early December, wiping out the rest of his season. Ashley Westwood performed well when he was given a regular midfield berth in February. Winger Aaron Lennon was a useful addition, too, particularly with his pace, which Burnley were short of. Phil Bardsley provided welcome physical resilience at full-back when called upon.

3. BOARDING THE ORIENT EXPRESS

Despite suffering a 0-5 thrashing at Arsenal on 6 May, in Wenger's valedictory game, only Spurs (0-3) and Manchester City (0-3) inflicted heavy defeats in 38 league games. Burnley scored 36 goals and conceded 39, winning seven times at home and away and keeping 12 clean sheets. It was a truly remarkable achievement that such a small club with such limited resources could attain seventh place in the Premier League.

Their reward was a place in the preliminary round of the Europa League. This would be their first European adventure since the mid-sixties. They were to face Aberdeen in July and August, and, if successful, Istanbul Basaksehir and Olympiacos of Piraeus, Athens, in the final two preliminary stages. Their oriental journey was about to begin.

Aberdeen 1 Burnley 1
26 July 2018
'Waterfront'

The weather was fair and serene, with the neighbouring North Sea unusually mellow, but the atmosphere inside Pittodrie was stoked. A crowd of 20,313 raucous fans packed into the stadium, determined to bawl their side to victory. The Home International tournament had been abandoned years before, but fierce Anglo-Scottish rivalry had not. Besides, Aberdeen had an illustrious history in European competition, having won the European Cup Winners' Cup in May 1983, under Alex Ferguson, beating Real Madrid in the Gothenburg final, and also going on to win the European Super Cup. Only a year before, Aberdeen had progressed to the third qualifying round of the UEFA Europa League competition, losing narrowly to AEL Limassol.

Burnley soon knew they were in an almighty scrap, for Aberdeen were big, strong, and aggressive. Burnley's cause was not helped when their brilliant goalie, Nick Pope, had to be taken off in the seventh minute with what appeared to be a serious shoulder injury. Tom Heaton was still not fully fit, having suffered a dislocated shoulder almost a year before, so Anders Lindegaard, a Danish international goalkeeper, replaced him. Just 12 minutes later, Lindegaard faced a penalty kick after Tarkowski was adjudged to have impeded brawny Sam Cosgrove. The decision seemed soft but right-winger Mackay-Steven showed no mercy, sending Lindegaard the wrong way. The resulting roar was tumultuous. The home fans proceeded to mock stuttering Burnley with the derisive chant: 'Premier League – you're having a laugh!'

But Sean Dyche's men were well versed in combating adversity and began asserting themselves more after the break. Aberdeen goalkeeper Joe Lewis had little to do in the first half, being well protected by his muscular defenders, but he was forced into making an instinctive save when Jack Cork threatened. He also had to paw away a dangerous cross from Lennon seconds later.

With Burnley pushing forward more, Aberdeen had more opportunities on the break. Nifty Mackay-Steven might have set up Cosgrove for a decisive second goal had he not delayed his pass. When Cosgrove got his shot away, Lindegaard saved with ease. Towering Aberdeen centre-backs, McKenna and Devlin, had largely snuffed out the Burnley attack in the first half, but a late loss of focus proved fatal. With ten minutes remaining, Wood won a critical aerial battle, allowing substitute Vokes to pounce on the second ball, take a touch, spin, and wallop the ball past Lewis. It was a superb strike, rightfully acclaimed by the ecstatic travelling fans. Importantly, it ensured that Burnley left Pittodrie on level terms.

Despite the febrile Anglo-Scottish rivalry inside the ground, afterwards fans of both clubs cordially drank and ate together in the local pubs, arranging to continue their newly formed friendships after the second leg in Burnley. The two clubs had much in common, striving to compete against wealthier opponents.

3. BOARDING THE ORIENT EXPRESS

Burnley 3 Aberdeen 1 (*aet*)
31 July 2018

'Glittering Prize'

It seemed as if Aberdeen had brought the balmy Pittodrie weather with them, for Turf Moor was bathed in glorious sunlight. But Aberdeen also brought bloody resolve on the pitch and in the stands. Their rowdy fans made a colossal din throughout this toe-to-toe fray.

Here, Dyche reverted to his preferred 4-4-2 formation with Vokes partnering Wood. His decision was soon vindicated. In the sixth minute Westwood's pinpoint long ball found Wood on the edge of the Aberdeen box with his back to goal. With no defender intervening, Aberdeen goalkeeper, Lewis, rushed from his line attempting to block Wood's shot. Sensing the goalkeeper was behind him, Wood dummied a shift to his left before suddenly twisting to his right, leaving Lewis stranded as he hammered a rising drive over two defenders guarding the goal. The thunderous roar from the home crowd momentarily silenced the visiting fans.

For a short spell Burnley were in total command, with the Scottish side left chasing the lengthening shadows. But their fans soon recovered their voices as their team fought back pugnaciously, repeatedly bearing down on the Burnley goal. Just before the half-hour mark, Aberdeen were level. A left-wing corner from Mackay-Steven passed over the heads of everyone except Chris Wood, at the far post. In a feeble attempt at clearing the ball, his misdirected header drifted back into the danger zone, allowing 18-year-old midfielder Ferguson to score with a stunning overhead scissor-kick. Dyche was furious with Wood, loudly berating him for his unforced error while the Scots fraternity went wild with elation.

This goal energised Aberdeen hugely. Lindegaard had to be at his best in saving Shinnie's goal-bound shot while Burnley fans slated Italian referee Irrati for not red-carding McKenna when he brought Wood down as the Burnley centre-forward was homing in on goal.

There was no let-up after the break. Although Burnley dominated possession, Aberdeen were excellent, counter-attacking with menace. Shinnie wastefully fired over from a fine cut-back by McGinn. Meanwhile Lewis denied substitute Barnes with an incredible point-blank save. With the contest swinging from end to end, Lindegaard pushed away Shinnie's powerful drive at his near post and Vokes's looping header was deflected over the bar by Lewis's magnificent fingertip save.

At full time the two sides could not be separated, so they went into extra time with us, the supporters, feeling almost as exhausted as the players. Eventually, fatigue played a crucial part in the outcome. Charlie Taylor's inch-perfect cross was intercepted by unmarked Cork, whose glancing header found the top right-hand corner of the net. Shortly after, Barnes, who had come on for Wood at the interval, sealed the game with a spot kick after McKenna had handled Gudmundsson's cross. This game will remain long in the memory.

Istanbul Basaksehir 0 Burnley 0
9 August 2018
'Holy City'

Burnley were bound for the Orient where they would meet Istanbul Basaksehir, a leading side in the Turkish Super Lig, despite their comparatively short history. (They were formed in 1990.) I could not travel to Istanbul, so I watched the game on a friend's dodgy channel on which goats were advertised at half-time. Just 4,231 were present in the huge Atatürk Olympic Stadium. Only the visiting Burnley fans made much noise. Watching the game from afar, this seemed a soulless affair.

With Pope and Lindegaard injured, and Tom Heaton only recently recovered, Burnley spent £3.5m in signing former

3. BOARDING THE ORIENT EXPRESS

England goalkeeper Joe Hart from Manchester City. Hart came with a high pedigree having made 75 appearances with the senior England team. He marked his Burnley debut with a clean sheet. He also received a yellow card as the Clarets held Istanbul Basaksehir to a dull, yet important, goalless draw. Hart played an important part, denying Brazilian defender Junior Caicara before tipping over a header from ex-West Ham defender Manuel da Costa. Burnley, who had only 29 per cent of possession, did not manage a shot on target. Chris Wood was unavailable because of an infected insect bite.

Burnley manager Sean Dyche said afterwards: 'I think overall, one of the more pleasing things is we had to bolt together a team and come somewhere like this where we've never been before and find a way of getting a result. You know, it's tough coming to a place like this, it's new to these lads, and we've come with 17 players – that's our lot. So, I'm really pleased, certainly with the shape and attitude, on a heavy, leg-sapping, old-fashioned pitch. Most clubs don't statistically dominate the ball away from home in the Premier League, so the basics, the shape, the energy, the will, is very important. We've had ten years of everyone saying possession wins – it doesn't, as the World Cup showed. It's less relevant now.'

Burnley 1 Istanbul Basaksehir 0
16 August 2018
'Hollow Talk'

Burnley moved within one round of the Europa League group stage as they beat Turkish side Istanbul Basaksehir after extra time. Following a goalless first leg, Jack Cork scored the only goal of the Turf Moor leg when he broke the deadlock in the 97th minute. Earlier, Ashley Barnes shot wide and Phil Bardsley's strike was saved by goalkeeper Mert Gunok. Burnley goalkeeper Joe Hart made fine saves to deny Edin Visca and Kerim Frei at the end of the first half.

The Clarets, in their first season of European football since 1966/67, had earned the right to play Greek side Olympiacos in a two-legged play-off, to decide which side qualified for the group stage. Dyche told BBC Radio 5 Live: 'The players are showing a desire for the competition, which is great because there is a lot of negative noise around it. It is a massive badge of honour to be in a European competition, as most fans thought those days had gone forever.'

This second-leg game attracted a crowd of 16,583 but none of these were Istanbul Basaksehir supporters. There were no away fans in the ground after Istanbul Basaksehir made the decision not to sell tickets to their fans. After the first leg, their manager Abdullah Avci criticised Burnley's 'long-ball' tactics. But there was nothing crude about Cork's 97th-minute winner. It was a fine curling shot from 22 yards after he received a precise pass from Jeff Hendrick.

'Tonight's was a sublime goal,' added Dyche. 'That is something we don't get enough credit for. If that is a trendier name than Jack Cork, it would be raved about.' Despite Joe Hart's smart saves, Dyche was keen for Hart not to become the focal point of the Clarets' season, chiding: 'I'm surprised you're not fed up; we've been talking about him for two weeks. I made a lot of the display of the team. There were a lot of really good performances, and they deserve just as many mentions. But Joe definitely played his part, just so you're happy.' Chelsea and Arsenal would join the competition in the group phase.

Olympiacos 3 Burnley 1
23 August 2018
'I Predict a Riot'

Dyche felt the officials succumbed to pressure from Olympiacos players during his side's first-leg defeat in the play-off in Athens. The Clarets lost 1-3 in a game in which their defender Ben Gibson was sent off and both sides were awarded a penalty.

3. BOARDING THE ORIENT EXPRESS

Dyche criticised the home team's conduct at half-time when it was 1-1 saying, 'They were waiting for the referee. You all saw the different feel of the game in the second half. The scenes I saw at half-time with all and sundry around the referee apparently on their side, left me scratching my head. All I keep getting told is respect the officials with your conduct around the referee.'

In the first half, Chris Wood's penalty – awarded after he was pushed over in the box – had cancelled out a superb free kick from home captain Kostas Fortounis. The hosts largely dominated the second half, regaining the lead quickly through Andreas Bouchalakis's header. Gibson received a second yellow card for handling in the box after an hour, leaving midfielder Fortounis to score the resulting penalty.

'I don't understand why he's booked Ben Gibson again,' said Dyche. 'The first one maybe, but the second one, he's gone to block a shot and it's hit his hip before hitting his hand. How can that be deemed deliberate handball? It's just an impossibility. Then he gives him the yellow card and it's probably the world record for how quickly he got it out of his pocket.'

Dyche was also unhappy with the distance the referee asked his players to stand back for the free kick that opened the scoring for the Greek side. He said: 'The wall is a strange distance from the ball,' adding, 'I feel for our fans. They've come a long way to see a balanced game and haven't seen that. Hopefully next week will be more even.' Sam Vokes thought he had made the second leg an easier prospect when he tapped-in late on, but it was ruled out for offside, to compound the Clarets' miserable night.

While the game was mired with controversies, it should be remembered that Olympiacos were dominant for much of the game, having 68 per cent of possession, and managed 17 shots on goal, seven on target, compared to Burnley's three shots on goal with only one on target – Wood's successful penalty. On home soil, Olympiacos were formidable opponents with a 100 per cent success record in the Europa League qualifying rounds, winning their six games by an aggregate score of 18-4. They had beaten Luzern 7-1 on aggregate in the previous round.

Burnley 1 Olympiacos 1
30 August 2018
'Suck the Blood from My Wound'

An outsider might have thought that Burnley left themselves with too much to do in the second leg, but had they not frittered away so many chances, they might well have joined Arsenal, Chelsea, Rangers, and Celtic in the group stage draw. According to a BBC sports journalist, 'Burnley created enough chances to turn the tie on its head inside the opening 45 minutes alone.' My recollection was similar. Burnley dominated from start to finish, having 60 per cent of possession with 20 attempts on goal, five on target, but it was not to be.

Vokes was unfortunate to see his curling attempt rebound off a post early in the second half, having missed two golden opportunities earlier. He headed agonisingly wide from a super cross from the impressive Dwight McNeil, making his first competitive start, before sending a header from point-blank range over the bar. Barnes saw his deflected first-time shot roll wide while McNeil, brought up in Manchester United's youth academy, forced a one-handed save from Andreas Gianniotis. Olympiacos used their vast European experience to progress.

Podence's away goal seven minutes from time sealed Burnley's fate, making the aggregate score an unreachable 2-4. Czech Republic forward Vydra marked his first Burnley appearance since signing from Derby with a goal after a scramble inside the Olympiacos penalty area. However, the goal came too late to be significant. After the full-time whistle, Dyche applauded the home fans who had roared their team on throughout the tie, while Olympiacos's players celebrated before their small band of travelling fans.

3. BOARDING THE ORIENT EXPRESS

Dyche concluded: 'The whole club will learn from this experience. It bodes well for the future, but we have got to use it wisely because we want these players to continue growing and we want to get stronger as the season progresses.' Dwight McNeil was clearly Burnley's man of the match. In the second leg he created four chances, more than any other Burnley player. It was his first senior start at the age of 18 years and 281 days. As for Olympiacos, their midfielder Kostas Fortounis was certainly their man of the tie, having been directly involved in all four of Olympiacos's goals over the two legs, scoring twice and assisting once in Greece, before setting up Daniel Podence's goal at Turf Moor.

On reflection, I was relieved we did not progress further. We seemed not to have enough high-calibre players to contend with demanding competition on two fronts. Leicester had already demonstrated the perils of this after their incredible Premier League title-winning season. Their excellent showing in the Champions League affected their EPL form so significantly that they were threatened with relegation. This led to the summary sacking of Ranieri, the manager who had guided them to this improbable triumph.

Burnley's league form also suffered badly in the aftermath of their European adventure. After an opening day 0-0 draw at Southampton on 12 August, a game they might have won, having spurned a litany of first-half chances, Burnley's subsequent four league games ended in defeat, conceding ten goals. Left-back Stephen Ward attributed their decline in form and uncharacteristic defensive frailty to insufficient time being available for preparation and recovery because of their onerous travelling commitments. He also felt that with the Europa League games starting in July, there was little opportunity for a proper pre-season programme. He conceded that players unselected for the away games in Turkey and Greece were reluctant to rest at home, wanting to experience the prestigious journey.

4. 'MY ZERO'

Burnley's resounding defeats in potentially winnable games against Watford (1-3) and Fulham (2-4) exposed their fatigue, tipping them into the relegation zone. A crushing home victory over Bournemouth (4-0) and a fortuitous win at Cardiff restored some self-belief, only for heavy defeats by Manchester City (0-5), Chelsea (0-4), and West Ham (2-4) to unsettle them once more. Subsequent losses at home to Newcastle (1-2), and away at Crystal Palace (0-2) were complemented by a home defeat against Liverpool (1-3) after Burnley had bossed the first half. The Clarets were once more in a relegation position.

Although they ragged an ugly 1-0 victory over Brighton on a freezing 8 December, this was followed by a late loss at Spurs (0-1) and an undeserved defeat by Arsenal (1-3). Worse still, on Boxing Day they were mauled by Everton (1-5) with Hart culpable for the size of the loss. Burnley were looking down the barrel with only the poor form of Huddersfield, Fulham, and Cardiff giving solace. Dyche's experimental employment of a 5-3-2 formation had almost won a point at Spurs and should have garnered something at the Emirates, but Everton tore this set-up apart. Neither Lowton nor Taylor could cope with their wing-back responsibilities, snuffed out by the aggressiveness of Everton's high pressing, while the addition of centre-back Ben Gibson did not provide greater defensive security. Our midfield was frequently overrun, and our forwards were merely ornamental. Hart did not command his goal area as well as Pope and Heaton, seeming slow to come off his line. His performance

4. 'MY ZERO'

against Everton suggested he was vulnerable in dealing with fierce ground shots. Many Burnley fans thought we were destined for the drop.

5. BACK TO BASICS

Burnley 2 West Ham 0
30 December 2018
'Total Football'

Six defeats in the previous seven games raised question marks over Dyche's position for the first time since early 2013. Burnley's seventh-place finish in the 2017/18 season had been largely built upon a solid defensive base. In stark contrast, that defence had become alarmingly porous – leaking 41 goals so far, two more than were conceded in the entire 2017/18 campaign. Dyche responded by making two big decisions in his team selection which comprised five changes for the following game against West Ham. These were the recall of Tom Heaton in place of Joe Hart, and the blooding of Dwight McNeil in a Premier League game. Rebuffing the fans' criticism of Hart's poor performance in the Everton game, Dyche insisted: 'Joe has been magnificent for us and credit to him because he was the first to jump up at the end when Tom made a big save from Carroll.'

More than 15 months had elapsed since Heaton had dislocated his shoulder against Crystal Palace – the last time he had featured in a league game for Burnley – but here the 32-year-old exerted his characteristic influence on those in front of him, barking instructions and providing certain organisation and leadership. This was apparently missing when Joe was in goal. Tom also directly contributed to Wood's opening goal in the 15th minute. Having calmly headed the ball out to Westwood while under pressure from West Ham attackers, a

5. BACK TO BASICS

goalscoring sequence was set in motion. A lovely sweeping move was continued by Westwood, McNeil, and Barnes, resulting in Chris Wood's decisive finish. Heaton underscored a good day's work late on by superbly tipping Carroll's header on to the woodwork, demonstrating again his remarkable agility.

Regarding the introduction of McNeil, Dyche commented: 'Dwight McNeil is a clever player who has some quality and ability. His family should take some pride in what he's doing. He'll get stronger and fitter and we hope he'll continue growing with the team.' Many fans had been clamouring for McNeil's introduction after his stellar display against Olympiacos. Against West Ham, McNeil repeatedly roasted his markers with nifty footwork and speed off the mark, scampering to the goal line and pumping a succession of dangerous crosses into anguished West Ham's box. It was entirely fitting that he should score the Clarets' second goal to cap a magnificent display. His devastating wing play reminded me of Leighton James in his pomp.

And with the hosts repeatedly carving through their visitors, they pressed home their advantage before the interval, when 19-year-old McNeil turned in Westwood's cross at the far post. With Wood and Barnes offering physicality in both boxes and club captain Heaton totally in command of the defence, West Ham managed just four shots on target. Their Brazilian midfielder Felipe Anderson had played a principal role in West Ham's recent upturn, but here he struggled to make any impact against well-drilled and determined opponents, winning only 31 per cent of his aerial duels while his passing accuracy was well below par at 64 per cent. Meanwhile, Burnley's Westwood produced a starring display, being involved in both goals and setting the tempo in midfield, completing 45 passes, more than any other home player. Both Wood and Barnes spurned several excellent opportunities after the break to make Burnley's win more emphatic. Importantly, though, this victory lifted Burnley above Fulham into 18th position, level on points with 17th-placed Southampton, who had lost 1-3 to Manchester City.

West Ham had arrived in Lancashire on the back of five wins from six games. Despite being boosted by the return of Marko Arnautovic, playing for the first time since injuring his hamstring at Cardiff on 4 December, Manuel Pellegrini's side were sluggish throughout, with their best chance, a header from substitute Andy Carroll, drawing a fine save from Heaton. Pellegrini's response to this comprehensive defeat was to whinge: 'We had a flight that arrived at 2am in the morning after playing Southampton. I was happy until two o'clock today. This was a game we were able to win – Burnley was in a bad moment but they played with intensity. Burnley recovered better because they had 30 or 35 hours' more rest.'

This victory transformed Burnley's season. Three days later they won 2-1 at relegation rivals Huddersfield with goals from Wood and Barnes, with McNeil again creating havoc on the left wing. On 12 January visiting Fulham again played homage to their Turf Moor fate after a brilliant goal from German international Schurrle gave them a second-minute lead. In atrocious conditions, cruel deflections from Hendrick's two shots in the 20th and 23rd minutes overturned this deficit. As hard as Fulham toiled in the buffeting wind and sheeting rain, they could not find a way back into the game.

A succession of draws at Watford (0-0), Old Trafford (2-2, having been 2-0 ahead), and at Southampton (1-1) reduced Burnley to 17th spot, but a controversial 3-1 victory at Brighton, followed by a 2-1 home win over Spurs, propelled Burnley into 14th position, their highest ranking since 20 October. Although four subsequent defeats pushed the Clarets back to the brink of the drop zone, fine wins at home to Wolves (2-0), away at Bournemouth (3-1), and at home to languishing Cardiff (2-0) moved them up to a position of almost certain safety. Despite losing their final three games, we had the thrill of holding

5. BACK TO BASICS

Chelsea to a 2-2 draw at Stamford Bridge on the evening of 22 April 2019, with a blistering goal from Hendrick and a superbly crafted one, finished by Barnes. Chelsea's David Luiz was livid, accusing Burnley of playing 'anti-football' whereupon his crass remark became the proud chant of the Burnley faithful.

Burnley completed the 2018/19 season with three defeats by Manchester City (0-1), Everton (0-2), and Arsenal (1-3) but Burnley's final place of 15th represented a remarkable recovery having been in the relegation zone eight times before their startling new-year recovery.

Burnley started the 2019/20 season brightly with a thumping 3-0 victory over and Southampton, and remained largely comfortable in or around mid-table for the first half of the season. Although Spurs, Manchester City, and Chelsea inflicted heavy defeats, Burnley hammered West Ham, Watford, and Bournemouth each by a 3-0 margin, although a controversial VAR decision sullied the Bournemouth victory. High-riding Leicester were also beaten at Turf Moor after a second-half recovery. A great win at Old Trafford followed on 22 January 2020 before proceedings were halted in March 2020 by the sudden onset of the Covid pandemic, bringing about many fatalities and transforming the lives of everyone both at home and abroad over the next two years.

Manchester United 0 Burnley 2
22 January 2020
'Shoot to Thrill'

Because a Burnley victory over Manchester United is a rare event I penned this account after the game.

Manchester United started brightly but could not take advantage of the openings they created. Martial wasted the best of these. But Burnley also exerted pressure, creating alarm among the United defenders as evidenced by Jones's clumsy challenge on Wood in the 39th minute. The resulting free kick enabled Burnley to pump a long lofted ball into the box, where Ben Mee outjumped his marker and headed downwards. Chris Wood spun off Harry Maguire to meet Mee's knockdown and tuck the ball into the top left-hand corner of the net.

Although United huffed and puffed in the second period, they could not find a way through a tightly organised Burnley defence. Jay Rodriguez then doubled the Clarets' advantage in the 56th minute when he played a one-two with Wood before unleashing a venomous strike that screamed into the top left-hand corner of the net, with David de Gea transfixed at his near post.

It was the third season in a row that Burnley had gone 2-0 up at Old Trafford, but this time they hung on for all three points. United, who were without the injured Marcus Rashford, were lacklustre for long periods and barely threatened Nick Pope during the second half. The United side were booed off at half-time and again at the end, with large parts of the ground emptied with five minutes left. While Ole Gunnar Solskjaer's side remained six points behind Chelsea, and out of the top four, Burnley rose to 13th position, seven points clear of the relegation zone. It was Burnley's first win at Old Trafford in 58 years and their first victory there in the Premier League. Burnley's tenacious second-half display against Leicester on the previous Sunday had enabled them to come from behind to beat the Champions League chasers, signalling a return to the grit and character that has been the Clarets' blueprint since they returned to the top flight in 2016.

Against United, Wood and Rodriguez showed the ruthlessness up front that had been sorely missing earlier in the season. Behind the front two there was a disciplined and well-organised display, with Mee and James Tarkowski superb at the heart of defence, assisted by belligerent midfield performances from Jack Cork and Ashley Westwood. Ben Mee was deservedly awarded the TV commentator's man of the match against

5. BACK TO BASICS

United. A delighted Sean Dyche exclaimed: 'I am very pleased with that. We know it's a tough place to come and it was a good performance from us. We scored two very good goals. United didn't find any killer moments, which was very pleasing. Strong, fit and organised will never go out of fashion.'

6. 'YOU WANT IT DARKER?' COVID CALLS 2020

The pandemic stopped play shortly after 7 March when Burnley drew 1-1 with Spurs at home. The Clarets dominated the first half with high-energy pressing, playing the ball largely to feet, with their players constantly finding space. With Burnley maintaining slick, one-touch football, I remarked to a friend: 'It's a pity that more pundits aren't here to witness this immaculate display of football when the club is so often derided as "hoof ball" merchants.'

The season was not resumed until 22 June, when Manchester City administered their routine 0-5 drubbing. Afterwards, an incensed Ben Mee reserved his ire for the plane trailing a banner inscribed with 'White Lives Matter'. He was clearly more distressed by this than the dismal result.

Burnley performed well in 'Project Restart', albeit compelled to play behind closed doors, winning four of their next seven games and drawing the other three. Jay Rodriguez revelled in the opportunity to lead the line, scoring match-winning headers against Watford and West Ham, and salvaging a point at Anfield, where Pope was outstanding. Had Gudmundsson found goal late in the game, instead of the bar, Burnley might well have ended Liverpool's long unbeaten home record. The downside was that Burnley suffered a succession of injuries which would blight their 2020/21 season. These casualties were almost certainly attributable to the lack of preparatory training before embarking upon an intense, squeezed league programme in the ensuing season.

Former Burnley chairman Mike Garlick commented: 'Most of the financial fears I had were regarding the season not getting completed, and then not starting again for the 20/21 season – which of course didn't happen but restricted the time we had to make decisions on who to release and re-sign and who to sign in the season going forward.' With the absence of fans, not only during the Project Restart games, but also for much of the following season, there were crazy anomalies in the results. Burnley managed to win only four home games, yet crucially beat Arsenal, Liverpool, Crystal Palace, Everton, Wolves, and Fulham away. Thanks to Dyche's resilience and the players' commitment, somehow Burnley survived. It was often hard to watch Burnley games on TV with so much riding on each game, and so much concern about the fitness of their players. However, there was one game which I particularly enjoyed, momentarily free from the angst caused by the ever-threatening Covid.

Wolverhampton Wanderers 0 Burnley 4
25 April 2021

'Boys in the Better Land'

Burnley took a huge step towards retaining their Premier League status when a first-half hat-trick from Chris Wood enabled them to thrash a lifeless Wolves at Molineux. It was an awful display from Wolves, who were ruthlessly torn apart by the Clarets in an excellent performance, after a barren run of three successive defeats. This victory placed Burnley nine points clear of Fulham, the highest-placed side in the relegation zone, with only 15 points left to play for. Wood was superb throughout but was also gifted his chances by a half-hearted Wolves display that smacked of mid-table complacency. Dyche again pointed out how hard it was to put out a competitive side given the glut of injuries in his squad and the lack of money to reinforce them. He pointed out that staying in the Premier League for another season was no mean feat. That goal was tantalisingly close after his side delivered one of their most accomplished away performances in recent years.

From the first minute, the Clarets were far more aggressive than Wolves, pushing their hosts back, and it was not long before Wood opened the scoring. Wolves centre-back Willy Boly had already got away with one error. In the 15th minute he was not so lucky when he inexcusably allowed a straight long ball to pass over his head. Wood was on it instantly, bringing the ball under his control and twisting England defender Conor Coady inside out before arrowing a low shot across the goalmouth and in.

Six minutes later, Wolves winger Adama Traore played a sloppy pass on the edge of the box; Dwight McNeil anticipated the error and ran through to square the ball for Wood to tap in. Another excellent cross from the left was volleyed over by Vydra as Burnley ramped up the heat. A third goal seemed inevitable and sure enough it came one minute before the break. Burnley forced a corner on the right. McNeil struck an in-swinging corner into the box where Wood outstripped the Wolves defenders, rising well above them, and heading powerfully past goalkeeper Patricio.

The Clarets had dropped 13 points from winning positions in the Premier League this season, but a repetition here appeared unlikely, particularly when, on the resumption, Vydra expertly rounded Rui Patricio to score. Unfortunately, he was adjudged just offside. Undeterred, right-back Matt Lowton let fly with the ball flashing narrowly past the post. With five minutes remaining, though, Burnley scored a merited fourth goal. Wood was provider this time, teeing up the former Aston Villa midfielder Westwood to hammer home from 20 yards.

In a post-match interview Dyche was asked how difficult it had been for him over this pressurised season. He replied: 'I've been sleeping all right. I don't tend to worry too much. It's a season's work. It's how you end up in the season and our focus is always the next game, in which we work really hard to try and get more points on the board.'

Burnley duly achieved Premier League safety with a 2-0 victory at Craven Cottage but it was generally a season of heart-stopping anxiety, not helped by the claustrophobic circumstances in which I watched all 38 league games. I suspect strongly that I was not alone.

EPILOGUE

WILL THE NORTH RISE AGAIN?

'Cold Days Of February'
(ISB)

No matter how well-endowed a football club is with business acumen, widespread and canny recruitment networks, skilled and clear-sighted management of staff and resources, inspirational leaders, tactical strength and perceptive planning and diligent preparations, the greatest factor in determining its success lies in its degree of financial strength, and security. The slogan 'it's the economy stupid' relates to Bill Clinton's successful presidential campaign in 1992, a strapline which emphasised the overriding importance of money and the wider economy in achieving electoral success. It is equally applicable to football management.

The abolition of the maximum player's wage in 1961 not only transformed a top player's earning potential, it also heralded a massive shift in players' power over their once autocratic clubs. As a consequence, a firmer line was drawn between the 'haves' and 'have nots' in the world of top-flight professional football, affecting both players and clubs. This division expanded exponentially after the creation of the Premier League in 1992 and the Bosman judgement of 1995, which enhanced player power even more.

There is another significant factor to be considered here. That is the relative strength of a football club's local and regional economy. If your club happens to be Manchester City or United or Liverpool, for example, the sheer weight of foreign investment in these gigantic institutions makes it largely irrelevant whether their northern economies are thriving or struggling. With top-flight clubs almost entirely dependent upon their owners' investments and TV money, it is unsurprising that 'turnstile' contributions amount to little more than eight per cent of their annual revenue. Potentially Newcastle will now join the ultra-privileged fraternity, irrespective of their flagging local economy. But if your club happens to be Blackburn, Blackpool, Preston, Bolton, Huddersfield, the Sheffield clubs, Middlesbrough, Sunderland, or Burnley, all of whom have had illustrious pasts, the strength of their local and regional economy has a more important bearing upon their prospects of success. With the northern economies trailing way behind those in the south, the biggest northern clubs can consistently outstrip their lucrative southern rivals. However, Burnley's top-seven finish in the 2017/18 Premier League season earned them a place in European competition. This was a remarkable triumph over unappealing odds, particularly when the club's locality is one of the most deprived areas in England and Wales. But why does the north lag so far behind the south in terms of prosperity?

Immediately after World War One, the economies of the north were almost on a par with those of the south-east, including London. The north contributed 30 per cent of GDP then, while the south-east provided 35 per cent. Yet by the end of the 20th century the south-east's share had climbed to 40 per cent while the northern contribution had fallen to 21 per cent. This is not simply the product of harsh global economics. Of course, it is true that the low-wage economies of Asia and eastern Europe have undercut and shrunk the manufacturing bases in all western European countries and in North American states. But the once powerful manufacturing base in northern Britain has fallen more dramatically than in any other comparable economy. British manufacturing as a share of GDP has flatlined at ten per cent since 2007, less than a third of the figure achieved in Germany, where manufacturing has benefitted from greater government support.

In sharp contrast, English governments since the late seventies have placed increasing economic reliance upon the financial and service sectors, largely located in London and the south-east. This trend not only explains why manufacturing has received relatively little support from English governments over the last 40 years, much to the detriment of deprived post-industrial areas, it also clarifies why the English government is centralist in outlook, with a heavy political bias shown towards London and the south-east. It may be tempting to blame Mrs Thatcher for this state of affairs but as Tom Hazeldine points out in his book, *The Northern Question: A History of a Divided Country*, the north has suffered from regionally discriminatory policies since the end of World War Two.

Had our governments seen fit to support British manufacturing, which was once prevalent in areas now described pejoratively as 'post-industrial', this might have had beneficial consequences, not only in reviving and sustaining British industry but also perhaps helping correct inequalities that now prevail in our deprived, once industrial cities, towns, and some villages. Instead, we in the north are patronised by our government's glib promises of a 'northern powerhouse' and improbable 'levelling up'. Meanwhile the London-oriented HS2 will eventually grind to a halt in Birmingham having cost in excess of £72bn.

But Burnley's tough, plain-speaking manager, Sean Dyche, was not one to moan and groan about the inequalities his small club was compelled to face. Based on interviews with him shown on Burnley FC Clarets Player I drew the following conclusions. He knew it was highly unlikely that Burnley would ever have benefactors who could pump large amounts of cash into the club and team. He recognised that he had to build a team within a tight budget. Taking this frugality into account Dyche seemed to believe that his success as a football manager should be judged upon the state of the club at his departure compared with that at his arrival, adding that his contributions to the general welfare of the club and its links with its community should be included within this assessment.

He suggested that one of the greatest pressures in football management was knowing what should be done when the best way forward was not obvious. During his time at Burnley, Dyche appeared to welcome other leaders, whether among the coaching or other staff or among the players. He cited how Joey Barton drove his team-mates on towards the Championship title in 2015/16 when the team was sometimes not firing on all cylinders. He questioned the expectation that the manager should always lead. He was also critical of the demands that managers should achieve success almost immediately after being appointed, pointing out that in business circles it is common to find progress resting upon mid-term and long-term planning with rigorous milestone reviews.

Dyche indicated his aversion to the prevalence of what he called a 'manager cult' seemingly created by a hyperbolic media, when a game between Liverpool and Manchester City is recast as a titanic battle between Klopp and Pep as if these individuals could singly determine what happens on the pitch. He remarked that previously the media focused on clashes between big-name players such as Roy Keane and Patrick Vieira.

Dyche said he endeavoured to avoid the heat that sometimes accompanies post-match inquests, with managers locking horns over the outcome. Dyche strove to maintain a cool demeanour when interviewed after a game. He seemed to prefer to give a measured, factual response to questions posed about his team's performance, emphasising the positives where possible and also considering whether his own contributions were good enough too. He recognised that the flak from the press, pundits, and keyboard warriors could be acidic, suggesting that those who cannot cope with this might be better off seeking a different job. As Burnley's former chairman Mike Garlick told me, Dyche tended to be cautious about bringing in foreign players, reasoning that he needed to be sure that such players were willing to live in the north, whether their families were content with the move, and whether the players could fit in with their new team-mates and were fully committed to relentless grafting whatever the weather.

In my opinion, Dyche was the finest manager Burnley FC has had in the 50 years I have followed them. Notwithstanding the disappointing 2021/22 season, he delivered six successive seasons of Premier League football, including a prestigious venture into a European competition. That is an incredible achievement given the limited resources available to him. Moreover, I cannot recall any other small-town club in Britain in such a deprived area achieving as much. Admittedly, Burnley's results had often been poor during the 2021/22 season, notably in his last game in charge at relegation rivals Norwich.

After Dyche's sudden departure, caretaker manager Michael Jackson achieved a startling revival with a more expansive style of play but unfortunately his courageous and severely depleted squad fell at the final hurdle in the last league game of the season against 'money-bags' Newcastle, consigning the club to the Championship once more. It is not my place, in this personal 50-year history, to comment upon the club's present circumstances, and its new owners' future plans. Obviously, I hope, like other Burnley supporters, that the club will continue to defy the odds and compete well with richer rivals, holding on to Dyche's mantra, 'minimum requirement is maximum effort'. I will remember Sean Dyche with great fondness, utmost gratitude, and massive respect. I wish him well.

Whether the north can rise again against the odds is uncertain; but if the region can emulate the canny, gritty, competitive drive exhibited at Turf Moor during much of Dyche's stewardship, it has at least an outside chance of achieving an improved future.

REFERENCES

Football books and journals consulted:
Berry, M. (Ed.), *Backpass* magazine: issues 1-50: PCP: (2007–20)
Bowler, D., *Winning Isn't Everything ... Biography of Sir Alf Ramsey* (Orion, 1998)
Butler B., *The Football League: 1888 – 1988* (Macdonald Queen Anne Press, 1987)
Cawley, S. & James, G., *The Pride of Manchester: A History of Manchester Derby Matches* (ACL & Polar Publishing, 1992)
Charlton, B., *Sir Bobby: The Autobiography: The Manchester United Years* (Headline, 2007)
Cummings, S., *Burnley Were Back!! One Fan's Perspective of Burnley Football Club's 1994–95 Season* (Janus, 1996)
Davies, H., *The Glory Game* (Mainstream, 1972)
Delaney, T. & Edelston, M., *Masters of Soccer* (Naldrett Press, 1960)
Docherty, T., *My Story: Hallowed Be Thy Game* (Headline, 2006)
Doherty, J. with Ponting, I., *The Insider's Guide to Manchester United* (Empire Publications, 2005)
Dougan, D. & Murphy, P., *Matches of the Day 1958–1983* (Dent, 1984)
Edwards, G., *Leeds United: Second Coat* (Mainstream, 2005)
Edwards, G., *Paint it White: Following Leeds Everywhere* (Mainstream, 2004)
Francis, T., *Clough: A Biography* (Stanley Paul, 1987)

REFERENCES

Gardner, J., *Johnny Haynes: Portrait of a Football Genius* (Pitch Publishing, 2017)

Gray, A. with Drewett, J., *Flat Back Four: The Tactical Game* (Boxtree, 1998)

Hayes, D., *East Lancashire Derbies* (Sigma Leisure, 2001)

Holgate, M., *The Rivals: Blackburn v Burnley* (Tempus Publishing, 2005)

Hopcraft, A., *The Football Man* (Aurum, 2006)

Hughes, S., *On the Brink: A Journey through English Football's North West* (deCoubertin Books, 2017)

Hunter, N., *Biting Talk: My Biography* (Hodder & Stoughton, 2004)

Kelly, S. F. (Ed.), *A Game of Two Halves* (Mandarin, 1992)

Law, D., *The King: My Autobiography* (Bantam/Transworld Books, 2003, reprinted by permission of the Random House Group Ltd.)

Lee, E. & Simpson, R., *Burnley: A Complete Record* (Breedon Books Sport, 1991)

Lord, B., *My Fight for Football* (Stanley Paul, 1963)

Lyall, J., *Just Like My Dreams: My Life with West Ham* (Penguin, 1990)

Mackay, D. with Knight, M., *The Real Mackay: The Dave Mackay Story* (Mainstream, 2005)

McKinstry, L., *Jack and Bobby: A story of Brothers in Conflict* (Collins Willow, 2002)

Matthews, T., *West Bromwich Albion: The Complete Record* (Breedon Books, 2007)

Morris, P., *West Bromwich Albion* (Sportsman's Book Club, 1966)

Mourant, A., *Don Revie: Portrait of a Footballing Enigma* (Mainstream, 1990)

Mullery, A. with Norman, T., *Alan Mullery: The Autobiography* (Headline, 2006)

Mullery, A. & Trevillion, P., *Double Bill: The Bill Nicholson Story* (Mainstream, 2005)

Nawrat, C. & Hutchings, S., *The Sunday Times Illustrated History of Football* (Hamlyn, 1994)

News of the World Football Annual: 1965–95 annuals (Thomson & Co./Invincible Press)

Nicholson, B., *Glory Glory: My Life With Spurs* (Macmillan, 1984)

Ponting: I., *Liverpool: Player by Player* (Crowood, 1990)

Potts, M. & Thomas, D., *Harry Potts – Margaret's Story* (Sports Books, 2006)

Prestage, M., *Blackpool: The Glory Years Remembered* (Breedon Books/DB Publishing, 2000)

Prestage, M., *Bolton Wanderers: The Glory Years Remembered* (Breedon Books/DB Publishing, 2000)

Prestage, M., *Burnley: The Glory Years Remembered* (Breedon Books/DB Publishing, 2000)

Prestage, M., *Preston North End: The Glory Years Remembered* (Breedon Books/DB Publishing, 2000)

Prole, D., *Football in London* (Sportsman's Book Club, 1964)

Quelch, T., *An End of Innocence: The Watershed Season of 1959/60* (Pitch, 2021)

Quelch, T. in collaboration with Burnley FC and the London Clarets, *Forever & Ever: A Rock 'n' Roll Years Diary of Burnley Football Club* (2000)

Quelch, T., *From Orient to the Emirates: The Plucky Rise of Burnley FC* (Pitch, 2017)

Quelch, T., *Never Had It So Good: Burnley's Incredible 1959/60 League Winning Triumph* (Know the Score Books, 2009/Pitch Publishing, 2015)

REFERENCES

Quelch, T., *Underdog! 50 years of Trials and Triumphs with Football's Also Rans* (Pitch, 2011)

Rothman's & Sky Sports Football Yearbooks 1973–2022 (Macdonald's & Jane's/Headline)

Signy, D. & Giller, N., *Golden Heroes: Fifty Seasons of Footballer of The Year* (Chameleon, 1997)

Simpson, R., with Bentley, D., Chadwick, W., Lee, E. & Simpson, P., *The Clarets Chronicles: The Definitive History of Burnley Football Club 1882* (Burnley Football Club, 2007)

Simpson, R., *Burnley Football Club 1882–1968: Images in Sport* (Tempus Publishing, 1999)

Simpson, R., *The Clarets Collection 1946–96: A Post-War Who's Who of Burnley Football Club* (Burnley Football Club, 1996)

Smith, M., *Match of the Day: 40th Anniversary* (BBC Books, 2004)

Soar, P. & Tyler, M., *The Official Illustrated History of Arsenal* (Hamlyn, 1997)

Taylor, R. & Ward, A., *Kicking and Screaming: An Oral History of Football in England* (Robson Books, 1996)

Thomas, D., *Champions: How Burnley Won Promotion* (Pitch, 2015/16)

Thomas, D., *No Nay Never: A Burnley FC Anthology* (Dave Thomas, 2004)

Thomas, D., *No Nay Never: A Burnley FC Anthology Volume 2* (Burnley FC, 2008)

Thomas, D., *Jimmy Adamson: The Man Who Said No to England* (Pitch, 2013)

Thomas, D., *Who Says Football Doesn't Do Fairy Tales?: How Burnley Defied the Odds to Join the Elite* (Pitch, 2014)

Thomas, D. & Smith, M., *Bob Lord of Burnley: The Biography of Football's Most Controversial Chairman* (Pitch, 2019)

Turner, D., *Fulham: The Complete Record* (Breedon Books/DB Publishing, 2007)

Tyrell, T., *Manchester United: The Official History* (Hamlyn, 1988)

Ward, A. & Williams, J., *Football Nation: Sixty Years of the Beautiful Game* (Bloomsbury, 2009)

Watts, D., *Football's Giant Killers: 50 Great Cup Upsets* (Book Guild, 2010)

Wheeler, K. (Ed.), *Soccer the British Way* (Sportsman's Book Club, 1965)

Widdows, R. (Ed.), *Book of Football: 60 Memorable Matches* (Golden Hands/first published by Marshall Cavendish Publications, 1973)

Wiseman, D., *A Case of Vintage Claret: Fifty of the Best Burnley Footballers of All-Time* (Hudson & Pearson, 2006)

Wiseman, D., *'Up the Clarets!': The Story of Burnley Football Club* (R. Hale, 1973)

Young, P., *Football in Sheffield* (Sportsman's Book Club, 1964)

Young, P., *Bolton Wanderers* (Sportsman's Book Club, 1965)

Football match reports and additional material from: *BBC Sport, Burnley Express, Daily Mail, Daily Mirror, FourFourTwo, Backpass, The Guardian, The Independent, Lancashire Evening Post, News Chronicle, Mail on Sunday, News of the World, The Times, The Observer, Observer Magazine, Sunday Express, Sunday Times, Daily Sketch, Daily Herald, When Saturday Comes*, club programmes and websites: Tony Scholes at Burnley's Up the Clarets website; Phil Whalley of Clarets Archive; Leeds 'Mighty Whites' site; BBC *MOTD*, ITV Hub, YouTube & David Hird's video footage of past games.

REFERENCES

Non-football reference works consulted:

Becket, A., *When the Lights Went Out: What Really Happened to Britain in the Seventies* (Faber & Faber, 2009)

Bracewell, M., *The Nineties: When Surface Was Depth* (Flamingo, 2003)

Chronicle of the 20th Century (Longman, 1998)

Footman, T., *The Noughties: A Decade That Changed the World* (Crimson, 2009)

Hazeldine, T., *The Northern Question: A History of a Divided Country* (Verso, 2020)

Hodgson, G., *The People's Century Vol. 2* (BBC Books, 1996)

Marr, A., *A History of Modern Britain* (Macmillan, 2007)

Marr, A., *Elizabethans: How Modern Britain Was Forged* (William Collins, 2020)

Sampson, A., *Anatomy of Britain* (Hodder & Stoughton, 1962)

Sampson, A., *Anatomy of Britain Today* (Hodder & Stoughton, 1965)

Sandbrook, D., *Never Had It So Good: A History of Britain from Suez to The Beatles* (Little, Brown, 2005)

Sandbrook, D., *Seasons in the Sun: The Battle for Britain: 1974-79* (Penguin Books, 2013)

Sandbrook, D., *The Great British Dream Factory: The Strange History of Our National Imagination* (Penguin Books, 2016)

Sandbrook, D., *White Heat: A History of Britain in the Swinging Sixties: 1964–70* (Abacus/Little, Brown Books, 2006)

Thomas, P., *The Golden Years of Burnley* (True North, 1998)

Turner, A. W., *Rejoice! Rejoice! Britain in the Eighties* (Aurum, 2010)

OTHER PITCH BOOKS BY TIM QUELCH

Never Had It So Good

Burnley's Incredible 1959/60 Title Triumph

'A superb book' *Trevor Meredith, Burnley's title-winning goalscorer in May 1960*

Underdog!

Fifty Years of Trials and Triumphs with Football's Also-Rans

'This is a major work, erudite, keenly observed. It is dripping with authentic atmosphere. I was captivated.' *Ivan Ponting: Backpass magazine*

Bent Arms & Dodgy Wickets

England's Troubled Reign as Test Match Kings During the Fifties

'Once we thought of the 50s as a golden age. We now look back and find snobbery, imperial arrogance, and racial prejudice. For looking at history differently Tim Quelch should be applauded.' *The Cricketer*

Stumps & Runs and Rock 'n' Roll

Sixty Years Spent beyond a Boundary

'Tim's descriptive powers regarding players are a treat.' *Andrew Roberts, CricketStatistics.com*

From Orient to the Emirates

The Plucky Rise of Burnley FC

'Burnley's inspirational, never-say-die recovery from the cusp of oblivion to once more competing against the top flight's big guns. To call the intervening 30-year journey a "roller-coaster" is an understatement. An abundance of comments from fans, players, newspaper reports and other contemporaneous accounts. An uplifting formula.' *SportsBookoftheMonth.com*

Good Old Sussex by the Sea

A Sixties Childhood Spent with Hastings United, the Albion and Sussex County Cricket

'Few have the skill of Quelch in describing the spirit of the times. He has also interwoven a commentary on current affairs and pop music to remind readers that sport was not the only activity changing fast. He ends with a few pen portraits of players he particularly liked. His quirky, highly personal book is an unexpected delight.' *Sussex Life magazine*

An End of Innocence

The Watershed Season of 1959/60

'Tim Quelch sets out to examine the truth of football's supposed age of innocence and what came after in a fascinating, detailed study.' *Backpass magazine*